Cities of the United States

Cities of
the United States

Studies in Urban Anthropology

Leith Mullings, Editor

Columbia University Press
New York

Library of Congress Cataloging-in-Publication Data

Cities of the United States.

Includes bibliographies and index.
1. Cities and towns—United States. 2. Urban
anthropology. 3. Urban policy—United States.
I. Mullings, Leith.
HT123.U733   1987   307.7'6'0973   87-5218
ISBN 0-231-5000-3 (cloth)
ISBN 0-231-05001-1 (paper)

Columbia University Press
New York   Guildford, Surrey
Copyright © 1987 Columbia University Press
All rights reserved

Printed in the United States of America
p 10 9 8 7 6 5 4 3 2
c 10 9 8 7 6 5 4 3 2

Contents

III. Urban Kinship: Generations and Gender

IV. The Study of the City: Theory, Ethics, and Advocacy

Preface

The articles in this volume are concerned with the anthropology of the contemporary urban United States. As such, this is the first volume of original essays to deal exclusively with the urban United States, although the analysis of both urbanism and the United States have an established tradition in anthropology. These studies are conducted in diverse urban settings, ranging from suburban to inner city, and cover a number of ethnic and socioeconomic groups. The book includes a variety of anthropological approaches, within the framework of a concern with the analysis of the political, social, and economic realities of the larger society.

The volume should be useful in the training of graduate and undergraduate students in anthropology and other fields of urban studies. While most of the articles will be of general interest, the volume also includes specialized articles (e.g., Smith) that will be of interest to graduate students of urban theory. Social scientists who are working in institutions and organizations should also find this volume useful. Several of the articles (Ogbu, Jones, Sanjek, Leacock) deal with institutions and bureaucracies, and some (Sanjek, Leacock) include extensive analyses of the problems encountered by anthropologists working in applied settings.

The organization of the volume reflects the traditional concerns of urban anthropology. The first group of articles focuses on the urban poor, as they are affected by public policy. The next section contains articles that take organizations, voluntary associations, institutions, and networks as their focus. Next we move to articles that concern urban kinship or gender roles. The volume concludes with a discussion of theoretical issues, ethics, and responsibility in anthropology.

I would like to thank Professor Roger Sanjek for his critical reading of the manuscript and helpful suggestions about the introduction. Special credit is due to Aisha Khan, my research assistant, who diligently assisted me in preparing the manuscript for production. I would also like to thank Beverley March for her careful attention to typing the manuscript. Finally, I would like to thank my parents, without whose provision of hospitality it would have been difficult to complete the volume.

Contributors

Robert Alvarez received his Ph.D. from Stanford University in 1979. His research has focused on issues concerning the U.S.-Mexico border, particularly immigration, adaptation, kinship, and family history. Alvarez is the author of *Familia* (University of California Press, 1986); his work has also appeared in the *Journal of San Diego History* and *The New Scholar*. He has co-produced a film on Mexican-American communities along the California-Mexico border for the Public Broadcasting System.

Delmos J. Jones is professor of anthropology at the Graduate School and University Center of the City University of New York. He has conducted research on the Papago Indians of southern Arizona, tribal peoples of northern Thailand, Australian Aborigines, and local organizations in the urban United States. His work has appeared in such journals as *Human Organization, Current Anthropology,* and *Urban Anthropology*. Dr. Jones is currently conducting research on intercultural marriage among U.S. and Caribbean blacks and also edits a series on ethnicity and cultural identity for Gordon and Breach publishers.

John Kreniske is assistant professor of community health at the State University of New York at Old Westbury, where he is a member of the Interdisciplinary Center for the Study of Aging. Dr. Kreniske is also a Fellow of the Research Institute for the Study of Man. He has co-authored, with Ida Susser, a book about industrialization, political movements, and local health issues in Puerto Rico, to be published by Oxford University Press.

Eleanor Leacock was professor of anthropology at the City College, City University of New York. Her urban-oriented research includes studies of schooling in New York City and Zambia and a study of race relations in suburban housing. Dr. Leacock's current research concerned the problems of youth in contemporary Samoa. Her publications include *Teaching and Learning in City Schools, The Culture of Poverty: A Critique* (editor), *Myths of Male Dominance: Collected Articles on Women Cross-Culturally,* and *Women's Work, Development, and the Division of Labor by Gender* (co-editor). Dr. Leacock died while this book was in press, and the volume is dedicated to her.

Iris Lopez received her Ph.D. from Columbia University in 1985. She is currently an assistant professor in the Latin American and Caribbean Studies Department at City College at the City University of New York. Her work on sterilization and prenatal care has appeared in such journals as *Genes and Gender* and *Sage Race Relations Abstracts.* Her recent research on prenatal care is to be published by the Community Service Society of New York City.

Gwendolyn Mikell is associate professor of anthropology in the Sociology Department at Georgetown University. Her research has focused on urban kinship and ethnic relations in the United States, as well as family structure and political economy in Ghana, West Africa. Dr. Mikell has edited a special volume of *Rural Africana* on African women and is the author of *Cocoa and Chaos in Ghana* (Paragon House Press, 1987).

Benjamin Miller holds an M.A. in anthropology from Temple University and has also done graduate work in anthropology at Columbia University. He is director of public policy for the New York City Sanitation Department's Office of Resource Recovery and Waste Disposal Planning. He is currently conducting research on the history of urban infrastructural planning.

Leith Mullings is professor of anthropology in the City University of New York Medical School and in the Ph.D. Program in Anthropology at the Graduate School and University Center of the City University of New York. She is the author of *Therapy, Ideology, and Social Change: Mental Healing in Urban Ghana* (University of California Press, 1984), and her articles on urban ethnicity and stratification, housing, health, kinship, and gender roles have appeared in a number of journals. Dr. Mullings is presently book review editor of *Medical Anthropology Quarterly: International Journal for the Cultural and Social Analysis of Health.*

John Ogbu is professor of anthropology at the University of California, Berkeley. He has conducted research in Malawi and Nigeria as well as in the urban United States. He is the author of *The Next Generation: An Ethnography of Education in an Urban Neighborhood* (Academic Press, 1974) and *Minority Education and Caste: the American System in Cross-Cultural Perspectives* (Academic Press, 1978). Both books won the Margaret Mead award in 1979. His work has also appeared in such journals as *Child Development, Africa, American Ethnologist,* and *American Anthropologist.*

Rayna Rapp teaches at the Graduate Faculty of the New School for Social Research where she chairs the Anthropology Department. Her current research focuses on the social impact and cultural meaning of prenatal diagnosis, and is based on fieldwork among multiethnic, multilingual patients and medical professionals in New York City hospitals. Dr. Rapp helps to edit *Feminist Studies* and *Signs,* and has been active in the women's movement for almost twenty years.

Helen I. Safa is professor of anthropology and Latin American studies at the University of Florida, Gainsville. She is the author of *The Urban Poor of Puerto Rico* and has edited or coedited a number of books, including *Migration and Development, Women and Change in Latin America, Toward a Political Economy of Urbanization in Third World Countries.* Her articles and reviews on migration, housing, race, ethnicity, education, and women and national development have appeared in a variety of scholarly journals and periodicals. Dr. Safa is past president of the Latin American Studies Association and former chair of the Advisory Committee for the American Republics, Council for International Exchange of Scholars (Fulbright).

Roger Sanjek teaches at Queens College, City University of New York. Following his work at the Over 60 Clinic, he studied the history of the Gray Panther movement in Philadelphia, Berkeley, and New York City, and is completing a book about this social movement. Since 1983 he and Jagna Sharff have co-led a team of anthropologists in a long-term study of two ethnically diverse neighborhoods in Queens, New York. Dr. Sanjek's work has appeared in *American Anthropologist, American Ethnologist, Comparative Studies in Society and History, Signs,* and other journals. A report, *Crowded Out: Homelessness and the Elderly Poor in New York City,* was published by the Coalition for the Homeless and the Gray Panthers of New York City in 1984. He also edits a series of books on anthropology and contemporary issues for Cornell University Press.

Jagna Wojcicka Sharff teaches at New York University in the Metropolitan Studies Program. Her earlier research includes work with long-distance commuting Mohawk construction workers, with the elderly homeless living in New York City and among families living in Spanish Harlem. Currently Dr. Sharff is completing a book based on the results of her team-led, long-term research on the Lower East Side. She is also co-directing field research in two ethnically diverse neighborhoods in Queens, New York, with Roger Sanjek, another contributor to this volume.

Raymond T. Smith is professor of anthropology at the University of Chicago. He has carried out extensive research on kinship, class, and race in Jamaica, Guyana, and Ghana, as well as in Chicago. Author of several works on family structure, he recently edited *Kinship, Ideology, and Practice in Latin America* (University of North Carolina Press, 1984). During the 1985–86 academic year he was director of the Consortium Graduate School of Social Science of the Universities of the West Indies and Guyana. He is at present a co-investigator in the Chicago Urban Family Life Project at the University of Chicago.

Ida Susser, who received her Ph.D. from Columbia University, is associate professor of community health education in the School of Health Sciences, Hunter College, CUNY. She is the author of *Norman Street: Poverty and Politics in an Urban Neighborhood* (Oxford University Press, 1982) and is co-author (with John Kreniske) of a book about industrialization, political movements, and local health issues in Puerto Rico, to be published by Oxford University Press.

Cities of the United States

1. Introduction: Urban Anthropology and U.S. Cities

Leith Mullings

For anthropologists doing ethnography in U.S. cities, perceptions of urban life have been significantly influenced by the changing social, economic, and political features of the cities they have studied. Problems that have been troubling in traditional anthropology—the selection of the unit of analysis, the conceptualization of the relationship of symbols to behavior (or culture to social structure), and the question of the involvement of anthropologists with their subjects—attain special salience in the urban arena, with its manifest class, racial, and geographic polarizations, and the conflicts such opposition engenders. The articles in this volume attempt to grapple with these issues, for the most part reporting on research conducted or updated in the late seventies or early eighties. This introduction will, in a somewhat selective manner, place this work in the context of trends in urban anthropology, as they are affected by the political and economic transformations of U.S. cities, and offer some perspectives on doing urban anthropology in the 1980s and beyond.

Urban Anthropology in the 1960s

In the United States, as well as in Europe, concepts of urbanism have been bound with images of industrial capitalism. It is not surprising then, that Engels' description of Manchester finds its echo in cities as far apart in time and space as industrial Chicago of the 1930s or "postindustrial" Newark and Boston (see Magubane 1985: 67). Thus the work that came out of Chicago between World War I and the 1930s, which was to leave its imprint on urban studies for the next several decades, was very much influenced by the structure of Chicago as industrial accumulation gave way to corporate accumulation (see Gordon 1984). While these studies attempted to grapple with the city itself as the unit of analysis, as several critiques have pointed out, the social effects of industrial capitalism, e.g., inequality and alienation, were frequently confused with those of urbanism (see Castells 1977; Eames and Goode 1977). Not surprising then was their emphasis on urban social "disorganization," which tended to be regarded as "everything but conformity with the standards of conventional society" (Hannerz 1980:56). As we shall note, the controversy about social and cultural "disorganization" continues to plague contemporary urban anthropology.

Although studies of the urban United States were carried out in the 1940s and 1950s, it was not until the 1960s that urban anthropology came into its own as a discipline. Around the world, the peoples traditionally studied by anthropologists experienced the massive and rapid urbanization of their societies; in the United States, urban poverty and urban ethnicity were "rediscovered."

In the sixties the effects of urban decline, which would culminate in even more significant transformations in later periods, had become evident. By the 1960s, the central cities were undergoing net losses in employment. Between 1954 and 1963 in the twenty-four metropolitan areas with populations greater than one million, more than 500,000 jobs were lost by the central cities (Ashton 1984: 65). In contrast to the job loss in the central cities, between 1954 and 1963, the suburbs gained over 1.5 million jobs (*ibid.*). Between 1958 and 1967, manufacturing employment increased by only 7 percent in the central cities but by one-third in the suburbs; and wholesale trade grew by only 11 percent in the cities but by 90 percent in the suburbs (Tabb 1984a:4).

The urban/suburban disparity had implications for ethnic inequality, as minority populations were concentrated in the central cities and experienced the economic crisis most sharply. Between 1940 and 1960, 3.1 million Afro-Americans had fled rural poverty in the South in search of better economic opportunities, and approximately 581,000 Puerto Ricans left the island of Puerto Rico for the United States between 1940 and 1959 (History Task Force 1979). To address the injustices of rural and urban racism, the civil rights movement was launched, reaching a high point with the 1963 March for Jobs in Washington, D.C. As frustrations mounted, rebellion took the form of burning and looting in several cities.

These confrontational politics, which were often racial in form, resulted in public exposure to the deterioration of conditions in the inner city. By focusing attention on urban poverty and threatening the social order, these protests brought some federal funds to the inner cities during the "New Frontier"/"Great Society" programs of the Kennedy and Johnson administrations.[1] While it is clear that the most needy populations were not the major beneficiaries of these programs, as I shall discuss, there were significant struggles for community control of schools, police, and other urban services that would have a significant effect on the communities studied by anthropologists in the seventies.

The urban research of the sixties, taking place within the context I have just described, often reflected concern about urban poverty. To a great extent, the urban anthropology of this period utilized the perspectives and methodologies of traditional anthropology, as anthropologists sought their "tribes" in the city by selecting ghettos and ethnic enclaves as bounded units for traditional ethnographic work. They brought to urban research the specialties of anthropology: holism, participant observation, and cultural relativism. While these studies were important additions to urban studies and sometimes produced unique ethnographic descriptions, it rapidly became clear that their limitations were also those of traditional anthropology.

Many of the studies published in the late sixties utilized ethnic considerations in defining their unit of analysis. Liebow (1967) observed Afro-American men who congregated around a street corner in a northern city; Oscar Lewis followed poor Puerto Rican families in New York City and San Juan (1966); Hannerz (1969) studied Afro-Americans in a neighborhood of Washington, D.C. Although the focus on ethnic groups in part reflected the convergence of ethnic and residential boundaries in a segregated society, it was for the most part a result of employing traditional anthropological approaches. Anthropologists were, to a great extent, influenced by the indigenous categories of their own society which held that ethnicity was primordial, and *a priori* bounded the unit of analysis. The problem was not that these studies were based on what were alleged to be ethnic groups, but rather that they failed to sort out what should be separate variables: the way in which ethnicity is conditioned by economic and political relationships, and the role of the larger social, political, and economic structure in defining the unit they selected for analysis.

Thus a major criticism of urban anthropology, elaborated early on by Leeds (1973), was the inadequate delineation of the relationship between the unit of study and the larger society. While to varying degrees researchers such as Lewis, Liebow, and Hannerz considered the constraints resulting from the lack of economic opportunity, urban anthropology often followed the community studies model (see Arensberg 1961), in which the community was held to be an object and a sample, a reflection of the larger society. In these studies where the unit of analysis is the family, block, or neighborhood, the holism of anthropology did not extend beyond the microenvironment.

Given the focus on ethnic boundaries and the use of the community studies model that often concealed the relationship between the community and the larger society, it is not surprising that the inextricable link between class and ethnicity was not adequately drawn (see Mullings 1977, 1984 [1978]). The historical and economic structures that defined ethnicity and gave it its salience were often analytically obscured, as these populations or communities were approached as self-contained, bounded groups locked into a set of cultural traits which perpetuated their "urban lifeways." Anthropologists studied the "powerless" without drawing the dialectic between power and powerlessness, between poverty and wealth, and explicating the way in which these relationships define and give meaning to ethnicity. It was but a short step from there to assume the independent determination of culture, to seek to analyze it apart from social relationships and to posit "urban disorganization"; to assert that poverty and the activities to overcome it result from subcultural values, passed down one generation to the next. And it must be added that the popularization of the "cultural" explanation for poverty reemerged at precisely the time that the disenfranchised were pressing for basic transformations in the inegalitarian structure of society (Mullings 1982) and when those in power were seeking to rationalize the failure of minor reforms (see Valentine 1971).

In summary, there is certainly some truth in Peattie's and Robbins' suggestion that urban anthropologists have done a service in describing "the world of little people in large complex places" (1984:95). Certainly the ethnographic approach, which strives to give a detailed account of real as well as ideal behavior, based on participant observation, is a significant contribution to urban studies, which are frequently based on survey data. Particularly important is that this approach often seeks to portray the culture in its own terms. Despite the problems associated with the concept of cultural relativism, the fact that it allows for the conceptualization of difference without the label of deviance is of great importance.[2] However, we must be critical about the degree to which such culture is accurately portrayed. To the extent that culture was described within the structural-functionalist model—as a functionally linked whole of unchanging traits—and behavior was seen as adaptive and unchanging, preserving the status quo (see Peattie and Robbins 1984:95), the urban anthropology of this period was inadequate.

Urban Anthropology in the Late 1970s and Early 1980s

In the 1970s the movement of capital and the dismantling of the social programs of the sixties had a qualitative effect on cities. The process of urban decline continued as plants moved out of the central cities to the suburbs, southern cities, rural areas, and overseas in search of low-wage, nonunionized workers, lower taxes, and cheaper land and energy (Tabb 1984a:5). The central cities experienced an absolute population loss (Sternlieb and Hughes 1983:456), increased unemployment, loss of services, and deterioration of the infrastructure. A bimodal job pattern became increasingly evident in the older industrial cities, with highly paid lawyers, executives, and professionals at one end of the scale, and low-wage service and clerical workers, maintenance personnel, at the other (Tabb 1984a: 5; Sassen-Koob 1984: 162).

Both the Nixon (Mollenkopf 1983:129) and Carter (Wilmoth 1984: 237) administrations took decisive steps toward privatization, dismantling the social programs of the sixties and opting for reliance on the private sector. Poor and working-class communities, often the loci of anthropological study, were demolished as the poor were removed from valued central city land and public resources were increasingly directed toward the renewal of downtown areas (Tabb 1984b:257; Mollenkopf 1983:261). As cities lost (or gave away) their tax base and federal policies placed heavier responsibilities on local governments while circumscribing their ability to retain monies raised by taxes (Hill 1978:218–219), the cities experienced fiscal retrenchment in deteriorating infrastructures and degenerating services.

Despite these circumstances, the effects of the social protests of the sixties continued to be evident. For example, concessions such as the Community Action Program were not so easily dismantled.[3] To a great extent, however, government-sponsored community organization can also be seen as an attempt to channel and defuse confrontational politics that are real attempts to gain power over urban services from a neighborhood base (see Jones, in this volume), and as Mollenkopf (1983:96) notes, the federal urban programs of the Great Society advanced the interests of upwardly mobile whites without trickling down to central city minorities (see also Mikell, in this volume). Nevertheless, almost one-fourth of Afro-Americans elected to local offices in the 1970s received their initial training in Community Action programs (Mollenkopf 1983:126). The electoral struggles, the attempts to gain community control over schools, hospitals, and other services, continued. Further, the momentum of the sixties, particularly the Afro-American liberation movement, inspired social protest among women, the elderly, and other minorities.

It is within this context that the contributors to this volume grapple with understanding the urban United States. The articles take various theoretical perspectives (e.g., social-historical, cultural-materialist, ethnoecological, Marxist), but are unified by their insistence on looking at the vertical links that connect the social groups studied by anthropologists to the larger society. I will review some of the more important themes raised in this volume. In taking this approach, I will give emphasis to the similarities rather than the differences among the contributors.

The most outstanding theme in the volume is the necessity of looking at the links between what Leeds (1973) has termed the microcosm and the macrocosm, and perhaps more to the point, at the reciprocal relations between populations and between processes. Many of the contributors select units of analysis and subjects of study that are familiar to anthropologists—communities, neighborhoods, schools, clinics, community organizations, occupational, ethnic, gender, and kinship groups—and make excellent use of the ethnographic method to provide a rich, detailed account of the people they study. As Sanjek suggests, there is no single correct unit of analysis. However, what one does with the unit selected for study has significant consequences, and these articles make the explicit point that the phenomena that have been of traditional concern to anthropologists cannot be understood without examination of how they are embedded in the political economy of the wider society.

Thus, as Sharff points out, "illegal" activities cannot be understood without explication of unemployment and underemployment and work in the secondary labor market. Susser and Kreniske draw the relationships between individual experiences and changes in public policy affecting welfare, which itself is determined by shifts in employment opportunities, the structure of industry, and the demand for labor. Jones investigates the way in which the functioning of a local community organization is conditioned by its relationship to state structures. Ogbu examines the links between the neighborhood, the school system, and those outside the neighborhood who control the school system. Sanjek explores the interplay of governmental bodies, community organizations, and various interest groups in determining the existence of a community clinic. Miller suggests that a polo club is not simply an arena for recreational activities, but is a node of national and international upper-class networks in which control over resources is maintained. Family, kin, and gender relationships are seen by Rapp and Smith as mediated by the class structure of the society; "choice" in fertility decisions is shown by Lopez to be conditioned by historical and contemporary socioeconomic relationships; and Safa looks at the way in which the history of industry and the structure of production affect the attitudes and behaviors of garment workers.

While many of the articles concern themselves with poor and working-class populations, there is an attempt to explicate the reciprocal relationships, the way in which populations are linked to each other. Thus Miller heeds Laura Nader's admonition to "study up" in his description of the upper classes who, through controlling the surplus from the city, are able to inhabit "the suburban-rural fringe." Ogbu portrays not only the culture of the Afro-Americans and Chicanos who supply the student population, but also the worldview of the middle-stratum Euro-Americans who control the school system, and examines the way in which they condition each other. Similarly, Mikell describes the interaction between middle-class and working-class blacks and Italians. Sharff not only investigates the illegal activities of small-scale drug sellers but points out their relationship to the established drug merchants, who make the real profits. The contributors not only discuss the welfare recipients but indicate that they function as conduits to "welfare beneficiaries"—the landlords, merchants, etc. (Sharff, Susser and Kreniske).

Despite the thrust toward "the new ethnicity" in social theory (see, for example, Glazer and Moynihan 1976), several of the chapters involve rethinking the adequacy of a concept of ethnicity as a self-contained, bounded group. The polyethnic populations described by several of the authors (e.g., Mikell, Ogbu, Leacock, Susser and Kreniske, Sharff, Sanjek, Safa) represent a significant departure from much of the urban anthropology done in the sixties and early seventies that sought out "tribes" or ethnic groups in segregated enclaves of the city. Mikell, using political relations in Newark, New Jersey, as a case study, is most explicit in arguing that race or ethnicity is a mechanism through which class relations are expressed.

A major proposition, then, explicit or implicit in several of the articles, is the use of class as a tool for analysis. The authors define class somewhat differently (cf. Rapp, Mikell, Smith, Safa), reflecting the variation in the anthropological literature (see R. Smith 1984). Although Rapp and Mikell differ somewhat in the way in which they designate specific classes, they tend to agree on the definition of classes being determined by access to the means of production, whereas Safa delineates an occupational group and seeks to assess class consciousness. Rapp underscores an important methodological point: that "social class is a short-hand for a process, not a thing. . . . class is not a static place that individuals inhabit. It is a process set up by capital accumulation."

Given this emphasis, it is not surprising that most of the articles are critical of concepts of culture that divorce symbols and ideology from social structure and action (see especially Smith, Sanjek, Rapp, Ogbu, and Lopez). Two propositions follow from this. First, these chapters depart from some of the studies of the late sixties with respect to the issue of urban disorganization. By eschewing the notion of culture as a set of bounded traits, and grounding their discussion of symbolic systems in social action within a field that includes analysis of the wider social structure, the contributors arrive at a different view of "cultural disorganization" and "deviance." For example, what is popularly considered to be criminal behavior is not a result of culture, passed from generation to generation, but a response to underemployment (Sharff) or to the welfare system (Susser and Kreniske).

Second, the fact that people are not simply passive recipients of the conditions thrust upon them but are engaged in acting on their own behalf is not lost on these contributors. They describe people acting to bring a community clinic into being (Sanjek); to manipulate the political situation (Mikell); to challenge the ideological images of "family pathology" and "patriarchal power" (Rapp); to build networks for mutual assistance in migration (Alvarez); to mobilize community action for education (Jones, Leacock). Though such attempts to address the system are not always successful, the important point is that people being studied are also actors, making choices within a structure of constraints that then modify that structure. Hence, one of Smith's major criticisms of the Chicago school is their neglect of the effects of praxis upon structure.

Finally, several of the contributors explicitly examine the role of anthropologists and their responsibilities to the people they study. A number of investigators (Leacock, Sharff, Lopez, Sanjek) point out that they made themselves available to advocate for the people among whom they worked. But for some, the issue is that of the political engagement of the anthropologist and how this bears on the question of values in research. For example, Sanjek's article includes an extensive discussion of the differences and complementarity among academic, applied, and advocacy goals, and Leacock describes the way in which she combined academic, applied, and advocacy work in studying schools in New York City.

These studies carry forward the ethnographic tradition in anthropology, but fieldwork is combined with a theoretical perspective that requires analysis of the larger structure and modification of traditional methodologies. Thus Sharff, for example, worked with an interdisciplinary team, and almost all of the studies supplemented participant observation with survey techniques (Lopez, Sharff), examination of documents (Jones, Sanjek), structured interviewing (Sanjek, Smith, Safa), collection of genealogies (Alvarez, Smith, Sharff), or analysis of budgets (Sharff). Given their theoretical perspectives, most of the chapters place the case studies in the context of historical or structural analysis.

In short, these studies build upon the strengths of anthropology but attempt to place the ethnographic descriptions in a wider context, to draw the link between the microcosm traditionally studied by the anthropologist and the macrocosm that in many ways determines the smaller picture. In their recognition of the importance of the political and economic realities of the urban context, these studies present a contrast to the anthropology of the United States presented in other volumes (see, for example, Arens and Montague 1976; Spradley and Rynkiewich 1975) that, as Sanjek points out, focus on analysis of symbols largely removed from a political and economic context and, for the most part, withdraw from the issues presented in this volume.

Urban Anthropology in the Post-Reagan City

The impact of Reaganomics on U.S. cities will be evident long after Reagan is out of office. It has now become clear that analyses projecting the decline of the old northern industrial cities and the rise of new southern and western cities were somewhat simplistic. As capital forsakes these cities for cheaper land and labor overseas, they too experience high unemployment and infrastructural deterioration. More to the point is the international division of labor and how this affects the forms and functions of cities as capital seeks the most profitable areas. Amid the fiscal crises caused by the mobility of capital, the policies of the Reagan administration have taken the direction of major cuts in federal aid to cities. This has been accomplished by reducing federal grants to local governments and giving back to state and local administrations as much responsibilities for programs as possible, without decreasing their tax payments to the federal government. As private interests increasingly control surplus through tax breaks and government subsidies and grants, the cost of the city falls more heavily on taxpayers and local governments are unable to maintain the services at previous levels (see Tabb 1984b:256).

The effects of this have been felt primarily by the urban poor and working people as the unemployment and underemployment described by the contributors to this volume have increased in the central cities. In addition to the "new poor"—people who have become poor as a result of losing their jobs in the most recent recession (Nathan 1983:58)—the working poor and minorities have been hardest hit by the economic policies, particularly as racial gaps have widened in the seventies. In 1984, the official unemployment rate was 17.2 percent for Afro-Americans, 11.6 percent for people of Hispanic origin, and 7.2 percent for Euro-Americans (Statistical Abstract 1984:407). A study in New York City concluded that Afro-Americans and Hispanics were virtually excluded from 130 out of 193 industries in the private sector, those industries representing 60 percent of the private sector work force and among the leaders in job growth (Stafford 1985). At the same time, entitlement programs have been significantly cut: in 1982, of a total of $11 billion cut from federal entitlement programs, 60 percent of those were cut from programs for the poor.[4] Many of the neighborhoods and communities studied by the contributors to this volume have been demolished, as almost all of the major cities undergo "gentrification." In 1981, the

Community Services Administration, the last vestige of the war on poverty, was closed (Dugger 1983:300). Block grants inexorably changed the nature of community organization by further diminishing the possibility of community control (Nathan and Doolittle 1984:27).

The anthropology of urban America of the next period will therefore take place within a context of increasing disparity between the affluent and the poor, between Euro-Americans and peoples of color. The anthropology of the next period, then, will need to build on the insights of the contributors to this volume in order to develop models that not only conceptualize the relationship between the populations being studied and the city state systems, but allow us to analyze such populations within the context of international systems. The necessity for such a model has been recently recognized by anthropologists who have called for the examination of the multinational enterprise (Wolfe 1980:83) and the search for causes at the level of the world system (Rollwagen 1980:128; Leeds 1980). I suspect that such models will increasingly require much of what we see as ethnicity to be viewed as a function of the international division of labor.

While many agree that such an approach is necessary, it remains to develop models and methodologies that can shed light on how international structural forces bear on the lives of individuals. While several of the articles in this volume give us an indication of the direction these might take, the task of adequately and convincingly drawing the relationship between international forces, modes of production, urban forms and functions, and the lives of individuals remains a challenging one.

In this endeavor, anthropology might draw on contributions from other fields of urban studies that have already taken up these issues. Boundaries of discipline increasingly become less important and theoretical perspective more so in explaining urban life. The urban geographers, for example, particularly those employing a Marxist perspective, have sought to analyze the organization of space as the product of social relations of production, and much of the recent work of the urban sociologists (see Zukin 1980) attempts to address these problems within a similar theoretical perspective.

Despite the contributions of these disciplines, many of the studies remain somewhat inert, without the feel for human agency that is one hallmark of anthropology. A central problematic remains that of drawing the dialectic between structure and action, between determinism and free will, between choice and constraints. Although anthropologists have also tended to see things in terms of structures and systems and to eschew analysis of the effects of praxis on these structures, it is perhaps in this area that anthropology can make an important contribution. The anthropological study of culture, of how symbols are used in action within the "historically specific contextual approach" (M. Smith 1984:14), if placed within the wider political economic context, can be a significant contribution to urban studies. With continued emphasis on ethnography and the study of human behavior at the microlevel analyzed with reference to macrostructural international relationships, we need to consider how to solve what is perhaps the last riddle of culture, demonstrating the way in which people create history within the constraints imposed by social structures and forces.

I suspect that the anthropology of the next period will continue to be an "anthropology of issues" (Messerschmidt 1981:5), despite Eddy's contention that the concern for social problems in American cities that gave impetus to the emergence of urban anthropology in the mid-sixties has largely disappeared (1980:142). With the deterioration of life for the majority of urban residents traditionally studied by anthropologists, urban "issues" will take on a clarity that will be difficult to avoid. As more and more anthropologists take nonacademic jobs and go to work for urban organizations, bureaucracies, governments, and the like, the problems of value orientation, advocacy, and political engagement discussed in this volume must be worked out in practice. As Sanjek and Leacock have noted, these developments have implications for training graduate students. Particularly in applied research, the issues raised by Sanjek and Leacock will be salient: the extent to which the values of the organization or funding agency under whose auspices the study is carried out become the values of the investigator, and the implications of this. At the very least, these issues will require renewed discussion of ethics and responsibilities in social research. The articles presented in this volume provide a foundation for these developments.

Notes

1. In 1960, 44 federal grant programs to cities totaled about $3.9 billion, and by the end of the Great Society years, there were over 500 programs totaling $14 billion (Mollenkopf 1983:93).
2. See, for example, Spradley's (1970) study of the subculture of men on skid row.

3. The Community Action Program dispersed $1.1 billion to central city areas in 1969; in 1974, $26.8 billion were dispersed in grant programs to cities despite the Republican administration (Mollenkopf 1983:91–93).

4. By fall of 1982, 660,000 children lost medicaid; 1 million people lost food stamps, and 20 million people had the benefits of food stamps reduced; 365,000 families with dependent children were cut from the Aid to Families with Dependent Children program, and another 260,000 had their aid reduced (approximately one of every six families on welfare was removed or had their benefits cut); 3.2 million children no longer participated in the school lunch program (Dugger 1983:287–288).

References

Arens, W. and Susan P. Montague, eds. 1976. *The American Dimension: Cultural Myths and Social Realities*. New York: Alfred.

Arensberg, Conrad M. 1961. "The Community as Object and Sample." *American Anthropologist* 63:241–264.

Ashton, Patrick J. 1984. "Urbanization and the Dynamics of Suburban Development Under Capitalism." In Tabb and Sawers, eds., *Marxism and the Metropolis*, pp. 54–81.

Castells, Manuel. 1976. "Theory and Ideology in Urban Sociology." In C. G. Pickvance, ed., *Urban Sociology*, pp. 60–84. London: Tavistock.

——1977. *The Urban Question*. London: Edward Arnold.

Collins, Thomas W., ed. 1980. *Cities in a Larger Context*. Southern Anthropological Society Proceedings, No. 14. Athens: University of Georgia Press.

Dugger, Ronnie. 1983. *On Reagan: The Man and His Presidency*. New York: McGraw-Hill.

Eames, Edwin and Judith Granich Goode, eds. 1977. *Anthropology of the City: An Introduction to Urban Anthropology*. Englewood Cliffs, N.J.: Prentice-Hall.

Eddy, Elizabeth M. 1980. "Discussion." In Collins, ed., *Cities in a Larger Context*, pp. 141–143.

Glazer, Nathan and Daniel P. Moynihan, eds. 1976. *Ethnicity: Theory and Experience*. Cambridge: Harvard University Press.

Gordon, David M. 1984. "Capitalist Development and the History of American Cities." In Tabb and Sawers, eds., *Marxism and the Metropolis*, pp. 21–53.

Hannerz, Ulf. 1969. *Soulside: Inquiries Into Ghetto Culture and Community*. New York: Columbia University Press.

——1980. *Exploring the City: Inquiries Toward an Urban Anthropology*. New York: Columbia University Press.

Hill, Richard Child. 1978. "Fiscal Collapse and Political Struggle in Decaying Central Cities in the United States." In Tabb and Sawers, eds., *Marxism and the Metropolis*, p. 213–240.

History Task Force, Center for Puerto Rican Studies. 1979. *Labor Migration Under Capitalism: The Puerto Rican Experience*. New York: Monthly Review Press.

Leeds, Anthony. 1973. "Locality Power in Relation to Supralocal Power Institutions." In Aidan Southall, ed., *Urban Anthropology: Cross-Cultural Studies of Urbanization*, pp. 15–41. New York: Oxford University Press.

——1980. "Towns and Villages in Society: Hierarchies of Order and Cause." In Collins, ed., *Cities in a Larger Context*, pp. 6–33.

Lewis, Oscar. 1966. *La Vida: A Puerto Rican Family in the Culture of Poverty, San Juan and New York*. New York: Vintage.

———1970. "The Culture of Poverty." In Oscar Lewis, ed., *Anthropological Essays*, pp. 67–80. New York: Random House. (Originally published 1966.)

Liebow, Elliot. 1967. *Tally's Corner: A Study of Negro Streetcorner Men*. Boston: Little, Brown.

Magubane, Bernard. 1985. "Engels: The Condition of the Working Class in England in 1844 and The Housing Question (1872) Revisited: Their Relevance for Urban Anthropology." *Dialectical Anthropology* 10:43–68.

Messerschmidt, Donald A. 1981. "On Anthropology 'at Home.'" In Messerschmidt, ed., *Anthropologists at Home in North America: Methods and Issues in the Study of One's Society*, pp. 3–14. New York: Cambridge University Press.

Mollenkopf, John H. 1983. *The Contested City*. Princeton: Princeton University Press.

Mullings, Leith. 1977. "The New Ethnicity: Old Wine in New Bottles." *Reviews in Anthropology* 4 (6): 615–624.

———1984 [1978]. "Ethnicity and Stratification in the Urban United States." In Berlowitz and Edari, eds.; *Racism and the Denial of Human Rights:Beyond Ethnicity*, pp. 21–38. Minneapolis: MEP Publications [originally published in *Annals of the New York Academy of Sciences* 318:10–22].

———1982. "Rationalizing Inequality." *Journal of Academic Skills* 3 (1):6–17.

Nathan, Richard P. 1983. "The Reagan Presidency in Domestic Affairs." In Fred Greenstein, ed., *The Reagan Presidency: An Early Assessment*, pp. 48–81. Baltimore: Johns Hopkins University Press.

Nathan, Richard P. and Fred C. Doolittle. 1984. "Overview: Effects of the Reagan Domestic Program on States and Localities." Manuscript. Princeton: Princeton Urban and Regional Research Center/Princeton University.

Peattie, Lisa Redfield and Edward Robbins. 1984. "Anthropological Approaches to the City." In Lloyd Rodwin and Robert M. Hollister, eds., *Cities of the Mind: Images and Themes of the City in the Social Sciences*, pp. 83–95. New York: Plenum Press.

Rollwagen, Jack R. 1980. "Evolutionary Perspective in the Study of Urban Anthropology." In Collins, ed., *Cities in a Larger Context*, pp. 123–140.

Sassen-Koob, Saskia. 1984. "The New Labor Demand in Global Cities." In Michael Peter Smith, ed., *Cities in Transformation*, pp. 139–171.

Sawers, Larry and William K. Tabb, eds. 1984. *Sunbelt, Snowbelt: Urban Development and Regional Restructuring*. New York: Oxford University Press.

Smith, Michael Peter. 1984. "Urban Structure, Social Theory, and Political Power." In Smith, ed., *Cities in Transformation*, pp. 9–27.

Smith, Michael Peter, ed. 1984. *Cities in Transformation: Class, Capital, and the State*, Beverly Hills: Sage.

Smith, Raymond T. 1984. "Anthropology and the Concept of Social Class." *Annual Review of Anthropology* 13:467–494.

Spradley, James P. 1970. *You Owe Yourself a Drunk: An Ethnography of Urban Nomads*. Boston: Little, Brown.

Spradley, James and Michael A. Rynkiewich, eds. 1975. *The Nacirema: Readings on American Culture*. Boston: Little, Brown.

Stafford, Walter W. 1985. *Closed Labor Markets: Underrepresentation of Blacks, Hispanics, and Women in New York City's Core Industries and Jobs*. New York: Community Service Society of New York.

Statistical Abstract of the United States. 1984. "Unemployment Rate by Sex, Race, and Educational Attainment: 1965–1984." *Statistical Abstract of the United States 1985*, pp. 407. Washington, D.C.: U.S. Bureau of the Census.

Sternlieb, George and James W. Hughes. 1983. "The Uncertain Future of the Central City." *Urban Affairs Quarterly* 18 (4): 455–472.

Szelenyi, Ivan, ed. 1984. *Cities in Recession: Critical Responses to the Urban Policies of the New Right.* Beverly Hills: Sage.

Tabb, William K. 1984a. "Urban Development and Regional Restructuring." In Sawers and Tabb, eds., *Sunbelt, Snowbelt*, pp. 3–15.

——1984b. "The Failures of National Urban Policy." In Tabb and Sawers, eds., *Marxism and the Metropolis*, pp. 255–269.

Tabb, William K. and Larry Sawers, eds. 1984. *Marxism and the Metropolis.* New York: Oxford University Press.

Valentine, Charles A. 1971. "The 'Culture of Poverty': Its Scientific Significance and Its Implications for Action." In Eleanor Burke Leacock, ed., *The Culture of Poverty: A Critique,* pp. 193–225. New York: Simon and Schuster.

Wilmoth, David. 1984. "Regional Economic Policy and the New Corporation." In Sawers and Tabb, eds., *Sunbelt, Snowbelt*, pp. 235–258.

Wolfe, Alvin W. 1980. "Multinational Enterprise and Urbanism." In Collins, ed., *Cities in a Larger Context*, pp. 76–96.

Zukin, Sharon. 1980. "A Decade of the New Urban Sociology." *Theory and Society* 9:575–601.

I.

PUBLIC POLICY AND THE URBAN POOR

Much of the urban anthropology in the United States has been concerned with the poor. The two chapters in part I examine the way in which public policy and the state structure affect the poor in two different urban communities. Sharff analyzes a predominantly Puerto Rican community in New York, in terms of the relationships between family needs, welfare inadequacy, and lack of economic opportunities on one hand, and participation in illegal and semilegal activities on the other. Using case studies from a polyethnic working-class community in Brooklyn, Susser and Kreniske investigate the way in which changes in welfare policy determine strategies employed by individuals. Both chapters make the argument that the poor contribute to the economy in ways that are generally unrecognized; and both draw conclusions that have implications for the "culture of poverty" theory.

2. The Underground Economy of a Poor Neighborhood

Jagna Wojcicka Sharff

At this point in history many metropolitan areas of the United States contain certain segments of population engaged in "underground," unreported or unreportable work. Conventional explanations for this phenomenon have not been very enlightening. For example, the "urbanism" school, principally associated with the work of Wirth (1938), suggests that urbanization per se leads to the destruction of traditional norms and values, creating a climate for illegal or delinquent activities. Conventional explanations usually also include some version of the "culture of poverty" hypothesis, first proposed by Lewis (1965), which suggests that poverty, and the activities people undertake to overcome it, results from subcultural values, passed on from one generation to the next. Various "deviance" and "psychosocial" explanations locate the impetus for participation in illegal activities in the individual or group's antisocial, thrill-seeking, or destructive impulses. All of these explanations fail to provide a rational, socioeconomic explanation of why some people do and *must* engage in "illegal" activities. This paper will offer such an explanation.

Empirical data collected over three years by ethnographic team research for thirty-six households and their kin suggests that:

1. Economically, the condition of chronic underemployment among the neighborhood's residents compels them to seek public assistance. The fact that the assistance levels are grossly inadequate even for sheer

subsistence requires the residents to seek additional sources of income in unreported or unreportable activities.

2. The systemic forces of monopoly capitalism which impose the condition of chronic poverty in the first place also provide the parameters within which indigenous social responses develop. Thus a situation in which men and women are effectively enjoined from the acquisition of equity and marital stability tends to produce strong mother-children links and specialized "investment" in the reproduction and socialization of children.

The research was conducted in a predominantly Hispanic neighborhood on the Lower East Side of Manhattan by a team of four researchers and two part-time consultants.[1] Utilizing the cultural-materialist strategy (Harris 1979), we began with a macrofocus mapping of the social and economic resources available to the residents. We then conducted a microeconomic and microsocial inquiry into the strategies utilized by households and individuals to secure viability and survival.

In the following pages I will first briefly describe the setting, the staff, and the methods of data collection. I will next discuss the concepts of underemployment and work in the secondary labor market because they provide the framework for the discussion of our empirical data. The paper will conclude with an analysis of the data.

The Research Setting, Staff, and Procedures

The first phase of the research, which lasted for fifteen months (June 1975 to September 1976), was primarily devoted to a census collection of the socioeconomic resources of the neighborhood,[2] and acquainting ourselves with the cultural and political leaders and institutions of the area. During the second phase we established a storefront office on Dolittle Street near the corner of Battery Avenue.[3]

We determined from our census work that the area was predominantly Hispanic. Utilizing a scale of twelve physical indicators, we concluded that the housing stock ranged from fair to uninhabitable. We found also that the area was deficient in commercial and social services, and suffered from one of the highest fire rates in the city.[4] Further, the area had the highest proportion of households with the lowest incomes in the city, and was characterized by a great deal of illegal economic activity.[5]

The block in which we established our office was rich in children. The boys capered on the sidewalk and street, riding skateboards and broken bicycles, sometimes into the oncoming traffic. They called out to each other while dangling from fire escapes or balancing on rooftops where they flew their pigeons and kites. They "hitched" rides on the bumpers of cars and on the backs of passing buses temporarily stopped for the traffic light. The girls played in slightly more demure groups, often darting off to wallop a teasing boy. Some tended younger children, participating in the life of the street from windows and doorways.

The children's vitality was striking in contrast to the dead-end setting of the street: the potted, disfigured sidewalk and street, the cool stench yawning from peeling entranceways, and the hum of biting insects, spawned in stagnant backyards and cellars. The children played and cavorted, breathing poisonous exhaust from speeding cars and the acrid smoke of yet another building burning down in the neighborhood. We selected our office site because of the children. The busy social life of the street, with mothers watching from stoops and windows, seemed like a protected base for excursions into more dangerous areas where "underground" activity might be taking place. As it turned out, however, we need not have gone farther than our storefront to acquire the information we sought.

For instance, as we discovered after a few months, the clumps of six to ten young men who seemed to be socializing on the corner from early morning until late at night were not there solely for convivial reasons. Nor was the little hole-in-the-wall cigarette store near the corner selling only tobacco cigarettes. Nor was the storefront next to ours just the home of a popular bachelor with lots of friends continuously dropping by; nor was the mechanic next door simply repairing cars. The social club across the street was selling more than drinks, and the *bodega* (small grocery store) next to it was selling more than groceries. And finally, as we learned much later, the mothers conversing in small groups and calling out of the windows were not simply occupied with housework and child care. Nor were the children simply playing. As we were to discover with the arrival of colder weather, almost every man, woman, and older child on the block was actively engaged in providing services or securing additional goods and income for his or her household through licit or illicit occupations.

Because the initial subject of inquiry, "the socioeconomic context of drug use and commerce," promised to be dangerous, the project director hired a predominantly female staff.[6] The lone male member of the staff, a national of the Netherlands who had resided in the neighborhood for the past seven years, had established residential credentials and networks. The other staff members included two bilingual Puerto Rican women, both raised in *El Barrio* (East Harlem), and a Spanish-speaking sociolinguist woman consultant who joined the project in its last year, as did a female nutritionist for a brief period of time. The project director was also a female who speaks Spanish.

From the outset we explained our research interest as wanting to know "how people make a living in this neighborhood." We also made it clear that we were interested in the economic, social, and psychological value and use of drugs. We made ourselves available as advocates to the residents and helped them with their many problems but especially in their dealing with bureaucratics in impersonal institutions.

It took a long time and a great deal of energy before the residents began to tolerate, accept, and finally trust us. Through observation, participant observation, and audio-taped interviews, we collected information from approximately 200 individuals. The data included genealogies, official budgets, and patterns of work and leisure. However, it was not until the last months of the third year of the research that we began to obtain "unofficial" budgets from some of the residents, who had by then become well acquainted with various staff members, through mutual visiting and continuous daily interaction.

The criteria for inclusion in the final sample of households on which this paper is based included a complete genealogy and a detailed account of the household's income, assets, and expenditures. Fertility data as well as the incidence of accidents and homicides were also collected. The most important criterion was that all the information be confirmed by repeated daily interaction and observation. The final group of thirty-six households containing 133 individuals who met these criteria was not a random sample, because the kind and quality of information sought cannot be obtained by random sampling. The information presented below cannot be matched for depth and accuracy by any survey or sampling method. It is also probably rather conservative. The individuals who provided us with the data were mutually selected. Those who had a great deal to hide avoided us or refused to be interviewed. In the following section the theoretical framework for the presentation of the data is discussed.

Unemployment, Underemployment, and the Dual Labor Market

According to the U.S. Department of Labor, "Unemployed persons are those who (a) were not working during the survey week and made specific efforts to find a job in the preceding four weeks; (b) were on layoff and waiting to be recalled; or (c) were waiting to report to a new job within 30 days" (Bureau of Labor Statistics, 1980).

In order to understand the economic conditions in which the households exist, a brief discussion of the concepts of underemployment and the dual labor market is necessary. Economic analysts have suggested that, especially for poverty areas, unemployment statistics simply do not begin to measure the extent of the problem. For example, Spring, Harrison, and Vietorisz write: "To gauge the degree of labor-market failure, it is necessary to know not only the magnitude of overt unemployment, but also the extent of worker discouragement . . . the number of people who can find only part-time work; and the number who hold jobs but at inadequate pay" (1977:67). They demonstrate that official unemployment statistics of 9.2 percent for ten ghetto areas in ten major cities "take a horrifying leap" to an average of 61.2 percent when the other underemployment factors are measured (1977:68). Thus official unemployment figures offer no clue as to how many workers earn salaries inadequate for the support of a family, how many are forced to work part-time, how many hold only seasonal jobs, and how many have simply given up looking.

The phenomenon of underemployment is well explained within the context of the dual labor market theory. The theory proposes that in the mature stage of the capitalist economy different labor markets develop. The "primary sector" is characterized by stable, heavily capitalized monopoly industries, which require and employ a disciplined, skilled labor force and allow unionization and promotional ladders. The secondary sector is composed of marginal, unstable industries which are labor intensive and in order to remain economically viable require a transient, unskilled, and nonunionized labor force (Bluestone 1977; Gordon 1977; Harrison 1977; Piore 1977, 1979). Harrison is even more specific and suggests that the primary or "core" sector is surrounded by "peripheral segments" of which the secondary sector is just one. The other periphery sectors include the training sector (federal training programs), the welfare sector, and the "irregular economy"—unreported and unreportable work (1977:103). He contends that underemployed workers frequently move from one segment of the periphery to another but are seldom able to penetrate into the primary work sector.

Further, recent economic developments have produced a situation where job security enjoyed by workers in the primary sector during the "boom" years of 1940–1970 has been severely undermined and is deteriorating. Layoffs in such key industries as the auto and steel industries are swelling the ranks of the unemployed and make it even less likely that the poorest segment of the population can find regular work.

Harrison and others suggest that the condition of underemployment helps to trap an available pool of potential workers who can be recruited to support low-wage, marginal, or faltering industries. Through the mechanism of discrimination, the workers are relegated to work in the secondary labor market at substandard wages. Furthermore, these authors suggest the welfare, training, and irregular economy sectors serve as stabilizers by feeding into, complementing, and reinforcing the secondary labor market.

The function of the underemployed (or subemployed) in monopoly capitalism is dual: they support marginal industries with their exploited labor and constitute a reserve labor pool. As Magdoff and Sweezy write:

> What has to be kept constantly in mind is that these workers are employed in highly competitive branches of an increasingly monopoly-dominated economy. The result is that a large part, and perhaps most . . . of the surplus value produced in these competitive industries is *drained off* and *realized* in the monopolized sectors of the economy. Nor is this the only reason why this substandard and superexploited part of the economy is important to big capital. The existence of a large number of low-wage workers who are always ready and anxious to move into better paying jobs if any are available acts as a drag on the bargaining power of the better-paid workers in the monopolized sectors of the system. (1977:83, italics in the original)

Let us now turn to the question of underemployment, how it affects working people in general and the households we studied in particular.

The Research Households and Underemployment

The general socioeconomic characteristics of the research households in 1979 were as follows: of a total of 133 individuals residing in the households, 56 percent were under the age of eighteen (see table 2.1 for the age and sex distribution). Thirty of the households were Puerto Rican

Table 2.1. Persons Residing in Research Households, 1979: Sex and Age Distribution

Age	Under 5	5-9	10-14	15-19	20-24	25-35	35-44	45-54	55-64	Total
Male	6	10	12	16	5	13	4	1	0	67
Female	7	3	17	9	3	12	7	7	1	66
										Total 133

(83 percent), two were black (6 percent), and four were white ethnic (11 percent). Of the latter, one was Italian, one was Jewish-Irish, one was Irish, and one was Polish. In 1979, the majority of the households resided in privately owned tenements; five lived in public housing, and only one household resided in moderate-income new housing. The residents who were able to work, and who did find work, earned (with some exceptions) wages at minimum or below-minimum rates ($3.10 per hour). I will consider below, in detail, how they made a living.

Since 1967, the Bureau of Labor Statistics has published a three-level list of family income needs adjusted for living costs in various cities in the United States. Its "lower budget" figure is considered by a number of analysts as a very modest level below which households are considered to be in poverty (de Lone 1979; Keniston 1977; Spring et al. 1977). For a family of four residing in New York City in 1979, that figure was $12,063 (Bureau of Labor Statistics 1979). How does this figure compare with earnings of persons in the secondary labor market?

Assuming that a man could find continuous steady work (which is rare) and worked forty hours a week, fifty weeks of the year, at the minimum wage of $3.10 an hour (most residents work at minimum wage or below), he would gross $6,200. That is a little over half of the amount necessary to support a wife and two children above the poverty level. A woman working under the same conditions and earning 60 percent of what the man earns would gross approximately $3,720.[7] Their combined annual income would be approximately $9,920, or still at three-fourths of the lower-level budget.

But these hypothetical figures assume that the two adults would be able to find steady work, and this is not the case for workers in the secondary labor market. As Spring et al. point out, "The majority of low-income families in America are unable to find enough work to occupy more than one 'full-time-equivalent' member" (1977:68). They write: "In 1970, the average number of 'full-time-equivalent' workers per low-income family was *less than one!* In other words, one person (usually the male head) worked nearly (but not totally) full-time, or several family members worked, but very sporadically. It is therefore useless—and cynical—to tell those for whom jobs do not exist that they could relieve their poverty if only they would be more willing to work" (*ibid.*, italics in the original).

Before presenting the data about work patterns in the research households, the question of whether there is evidence of underemployment or work in the secondary labor market among the city's poor should be addressed. The kind of statistics which enabled Spring et al. to calculate the "horrifying leap" from unemployment to underemployment figures is no longer collected.[8] However, there are some data available on Puerto Rican New Yorkers that would permit plausible extrapolation.

According to a Bureau of Labor Statistics report for New York City, "All of the occupational data point to the conclusion that New York Puerto Ricans are disproportionally employed in semi-skilled or unskilled jobs at the bottom of the occupational distribution" (Bureau of Labor Statistics 1975:97). The report notes that New York City's loss of jobs, especially in manufacturing, would have the heaviest impact on Puerto Ricans. The report also indicates that in addition to work in manufacturing, most Puerto Rican workers were concentrated in secondary market jobs, as packers and wrappers in the retail trade, and as cooks, cleaners, and health service workers in the service trades. They accounted for one-fifth of the area's busboys and dishwashers (1975:85). The official unemployment rate for Puerto Ricans in New York City in 1979 was 11.3 percent. A plausible estimate of underemployment in poor neighborhoods of the city should approach 70 percent (Gordon 1977).

Table 2.2 shows the "regular" work performed by the household members and their kin during the year 1978—79. By "regular" work I mean all of the wage-earning activities which are not illegal per se. It includes steady, temporary, and part-time work in manufacturing, service trades, and self-employment. The "manufacturing" category is self-explanatory. Of the four men under thirty years of age who worked in manufacturing, only one worked during the entire year, and another worked almost a year. The latter "commuted" to a factory in Connecticut, which entailed a long subway ride to East Harlem whence he traveled by car with a friend to the factory. Aside from his high expenses for transportation, shared with his friend, he spent five hours daily in travel. A family emergency forced him to miss a week of work and he was fired. The two other young men worked only for a few weeks before they were laid off. Among people over thirty years old, three of the men worked steadily, one for only half of the year, and the woman for only two months. The latter worked using a "borrowed" social security card (more about that later) for a seasonal producer of Christmas ornaments.

The "service" category in table 2.2 is also self-explanatory with the exception of the CETA/MFY category. These are federally funded "training" programs which pay stipends to the "trainees." The two teenagers

Table 2.2. "Regular" Work of Household Members and Kin, 1978–1979

Type of Work	Age 8–12 M	F	13–16 M	F	17–21 M	F	22–30 M	F	31–40 M	F	41–50 M	F	50–60 M	F	Weekly Earnings Range[a]
Manufacturing															
Accessories							1		1						$90–$120
Clothing					1						1				90–120
Other					1		1				2	1			90–120
Service															
CETA training/MFY			1	1			2	1	1	1					65–90
Community worker					2			1							50–200
Dry Cleaners							1	2							90–150
Guard (police)									1						200–300
Hospital aide											1				120–200
Office cleaner	1			1											5–10
Retail cashier p/t			2												35–45
Clerk p/t				1				1							35–45
Packer p/t		4													5–15
Restaurant/bar waitress										1		1			60–140

Self-Employed								Earnings[a]
Baby-sitter	1				1			5–20
Carpenter		3			1			60–90
Dog breeder	1					1		5–10
Handy man/janitor					1	1		40–60
Home sales				1	1			10–15
Landlord							1	250–300
Legal suits		1	1	1		1		10–15[b]
Musician		1	1	1				20–40
Paid advocate							1	80–120
Painter				1	1			5–10
Police "line up"				1				5–10
Religious specialist						1		10–20
Street mechanic				1				40–50
Street vendor						1		10–20
Total[c]	25	56	50	96	55	74	20	

[a] Represents earnings when work is available, which it often is not.
[b] Difficult to estimate, since individuals sue occasionally.
[c] Represents number of jobs, since individuals may perform more than one job.

who had summer jobs with MFY earned sixty-five dollars a week and spent most of the eight weeks of the program without receiving any useful training. The older people enrolled in the CETA program received ninety dollars per week for the full-time, arduous work of sealing up vacant buildings and demolition and renovation work. The program "terminated" most of the workers before the year was finished. Of the other workers in the "service" category, the man employed in the dry cleaning plant, the police guard, and the hospital aide were the only ones who worked full-time the entire year. The other residents were only able to find either sporadic or part-time work.

All of the jobs in the "self-employed" category are low paid and sporadic, except for the landlord who owned a dilapidated building and realized a moderate income from rents. Some of the more unusual jobs in this category require an explanation. "Dog breeding" entails the purchase or acquisition of a "hot" (stolen) pure-bred dog. Twenty-five dollars can be realized from stud services of the male, or twenty-five dollars per puppy sold, from a female. "Home sales" work is done by women who sell Avon, Tupperware, and similar products to their friends and neighbors. One woman (not listed in the table) worked as an itinerant peddler, buying bluejeans wholesale and retailing them door-to-door. Several people involved in accidents initiated legal suits and earned half of the money in the settlements. (The other half was kept as "fees" by the lawyers.) A "paid advocate," usually a man, accompanies people (recent immigrants) to institutional settings such as a court, police station, welfare office, public housing office, or employment office. His function is to guide, translate, and in general give comfort in these anxiety-provoking situations. Another job, performed by one of the male residents, is that of an "extra" in a police lineup. He stands in a line with an arrested suspect and other "extras" for identification by the victim.

The "religious specialist" was an older woman with a reputation for celibate and devout conduct. Among the services she performed was leading the *rosario* (rosary) prayers for nine consecutive nights following a death, in the home of the bereaved. Another woman earned money as a "street vendor," selling home-cooked foods from a make-shift stand on the street. The "street mechanic" (of whom there are several on every block in the neighborhood) worked directly on the street diagnosing and solving the car's problem by a hit-or-miss method. Street mechanics are usually backed up by a chorus of consultants.

It should be evident from the foregoing discussion of table 2.2 that most of the households' residents, through no fault of their own, are underemployed and that their incomes from "regular" work are paltry. In the following sections I will explore the household strategies for obtaining additional income supports to assure a modicum of economic security.

The Research Households and Income Maintenance Supports

Two-thirds of the households received some assistance in 1979 either from AFDC (Aid to Families with Dependent Children) or from the SSI (Supplemental Security Income) or both (see table 2.3 for the age and sex distribution of the persons receiving assistance in our research households). Women and children under eighteen years of age accounted for 97 percent of persons receiving assistance. Among children receiving assistance, 68 percent were fourteen years old or younger, and of those, 36 percent were under the age of eight. These figures are comparable with citywide figures which show that in 1979, 87 percent of welfare recipients were women and their children (Downtown Welfare Advocate Center 1979:2). Only 3 percent of persons receiving assistance were males over eighteen years old. For reasons too lengthy to discuss here, a number of people, including four children, who were eligible for assistance were not receiving any aid (see Susser and Kreniske, in this volume).

Table 2.3. Household Residents Receiving Public Assistance in 1979

Number Persons under 18		% of Total Persons	Number Receiving Aid	% Receiving Aid	% of Total Persons Receiving Aid
Males	41	31	35	85	38
Females	34	25	30	88	32
Number persons over 18					
Males	26	20	3	11	3
Females	32	24	25	78	27
Total	133	100	93		100

What were the benefits received by households on public assistance? In 1969, the New York State Welfare Department established a flat grant called the Pre Add Allowance (PAA), which set the "standard of need" at a sum barely adequate for survival. Since then the grant has been

Table 2.4 PAA Semimonthly Allowance

			Number of Persons in Household			
One	Two	Three	Four	Five	Six	Each Additional
$47	$75	$100	$129	$159	$184	$25

Source: HRA 1975.

increased by 11.85 percent, while the cost of living has more than doubled (Downtown Welfare Advocate Center 1979:3). Table 2.4 shows the
1979 allowance for all the necessities except rent and medical costs. In
addition to the flat grant, most of the households receiving aid were also
receiving food stamps. But because of the recent changes in the eligibil-
ity standards and a very complex method of calculating need, most of
our research families were not receiving as much as they were entitled
to. Using the information in table 2.4 and an average calculation for the
food stamps received by the households, an average family of four in our
households was receiving $258 per month from PAA and $88 in food
stamps, or $346 a month. This sum was supposed to cover food, gas,
electricity, telephone, clothing, transportation, furnishings, cleaning materials, personal care items, school supplies, and miscellaneous expenses.
Yet during the month of July 1979, when most of our household budgets were completed, the cost of *food alone* for a family of four residing in
New York City was $352 a month (Consumer Price Index 1979). In
addition to the fact that all the items covered by the PAA are grossly
underbudgeted, the Human Resources Administration (HRA) has specific limits for the rent allotment. Landlords are very familiar with these
maximums and charge maximum rents for substandard or uninhabitable dwellings (see Susser and Kreniske, in this volume). Often, however, because of the shortage of vacant apartments, a household must
pay more than the allotment, which must then be teased out from its
food budget. Table 2.5 shows the maximum rent allotments set by the
state standard.

Of the twenty-four households with children receiving AFDC, eight
(34 percent) were paying more than the maximum allotment for rent.
Thirteen of these households (45 percent) were paying the maximum,
while five households (13 percent) residing in the public housing paid
considerably less. The latter had an additional advantage in the fact that
these state and federally subsidized houses included gas and electricity in
the rent.

Table 2.5. Maximum Monthly Shelter Allowance—with Heat

Number of Persons in Household							
One	Two	Three	Four	Five	Six	Seven	Eight and Over
$152	$183	$194	$218	$226	$249	$303	$317

Source: HRA 1975.

We calculated the percentage each household spent on food and rent from the combined allotment of PAA, rent, and food stamps. The average spent on food was 51 percent of the total budget. The average spent on rent was 36 percent (41 percent in private housing). Thus the average spent on food and rent together was 87 percent.[9] This left 13 percent for all of the other necessities!

Comparing the official income with the actual expenditures, we calculated the annual "deficits" experienced by the households. They ranged from nearly $4,000 for one household to none in another. The other household deficits ranged between these numbers, with an average annual household deficit of $1,633. Households receiving SSI and/or living in public housing received support which was more realistic. In general, households with several male adolescents experienced the highest deficits, primarily because of the caloric requirements of this sex/age group. The only other group approaching the caloric needs of teenage boys are pregnant and lactating women (Burton 1976). But although the latter group's special needs are recognized by welfare programs, there is no such recognition in special food allotments for adolescent boys.

Three of the households had high deficits because of unusual expenses. One had a serious fire, and while the HRA contributed $400 in emergency funding, the actual cost of replacement of basic furniture and clothing was over $2,000. The other two households each lost a young adult male, victims of homicide. In this neighborhood a proper burial is the only ceremony a resident can look forward to with confidence, and although kin and neighbors take up a collection, the immediate household is expected to bear the major burden for this most important "rite de passage."

The Research Households' Additional Income Strategies

Given the condition of underemployment and inadequate income assistance, what were the individual and household strategies for reducing

budget deficits and avoiding destitution? Pooling of resources and sharing of living space was one of the several strategies used. Another was
the deployment of household members including children into regular,
but unreported, and irregular work.

All of the twenty-four households with children receiving AFDC represented themselves as "female-headed" to the HRA. However, fifteen of
them (62 percent) had a male resident performing the husband-father
role, while nine (38 percent) did not. For a mother to report herself as
single and deserted is a realistic choice (also discussed by Valentine
[1978]) because it is only by claiming to be abandoned and helpless that
she can obtain the maximum of the already inadequate assistance. Also,
because she cannot depend on the support or continued presence of a
man whose income is determined by his work in the secondary labor
market, she is, in effect, the head of household. While it is very important for a man's self-esteem and his role in the household to be able to
bring in an income, the jobs available to him are so insecure that he can
expect to be unemployed at any moment. When this occurs his position
in the household becomes untenable, and if he cannot find work
promptly he withdraws from the household. This is the major factor
underlying marital insecurity in the research households. (It has been
discussed in detail from a male point of view by Liebow [1967].)

Household structure in a poor neighborhood changes rapidly because
of economic exigencies. Within the period of a year, households may
change from nuclear to extended, from conjugal to consanguineous
(Gonzalez 1970) and vice versa (Sharff 1979; Stack 1974). Among the
research households, for example, all the common-law couples lived in
stable, monogamous unions, and presented themselves in the neighborhood as husband (*esposo*) and wife (*esposa*). The men paid for their share
of food and other expenses and made additional contributions to the
household budget. The contributions were proportionate to the number
of children fathered—one-third of the men were not genitors of any of
the mother's children, and they contributed less than the ones who
were. However, within the research period there was a considerable
change in the composition of the households.

Two of the households which did not have husband-fathers acquired
them. Four of the households who had them lost them. Of the latter,
one man committed suicide, another was murdered, and a third was
imprisoned. The fourth became discouraged by his low-wage factory job
and the long time spent "commuting." After a "grace period" of a few

months during which time he could not find another job, his common-law wife verbally drove him out of the house.

Most women feel that the well-being of the children is of paramount importance, and they act on it. And although they are shy and easily intimidated by the agents of superordinate institutions, they overcome their anxiety and persist in seeking aid (usually by bringing along advocates as reinforcements). Almost any activity or action is understandable if it is done for the children, *para el futuro* (for the future). So they do not consider representing themselves to HRA as single a form of cheating. They pitied one woman (a white ethnic) who had given up her child and, having been certified as "mentally ill," was receiving Home Relief. She was a poor *loca* (crazy one), they said. But another woman (a Puerto Rican) they considered a "welfare cheater." The woman had been collecting assistance for herself *and* her three children, even though the children were not living with her. She was denounced to the HRA by one of the women. Whatever actions are undertaken for the sake of children, even if not laudable, are excusable as far as the women are concerned.

Thus contributions from common-law husbands and children who had regular work (see table 2.2) were not reported. Neither was the work of the mothers themselves. Women who got jobs in manufacturing used either borrowed or purchased social security cards (stolen social security cards can be purchased for twenty-five dollars), and worked for a short period of time to avoid HRA detection. In the service industries, the employers themselves suggest working "off the books" so that they can avoid paying social security and other insurance payments, and in addition pay below-minimum wages. And finally, none of the income derived from self-employment was reported. It should be stressed again that the income earned by the mothers was very small, but a crucial addition to the household's income. The cumulative effect, however, of having to hide their productivity is that they cannot look forward to an old age buffered by social security income.

The final category of work with which the households supplement their income to be considered here is "irregular work." By "irregular" work is meant all quasi-legal or "illegal" income-generating activities which, if reported or discovered, might put the person in jeopardy of a penalty or criminal prosecution. The use of the word "irregular" in preference to "illegal" or "criminal" is suggested by the previous discussion of Harrison's analysis of the "peripheral" sectors of the economy.

The irregular sector shares the work characteristics of the other peripheral sectors: nonspecific skills, high turnover rates, low annual incomes, and a small chance of upward mobility. For example, household residents engaged in sales of illegal drugs participated in this commerce on the lowest and most visible (therefore most exposed to arrest) levels. The structure of the illegal economy closely parallels the structure of the legal one, with high monopolistic earnings at the top and low, unstable, risky jobs at the bottom.

Our awareness of irregular work in the neighborhood grew with the increase of those activities as cold weather approached. The idyllic romping of children, browned by the sun and nourished by summer lunch programs, was slowly replaced by growing gloom and anxiety. The children and mothers began to worry about proper school clothing, school supplies, winter jackets, and tighter food budgets. Older boys, who had spent the summer wearing cut-off jeans, became anxious about fashionable trousers and shirts which they considered requisite for returning to high schools located in the "outside" world. And although *all* of the children over the age of fourteen had applied for the MFY summer jobs, only two got them. Some of the girls were able to get jobs as packers in the local supermarket, but not all, and none of the boys were even allowed in the store. The huge Jamaican guard at the store, nicknamed "Jumbo" by the children, knew from experience the boys' big appetites and nimble fingers.

Toward the end of August, the merchants in the outdoor stall markets on Orchard Street began hiring extra "toughs" to protect their merchandise, and the boys started their raids. It was not uncommon to see a party of three to five boys setting off as if for a hunting expedition, and return a few hours later with several pairs of socks, trousers, and shirts. They called it "geesing," but they did not brag about it except in their peer group. The mothers avoided inquiring into the source of the spoils. Not all of the adolescent boys participated in these activities. Some had fathers or stepfathers whose special contributions at this time were essential; some had mothers who bought their clothes as they themselves began earning money in regular or irregular work.

As winter approached, the misery and anxiety deepened, and irregular work increased. Before Thanksgiving, as the weather grew really cold, the boys took bigger risks to acquire winter jackets and extra money for food. Several of them were arrested, and we spent long days in the courts with the mothers trying to get them released. The coming of Christmas was the lowest period for everyone. There was no money for gifts or for festive food. Also, the landlords began "saving" heating fuel. For a third of the winter months, in spite of constant protests, the building in which our office was located was not heated. The staff worked wearing sweaters, jackets, gloves, hats, scarves, and leather boots.

The mothers improvised. They dressed the children in sweatshirts and double layers of clothing under their cheap winter jackets. The most pathetic sight was that of the children putting plastic "baggies" over their socks to keep their sneakered feet dry. No one could afford boots or leather shoes. As we visited the homes during those cold days, we often found mothers with their preschool children in bed, trying to keep warm under thin coverlets. The incidence of fires also increased, as the residents began warming their kitchens with *ladrillos* (a brick placed on top of a burning gas ring to radiate heat) and electric heaters. And the utility bills, already grossly underbudgeted in the PAA allotments, soared. Even during the coldest months, Con Edison methodically continued to cut off utility lines for households in arrears in their payments. The HRA advanced emergency money to pay the bills and then systematically "recouped" the advance from subsequent allotments. This plunged the households into deeper deficits.

Table 2.6 shows the irregular work in which some of the household members participated. The total at the bottom represents the number of jobs people worked in, not the number of people who worked, because some people were engaged in more than one job. As can be observed from this table, adolescent boys and young adult males performed the most visible and most risky of these jobs, and they also earned the least. Women are low-level participants in irregular jobs. When they do participate it is in the relative security of the home. The most secure of the jobs are in the *bolita* (illegal lottery) business, which is controlled by conglomerates outside of the neighborhood. The latter skim off most of the earnings of the operation but also protect it from raids with regular bribes to the police. Only a few people, most of them middle-aged, hold these steady jobs.

Bolita (the little ball) is geared to the Puerto Rican community by the illegal numbers racketeers. The name itself has antecedents in Puerto Rico. Thirty years ago, Mintz observed and described its operation among workers on a sugar cane plantation. Illegal then, as it is now, the winning numbers were based on the results of the legal Dominican state

Table 2.6. "Irregular" Work of Household Members and Kin, 1978–1979

Type of Work	8–12 M	8–12 F	13–16 M	13–16 F	17–21 M	17–21 F	22–30 M	22–30 F	31–40 M	31–40 F	41–50 M	41–50 F	50–60 M	50–60 F	Weekly Earnings Range[a]
Bolita (Numbers)															
"Bank" manager										1	1				$260–300
Cashier/accountant									1						150–200
Telephone operator						1						1		1	75–90
Street collector									1						90–100
Home gambling est.												1			50–75
Drugs															
Street vending					4		6								25–50
Touting			1		3		2								15–30
"Guarding"					1		1								40–50
"Drug-o-matic"									1		1				500–750
Drug stand							1								200–300
Shooting gallery												1			100–125
Home sales to friends								1	1	2					15–30
Drug store								1							150–200

Criminal														Weekly earning range[a]
Stealing			8		2		1								0–15
Mugging			2		1										0–20
Robbery			5		2										0–15
Armed robbery					1										1–50
Street fencing			3		1		4								10–15
Fencing							1		1						25–35
TOTAL[b]	0	0	19	0	15	1	17	1	5	3	1	4	0	1	

[a]Represents the weekly earning range in work which may be sporadic.
[b]Represents number of jobs, not persons, since individuals move between jobs or may perform several at the same time or during the year.

lottery. Mintz observed (as did Padilla Seda on another plantation) that during the "dead season" between the harvest and planting of the sugar cane, participation in the *bolita* and selling of illegal rum, among other activities, were an important source of income for some of the impoverished cane cutters (Padilla Seda 1956; Mintz 1956). In the very different context of the Lower East Side, where the "dead season" lasts all year long, *bolita* and the selling of illegal drugs perform a similar function.

The New York *bolita* is based on the last three digits of the winning numbers in horse racing. People place their bets, usually ranging from $.25 to $1, with the "street collector" who goes from door to door or from one store to another, taking the money and writing down the name and the number his customers bet on. The bets must be placed before 12:45 p.m. for day races and at two separate times for the night races: 8:20 p.m. for the singles and 9:20 p.m. for the doubles. The "telephone operator" then phones the numbers to the central office. The "cashier/accountant" counts and enters the money, and the "manager" makes sure, as all managers do, that everything is properly done. When the winning numbers are announced, the street collector delivers the winning sum (usually on the following day) to the winner. The collector receives *una propina* (a tip) from the winner as follows: $100 on a $600 win, $50 on a $300 win, and $25 on a $150 win. The respective bets for winning each of these sums are $1, $.50, and $.25.

The staffing of a *bolita* business is usually home and kin based. Two of the residents, an older man and an older woman, operated the business from their apartments and hired kin for the telephone and collection work. On our block, a middle-aged man whom everyone knew went from one establishment to another collecting bets and joking with everyone. Mintz writes that in Puerto Rico the *bolita* can be seen as a form of investment (1956:366). Small amounts of money which would not be otherwise saved eventually result in a large lump sum of cash. This is of importance to people who by definition lack credit and equity. The cash can be used to settle debts or to invest in durable goods. Since the HRA regulations prohibit saving in banks, this should be even more true in New York. However, we found that only people who had some margin to spare played the *bolita*. The mothers played occasionally, especially if they had a dream in which special numbers appeared. However, they had devised better methods of saving and investing. The most important one was to "purchase" furniture or a washing machine in one of the furniture stores which abound in the neighborhood. They would pay a few dollars a week, for as long as ten years in some cases, until they were finally assigned to their "dream-come-true" apartment in public housing. Then the article would be claimed.

The drug business is controlled and supplied by people outside of the neighborhood. We saw no evidence of neighborhood indigenous drug networks of the kind described by Ianni (1975) nor of passage of power in these "criminal occupations" from one successive immigrant group to another. In fact, the evidence points to continued control by whites of wholesale distribution and high earnings. The residents work in the most visible and vulnerable lower-level, retail distribution jobs. Perhaps the most lucrative of these lower-echelon jobs is what we have termed the "drug-o-matic." It is a cash-and-carry operation carried on through a hole in the door of an apartment. The customers, who are sometimes steered to the location by "touts" (local guides) knock on the door, state their preference into the hole, and pass their money through it, and the merchandise is passed to them through the same hole. The operation resembles the automatic cash-checking bank machines. Several kin of the research households operated a "drug-o-matic" elsewhere in the neighborhood, but we had an opportunity to observe the operation when one moved into the apartment behind our office.

Two "guards" wearing green khaki "uniforms" (with "hardware" bulging in their pockets) posted themselves in front of the building's entrance from early morning until late at night. We counted the numbers of customers entering and leaving: each day they were 50 to 150 men and women of all ethnicities, many of them well dressed. Mothers in the building, anxious about the possibility of violence, informed the police, with the result that the police staged a raid.

But next day the operation was back in business and continued for several months. There was, however, a change of managers. A young man, who arrived several times a week in a gray Porsche with out-of-town license plates to check the operations and pick up the cash, one day was murdered. The next morning the "guards" were dressed in somber funeral clothes, but business went on as usual. The greatest danger to this business appeared to come from middle-level competitors and not from "law enforcement."

"Street vendors," the young men who stand on street corners all day selling marijuana cigarettes, are more likely to be arrested. Small home operations which include "shooting galleries" are also at more risk of arrest. These are apartments where a heroin user can buy the drug, and for an additional five dollars perform the injection in the apartment and rest until he is able to leave. The other drug operations in which several of the residents were involved were the "drug stand," "the drug store," and "home sales" to friends. All of the operations were principally engaged in the sale of marijuana; the "drug stand" was a small kiosk also selling regular cigarettes, often by the piece; "the drug store" was the storefront home of our bachelor neighbor, where people could buy and smoke marijuana; and the "home sales" were carried out by women selling small amounts of marijuana to neighbors.

The "criminal" category is self-explanatory. Adolescent boys who are not allowed by the traders to participate in the drug-dealing activities (except as couriers, but none of the boys in our households did this) participated in these activities. Most of the stealing was of useful items: food and clothing. The boys lacked skills for larger "jobs." For example, one day a rowdy crew of five of them set out to "geese" in a fashionable department store on Fifth Avenue. They were after gold necklaces, which are a very desirable durable good in the neighborhood (they can be pawned in emergencies) and which the local "fences" (dealers in stolen goods) have no trouble selling. The boys must have been spotted by the store detectives as soon as they entered. No sooner was the deed done and a handful of imitation gold necklaces in one of the boys' pockets, when they were surrounded and arrested. On another occasion four boys were apprehended just as they were exiting, via the fire escape, with the owner's television set. Seemingly endless days were spent at the precinct stations and the courts by the mothers and staff members following each of these bungles. The mothers swore they would let the boys "rot in jail the next time." The boys regaled each other and the younger children with horror stories of jail life. The one instance of "armed robbery" was done by a seventeen-year-old who participated with older young men in holding up a Chinese landlord as he was leaving his office with "fresh" rent money. The boy, who was "holding the bag" (literally, a brown paper bag), was caught by the police in the ensuing chase. He spent some time in prison and was eventually released on parole because this was his first (recorded) offense.

One additional explication should be made about the "criminal" category. "Fencers" are mature (usually single) men who pay cash for stolen goods and whose living quarters are turned into "show rooms" in which the customers can examine and purchase the desired goods. "Street fencers," on the other hand, are younger men who hawk stolen goods from house to house, from one business establishment to another, and to people on the street.

It should be evident from table 2.6 that all of the activities in the "criminal" category earn minimal incomes and place the individuals engaged in them at very high risk for incarceration. A few individuals obtain relatively secure, steady work in the *bolita* business. A few people can rise through the ranks to obtain high earnings in the drug business, but competition for these well-paying jobs is fierce and deadly. Table 2.7 summarizes the most recent casualties sustained by the households we studied. High death rates among young people, especially the males, are not limited to our households. They are endemic to the entire neighborhood, and the staff members attended many wakes and funerals of people we had known and liked. Neither is this pattern limited to the neighborhood. A recent Fordham University study shows that in the city as a whole, "for the Puerto Rican born population, homicide is the greatest killer, accounting for almost 20 percent of all deaths" (Oscar Alers, 1978). In the next section I will briefly consider some of the social concomitants of low-income living.

Some Social Adaptations to Systemic Poverty

In this paper I have attempted to show that the condition of chronic unemployment compels the neighborhood's women to seek public assistance for themselves and their children. I have also attempted to show that the public assistance levels are grossly inadequate, even for sheer survival. I have presented data which catalogues income-generating activities of the residents and suggested that most of the work in the peripheral sectors of the economy shares similar characteristics: low income, small chances of upward mobility, high turnover rates, and sporadic employment. I also described some of the strategies, such as income pooling and common-law unions, employed by the households to avoid destitution, possible starvation, and death. I have pointed to the ironic fact that in the quest for household viability, a specific sex and age group is at high risk for incarceration or violent death. I will now briefly discuss some additional adaptive strategies which may help to illuminate the data; namely, the value of children to the households and the role of drugs in the neighborhood. These subjects require a more extensive discussion than is possible here, but must be briefly raised.

To begin with the issue of the value of children, it is first important to

Table 2.7. Violent Death of Household Members and Kin

Household Number	Sex	Age	Date of Death	Immediate Cause of Death
01	F	23	1976	Stabbed in drug-related incident
01	M	25	1979	Shot in drug-related incident
03 (01)	M	19	1979	Shot in a dispute in grocery store
07	M	21	1977	Shot in drug-related incident
12	M	28	1976	Stabbed in drug-related incident
13	M	32	1979	"Suicide" in a police precinct
14	M	19	1978	Tortured and stabbed in drug related incident
20 (21)	M	30	1977	Stabbed in drug-related incident
23	M	28	1976	Poisoned by heroin additives
23	M	30	1976	Arson victim
33	M	24	1979	Shot in drug-related incident

note that the household mothers have a large number of children. The average number of children for all of the mothers was 3.3 children per mother, and for mothers over thirty-five, it was 4.38. Comparable figures for women (over forty-four years of age) residing in New York City are 2.4 children for mothers of all ethnicities, 2.6 for black mothers, and 3.3 for Puerto Rican mothers (Bureau of Labor Statistics 1975:47).

Mothers develop their children's potential contribution through differential specialized socialization. From infancy most of the male children are trained to become "macho" men and the girls gentle, competent mothers. This is traditional in most Latin societies and among most working-class populations. However, a surprisingly large proportion of young children, at least a fourth, are identified at an early age and encouraged to develop nontraditional skills and attributes—some girls become "strong" or dominant, while some boys are allowed to develop "gentle," passive qualities, as *patos* (homosexuals).

The children are then chaneled according to disposition and training into various roles which they will perform for the household. We have labeled some of these roles as "street representative," "young child reproducer," "scholar/advocate," and "wage earner." These roles parallel the specialized socialization which children undergo. For example, the "street representative" must be a "macho" man. He protects his siblings and mother, is the household's defender and avenger, and works in irregular work which allows him to remain close to home. The "young child reproducer" brings in additional assistance money, helps the mother with household chores, and provides replacement for lost members of the household. (A fourteen-year-old girl gave birth to a son within a year of her older brother's death. The child was named after the latter.)

Gentle boys and strong girls are also productive for the household's maintenance. They are, in a sense, "let off the hook" of traditional roles; the boys do not have to prove their manliness in risk-taking behavior, the girls are not trapped into premature reproduction. Strong girls usually begin their training as "advocates" by accompanying the mother to institutional settings (Sharff 1979). A dominant girl or a passive boy may be subsidized by the household to finish her/his high school education and will eventually contribute to the household's income with wage earning. This is only made possible at the expense of the "street representative," who begins his economic contribution earlier and has to "play hooky" to engage in income earning. Most of the "street representatives" drop out of school at the ages of sixteen or seventeen. The "child reproducer" usually drops out even earlier at the ages of fourteen or fifteen. It is from the ranks of the "wage earner" and "scholar/advocate" that there is occasional upward mobility through better-paying jobs or hypergamy.

It appears from the data, which has been only sketchily presented here, that children are valuable socially and economically to the households. They are raised inexpensively, on poor diets, sharing rooms, beds, and clothing. They begin contributing to the household's economy by the age of twelve, sometimes earlier. Their numbers expand the household "domain," which is mobilized and directed by the mother for income gathering and further network expansion. The children are the mother's "investment portfolio" organized with the hope that at least one or two children will "make it." At the very least the mother (and sometimes the father) can expect a modicum of security in her old age, since Puerto Rican families never send their parents to old-age homes. The certainty that some boys will not survive to maturity makes it important to have several sons. At a given time in the developmental cycle of the household there is usually a trainee for the role of the "street representative" who is learning the role from his older brother, a "street-rep-in-waiting." And finally, from a systemic point of view and contrary to conventional wisdom, the large numbers of children raised by the households are an asset to the economy in several important ways. First they are raised cheaply, through the uncompensated labor of their mothers and at very thrifty welfare rates. As they grow up they provide cheap labor for marginal industries and small competing businesses. They constitute a surplus labor pool which makes it possible for monopoly capitalism to keep the regular labor force on a short leash. Also, along with blacks they are statistically overrepresented in the U.S. armed forces and are easily disposable in the defense of capitalist expansion.

The role which drugs play in the neighborhood can also be viewed from several perspectives. First, from the individual point of view, the use of drugs has been shown to be related to continuing stress (Peele 1978). The stressful living conditions which the residents experience are especially pronounced for a household's "street representative." This is the sex and age category which has the easiest access to illicit drugs and uses drugs most frequently and in the highest doses. A few of the young men are or were heroin users. Most of the others use marijuana daily. It is used sociably and openly, and seems to perform several functions. It supports peer group networks on the social level, and on a personal level seems to allay feelings of hunger and anxiety. Its use seems to enhance the young men's ability to continue working in hazardous jobs and confronting the constant threat of incarceration or death.

Second, drugs play an important economic role in the neighborhood, as has been shown in the previous pages. Drug commerce on the lowest-echelon level is an important source of income to the residents. But from the systemic point of view, the ultimate gain from the drug trade enriches only the monopolistic top of the trade. The organization and ultimate profits of the drug trade are a caricature of the "legitimate" business. It is a distorted mirror-image of monopoly capitalism. And for the residents, as in other work, it provides low earnings coupled with high risk.

Recently, the Lower East Side neighborhood has changed drastically. Large real estate companies began to buy up the area in the early 1980s at the same time as Reagan's budget cuts caused the benefits to plunge, and many families lost their benefits altogether. As the rents in the remaining tenements skyrocketed, families lost their shelter because of the lowered value of the benefits and the HRA's policy of "churning" the caseloads (Dehavenon 1985). The stage was set for the gentrification of the neighborhood. Some families moved (or more precisely, were removed) to the outer boroughs. Others doubled up with relatives in public housing on the fringes of the area. A few were lucky enough to remain in housing renovated through "sweat equity," (the investment of physical labor), while others became homeless and now exist in welfare hotels and public shelters.

Denuded of its familial component and social constraints, the area became this country's biggest drug retail market. Middle- and upper-class buyers converged daily on the neighborhood from outlying districts and suburbs, while the young men continued returning to "work" in their old neighborhood. These jobs had grown even more competitive, frantic, and hazardous. Some of the street sellers became addicted to the substances they were selling as they attempted to allay the anxiety and stress of their working conditions. Ironically, it was the very nature of the drug transactions and the attendant danger that was the final barrier to full-scale gentrification of the area. Mayor Koch, newly reelected with the financial support of the real estate industry, removed this final obstacle to gentrification. Early in 1984, the city launched a massive, military-type campaign on drug dealing in the neighborhood with regular, housing, and transportation police and undercover agents. They were supported by mounted police as well as motorcycle, canine, and helicopter units. During the next two years, over 17,000 young men were arrested in the neighborhood, of whom the overwhelming majority were street dealers. Many of them now languish in city and state prisons and in federal penitentiaries. The fact that these institutions are so overcrowded means that most of the prisoners cannot be reached by training or rehabilitative programs. The stressful life in prisons with its chicanery and debasement of every detail of daily life ensures that very few lucky and persistent men will profit from the existing educational programs. And most of the men, once caught in the wheels of criminal justice, are certain to stay hooked up to the system. The women remain, raising children and hoping.

Conclusion

In the foregoing pages I have provided a rational, socioeconomic explanation of why a segment of the population *must* engage in unreported or unreportable work. I have briefly presented empirical data on the economic and social responses of a group of people to conditions of chronic poverty imposed upon them from above. I have also shown that the residents' ingenuity and aspirations are not different from other working people's, but that their chances of success are small. I have suggested that from a systemic point of view, the poorest people perform functions important to the economy as a whole. They produce and reproduce cheap labor. They subsidize small business by working for low wages and also by serving as "conduits" in transferring public funding into the hands of private business. They perform a similar "conduiting" function for slumlords who can be assured of steady rent incomes regardless of the conditions and services they provide, and for utility companies, regardless of the rates they charge.

The residents perform the most insecure and menial work in the regular economy and the most insecure and risky work in the irregular economy. Their rational, socioeconomic adaptations to these constraints have been analyzed by the social science establishment as the result of a deviant or subcultural mind-set. This sort of stigmatization is very useful to the few who gain the most from the misery of the poor.

Notes

1. The research team was composed of Nilsa Velazquez Buon, Nilda Cortez, Paul Van Linden Tol, research assistants, and Jagna Wojcicka Sharff, coprincipal investigator and project director. The consultants included Bonnie Urciuoli,, a sociolinguist, and Ronna Berezin, a nutritionist. Dr. Marvin Harris was principal investigator. The research was funded by a grant from NIDA (1-RO1 1DAO 1866), whose support is gratefully acknowledged.

2. The first phase of the research was funded by Narcotic and Drug Research, Inc.

3. The names of the streets are fictitious.

4. See the Hispanic Study Project Report (1976) for a detailed description of the area. The reasons for and consequences of high fire rates in the neighborhood are detailed in a separate paper by J. W. Sharff and P. Van Linden Tol (1976).

5. For a discussion of this see the Hispanic Study Project Report (1976).

6. The neighborhood is honeycombed with illegal economic activity and permeated with "law enforcement" undercover operations. Fierce competition, constant suspicion, and "busts" or raids by the police often result in violence. In these male-dominated activities females tend to operate in the background and are thus somewhat protected, at least from public assault, by nonkin males.

7. Puerto Rican women working full-time and in similar occupations as men earned approximately 60 percent of a man's income (Bureau of Labor Statistics 1975).

8. The Census Employment Survey which collected this information from 1967 to 1970 was disbanded by the Nixon administration.

9. Although the household members benefit from these allotments, they do so at the cost of poor diets and poor housing. The ultimate beneficiaries are the landlords and the grocery chain markets. This has been termed "conduiting" by Hamilton (1976).

References

Bluestone, Barry. 1977. "The Characteristics of Marginal Industries." In Gordon, ed., *Problems in Political Economy*, pp. 97–101.

Bureau of Labor Statistics. 1975. *A Socio-Economic Profile of Puerto Rican New Yorkers*. Washington, D.C.: U.S. Labor Department.

——1979. *News*. New York: Middle Atlantic Region, U.S. Labor Department.

——1980. *Employment in Perspective: Minority Workers*. Washington, D.C.: U.S. Labor Department.

Burton, B. T. 1976. *Human Nutrition*. New York: McGraw-Hill.

Consumer Price Index. 1979. *Bulletin*. New York: Bureau of Consumer Affairs, August.

Dehavenon, Anna Lou. 1985. "The Tyranny of Indifference and the Re-institutionalization of Hunger, Homelessness, and Poor Health." East Harlem Interfaith Welfare Committee.

de Lone, Richard. 1979. *Small Futures: Children, Inequality, and the Limits of Liberal Reform*. New York: Harcourt Brace Jovanovich.

Downtown Welfare Advocate Center. 1979. *Children on Welfare, Families in Need: The Case for a Welfare Grant Increase*. New York.

Gonzalez, Nancie. 1970. "Toward a Definition of Matrifocality." In N. E. Whitten, Jr., and J. F. Szwed, eds., *Afro-American Anthropology*, pp. 231–243. New York: Free Press.

Gordon, David M., ed. 1977. *Problems in Political Economy: An Urban Perspective*. Lexington, Mass.: Heath.

Hamilton, C. 1976. "Public Policy and Some Political Consequences." In M. Barnett and J. Heffner, eds., *Public Policy for the Black Community*, pp. 237–255. New York: Alfred.

Harris, Marvin. 1979. *Cultural Materialism: The Struggle for a Science of Culture*. New York: Random House.

Harrison, Bennet. 1977. "Institutions on the Periphery." In Gordon, ed., *Problems in Political Economy*. pp. 102–107.

Hispanic Study Project Report. 1976. "Phase I." Albany, N.Y.: Narcotic and Drug Research.

HRA (Human Resources Administration). 1975. *Handbook for Case Units in Public Assistance*. New York.

Ianni, Francis. 1975. *Black Mafia: Ethnic Succession in Organized Crime*. New York: Pocket Books.

Keniston, Kenneth. 1977. *All Our Children: The American Family Under Pressure*. New York: Harcourt Brace Jovanovich.

Lewis, Oscar. 1966. *La Vida: A Puerto Rican Family in the Culture of Poverty, San Juan and New York*. New York: Vintage.

Liebow, Elliot. 1967. *Tally's Corner: A Study of Negro Streetcorner Men*. Boston: Little, Brown.

Magdoff, H. and P. Sweezy. 1977. *The End of Prosperity: The American Economy in the 1970's*. New York: Monthly Review Press.

Mintz, Sidney. 1956. "Cañamelar: The Subculture of a Rural Sugar Plantation Proletariat." In Steward, ed., *The People of Puerto Rico*, pp. 314–417.

Oscar Alers, José. 1978. *Puerto Ricans and Health: Findings from New York City*. New York: Fordham University.

Padilla Seda, Elena. 1956. "Nocorá: The Subculture of Workers on a Government-Owned Sugar Plantation." In Steward, ed., *The People of Puerto Rico*, pp. 265–313.

Peele, Stanton. 1978. "Addiction: The Analgesic Experience." *Human Nature* 9:61–67.

Piore, Michael J. 1977. "The Dual Labor Market: Theory and Implications." In Gordon, ed., *Problems in Political Economy*. pp. 93–97.

——1979. *Birds of Passage: Migrant Labor and Industrial Societies*. Cambridge: Cambridge University Press.

Sharff, Jagna W. 1979. *Patterns of Authority in Two Low-Income Puerto Rican Housenolds*. Ph.D dissertation, Columbia University.

Sharff, Jagna W. and Paul Van Linden Tol. 1976. "Burning a Historic Area for Profit." Unpublished paper.

Spring, William, B. Harrison and T. Vietorisz. 1977. "The Crisis of the Underemployed." In Gordon, ed., *Problems in Political Economy*, pp. 66–69.

Stack, Carol. 1974. *All Our Kin: Strategies for Survival in a Black Community*. New York: Harper and Row.

Steward, J., ed. 1956. *The People of Puerto Rico*. Urbana: University of Illinois Press.

Valentine, Bettylou. 1978. *Hustling and Other Hard Work: Life Styles in the Ghetto*. New York: Free Press.

Wirth, Louis. 1938. "Urbanism as a Way of Life." *American Journal of Sociology* 44:1–24.

3. The Welfare Trap: A Public Policy for Deprivation

Ida Susser and John Kreniske

In this paper, we are concerned with the way the welfare system responds to political and economic change.[1] We are also concerned with the way public assistance exercises a controlling and constraining influence on those who rely upon it. From this point of view, publicly financed aid may be considered to be a political and economic mechanism which, while it may serve a variety of purposes, is frequently turned against those who depend upon it. Because of the disparity between its announced function—the aid of the poor—and the actual role the welfare system plays, welfare officials and regulations frequently force people into breaches of rule and law. In this sense, the welfare system may be seen as contributing to, or even creating, much of the ineligibility that figures so prominently in discussions of the provision of public assistance.

In this study of welfare provisions in New York City in the 1970s, we trace the links between individual experiences at the welfare office and the change in the general direction of the administration of public assistance. These factors, in turn, may be related to shifts in employment opportunities, the structure of industry, and the demand for labor—all of which, in the case of New York City, may be shown to have a direct relationship to changes in the urban financial structure (Susser, 1982).

Between 1970 and 1974, New York City lost 68,000 manufacturing jobs per year, and unemployment rates rose from under 5 percent in 1970 to over 11 percent by 1975. This industrial decline left many families in need of public assistance. However, welfare rolls did not reflect this increased need. In 1972, at the peak of registration, 13.7 percent of the population was receiving AFDC (Aid to Families with Dependent Children) or Home Relief (Congressional Budget Office 1977). By 1976, while unemployment rates had almost doubled, welfare registration dropped to 13.2 percent (New York State Department of Social Services 1976:19).

In the following pages, we will examine the processes which led to this reduction in welfare rolls despite the apparent increased need of New York's population. We will analyze several cases and various stages of the actual welfare process as they occurred in Greenpoint-Williamsburg, in the borough of Brooklyn. In our concluding remarks, we will suggest some reasons why changes in welfare policies might be taking place, as well as the way in which these changes may be considered to be consistent with shifts in the economy of New York City.

Greenpoint-Williamsburg is an industrial section of New York City that has housed a working-class population since the 1890s. In 1969, one-quarter of the industry of New York City was located in Brooklyn and one-half of this was in Greenpoint-Williamsburg. There were 95,000 jobs in the area, and the median income in 1970 was $6,879. The population was a mixture of ethnic groups: Italian-American, Polish-American, Hispanic, and black; these last two groups were located in areas fairly distinct from the white ethnic areas. However, poverty and the need for public assistance was not confined to any one group.

During the period in which fieldwork was conducted, unemployment increased throughout New York City. The unemployment rate for Greenpoint-Williamsburg—usually slightly higher than for the city as a whole—rose from under 6 percent in 1970 to over 12 percent by 1978 (Department of Labor Market Information 1978).

In our discussion of the welfare process, our observations and cases are drawn from fieldwork among all the ethnic groups of Greenpoint-Williamsburg. Although the descriptions will be restricted to one welfare center, our own observations of other welfare centers as well as documentation from other studies confirm that these experiences are representative (see, for example, Shewbridge 1972; Elman 1966).

The Welfare Process

The events described here occurred at the Williamsburg Income Maintenance Center in 1975–76 in connection with applications for assistance
made within the dictates of the regulations for AFDC and Home Relief.

Although people were not admitted to the welfare office until nine
o'clock, a crowd began to gather around eight a.m. Those who arrived
after ten were denied service. At nine sharp, a receptionist began to
hand out numbers. Each person received a number and was then directed to sit on wooden benches in the main hall. The length of time any
individual might wait was completely unpredictable. After a couple of
hours, the welfare officers and workers would begin to take staggered
lunch breaks; but for the applicant there would be no relief. If one's
number had not been called by two or three in the afternoon, there was
every possibility of waiting until five and then having to return the next
morning to begin waiting again.

When a number was called, the individuals concerned were directed
to the line for "groups"; on any one day, there might be between one
and two hundred people waiting on the serpentine line stretching from
the receptionist's counter and coiling interminably through the room.
The "group" receptionist checked forms to certify the client had the
correct information and identification. If something was missing or not
in the proper order, the applicant would be sent home—regardless of
the hours spent in waiting—to begin the process anew the next day.

If the client had the correct forms, the group receptionist directed
them to the welfare officer on the second floor. Making their way up-
stairs, people took seats on chairs arranged along two walls. In the
center of the large hall were long rows of desks, each with a telephone
and covered with papers. Welfare officials were seated at only about ten
of the more than twenty-five desks; about five of those officers present
were actually engaged in interviewing clients. For the clients, the waiting time was again unspecified. The wait might be fortuitously short or
mercilessly long.

Whether the wait was long or short, the interview was only the initial
step in a tedious and lengthy process. If the client had already filled out
an application, he would present it to the officer when his name was
called—along with an assortment of other documents (a rent stub,
information and evidence concerning previous jobs, and any forms of

"prior maintenance"). Even if the client or prospective client had complied with all of the written requirements of the welfare office, the evidence he presented might still be considered insufficient; other letters might be requested, depending on the attitude of the worker and the nature of the case. For example, officers required that letters certifying the status of the applicant be notarized. This, however, was not a legal requirement; despite the fact that a departmental supervisor had circulated directives informing officers this was not expected, case officers continued to require notarization of letters about previous maintenance. If letters were not notarized, the client was instructed to return another day.

If documents were in order, then discussion, wrangling, or, again, waiting while the officer made inquiries proceeded for an hour or more. If the client presented the requested documentation, including notarized letters, they might still be informed that this was insufficient information and be required to return another day. When, as often occurred, the client was not able to obtain the documents, the application was simply terminated.

If the applicant managed to successfully navigate this initial interrogation, he would then be sent for a medical examination. This required additional waiting in a different section of the building. This would be followed by an interview about possible employment and further waiting; he might then be sent to several compulsory and generally fruitless job interviews—after which the applicant would have to return again for an additional interview. To register usually requires four or more visits, all of which may entail a full day spent primarily waiting. The sequence of visits and the amount of time they will require is unpredictable, but may spread over weeks.

The indeterminate periods of waiting and the frequent return visits required by officials were the direct result of regulations and policies of the New York State Department of Social Services. Each of the welfare officers had been given training programs aimed at tightening welfare registration and eliminating "ineligible" candidates (New York State Department of Social Services 1975). They were taught to doubt clients who presented formal, legally adequate evidence of their situation. Their training resulted in making their own requirements even stiffer than the format outlined in departmental policy. In a sense, the welfare officers were right. The clients were not providing them with *completely* accurate information. It was difficult, often impossible, for any applicant to conform in every detail to the multitude of regulations—regulations that could be subjectively interpreted and modified according to the disposition of the officer handling the case.

The problem of subjective interpretation on the part of welfare officials is not the only stumbling block inherent in the system. By the very rigidity of their formulation, welfare regulations defy direct imposition on the day-to-day lives of people subject to the vagaries and contingencies that are a part of life in poverty. Despite the fact that people who pass through the welfare system are in legitimate, often desperate need of money and are legally entitled to assistance provided as a "last resort" for all, the very regulations which should assist them often make the process more difficult or impossible. In fact, the regulations, with which clients cannot possibly comply, *create* the conditions under which recipients may be classified as ineligible or forfeit assistance through charges of fraud. In the long run, such unreasonable regulations serve to deny clients welfare and reduce the budget of the welfare department. Concurrently, the lives of welfare recipients become strictly controlled and subject to harassment and public scrutiny.

But we have sketched only the application process. In order to understand the way in which the welfare system, the behavior and attitudes of officers, and the necessities of clients' lives interact to keep people from receiving welfare, we must consider some case histories. The following cases demonstrate that difficulties with the welfare system may begin with the application process but do not end there. The families depicted here each made different choices in their attempts to deal with the welfare system and circumvent the burdens of restrictive regulations.

The Ferguson Household

In 1975, Jenny Ferguson was twenty-one years old and receiving public assistance for herself and her two children, aged one and four. Her mother was the daughter of Euro-American parents (Jenny's grandmother still lived in Greenpoint), and her father had been borne in Puerto Rico. At the age of seventeen, Jenny left high school, where she had been doing well academically, to marry John, a twenty-four-year-old military recruit. John, who was of Irish descent, had grown up in Greenpoint-Williamsburg, where both his parents were born. Although

John wanted to leave the army to stay in New York City with his wife, he could not find another job. Jenny found work as an operator in an electrical parts factory. When she was pregnant with her first child, John was transferred out of New York State. Jenny quit her job and moved in with John's father, where she lived on the military stipend ($160 a month) allotted to wives. After a year, John left the army, since both felt the separation was destroying their marriage. However, for the year that followed he was unable to find a permanent job. He had no training and had not completed high school, although he and Jenny subsequently passed the high school equivalency examination. During this year, the couple were unable to pay rent and were evicted from their apartment. Jenny registered for welfare assistance. She described her situation as follows:

Me and John and Christopher [her son] lived with my aunt until John got a job. But he was fired for being late a couple of times. We were up all night with Chris being sick and he was late and then he was fired. Then he got a job window cleaning. They fired him because there was a slowdown at work and they had to keep the guys in the union working there longer. Then he didn't have a job for one year except for jobs on the side, that you couldn't count on. So I went on welfare. I had to lie that he wasn't there.

Jenny had to lie about the presence of her husband because the family could not have received AFDC were she to have admitted to his presence. On the other hand, were they to receive Home Relief the status of their aid would have had to be changed each time her husband found employment—no matter for how short a time or for what menial wage. In an insecure job environment, it is reasonable to be hesitant to report new employment; the changing of status exposes one anew to inquiries from the welfare department and can result in delays in payment one simply cannot afford. It was not unlikely that by the time the welfare department finished processing the change of status, the new employment was lost. The client would then be subject to red tape, prying questions, and delay, only to have to begin the process again.

There are additional factors the welfare recipient must weigh when deciding whether or not to report income. While welfare payments are lower than subsistence requirements, wages from temporary, nonunionized work are also low (see Sharff, in this volume). For example, when Jenny's husband worked, his wages amounted to less than $110 a week. Neither welfare payments nor wages were sufficient for a family to live on. In order to obtain a meager subsistence, families are forced to com-

bine low-wage employment with inadequate welfare benefits, thus laying themselves open to charges of fraud.

Jenny Ferguson was caught in a second situation fraught with difficulties created by the regulations of the New York State Department of
Social Services. When she requested permission to move from an unheated apartment in which water dripped from a ceiling leak onto the
children's bed, welfare refused to grant a raise in her rent allowance.
She and her husband moved anyway. Jenny expressed her position this
way: "My kids—if I have to go on the corner and sell myself they're
gonna have everything I didn't. I would steal. I'm already doing something illegal with the welfare. They didn't want me to move. They're
only paying rent from the other apartment [$104 per month]. They
don't know I moved." (Her new rent was $200.)

If she had accepted the welfare department decision, Jenny Ferguson's
family would have had to live through the New York winter in a damp,
unheated apartment. By insisting that the Ferguson family remain in an
unheated apartment, the Department of Social Services was in essence
condoning criminal neglect on the part of the landlord. In order to
improve conditions for her family, Jenny Ferguson was forced to ignore
restrictive regulations.

It is important to note in this connection the way in which the welfare system interacts with landlords who are attempting to maximize
their gain from substandard apartments. The rents charged to welfare
clients are competitive market rents, despite the fact that lodgings are
often substandard. Not all landlords will rent to those on welfare; those
who do quickly perceive the advantages to be gained by one who under-
stands and can manipulate the welfare system. Aware that welfare tenants are excluded from many apartments, landlords charge high rents
to a trapped clientele. The landlord can neglect necessary services and
repairs while still receiving full rent for an apartment that no one but a
welfare recipient would consider renting. (For a detailed analysis of the
proliferation of deteriorated "welfare" housing and the exclusion of welfare recipients from other neighborhoods, see Sternlieb and Indik 1973.)

Jenny's decision to move without the permission of the welfare department was typical of the actions of many welfare recipients—actions
that may place them in a vulnerable position with both landlords and
the welfare system. In their attempts to cope with untenable conditions,
welfare recipients open themselves to charges of fraud on the one hand,
and intimidation by landlords on the other.

The Johnson Family

Gloria Johnson's case provides another illustration of the way job insecurity affects a client's ability to comply with welfare regulations. Gloria
was a black woman who lived with her husband, her two children aged
seven and two, and her two brothers in an apartment owned by the
New York City Housing Authority. All of them had been born in Brooklyn, and Gloria had "inherited" the apartment, a prized residence, from
her mother when she died. Gloria's husband was a maintenance
worker. Unable to find continuous employment, he would work for a
period of days or months before being laid off. Gloria was enrolled in a
college program for working-class women which was funded by CETA
(Comprehensive Employment and Training Act).[2] Gloria's youngest
brother was in college and her other brother was an unemployed alcoholic. The household was largely supported by the biweekly welfare
checks which Gloria received for herself, her two children, and her
younger brother. Her second brother lived on the income but was not
receiving a welfare stipend, because the procedures for registering as an
alcoholic were both punitive and uncertain. Since alcoholics were the
responsibility of two separate departments (Supplemental Security Income and public assistance), they tended to be shunted from one department to the other. Thus, the Johnson family was trying to support six
people on a welfare stipend of $248 every two weeks, and consequently,
the family was in debt.

When Gloria found a job as a secretary, through the CETA program,
she did not report her new job to welfare immediately. However, after
three months, when harassed by her landlord, she did inform welfare
that she was working. A month after reporting, she was fired. She reap-
plied for welfare. Three months later she was rehired for the same job—
while still receiving welfare. Six months later she was laid off. Two
months later she found another job and again waited three months
before reporting her employment. The insecurity of Gloria's work was
compounded by the insecurity of her husband's employment. Both factors, combined with the debts incurred while Gloria was relying solely
on insufficient welfare assistance, contributed to her continuance of welfare beyond legal limits.

For Gloria, who had several dependents registered on her welfare
case, changing her status was not a simple matter. She had to consider
not only how she would be affected, but how the status of every mem-

ber of the family would be altered. She then had to consider what this would mean for the New York City Housing Authority (her landlord) and whether her subsidized rent would be raised. If her income went up, her rent would be raised and would be likely to cancel out the raise. The welfare regulations did not allow for instability of employment or take into account changing family relationships or fluctuating household composition. Thus the welfare client was almost inevitably drawn into conflict with welfare regulations. If Gloria Johnson canceled her welfare stipend, her younger brother would also lose his income. However, if she did not cancel it and continued to work, her rent would be raised in accordance with her increased income. Such were the calculations which drew the welfare recipients into jeopardy of legal prosecution in order to receive the financial assistance guaranteed them under law.

The Face-to-Face

The welfare department is not unaware of the circumstances that might draw—or force—a person into infractions of the regulations. In 1973, the New York State Department of Social Services instituted a procedure known by clients and staff as the "face-to-face," specifically to expose "irregularities" and thereby reduce welfare rolls. The scheduling of a face-to-face was an intimidating, panic-creating event for the people of Greenpoint-Williamsburg. Even if the client had been scrupulous in her attempt to remain within the law, it was likely that there was some regulation she had not complied with.

Mary Sanchez lost her job when a dyeing factory moved out of New York City, and was supporting two children who were not registered on her welfare case (for more details on the life of Mary Sanchez, see Susser 1982). She did not show up for her face-to-face interview because she was concerned that her budget might be lowered to pay her gas and electric bills. If the welfare department had discovered her large unpaid bills, they would have paid them and reduced her budget to reimburse the department. The situation arose because Mary had been unable to meet contingency expenses, subsistence costs, and her utilities bills; she therefore failed to pay the utilities bills. Rather than considering the possibility that Mary's allotment was too low to begin with, the welfare department would have reduced her payments further. This would have made Mary's situation still worse and would have increased the likelihood of further unpaid bills. Thus, Mary and her family preferred to live in fear and by candlelight rather than have their allowance further reduced. When Mary finally appeared for a rescheduled face-to-face, she concealed her unpaid bills in order to preserve her stipend at its current inadequate level. This left her vulnerable to a charge of fraud at some later date.

The Fair Hearing

In addition to the necessity of the face-to-face and the possibility of visits from case workers each time their status changed, the welfare recipients' lives were further complicated by the complexities and uncertainties of the "fair hearing." A woman who wished to bring a complaint and request a fair hearing had to master the technical details of filing a complaint form and overcome the myriad, ill-defined fears produced by the day-to-day rebuffs and dealings with the department. For this reason, clients did not often initiate such cases spontaneously; rather, they acted on the promptings of community organizers or social workers. As Piven and Cloward note (1971), such "outside" agency workers play an important role in assuring access of eligible people to the rather forbidding system of state aid. In fact, according to Piven and Cloward, much of the rise in the welfare rolls during the 1960s was due to an increase in community organizing, and it was community workers who began to encourage the use of the fair hearing as a legal recourse for applicants who were unfairly treated (Piven and Cloward 1971).

Joannie Gonzalez's case demonstrates the way in which welfare regulations and allegations of fraud can be used to harass clients even when they have recourse to a fair hearing. Joannie was born in Williamsburg of second-generation Italian-American parents. At the age of sixteen, she married a Puerto Rican man; they had three daughters and separated four years later. At the time of this study, Joannie was suffering from agoraphobia and never left the house. She was receiving welfare for herself and her two teenage daughters. Her oldest daughter had a child of her own and was not living with Joannie. Joannie's husband had not had a permanent job or supported the family since he left them. Their marriage was clearly a casualty of the high levels of unemployment and destruction of the male role described by Liebow in his study of street corner men (1967). In accordance with the requirements of welfare, Joannie had filed a case against him in family court. As she had expected, he had not responded to the summons and the welfare department accepted her case.

While she was receiving welfare, Joannie's landlord attempted to force her to move from the apartment she had occupied with her family for more than twenty years. She was the only tenant remaining in a rent-controlled apartment, and her eviction would have meant the landlord could have raised the rent for the apartment substantially. Both her mother and her brother's family had already been evicted from apartments in the building. However, Joannie took the landlord to court and won the case.

Having failed in the courts, the landlord began a campaign of harassment involving the welfare department. The landlord claimed that Joannie's husband had not really left. The welfare department found they could not substantiate the landlord's claim. Later, the landlord again claimed that Mr. Gonzalez was still living in the apartment and that he was working. A welfare official was sent to investigate, could not substantiate the claim and recommended that Joannie should continue receiving welfare. Again, the landlord complained; this time he claimed Mrs. Gonzalez was consorting with male tenants of the building. If this were so, Joannie's consort would have been responsible for Joannie and her family. There was still another investigation, and again the claims of the landlord were not substantiated.

Despite the fact that the welfare department consistently found Joannie to be without fault, her case was not cleared. Four years later, Joannie was served with "a notice of intent" to reduce her welfare stipend. She had been charged with fraud and was told her check would be reduced in recompense for monies she had allegedly claimed illegally. The welfare department charged that Joannie owed over $27,000 which, they claimed, had been collected fraudulently over a period of ten years. With considerable trepidation Joannie filed for a fair hearing. By the time the hearing actually took place she had been receiving a reduced check for nine months.

At the hearing, Joannie was told the evidence against her was presented in the letter of intent from the welfare department. The evidence was the unsubstantiated allegations of Joannie's landlord. The hearing officer suggested that there was insufficient information and the case should be closed. But the welfare prosecutor refused to drop the charges, claiming that evidence was missing because the file had been placed in storage. Again, the hearing officer suggested that the hearing be canceled and noted: "Why harass this poor lady. . . . Why should we put her through the whole procedure when you have no evidence anyway? Why don't you just call your supervisor." The welfare prosecutor remarked that her supervisor was new and knew less about the case than she did. She did, however, phone her supervisor and was told to continue the case. Joannie was then questioned about every aspect of her personal life. After almost an hour of interrogation, Joannie pointed out that her husband was in prison and could not possibly visit her. The welfare prosecutor reintroduced the letter containing the landlord's allegations as evidence. Finally, the hearing officer was able to override the welfare prosecutor's objections and close the case. The verdict was in favor of Joannie.

Joannie's case not only represents the difficulties a client may experience in a fair hearing—even in the absence of concrete evidence against her—but also the determination of the welfare officers to reduce their rolls and conform to state budgets. The case also illustrates one of the sources of fear and insecurity for the welfare client. The allegations against Joannie had been made four years before her check was reduced. None of the allegations had been supported and had, in fact, been previously refuted. There was no apparent reason for Joannie to worry that her welfare standing would be called into question . . . yet it was.

It should be apparent from the cases we have presented that the recipient of welfare assistance is enmeshed in an extraordinarily complex web of constraints. On the one side there is the welfare department with its rigid, even punitive, regulations; on the other, there is the Housing Authority or the landlord, each seeking to manipulate the welfare client to their ends. Any move the client makes may have indirect and unforeseen consequences; any move may bring to the fore a vulnerability, opening the way for charges and retribution.

Planning and Policy in the New York State Department of Social Services

We have cited a number of case studies in order to demonstrate how the welfare system operates. While some of the features are specific to the case cited, the cases are also indicative of the general workings of the welfare system. The difficulties which welfare clients experience are not simply a reflection of the inefficiencies of a mushrooming bureaucracy or a problem of policy implementation. They are a direct result of planning. In the 1973 annual report of the New York State Department of Social Services, the matter was stated in the following way:

There was a sense of urgency to the need for welfare reform. Beginning in 1962, national and state caseloads began to skyrocket. In less than ten years, they had tripled. By March 1972, they had peaked in New York State to a record high of 1.8 million. . . .

Since March 1972, when the first inroads under the reform program began to be seen, there has been a continuing decline in the State's welfare rolls. (1973:1)

In their alarm about the large numbers of people receiving public assistance, the welfare department instituted arbitrary changes which resulted in a reduction of the rolls.

In spite of the fact that the New York State–commissioned study of public assistance noted that

in the field of publicly assured general social services, New York City is so underserved and so poorly provided for that many of its troubled and endangered citizens can find no aid. There is no evidence of any commitment to the delivery of social services to people who need them. Despite a long period of planning and high expenditures in the public and voluntary sectors, the City lacks the capacity to deliver even those social services currently mandated by Federal law and State policy. (New York State Study Commission for New York City 1973: 1),

reforms were directed specifically toward extending the application process and trying to track down information which would prevent applicants from receiving assistance. They were not directed toward increasing accessibility of desperately needed resources.

In 1973, reforms included a lengthening of the application form, the introduction of face-to-face interviews to check up on individuals already receiving public assistance, a screening policy requiring mothers to document the absence of the father, and an increased effort to track down missing fathers. Each of these procedures was aimed at tightening regulations rather than increasing the efficiency of management or benefiting the recipient.

In 1975, there were significant layoffs in the Department of Social Services. At about the same time, the number of people receiving welfare assistance began to rise. The director of the Department of Social Services maintains, paradoxically, that it was the *decrease* of Social Services staff that allowed the increased enrollment (New York State Department of Social Services 1975). Yet there is no evidence of increased fraud for this period. This would seem to indicate that the function of the welfare worker was to act as a barrier between the potential recipient of welfare and public assistance.

To overcome the shortage of personnel, a computerized system was introduced to uncover other benefits welfare recipients might be receiving which would disqualify them from public assistance. The major thrust of the Department of Social Services for 1975 was "reducing the rate of ineligibility." What was meant by this was that the department intended to scan the rolls for people previously determined to be eligible but who did not actually meet the new and more rigid interpretation of assistance requirements. Thus at the very time welfare rolls were beginning to increase because of worsening social and economic conditions, the Department of Social Services redoubled its efforts to keep low-income people from applying for or receiving aid.

Conclusion

Rigid regulations and bureaucratic delays combined with a pervasive atmosphere of hostility exacerbate and at times create problems in the already difficult lives of low-income working-class people. The workings of the welfare system also contribute to a sense of dependency, insecurity, and fear on the part of the welfare recipient. Such feelings are intensified by welfare officers who are required to suspect and harass clients as a normal part of their daily work. The regulations of the New York State Department of Social Services also contribute to exploitative landlord-tenant relations and play a part in the profusion of substandard housing.

Welfare regulations are not designed to assist poor people; rather, they are intended to discourage them from requesting relief and make it difficult for those obtaining assistance to remain within the strictures of the regulations. Unrealistic, punitive regulations breed ineligibility and propel welfare recipients toward fraud, because the very structure of the welfare system makes it likely one will at some time be guilty of some irregularity.

Thus the atmosphere of demoralization, disbelief, and harassment created by welfare regulations discourages application, accurate reporting, and changing of status with regard to welfare enrollment. The arbitrary application of welfare regulations discourages clients from asserting legal rights or pressing cases where they have a clear grievance.

Welfare, however, is sensitive to the political and economic climate in which it is granted. Piven and Cloward (1971) have shown that, over time, public assistance has responded to local political and economic conditions (see also Jackson and Johnson 1974 for a similar conclusion for New York City). Since the turmoil of the 1960s and the protests of the National Welfare Rights Organization—when the welfare rolls rose precipitously (Piven and Cloward 1971, 1979)—the New York State Department of Social Services has organized a counterattack. In particular, the concept of "ineligibility," which has been operationalized in a variety of ways and finds frequent expression in long, complicated application procedures and accusations of fraud, has been the main tool employed both to reduce welfare rolls and to quiet dissent. As a result, the first decrease in welfare rolls in twenty years occurred in 1973, a year in which economic conditions in New York City, and nationwide, were deteriorating.

The social costs and repercussions of such policies have far-reaching consequences. In the absence of decent job opportunities, householders are forced to live on marginal incomes and to employ dangerous strategies in order to survive. Alternatives are harsh and limited. The choice for many rests either in the dwindling temporary work of labor-intensive industries or in hustling and street crime (see Sharff, in this volume, for additional discussion of the relationship between employment opportunities and hustling; see also Belmonte 1979; Burawoy 1976; Valentine 1979).

Within a larger context, increase in welfare regulation corresponds to the general reduction of services for working-class people in New York City. There has been an overall shift in New York City's need for workers and the kinds of employment available. Between 1970 and 1975, municipal employment was the only area in which employment opportunities increased, but since that time even municipal employees have been losing their jobs. As job opportunities decrease, welfare rejections increase and members of New York's unemployed labor force are pushed into either illegal hustling or leaving the city.

At the same time as the decline in employment opportunities, there has been an increase in rents, and areas which once harbored inexpensive housing have been burned to the ground (Susser 1982). As the standard of living of working-class people has been lowered, these people have been moved to make way for new and more profitable developments. These developments have, in turn, contributed directly to the renewed "vitality" of the city in the form of the concentration of large plots of land—acquired cheaply after suffering devaluation as "slums"—in the hands of a few extraordinarily powerful landholders.

This land is being developed as high-rent housing and commercial office buildings (Susser 1979).

The policies of the New York State Department of Social Services were only one aspect of changes that were taking place throughout the economy of New York City. Welfare represents only one institutional aspect of intervention in the direction of reducing living standards of working-class people in the city with a concomitant reduction of their political and economic power. The decrease in public assistance benefits, the reduction of social services, the closing of public hospitals, the decline of schools, and the reduction of the availability of low-income housing are all indicative of a reworking of investment within an advanced capital-industrial system.

As a result of the processes of capitalism, many cities in the world are being transformed from industrial to corporate-financial forms (see Gordon 1978 for a discussion of industrial and corporate cities). Changes in financial structure, the trend toward gentrification, and investment in urban land all signal this shift (Kreniske 1979). Viewing developments in New York from this perspective, it is clear that the characteristics of public assistance in the late seventies coincided with and facilitated the broad-scale changes in the economy of New York City.

In the absence of alternatives and in the face of the prevailing politics and attitudes of workers within the welfare system, the low-income population of New York City has witnessed the systematic physical destruction of its livelihood and its neighborhoods on a scale that is seldom experienced in the absence of civil strife or foreign invasion. Without viable work and in the face of steadily worsening conditions, working-class people must either move to make way for the middle class or stage persistent and effective protest. Welfare continues to play an important part in this process—and insofar as it does, it continues its historical role, that of moving, manipulating, quieting, and quietly constraining the low-income worker. It is in this sense that welfare may be seen in terms of the larger economy and society; and it is in this sense that the apparent irrationalities of the welfare system begin to become comprehensible.

In the preceeding pages we have described the situations of people attempting to deal with public assistance in the mid and late 1970s. Much has happened since then—and virtually none of what has occurred has benefited poor people subsisting on public assistance (for a current description of the plight of poor women, see Sidel 1986). Since the initial study, trends that were emerging in real estate have become established, and the pressures that the New York City real estate boom have exerted on the low income, public assistance dependent have serious consequences.

In the last few years, the population of homeless people has changed demographically and numerically. Hopper, Susser, and Conover observe:

The changing constituency of New York City's homeless has been documented in unusual detail. . . . Early casualties of a housing market increasingly hostile to low-income tenants were apparent by the mid-1970s, when the population in the city shelters began to get younger, to contain more minority males, and to show increasing evidence of psychiatric disability. . . . Homeless women also made their appearance on the streets, in numbers not seen since the Depression (if then). (Hopper, Susser, Conover 1986:4)

Also, among today's homeless are entire families, no longer able to hold on to even the sub-standard housing we described in our study. Further, for the low-income person living on the margins of society, rising rent is not the only problem: in the last few years, hunger has been "rediscovered." With a government that has introduced profound changes in public assistance regulations and, as important, contributed to a changed climate in service agencies, it is difficult to be optimistic about the future of the poor in American cities.

Notes

1. Some of the case studies presented in this paper appear in Susser, *Norman Street: Poverty and Politics in an Urban Neighborhood*, (New York: Oxford University Press, 1982).

2. The Comprehensive Employment and Training Act funded employment in Greenpoint-Williamsburg from 1975. Greepoint was allotted over 250 jobs, funded through CETA, for workers in community service agencies. Funds for the CETA program were completely eliminated in the 1980s and the program no longer exists.

References

Belmonte, Thomas. 1979. *The Broken Fountain*. New York: Columbia University Press.
Burawoy, Michael. 1976. "The Functions and Reproduction of Migrant Labor: Comparative Material from Southern Africa and the United States." *The American Journal of Sociology* 81 (5): 1050–1087.
Congressional Budget Office. 1977. "New York City's Fiscal Problem." In Roger Alcaly and

David Mermelstein, eds., *The Fiscal Crisis of American Cities,* pp. 285–295. New York: Vintage.

Department of Labor Market Information, personal communication, 1978. New York City.

Elman, Richard. 1966. *The Poorhouse State.* New York: Pantheon.

Gordon, David. 1978. "Capitalist Development and the History of American Cities." In William Tabb and Larry Sawers, eds., *Marxism and the Metropolis,* pp. 25–64. New York: Oxford University Press.

Hopper, Kim, Ezra Susser, and Sarah Conover. 1986. "Economies of Makeshift: Deindustrialization and Homelessness in New York City," *Urban Anthropology* 14(1–3):183–236.

Jackson, Larry and William Johnson. 1974. *Protest by the Poor.* Lexington, Mass.: Lexington Books.

Kreniske, John. 1979. "The Political Economy of Tokyo." paper presented at the Annual Meetings of the American Anthropological Association, Cincinnatti.

Kreniske, John. "The Economic Anthropology of Development: New York City and the Corporate Transition." Manuscript.

Liebow, Elliot. 1967. *Tally's Corner.* Boston: Little, Brown. New York: The Commission.

New York State. 1973. Study Commission for New York City. *Task Force on Social Services in New York City.*

New York State Department of Social Services. 1973. New York State Department of Social Services, *Annual Report,* Albany.

——1976. New York State Department of Social Services, *Annual Report,* Albany.

Piven, Frances and Richard Cloward. 1971. *Regulating the Poor.* New York: Vintage.

——1979 *Poor People's Movements.* New York: Vintage.

Shewbridge, Edythe. 1972. *Portraits of Poverty.* New York: Norton.

Sidel, R. 1986. *Women and Children Last.* New York: Viking Press.

Sternlieb, George and Bernard Indik. 1973 *The Ecology of Welfare.* New Brunswick, N.J.: Transaction.

Susser, Ida. 1979. "Capital Development, Neighborhood Destruction, and Local Protest: New York City, 1975–1980." Paper presented at the Annual Meetings of the American Anthropological Association, Cincinnatti.

——1982. *Norman Street: Poverty and Politics in a New York City Neighborhood.* New York: Oxford University Press.

Valentine, Bettylou. 1979. *Hustling and Other Hard Work.* New York: Free Press.

II

URBAN JUNCTURES: ORGANIZATIONS, INSTITUTIONS, AND NETWORKS

The next set of articles examines a variety of urban organizations, institutions, and networks. Community organizations are the object of study for both Mikell and Jones. Mikell analyzes the class interests that give rise to ethnic politics and organizations in Newark, New Jersey, arguing that ethnic conflict and cohesion among Italian-Americans and Afro-Americans is not a cultural phenomenon, but is closely related to fluctuations of the economy. While Mikell emphasizes the political economy of the city, Jones focuses on the internal politics of a community organization in New York City. He concludes that although community organizations might initially function as advocates for the community, they often shortly become instruments of the state, operating to increase control over the community.

Ogbu and Sanjek examine service institutions. Ogbu's chapter describes a school system in California where the students are from Afro-American and Mexican-American working-class families and the teachers and administrators are middle-stratum Euro-Americans. He elucidates the historical roots of the differing "cultural definitions of reality" and the way in which these perceptions influence behavior. A free Gray Panther community clinic is the focus of Sanjek's study. Like Jones, Sanjek looks at the relationship of the center to higher-level institutions, as well as to the population. His self-conscious description of his role as an academic, applied anthropologist, and advocate for the clinic provides provocative questions and answers for anthropologists working in institutions or for community groups.

All four articles (and Leacock, in this volume) raise important questions about institutions and who controls them. The institutions described by Mikell, Jones, and Ogbu, to greater and lesser extents, have leadership sponsored from above, while the clinic described by Sanjek is to some degree controlled by the users. The contrasting situations of alliances and conflicts described by the authors allow us to consider some of the issues that may contribute to the successes and failures of organizations.

The article by Alvarez picks up some of the themes of the other articles in looking at praxis, or action, within externally imposed constraints. In tracing the history of network formation among Mexican immigrants, he applies approaches in migration research used elsewhere in the world to the study of Mexican immigration in the United States.

These five articles describe organizations and networks of poor, working-class, and middle-income people, formed for the purpose of gaining or sharing services and resources. Then in one of the few studies we have of the upper class, Miller describes a voluntary organization of executives, businessmen, and bankers. He analyzes a polo club, arguing that its underlying function is to help maintain patterns of upper-class dominance and conservation of resources through closure, status marking, and networking. An interesting issue, implicit in Miller's study, is the researcher's difficulty in gaining access to upper-class informants, who, as Rapp (in this volume) tells us, do not answer questionnaires—they fund them. This raises the problematic issue of whether anthropological methods work best for the study of the powerless, who are less able to defend themselves against researchers.

4. Class and Ethnic Political Relations in Newark, New Jersey: Blacks and Italians

Gwendolyn Mikell

This paper posits a theoretical framework for the investigation of political power relationships in ethnically diverse urban areas. The underlying assumption is that the effectiveness of many contemporary urban anthropological studies may be enhanced by further specificity in the selection of the units of analysis, both spacial and social. It is also suggested that the use of a class analysis will introduce clarity into what appears to be conflictual and competitive relationships between urban ethnic groups vying for control over urban resources and political power.

I will present a case study of Newark, New Jersey, where ethnic conflict, characteristic of the late 1960s and early 1970s, has its roots in the historical class development and in interethnic relations since 1900. As economic conditions changed in the mid-1970s, allowing for the penetration of professionals into public and private bureaucracies, the competition between blacks and Italians was tempered.

Theoretical Approaches

Anthropologists such as Haaland (1969) have recognized the use of cultural and ethnic differences as factors in competition for scarce resources. Although Haaland discusses the changing of ethnic boundaries and mechanism of incorporation over time as economic changes make it advantageous for purposes of social mobility, he hesitates to recognize the centrality of class and socioeconomic interest in explaining social behavior.

Applied anthropological studies such as Holmberg's (1965) of the Vicos project convincingly demonstrate that by changing power and economic relationships, it is possible to change social patterns and intergroup dynamics even for poor peasants. Yet the implications of such findings are seldom explicitly stated in these analyses of agrarian societies, and equally as rarely stated in urban anthropological studies. The preponderance of the data notwithstanding, anthropologists have often, as Firth asserts (1975:30–31), tried to escape the ideological implications of their findings if these findings parallel Marxian analyses of society in which class structure and dynamics is a dominant element.

An effective use of the class analysis in anthropology has, however, been demonstrated by the French anthropologist Terray, who states: "Class is, as it were, the place where the various dimensions of social life—economic, political, and ideological—intersect" (1975:86).

It is important at this point to specify the usage of the various class designations which appear in the following analysis. In application to contemporary events in Newark, these categorizations imply significant interests which are reflected in sociopolitical behavior. *Working class* refers to those whose relationship to the productive forces within their society involves them as sellers of their own labor power, not as owners of the value-generating property and resources, or as employers of labor.[1] The *nonworking poor* are those who are excluded from the job market, and who, unable to sell their labor power, are dependent upon social services and welfare institutions for their existence.[2] The *petite bourgeoisie* are those who play an intermediate role between capitalist owners of industry and resources, and the working class. While some may own property which generates surplus value, they are not large-scale employers of labor. Usually, they possess skills with which they provide services, and while often classified as professionals, they are still dependent upon their own labor to maintain their structural position (doctors, lawyers, small store owners, independent small farmers, politicians, etc.). The *bourgeoisie* are those who own the major productive forces of society (industry, capital, etc.) and who are employers of labor, extracting surplus value from the productive process. This group includes those directly controlling the capitalist sector as well as those who control the apparatus of the state in the interest of the capitalist economy. The *middle class* is a popularized but vague category often used to indicate social status as indexed by life-style, education, and/or income. It is used here to refer to a heterogeneous group sometimes composed of both *petite bourgeois* individuals and upper-income white-collar members of the working class.

Many earlier sociologists avoided recognition of class and socioeconomic divisions within the "community" by identifying political leaders (Dahl 1961:102) or types of influentials (Banfield and Wilson 1972:278), without differentiating between those who own and control resources and those who only administer. A classic situation is the location of these "elites" within federal and local private bureaucracies which are the base of urban resources (jobs, housing, social services, educational institutions). Allen (1969:117n) quotes Newark's former mayor Richard Hatcher's observation that because of their middleman role as administrators of power contained within the bureaucracy, there is often the incorrect perception that they are capable of directly utilizing the power of these public institutions and private corporations in the interest of their constituents. When they are located within the community-based associations and organizations, or operate as small businessmen, the appearance of ability to control and manipulate federal and local resources in the interest of their constituents is greater. However, their ability to undertake independent benevolent actions on behalf of their ethnic constituents is falsely perceived, often by the actors themselves. Tabb (1970:80) discusses the way in which these institutions perpetuate relationships of dependence by doling out limited resources to the upper strata of the black working class and the petite bourgeoisie to support notions of "black capitalism," and to utilize this sector as "middlemen" in the exploitation of the poor.

The following analysis of Newark demonstrates the circulation of white-collar and petite-bourgeois blacks and Italians into positions in local institutions and bureaucracies in response to developments in the U.S. economy and their regional reflections. This process was by no means unique. The consolidation of the Irish and German politicians and petite bourgeois elements in Newark around 1900 stands out in sharp contrast to the earlier competition and conflict between the two groups, and the development of segregated Irish and German working-class communities during the 1860s.

The case also reflects the fact that in times of consistent economic growth the petite bourgeoisie often speak with one voice, having relatively little regard for the internal ethnic diversity. However, as the economy tightens, intense competition is encouraged within the petite bourgeoisie on an ethnic basis, and the petite bourgeoisie begin to polarize the ethnic working-class communities in urban areas such as Newark. As the petite bourgeoisie push for "black power" or "Italian power," they often justify their actions by false assertions that they can manipulate urban institutions and economies in such ways as to benefit their communities.

In many urban studies the "community" is defined geographically by the selection of the poor ethnic *ghetto* as the unit of analysis, and the reflection of social networks (see, for example, Liebow 1967 and Stack 1974). The ghetto community is usually portrayed in miniature, excluding those institutions which link ghetto to wider society, and those persons whose social roles in these institutions involve them in a constant interaction with the poor.

The fact that the petite-bourgeois elements often do not reside there reinforces the notion that they are peripheral to the culture within the ghetto. Thus, there are few urban studies which capture the dynamic process of interaction between classes within an ethnic group; and by extension, few studies capture the links between the working class, the poor, and the institutions of the urban area. The absence of a class perspective in most urban studies leaves the reader unable to give depth to social patterns and attitudes, as well as changes in perception of other groups which are reflected in urban behavior and political orientation.

Since the social-class composition of most large U.S. urban areas increasingly conforms to the composite of well-defined ethnic/racial communities which are economically distinct, it is important that at some point community studies expand the unit of analysis to that of the metropolitan area, the city or the locality, depending on the situation. This expansion allows us to include in the analysis consideration of middle- and upper-class suburbs as well as working-class fringe areas, all of which may be tied into strong geographical and economic relationships with the central city. Rather than delineating the geographical range of social dynamics within the area under study, this approach is likely to identify those actors and social groups representing the various power-class levels, and the social dynamics between them in the locality.

The concept of the "locality" in defining power relationships is derived from Leeds' analysis (1973) of supralocal power relationships.

Leeds accepts the thesis that there are various levels of power, each controlled by various classes: control of resources, organization and administration, and mobilizable masses of people. This last level of power, Leeds argues, is that which the locality can most effectively control through sanctions such as mass protests and violence. For Leeds, locality power and mass power are more durable, since state power increases or decreases according to groups in control, despite the state's potential for power dominance. To the extent that Leeds' position leads to the conclusion that in the power dialogue the interests of all the various groups which hold forms of power are resolved, my analysis differs from that of Leeds.

The position which state and corporate capitalist institutions hold as owners and controllers of the means of production invests them with greater power than that of the petite bourgeoisie; these institutions have the control of capital, and therefore are able to place limits on working-class initiatives. The demise of the community control movements of the 1960s was an example of frustrated attempts by the poor and trained minority professionals to make local bureaucracies (schools, hospitals, etc.) responsive to the needs of the community by involving community personnel in the decision making (Kenny and Ehrenreich 1971).

Within institutions and bureaucracies, the tendency of petite-bourgeois and white-collar elements to identify with bourgeois interests can also limit the ability of the poor to control these institutions. However, even if minority personnel within bureaucracies opt for a pro-community position, the raison d'être of the bureaucracy may frustrate such internal attempts at redirection (see Jones, in this volume).

Therefore, in urban localities, there are likely to occur fluctuations between periods: (a) in which working-class groups and communities rally enough strength to gain important concessions from public and private institutions and to work jointly with minority petite bourgeoisie to influence the actions of these bureaucracies and institutions to achieve positive goals (witness the outcome of the 1967 riots which increased minority representation in mid-range jobs and public offices in Newark); and (b) in which the petite bourgeoisie can control the flow of resources to the locality and, based on their own sectional interests, can encourage ethnic competition which is disruptive of working-class unity (but which generates personal ethnic identification and mass support).

Using Newark as our unit of analysis, it is possible to examine the relationship of the members of the petite bourgeoisie to local institutions and to each other on an ethnic basis. This case will demonstrate that particularly in times of social and economic crisis (such as occurred in Newark during the 1960s), the limited availability of social resources prompts the division of the petite bourgeoisie along ethnic lines; they therefore seek to consolidate ethnic identification as a means of mobilization of the entire ethnic group in order to gain influence over various institutions of the state. This ethnic emphasis is possible because of divisions which exist within the working class as a result of racism and competition for jobs and resources. Thus, these temporary but recurrent cycles of inter-ethnic/racial conflict and competition disrupt other, more significant cooperative links which have historically existed between ethnic communities within localities such as Newark.

Such an analysis has particular theoretical significance, given the trend of social scientists such as Glazer and Moynihan (1975) to assert the increasing replacement of class identification by ethnic identification. Glazer and Moynihan state that ethnicity can be a more effective tool in political power competition than class, since it narrows the constituency, i.e., the group among whom power and resources must be distributed (1975:8–10). Bell, for example, claims that given the embourgeoisment of the working class and the institutionalization of its organizations, it now searches for emotional satisfaction within the primordial ties of the ethnic group, rendering ethnicity more salient than class (1975:169). Marxists, on the other hand, have been extremely critical of such analyses (Winston 1977).

A class analysis should by no means deny the critical significance of race in the distribution of social resources. It does not declare, as Wilson does (1978), "the declining significance of race." Rather, it asserts the use of race as an instrument by which class and intraclass competition, exclusion, and exploitation take place. The unique racial history of slavery and indentured service in the United States and the Caribbean amply demonstrate the use of color and background as factors in the competition for resources (see, for example, Remy 1973).

The analysis of Newark presented here is only a preliminary overview, yet it suggests cycles of social interaction which are highly correlated with fluctuations in a capitalist economy. It is suggested here that these recurrent, temporary phases of ethnic conflict (such as in Newark) are superficial responses by the multiracial/ethnic working classes to their historical exploitation and to the corresponding pressure of competition between racial/ethnic segments of the working class and between elite segments of various ethnic groups for resources and control over local and state institutions. Although there are a number of ethnic groups represented in Newark the case presented here focuses on the dynamic interaction between the two largest groups: blacks and Italians.

Ethnic and Class Development in Newark, New Jersey

Pre-1967. A review of the history of Newark reveals that relationships between immigrant and migrant communities on an ethnic basis have been the order of the day. However, these relationships have fluctuated depending on the particular needs and conditions dictated by business and industry in this area. Accordingly, relationships between working-class blacks and Italians and between petite-bourgeois segments of both groups have been characterized over time by socioeconomic alliances as well as schisms, in order to guarantee greater access to the social resources of the city.

The pursuit of economic interests on an ethnic basis was largely determined by the nature of the American economy. The native Protestant industrialists branched out over the state of New Jersey, and labor needs increased as industry grew. Despite the availability of native black labor, immigrant labor was recruited to fill the lowest-ranked jobs at rock-bottom wages, thus pushing the native white worker higher up the occupational scale, but lowering relative wage increases. Schwartz and Prosser (1977:vi) discuss the influx of Irish and Germans after 1830, and the eventual replacement of native born by Irish, German, and Jewish textile workers, brewers, and metalworkers after the Civil War.

The occupational movement coincided with residential movement. Fleming cites an oft-repeated quote about post–World War II Newark: "The people who work in Newark don't live there, and the people who live there don't work there" (1977:195). The quote is also applicable to the period 1870–1890s in that the merchants, bankers, owners of Prudential Life Insurance, transit owners, real estate speculators, etc., who controlled Newark's industry lived in the suburbs of Orange, East Orange, and Montclair, and commuted to their establishments in Newark and Manhattan (Schwartz 1977:54). Immigrants pursued jobs in industries that were expanding into the suburbs, while residing in the central city wards. As the Irish and Germans found their way into the lower ranks of business and politics in the 1860s, they abandoned the central city and occupied fringe areas of these suburbs (Hirsh 1977:9).

Schwartz describes the clear class distinctions between the suburbs and the city (1977:55), and the politics of containment in the 1890s practiced in order to keep the immigrant populations of Newark from expanding outward. Without a political or economic base, the early Italians and blacks lacked control over social services, housing, and jobs, and were clearly dependent upon the Irish and Jewish ethnic machines which dominated New Jersey life.

The dynamic growth of industry in this area attracted large numbers of unskilled European immigrants and black migrants from the South into the area. Although Italians had no visible representation in Newark before 1850, they had a significant presence there by 1910, and they had become the single largest ethnic group in the city by 1930. Their initial settlement patterns reflected the fact that they had come from a number of different towns and cities in Italy; there were scattered communities representing Sicily, Calabria, Lombardy, etc., whose social interaction was initially minimal, or even conflictual. In the later phase of Italian immigration (after 1910), the crowded urban ghetto often contained numerous other ethnic groups, and family ties as well as nationality served as cementing forces, rather than regional affiliation in Italy. Given the initial intragroup conflict, and the subsequent consolidation of these cultural factions into a cohesive "Italian" group as they struggled for social mobility in Newark, Mullings' assertion (1978:20) that U.S. ethnic groups are secondary phenomena which arise through the operation of the U.S. social structure is underscored.

Northern Italians had traditionally enjoyed educational and economic benefits denied to southern Italians, resulting in their earlier penetration of business and the professions (Whyte 1943:xvii). Most Italians were, however, of peasant background, and formed the bulk of manual laborers on the railways, sewerage constructions, and street maintenance crews in the 1890s. Despite references to the exploitation of the working-class elements in the group, Churchill notes their steady rise in living standards, involvement in education, integration into the wider society, and development of political organizations and professional ties (1975:27). Manzi relates a life history from another area which also documents this process (1980:18–20).[3]

Literate Italians with ties to and financial backing of industrialists or underground figures often became *padrones* (middlemen-type recruiters of labor) who allocated workers to various jobs, exacting a fee or exploiting them for a percentage of their wages. This also became a route to petite-bourgeois status within the group. Lipari compares the *padrone* system to the system of peonage practiced against black freedmen on Southern plantations after emancipation, and she links both phenomena to characteristics of the U.S. economy (1974:373–388).[4] It is clear that despite the exploitation of Italian workers, and the high levels of unemployment and reliance on welfare services among first-generation Italian immigrants, by the 1930s there was evidence of mobility and socioeconomic differentiation among second- and third-generation Italians (D'Alesandre 1974), which was reflected in political leadership and ethnic consolidation in Newark (Churchill 1975:52). Italian political leaders could, and did, deliver votes to the Irish Republican political machine in exchange for patronage jobs (1975:117). By the 1950s, they were competing for political office in their own right.

The concentration of blacks in Newark came after the Italian penetration and took place during two phases, both following the world wars. In 1910, the black population was 9,475 out of a total of 347,469 (Curvin 1977:146). The Italian population during that period was 20,000. Newark's black population rose from approximately 11 percent in 1940 to approximately 35 percent by 1960. Although blacks were originally spread out through all the wards of Newark, they became concentrated in the third ward of the city as the population grew and landlords in outlying areas became resistant to black tenants (Price 1975). In addition, the placement of Newark housing authority projects in the third ward, all within a one-mile radius, and the subsequent allocation of residence by race tremendously increased the black concentration in this ward (Curvin 1977:146). By 1959, ghetto conditions in the third ward among the growing black and Hispanic population had been increased by the slum-clearance policies of the city housing authority.

The bulk of the black migration took place after World War II. This was the period when the Italian petite bourgeoisie was beginning the process of suburbanization, as well as active political participation in Newark. Stable Italian working-class communities existed in the north ward, and more prosperous Italians sometimes resided in the prestigious Forest Hills–Silver Lake community where some of the oldest European families resided. By the 1950s, sectors of the Italian petite bourgeoisie which had moved into the arena of city politics had taken up residence in the remote Vailsburg section of Newark where Irish corporate officials

Table 4.1 Race and Ethnic Composition of Newark

Year	TOTAL	Whites		Blacks		Hispanics		Other Minorites	
	No.	No.	%	No.	%	No.	%	No.	%
1940	429,760	384,000	89.5	45,760	10.5	—	—	—	—
1950	438,776	363,149	82.9	74,965	17.1	—	—	—	—
1960	405,220	265,706	65.6	138,009	34.4	—	—	—	—
1967[a]	398,000	138,000	45.0	220,000	55.0	20,000[b]	—	—	—
1970	382,000	96,000	32.4	207,000	54.2	45,000	11.7	4,000	1.7

Sources: U.S. Census of Population 1940, 1950, 1960; Wright 1968:12.
[a]Adjusted social agency projections for 1967.
[b]Only Puerto Ricans were enumerated by census.

were reputed to live (Wright 1968). But the north ward was unique in that it retained a substantial percentage of the mobile Italian petite bourgeoisie who had grown up in the area.

The predominantly working-class character of the north ward and the presence of this politically active petite bourgeoisie predisposed the ward to an active role in local politics, both formal and informal, after 1930. Churchill describes this political phenomenon as "Italianism," or an ethnic political identification irrespective of issue or party (1975:121). This political involvement placed the north ward in greater contact with black and other minority working-class elements in Newark. Italians and the small proportion of blacks in the garment workers union (Local 144) engaged in joint activities in 1939 (Churchill 1975:72). Also significant were links which the criminal elements had established with blacks, alliances which included the Jewish underworld and the fledgling underworld segment of the black petite bourgeoisie. These alliances were a major source of jobs for poor blacks in the third ward after 1930.

Although the black population in Newark was predominantly poor and uneducated, and relied heavily on welfare because the job market was generally segregated, until the 1960s there was also a significant segment of "middle-class" blacks within the area. Many were descendants of freedmen who had been settled in Newark since the turn of the century. Some were teachers and ministers who dominated the black churches, social service institutions in the black community, and black schools in Newark; some were more clearly of petite-bourgeois status in that they owned small businesses, medical or legal firms, clubs, and rooming houses. They were actively involved in organizations such as the NAACP and the National Urban League.

The size of the black petite bourgeoisie grew during the 1930s and 1940s as the new leaders became entrenched in politics or business with the assistance and control of the underworld. After 1930, the patronage jobs which flowed from these underworld links helped to guarantee the new leaders a black constituency within the third ward. "They provided more jobs for blacks than city government could provide. They had various plants and contractors that they controlled. They put blacks in the brewey, an aeronautics factory, or other companies. Blacks were nonentities . . . and they were the only ones who gave them some kind of opportunity" (Curvin 1977:150).

The black-Jewish-Italian underworld alliance was not one which safeguarded the interests of the black working class in a consistent manner, based as it was on the needs of the larger corporate-political interests within the state. Although one positive outcome of the alliance was increased black political participation and representation after 1950, this was not easily translated into economic control. Blacks remained junior partners in an alliance in which many of the underworld associates with heavy economic and business interests were Italian, with a strong base in the north ward community.

The black petite bourgeoisie were therefore by no means equal (in terms of economic strength or historical roots) to the Italian petite bourgeoisie. The black votes which they could deliver were often used in their own interests. Some of these votes, for example, were responsible for the shift from Republican to Democratic dominance in 1948, when black votes were a deciding factor in the election of Hugh Addonizio as mayor.

Following the decline of the rackets, the increasing strength of the Italian political machine with its links with big business prevented black politicians from making significant economic gains. While black representation in white-collar jobs and in the professions increased during the 1950s, the flight of industry to areas of the state where tax conditions were more favorable adversely affected working-class blacks and the small businesses of the emerging black petite bourgeoisie. As the black petite bourgeoisie struggled to maintain political and economic control in Newark, they often opposed the young working-class or professional blacks who ran for political office from the third ward (Curvin 1977: 154), helping to increase the dominance of the Italian petite bourgeoisie over jobs as well as political positions.

The old black middle class had departed for the suburbs during the 1940s, leaving the most depressed sectors of the working class and non-working poor concentrated in the central wards of Newark (see table 4.2). In terms of occupation and income, the suburban groups were far better off than blacks in Newark. This suburban movement continued into the late 1960s, and in this respect was reflective of a national trend toward middle-class suburbanization in the 1960s. The black suburban group tended to derive much of its income from Newark industries and public-private institutions, just as did the Italian petite bourgeoisie, but played limited roles in the fight for political rights for black Newark residents (see Curvin 1977:151).

In contrast to the gradual mobility experienced by the black middle class during the 1960s, conditions in the poor black third ward were

Table 4.2. Black Movement Into Suburbs

	% Black in East Orange		% Black in Montclair
1940	11%	1940	18%
1960	25%	1950	20%
1966	37%	1960	23%
1970	36%	1965	27%

Sources: U.S. Census of Population 1940, 1950, 1960; Wright 1968.

legend. Deteriorated and congested housing, unemployment, insufficient state funding for the public school system, and racism in municipal hiring practices all contributed to black unrest. In addition, police violence, corruption in the city administration of Addonizio, and political neglect of the black community were creating conditions that exacerbated the Italian "law and order" forces in Newark—forces which were overtly antiblack. As the black community organized to address these problems, it was perceived as threatening by city hall and Italian ethnic forces.

1967–1973. The 1967 riots, when they came (Hayden 1967), were an expected prelude to the development of a more comprehensive black platform. Clearly demonstrated was the desire of blacks to destroy the former pattern of white control and suburban influence over Newark politics. Political organization after the riots also aimed at increasing opportunities for black business in Newark. When the Committee for a Unified Newark met to determine political strategies, Leroi Jones (Imamu Amiri Baraka) played a leading role (*New Jersey Afro-American* 1970). Newspaper reports from this period indicate that black groups were moving in a direction which allied the young, progressive petite bourgeoisie and the working class against the established petite bourgeoisie which had ties to corporate bourgeois interests in Newark. This would have undermined the former role of the old black elite and the underworld sector of the Italian petite bourgeoisie. However, the United Brothers (a Baraka-led group of black professionals and businessmen supporting Kenneth Gibson for mayor) succeeded in unifying the black community, although they appeared to place more emphasis on business reforms than on working-class reforms.

The "law and order" stance of the Imperiale forces in Newark often masked the severe economic and social deterioration faced by sectors of the Italian north ward community and other ethnic communities during the Addonizio administration.[5] Rice reports that during the 1967 riots, violence and looting by white youths also occurred in these areas (1977:120). The political response to these common pressures was ethnic competition between blacks and Italians, rather than initial unification around common problems.

Table 4.3 reflects some of these problems. It groups low-income census tracts into neighborhoods, and allows us to compare social conditions between neighborhood 01 (which includes parts of the Italian north ward), neighborhood 02 (which includes the older black central ward), and neighborhood 03 (including the predominantly black west ward). Irrespective of race, it is clear that roughly one-third of those who live in these areas are below the poverty level ($3,748 for a family of four in 1969). Yet median school years completed are higher for blacks than for whites in all three neighborhoods, and they are highest in the 01 neighborhood. That for blacks, more education does not result in higher incomes is evident in the higher median incomes of white families as compared with black families in these areas. Perlo provides statistics which show that in New Jersey, per capita income of blacks was 57 percent that of whites in 1969 (1975:33). He also shows that in 1971, median family income of blacks on a national level was lower than that of any other ethnic group (1975:40), and that in 1970, while median school years completed for blacks equaled or surpassed median school years completed for whites in many states, median income for black males was far lower than that of white males (1975:43; see also Ogbu, in this volume).

Blacks outnumber whites in Newark, and correspondingly, more black families than white families are receiving public assistance income in all three neighborhoods. Yet of those receiving public assistance, slightly more whites than blacks were below the poverty level in 1970. When one examines the occupational breakdown for neighborhood 01 where the racial balance is fairly equal, the concentration of whites as professionals or as skilled mechanics and construction craftsmen becomes obvious. The flight of business and industry from Newark seriously affected this group of workers, and had an impact on unemployment and public assistance figures for these neighborhoods.

During the late 1960s, Italians of the north ward had been unable to maintain the modest homes which were characteristic of the area. The more affluent fled to the suburbs. The numbers of Italians relying on

Table 4.3 Characteristics of Neighborhoods with Poverty Rates of 20 Percent or More, 1970

	01 Neighborhood				02 Neighborhood				03 Neighborhood			
	All	White	Black	Sp. L.[a]	All	White	Black	Sp. L.[a]	All	White	Black	Sp. L.[a]
All persons with income	62,789	30,041	31,556	12,149	71,789	10,351	60,953	6,341	68,002	7,396	60,248	4,062
% below poverty level	27.9	29.4	26.3	39.8	33.2	31.6	33.4	41.0	30.2	36.3	29.5	35.7
Median school years completed												
Males	10.0	9.5	10.4	8.2	9.6	8.9	9.7	8.1	10.2	9.0	10.3	8.7
Females	9.7	8.7	10.8	7.9	10.0	8.5	10.2	7.4	10.3	8.4	10.5	7.9
Median family income	$6,617	$6,630	$6,571	$5,140	$5,699	$5,805	$5,693	$4,634	$6,387	$5,942	$6,435	$5,559
Mean family income	$7,573	$7,857	$7,260	$6,189	$6,502	$6,791	$6,463	$5,276	$7,285	$7,026	$7,026	$6,238
Families with public assistance	3,252	1,246	1,960	812	5,041	530	4,495	458	4,387	323	4,050	259
Mean public assist. income	$2,737	$2,134	$2,301	$2,178	$2,449	$2,423	$2,441	$2,668	$2,426	$2,556	$2,417	$2,814
% below poverty level	50.5	51.6	48.8	64.5	54.2	58.1	53.7	59.8	53.6	57.0	53.3	50.2

Source: Table A-1, Low Income Neighborhoods in Large Cities: 1970. Newark, N.J. Supplemental Report. 1970 Census of Pop. U.S. Dept. of Commerce, Social and Econ. Statistics Admin., May 1974.
[a] Sp. L. = Spanish language.

welfare support and public housing went up, and drug and youth problems within the area increased (Shipley 1972:72–83). Fewer young people could find jobs and fewer could afford to go to college, or were prepared to go. The area had begun to reflect more closely many of the social problems long reflected in the poverty areas of the black central-west wards. The Newark *Evening News* of August 21, 1969, reported "The North Ward Feels Neglected" (p. 13). In addition, north ward residents had come to see the influx of blacks and poor Latinos from the over-crowded central areas as a threat to their sense of community identity.

The Italian community was, however, unique in the strength of its petite bourgeoisie which was born in the area, and which maintained close ties with the community, playing an integral part in community life. Political figures such as Imperiale, Adubato, and Cundari traced their roots from twentieth-century immigrants who acquired stable economic status and political visibility in Newark during the 1930s. The retention of this group was not entirely arbitrary, since the high cost of living in the suburbs, and access to roles in Newark politics, made it advantageous for them to remain. Instead of fleeing to the suburbs, as the older black petite bourgeoisie had done, they remained to engage in a fight for administrative roles in the Newark bureaucracy and political structure. This required them to maximize ties with the Italian community, and they thereby shaped the community position on many issues. The 1970 elections which brought Gibson to office were a reflection of the intense competition of black and Italian young, petite-bourgeois elements who had the backing of their ethnic communities in which they resided.

The new style of politics during the Gibson administration began to engage a larger percentage of young, upwardly mobile blacks (both indigenous and new), in government administration or business. Thus, not only was the structural position of both black and Italian elites changed, but the elites were also of a qualitatively different character in terms of the skills and training which they possessed. Others have referred to an elite of this nature as "technocrats" (Allman 1979).

Political gains were, however, illusory. Italian city council control during the early 1960s had been maintained only on condition that the tax laws, land arrangements, and city government structure were conducive to economic interests of other parts of the state. Insurance company dissatisfaction with the performance of Mayor Addonizio, whom they formerly backed, was responsible for the fairly explicit search for a "clean" Italian candidate who would carry the 1970 elections. Addonizio had, by 1969, been indicted for corruption. A *Village Voice* article of April 8, 1970, chronicled the dealings between the Chamber of Commerce, Mutual Benefit Life and Prudential Life, Governor Cahill, and their candidate, Senator Alexander Matturri, as well as the counterstrategies by Imperiale on the one hand, and the United Brothers (represented by Baraka) on the other hand. The politicking was complete with large campaign contributions, bribes, and promises for later political favors to the corporate structure. In the wake of this kind of political and ethnic maneuvering, all working-class groups experienced a worsening economic situation.

Mass reaction to this kind of corporate control and exploitation had surfaced during the 1967 riots. Using Leeds' analysis, the masses exerted the local power of mass violence which they had at their disposal. The concessions which resulted were increased social services to the working-class sector; drug programs and recreational and health facilities were quickly initiated and gave rise to additional job positions for the white-collar working class (greater integration of blacks in the police department, for example). These programs did not, however, significantly better the social and economic situation of the working-class population in Newark.

Between 1960 and 1970, some of the differential between black and white family income had lessened, but by 1969–70, median family income was not significantly higher than it was in 1959–60. Although median income for unrelated individuals was rising, the percentage of those below the poverty level was rising higher in minority areas than it was throughout the rest of the Newark metropolitan area. Despite increases in income, the rise in unemployment and in poverty status resulted in illusionary gains to the working class.

The middle class appeared to be the major beneficiaries of the mass protests of 1967. Rather than achieving a power balance through local mass action as the Leedsian analysis might assert, the riots succeeded in increasing the visible representation of blacks in government and in local bureaucracies.

The "neo-class collaborationism" to which Winston refers (1977:61) was prevalent in the period after 1968 as the middle class received payoffs which were the outcome of the riots. The most immediate gains were made by the black "technocrats" and petite bourgeoisie who acquired new inroads into the city administrative structure. The composi-

Table 4.4. Newark Social Indices, 1960

	All	_Nonwhite_
Median school years completed		
1960	11.1	9.0
1970	10.0	—
Median family income		
1960	$7,149	$4,807
1969	$7,734	$6,742 (Black)
Median income		
Male	$5,221	$3,642
1960		
Female		
1960	$1,992	$1,822
Both sexes		
1960	$2,391	$2,689
1970	$3,429	—

Source: Table 73, "Education, Employment Status, and Selected Labor Force Characteristics, 1960," New Jersey, from _General Social and Economic Characteristics_, Census of Population—1960, New Jersey, no. 32, p. 207, Bureau of Census, U.S. Department of Commerce.

tion of the city council changed from predominantly Italian (6–3) in 1970 to predominantly black (5–4) in 1974. Between 1970 and 1972, fierce battles took place in city council meetings over business occupancy tax arrangements which would require business to take a larger responsibility for solving economic problems of Newark. The increased black representation and demands from the poor and working classes intensified the reaction within the corporate sector, allowing for the continued flight of jobs and business. Increased black administrative control had not meant real power or benefits to the working class, since the state and corporate interests retained control over the purse strings of Newark, often operating through Italian middlemen. It verifies Baron's observations in Chicago that as minority representation increases, there is a tendency for structural changes to cause the power invested in those positions to decrease (1972:381–389).

When, soon after the 1970 elections, Gibson began to outline programs for increasing black representation in the building trades and in city contract jobs, there was considerable opposition from the Italian community and their political representatives in Newark. Despite the greater concentration of Italians in well-paid skilled and semiskilled jobs, Gibson's move was interpreted as partisan political action and was opposed by the Italian power structure. The economic position of Italians in Newark and the suburbs was substantially better than that of blacks. However, the Italian power structure emphasized the political visibility of blacks more than the economic needs of the two ethnic groups. The increased black political representation did, however, lower the mass reaction level, allowing the Gibson administration to provide a climate more conducive to business interests after 1972.

1973–1976. Under increasing pressure, the Gibson administration began to work more closely with the corporate sector, and the administration incorporated more Italians and Jews rather than blacks into high-level jobs. There was vocal opposition to his administration from the United Clergy of Newark, a multiracial organization. Within this group, black ministers actively opposed Gibson's reelection, throwing their support behind Imperiale. "Gibson has been bad for Newark," they claimed, citing poor housing, increased poverty, and his tendency to spurn "offers of aid from black clergy" (*New York Times,* April 20, 1974). Central to the opposition was the realization that Gibson's style allowed no room for the established black middle class to influence Newark politics. Imperiale seemed to offer that possibility, despite the dangers of his "law and order" stance.

By 1974, Gibson was courting the "alienated" white ethnic groups within Newark, claiming, according to a *New York Times-N.J.* article of January 13, 1974, that he was "running again, but not as black". The north ward Democrats under Adubato's leadership helped to reelect Gibson (Sullivan 1974), openly acknowledging that economic benefits must often override ethnic political allegiances to candidates such as Imperiale. The tangible benefits they referred to were, however, political offices and bureaucratic positions, rather than working-class jobs.

By 1975, business interests could point out the potential of the Newark area based on the high level of integration between the Newark business community and other corporate and residential areas of the state (Bureau of the Census 1970:29). The economic regeneration of Newark had begun, and the phase of overt black/Italian conflict was on the decline. The conflict had effectively been difused by the growing alliance between black and Italian petite-bourgeois groups who were being incorporated into the middle levels of the metropolitan political structure.

Ethnic-Class Politics

In light of the general thesis of economic retrenchment as the main stimulus of ethnic competition and conflict in the contemporary period, it is instructive to recognize that there were several developmental *phases* in the alignment and realignment of ethnic/class forces in the Newark area.

The historical evidence indicates continual alliances and schisms between the black and Italian communities in the period 1930–1967. This case study challenges the assumption that ethnic communities in the United States must, by virtue of their plural existence, stand as competitors in the political process. It suggests, rather, that changes in economic situations and the existence of divisive pressures generated by state and corporate bureaucracies lead to conflict between ethnic communities.

The relationship between blacks and Italians was not, however, one between equals given the greater strength of the Italian petite bourgeoisie, and the more stable working-class position of Italians as compared with blacks. In the 1930s, racism gave rise to conditions of economic dependency between what Mullings describes as an "oppressed minority" (1978:20), i.e., blacks, and a white ethnic group (Italians). In the 1950s, the relationship was one of political dependence as blacks supported Italian candidates in hopes of increased access to jobs and political representation.

Because of their stable working-class status, the other white ethnic communities such as Ironbound and Vailsburg tended to feel little threat from black unrest during the 1960s. As economic conditions worsened, sectors of these communities even participated in the 1967 riots, demonstrating their opposition to oppressive conditions. This kind of tacit support subsided after 1972 when press reports on the Gibson administration and the lack of effectiveness of social services led whites to believe that their economic position was threatened by "black favoritism" in distributing funds and resources. The group most in competition with blacks for decreasing resources and with the most to lose in comparison with the white working class was the Italian group. It is not surprising, therefore, that (given the encouragement from corporate institutions in the area) the temporary "ethnic reaction" in Newark was primarily based in the Italian community, although reflected to a lesser degree in other white ethnic communities.

The ethnic middle classes as power brokers played a key role in both the escalation and subsequent defusing of ethnic conflict in Newark. During the early part of the Gibson administration, there were attempts to service and build up a black constituency; at the same time, black politicians hoped to retain and attract business to the area. Despite the administration's endeavors to moderate the demands on the business sector, the general mood for reform caused the business-corporate sector to attempt the rebuilding of its Italian power base in order to offset the potential power of blacks in City Hall. The economic crisis thus precipitated by corporate-business reaction intensified the ethnic tensions between blacks and Italians. Political leaders within the New Jersey Italian American Association and the Italian American Civil Rights League led a recall movement against Gibson in 1973.

The fact of marginal black administrative control in the city council meant that they were often accused of engineering the economic crisis, experienced by Italians and other white ethnic groups as well as blacks. There was a peculiar historical blindness about the impact of the Addonizio period and the U.S. economy in general. When a journalist interviewed Italian construction workers, factory foremen, and housewives in the north ward in 1972, they openly blamed the black power movement and the Gibson administration for the economic and social hardships they experienced (Shipley 1972). Between 1970 and 1974, these perceptions and accusations affected the relationship between black and Italian residents of Newark. While the roots of the problem lay in the nature of the corporate control over capital in Newark, the roles of ethnic petite bourgeoisie as local administrators and power brokers perpetuated ethnic competition.

The most overt competition tended to occur within the city council, as Gibson opposed moves to expand the Italian-dominated council's control over federal- and state-funded programs and city contracts. Less visible but very significant in the ethnic competition was the development by Italians of a new organization that would have a constituency among the diverse Caucasian elements in Newark in order to offset the strength of the black political consciousness developed in the early years of the Gibson administration.

The need for a community or civic organization to service Italian-Americans and other white ethnics within the north ward was discussed by a number of young, politically astute Italians in the early 1970s, and the North Ward Educational and Cultural Center (NWECC) was founded in 1971 following Gibson's election as mayor. On the surface, the internal dynamics of NWECC are vaguely reminiscent of the ethnic and voluntary or civic associations of an earlier period, with its emphasis on the preservation of Italian or Slavic culture and community (NWECC Annual Report 1972). In addition to providing job training, educational counseling, crime prevention, etc., the center emphasized its potential as the base of a white supra-ethnic urban power bloc. Although NWECC did not advocate the active vigilantism against Afro-Americans which was in process, its crime prevention emphasis gave tacit support to such occurrences.

NWECC found its constituency among Slavic construction workers, factory workers, and small businessmen as well as working-class Italians. Its leaders, most of them Italians, appeared, on the surface, to fit the classic model of concerned activists who contribute their time and who achieve nonmaterial rewards for their constituency. Yet many of these leaders were members of the North Ward Democratic Committee, and NWECC's ties to the political party structure and, through funding, to the Newark corporate structure was obvious.

NWECC actively appealed to other civic and business organizations, the chamber of commerce, and state funding sources for money to support its activities. It gained the support of state institutions of higher learning, and many of its educational projects were initially administered by affiliate members of NWECC who were within local branches of New Jersey universities. By 1973, NWECC had received a $264,000 LEAA crime-prevention grant, and by 1975 they were to be centrally involved in the creation of a new university campus for white ethnics of the north ward and nearby suburuban areas.

The center's community support was already assured, and the financial institutions such as Prudential Life and Mutual Benefit contributed to the center. To the extent that NWECC continued to place itself and its interests in structural opposition to the Gibson administration and other minority interests, the political effectiveness of NWECC was limited. It chose to apply more subtle economic and political pressure on Gibson, which proved an effective strategy. The dilemma was resolved by 1974 when NWECC convinced the north ward to throw its support behind Gibson for a second term in office.

It is not surprising to find that the widespread conflict between the black and Italian communities dissolved in the period between 1973 and 1976. While the return of a considerable portion of industry and business to the area helped to decrease the tensions, the increase in availability of positions for the elite caused a restructuring of NWECC's political stance toward the Gibson administration, and accounts for the guarded cooperation between the two communities after 1974.

When one examines the community and local success of NWECC, what stands out is the "ethnic" basis on which community support was mobilized. NWECC projected its struggle as being one against a black administration which utilized political dominance to channel services and jobs to the black community, ignoring the "white ethnics" of Newark. It failed to pinpoint the origin of the social and economic crisis in the pre-Gibson administrations. It called for, and achieved, a unification of white ethnics to reassert their cultural pride in order to prevent "community disintegration and economic exploitation." Although there was initially little emphasis placed on the political structure which was being built to support the cultural effort, NWECC's ultimate goal of regaining economic and political control over the city apparatus surfaced by the mayoral elections in 1974.

By identifying the "power holders" as black city administrators instead of industry and financial institutions, an ethnic petite bourgeoisie can, through use of ethnic symbols, act in the interests of the corporate sector and assist them in the process of dividing the urban working class on an ethnic basis. All ethnic working classes in the long run lose in this process, although the group which undergoes this temporary ethnic revitalization experiences short-run gains.

Again, the individuals who gained most despite the interethnic conflict and rivalry were the middle class who, through manipulation of the organizations and mobilization of the larger ethnic community, assured themselves a vital position in community politics and affairs, and a constant source of visibility and income. The jobs which went to NWECC's constituency as a result of NWECC's activities and influences were limited. Most of them resulted from the return of industry, not the additional skills provided to young people and job seekers by NWECC.

NWECC did not seek changes in the socioeconomic structure that would relieve pressure in the north ward and other wards. NWECC's presence had, however, introduced competition into the political process, requiring the new black politicians to achieve a power balance favorable to the Newark business climate. The actions of NWECC, under the direction of its elite leaders, have been a capitulation to the divisive pressures of the corporate and state structures in Newark.

Conclusion

It is difficult to understand the competition for political power between ethnic groups and the resort to ethnicity as a tool for political mobilization within urban areas, unless one takes into consideration several factors: (a) the class structure of the ethnic groups involved as well as their historical relationship to each other; (b) the geographical dispersal of the class and ethnic groups within the locality under study; (c) the operation of the capitalist process which constantly divides and exploits ethnic working classes; and (c) the dependence of the petite bourgeoisie on the corporate structure, and the implications of this dependence for their roles within their ethnic group.

From the example of Newark, it is possible to see that ethnicity in political competition is more than a useful tool for achieving political goals (cf. Glazer and Moynihan 1975:18). I suggest that ethnicity emerges as a political strategy at those times when the economic conditions are most difficult. Once the working-class sector has been sufficiently deprived of alternative strategies, the efforts of the petite bourgeoisie to mobilize the group on an ethnic basis to achieve short-run goals may be successful. The consequences for the entire multiracial and multiethnic working class are, however, quite severe.

It is necessary to make a clear analysis of demands put forth by a historically oppressed ethnic group which occupies an exploited class position within the U.S. economy. Blacks and Latinos were, of course, in this position in Newark, and their demands for redress of the economic situation are clear, even though phrased in terms of race. If these demands had received more than token redress, they could have resulted in a bettering of the condition of all working-class groups in Newark as well as the nonworking poor.

Thus, all demands by the ethnic poor cannot be classified as ethnic demands. Some may indeed be class demands even if voiced by one racial and ethnic group. The demands made by the North Ward Educational and Cultural Center have, for the most part, addressed themselves to interethnic cultural rivalries and ethnic loyalties, i.e., to the building up of supra-ethnic affiliations, rather than to redressing the entire economic and class structure in Newark.

Little distinction can be made in Newark, however, between the actions of the black and Italian middle classes after 1970. Neither group moved consistently in the interests of the working poor of their own ethnic group. Their actions were aimed at building an ethnic middle-class power bloc which, it was felt, might exert pressure on the state bureaucracy to release to them a greater portion of state and local resources.

When cooperation between ethnic elites was necessary to achieve some goals, cooperation took place in such a way as to assure each elite the continual support of its ethnic constituency. In those urban areas where minorities are acquiring administrative positions in city and local government, such processes quickly reveal the economic powerlessness of this oppressed minority group, despite its increased political visibility.

An ethnic analysis of the political actions of various groups is clearly insufficient, and must be coordinated with an analysis of class factors. Such an analysis clarifies the interdependence of the black and Italian elite with other petite-bourgeois administrative groups both inside and outside of Newark. Hence the importance of the "locality" concept. Equally obvious in the case of Newark is the ultimate dependence of both black and Italian groups (despite ethnic support systems) upon the corporate and state structures, which, as the true representatives of economic and political power, perpetuate the process of ethnic divisiveness.

Notes

1. There is, of course, stratification within a class based on income and occupational status which is often reflected in the appearance of polarized interests between blue collar (factory workers, laborers, etc.) and white collar (clerks, teachers, foremen, administrators, etc.).

2. Piven and Cloward (1971:1–7) assert that this group is to a large extent exploited by capitalist industry—i.e., supplied with relief services to quell discontent in crisis periods, and alternately utilized as a surplus labor pool which acts to lower the rising wage levels of the working class during more prosperous times. A smaller sector of the non-working poor are engaged in criminal and extralegal activities, and are often classified as the lumpen proletariat.

3. "My grandfather, a peasant from Quindici, a commune in southern Italy, was driven from his homeland by poverty. . . . After working as a common laborer on the railroad in Hackensack, New Jersey, followed by a stint in the sewers of New York City, he finally found his way to Lawrence. He worked in the textile mills . . . for approximately twelve years. During that time he was effectively assimilated. . . . Consequently, he was able to obtain employment as a bartender in an eating and drinking establishment in Lawrence. With the money he saved, he bought a parcel of land and built tenement houses on it. On the ground floor of the tenement my grandfather started a restaurant and rented the rear area dwellings to other immigrants. With the money they saved [they] moved into a large

house in an Italian neighborhood in one of the outlying districts of Lawrence" (Manzi 1980:18–20).

4. Lipari states that in the early phases, the *padrone* brought children of the poor as indentured servants; after passage of labor laws, however, men were recruited to the United States and were subcontracted by *padrone* to various jobs (1974:382). The *padrone* often owned stores and tenements that workers were required to frequent at exorbitant prices, which guaranteed their indebtedness. Lipari says of the U.S. economy:
"The freedom of movement of labor had always been too limited to meet the excessive demand which always characterized our economic development. Since labor did not flow in sufficient quantities to the places where it was needed, either from other sections of the country or from abroad, our employing classes resorted to coercive methods to draw upon available sources for their labor supply. These forms of coercion had a common foundation characteristic of our economic system—the inequality between employer and worker. These practices, deliberate or not, were in effect attempts to maintain a sufficient and permanent supply of propertiless wage earners" (1974:382).

5. Anthony Imperiale was a militant leader of white working-class and vigilante groups in the North Ward of Newark during the late 1960s and early 1970s. He became a state assemblyman from the North Ward and gained notoriety for his pro-white and allegedly racist political stance (Shipley 1972:81).

References

Allen, Robert. 1969. *Black Awakening in Capitalist America.* New York: Doubleday.

Allman, T. D. 1979. "Newark—1979." *New Jersey Monthly,* January, p. 55.

Banfield, Edward and James Q. Wilson. 1972. "City Power Structures." In J. Palen and Karl H. Flaming, eds., *Urban America: Conflict and Change,* pp. 277–290. New York: Holt, Rinehart and Winston.

Baron, Harold M. 1972. "Black Powerlessness in Chicago." In N. Yetman and C. H. Steele, eds., *Majority and Minority: The Dynamics of Racial and Ethnic Relations,* pp. 391–401. Boston: Allyn and Bacon.

Bell, Daniel. 1975. "Ethnicity and Social Change." In Glazer and Moynihan, eds., *Ethnicity: Theory and Experience,* pp. 141–174.

Berlin, Irving. 1972. "Professional Participation in Community Activities." In D. Hegeman, ed., *Anthropology and Community Action,* pp. 40–48. New York: Anchor.

Bloch, M., ed. 1975. *Marxist Analyses and Social Anthropology.* New York: Wiley.

Bureau of the Census. 1970. "Journey to Work Survey." Newark, U.S. Department of Commerce. Newark, N.J.: Supplemental Report.

Churchill, Charles. 1975. *The Italians of Newark: A Community Study.* (1942). New York: Arno Press.

Cordasco, F. and E. Bucchioni, eds. 1974. *The Italians: Social Backgrounds of an American Group.* Clifton, N.J.: Augustus Kelly.

Curvin, Robert. 1977. "Black Ghetto Politics in Newark After World War II." In Schwartz and Prosser, eds., *Cities of the Garden State,* pp. 145–159.

Dahl, Robert. 1961. *Who Governs? Democracy and Power in an American City.* New Haven: Yale University Press.

D'Alesandre, John. 1974. "Occupational Trends of Italians in New York City." In Cordasco and Bucchioni, eds., *The Italians,* pp. 417–432.

Firth, Raymond. 1975. "The Skeptical Anthropologist? Social Anthropology and Marxist Views of Society." In Bloch, ed., *Marxist Analyses and Social Anthropology*, pp. 29–60.

Fleming, Thomas. 1977. *New Jersey: A Bicentennial History*. New York: Norton.

Glazer, Nathan and Daniel P. Moynihan. 1975. Introduction. In Glazer and Moynihan, eds., *Ethnicity: Theory and Experience*, pp. 1–26. Cambridge: Harvard University Press.

Haaland, Gunnar. 1969. "Economic Determinants in Ethnic Processes." In F. Barth, ed., *Ethnic Groups and Boundaries*, pp. 58–73. Boston: Little, Brown.

Hayden, Thomas. 1967. *Rebellion in Newark: Official Violence and Ghetto Response*. New York: Random House.

Hirsch, Susan. 1977. "Newark in Its Prime: Private Wealth and Public Poverty." In Schwartz and Prosser, eds., *Cities of the Garden State*, pp. 1–15.

Holmberg, A. 1970. "The Changing Values and Institutions of Vicos in the Context of National Development." *American Behavioral Scientist* 8:3–8.

Jones, Delmos. 1976. "Applied Anthropology and the Application of Anthropological Knowledge." *Human Organization* 35(3):221–229.

Kenny, Maxine and Barbara Ehrenreich. 1971. "Health: The Community Mental Health Center Controversy." In J. Bellush and Stephen David, eds., *Race and Politics in New York City*, pp. 164–202. New York: Praeger.

Leeds, Anthony. 1973. "Locality Power in Relation to Supra-local Power Institutions." In Aidan Southall, ed., *Urban Anthropology: Cross-Cultural Studies of Urbanization*, pp. 15–51. New York: Oxford University Press.

Liebow, Elliot. 1967. *Tally's Corner: A Study of Negro Streetcorner Men*. Boston: Little, Brown.

Lipari, Marie. 1974. "The Padrone System: An Aspect of American Economic History." In Cordasco and Bucchioni, eds., *The Italians*, pp. 373–384.

Manzi, Lisa. 1980. "The Italian-American Experience in Lawrence, Mass." Georgetown University, manuscript.

Mullings, Leith. 1978. "Ethnicity and Stratification in the Urban United States." In *Annals of the New York Academy of Sciences* 318:10–22.

Newark Evening News. 1969. "The North Ward Feels Neglected" August 21, p. 13.

New Jersey Afro-American. 1970. "Mayoralty Win: RRIC Report Says B-P Convention 'Quite a Show.' " March 21, p. 1.

NWECC (North Ward Educational and Cultural Center). 1972. *Annual Report* (synopsis). File on Newark Ethnic Groups. New Jersey Room, Newark Public Library.

Perlo, Victor. 1975. *The Economics of Racism*. New York: International.

Piven, Frances F. and James Cloward. 1971. *Regulating the Poor: The Functions of Public Welfare*. New York: Vintage.

Price, Clement. 1975. "The Afro-American Community of Newark—1917–1947: A Social History." Ph.D. dissertation. Rutgers University.

Remy, Anselme. 1973. "The Unholy Trinity." *Caribbean Review* 6(2):14–18.

Rice, Arnold, ed. 1977. "Newark: A Chronological and Documentary History (1666–1970)." New York: Oceana.

Schwartz, Joel. 1977. "Suburban Progressivism in the 1890s: The Politics of Containment in Orange, East Orange, and Montclair." In Schwartz and Prosser, eds., *Cities of the Garden State*, pp. 53–70.

Schwartz, Joel and Daniel Prosser. 1977. Introduction. In Schwartz and Prosser, eds., *Cities of the Garden State*, pp. v–xiii. Dubuque, Iowa: Kendall-Hunt.

Shipley, David. 1972. "The White Niggers of Newark: The Other Side of Prejudice." *Harpers Magazine*, August, pp. 77–83.

Stack, Carol. 1974. *All Our Kin: Strategies of Adaptation in a Black Community*. New York: Harper and Row.

Tabb, William. 1970. *Political Economy of the Black Ghetto*. New York: Norton.

Terray, Emmanuel. 1975. "Class and Class Consciousness in the Abron Kingdom of Gya-man." In Bloch, ed., *Marxist Analyses and Social Anthropology*, pp. 85–136.

Whyte, William F. 1943. *Street Corner Society*. Chicago: University of Chicago Press.

Wilson, William. 1978. *The Declining Significance of Race*. Chicago: University of Chicago Press.

Winston, Henry. 1977. *Class, Race, and Black Liberation*. New York: International.

Wright, Nathan. 1968. *Ready to Riot*. New York: Holt, Rinehart and Winston.

5. The "Community" and Organizations in the Community

Delmos J. Jones

The major goal of this paper is to argue that an understanding of the social organization of urban localities must include analysis of the structure and function of local organizations and their linkages.[1] I analyze these local groups as centers of organization that link the population of the locality and higher-level institutions of the city. Such organizations are viewed both as advocates of change on behalf of the local population, and alternatively, as potential components or instruments of higher-level institutions.

The data used to analyze the relationships among the population of a locality, organized groups in the locality, and higher-level institutions are derived from an intensive study of the Community Action Group, a local organization running a Head Start program in an inner city area. The history of this organization is an example of a local group that began as an advocate acting on behalf of the local population, but was transformed into a component of higher-level institutions of the city. The dynamics of this transformation will be described below.

The concept of community used here is derived from Leeds' "Locality Power in Relation to Supralocal Power Institutions" (1973). Leeds disavows the use of the community as the object of study in complex society, especially as it is assumed to be a minimal social structural unit or a microcosm. He employs the term "locality" rather than "community" to refer to urban subgroups "because of the prevailing confusions regarding the latter term as it has been used to designate the ethnographies of particular places" (1973:20). Locality, in Leeds' terms, refers to any sensorily distinct settlement, and does not make assumptions about the nature of the interrelationships that exist within it. "It may be the case, ideally, that no personalized relationships exist in the locality, that there are solely impersonal and secondary ones without community characteristics or feeling" (1973:21).

The ideas of voluntary contact on one hand and discontinuity and disconnection between individuals and groups on the other are central to other conceptualizations of urban community (see Bahrdt 1966:81). According to Mayer, the urban community is an economically and socially heterogeneous situation in which collections of people are found that do not, *as a whole*, form groups (1966:102). Groups and networks of various kinds exist, but they are not continuous. Thus, the existence of organizations does not imply the organization of an entire community. An individual or group of individuals must activate organizations in urban localities. That is, organization is not a quality that is given, but must be generated by the effort of individuals. In short, while the locality is not disorganized, it is not characterized by a continuous network of interrelationships. It is this quality that gives local organizations such a key role.

According to Hammond, associations develop in most societies with some degree of surplus and notable population density, and achieve goals that could not be achieved by the individual or family (1972:19). She goes on to suggest that associations are the growing tip of a society, and "the most responsive and dynamic segment of its social structure" (*ibid.*). The mobilizations for change that take place in urban areas are, other than on very special occasions, not mobilizations of total urban communities, but the actions of highly organized local groups. The goals of these organizations are often to improve the economic conditions and social status of the population as a whole (Little 1970:108,109,166–167; Gonzalez 1970:3; Leeds 1973:33). It is for this reason that the kinds of organizations that develop are of temendous concern to those who are involved in establishment institutions (Jones 1972).

Local organizations occupy an interface position between the local population that they attempt to represent and higher-level institutions concerned with coordination, administration, and the maintenance of order (Leeds 1973:28). While local organizations often apply pressure on higher-level institutions on behalf of local populations, the control of key organizations by these same institutions becomes an important means of controlling a local population. An important issue is whether these organizations stand in opposition to the state or whether they function as instruments of the state. It is on these grounds that the nature and function of local organizations and their leadership, in the context of their linkages with the larger society, require careful analysis.

Local groups that emerge risk being transformed into components of higher-level institutions. This transformation of local organizations into "components of" is especially important when the subgroup involved is one that poses a potential threat to the society. The common notion that the poor are a potential threat is, in part, derived from the popular fear that slums are potential seats of riots and uprisings that must be constrained and actively repressed (see Leeds 1973:34; Portes 1972:272; Goldfield and Lane 1973:5,7).

The Economic Opportunity Act of 1964 coincided with eruptions of social disorders in ghetto areas. Clearly the activities of this era posed a threat to the stability of the social system (Buckley 1968). One of the important consequences of the poverty program was that it created hundreds of community organizations and influenced others that had developed independently. The nature of these groups, their operations, and their transformation are the focus of this essay.

Between 1973 and the present, research has been conducted on four different local groups. One of them, the Community Action Group Child Development Center, has been studied in considerable detail. The Community Action Group's history spans the period between 1966 and the present, a period that overlaps with the war on poverty. The activities and transformation of the group during this period may be seen as a microcosm of larger sociopolitical processes. This paper will present the results of an intensive case study. I will explore the origins, structure, and transformation of the Community Action Group.

The Community Action Group had been in existence for six years when the study began in 1974. As the ongoing relationship between the organization and the local population was being investigated, the stages in the development of the organization were reconstructed. Three different types of information were collected. First, data from documents in the files of the organization were collected and analyzed.[2] Second, data was obtained from interviews conducted with individuals still active, and with people no longer involved in the organization. And third, information was obtained from participant observation. A great deal of time was spent in the office of the organization while the documents were being collected and organized. A large number of meetings and social affairs held by the group were also attended. During the research period, then, direct observation was combined with inspection and analysis of documents.

The Origin of the Community Action Group

The Action Group came into existence in 1967. Space does not permit a detailed discussion of the origin of the group, but certain aspects of this initial stage are important to understanding the relationship of the group to the community and to higher-level institutions of the city.

The Community Action Group was a grass-roots organization. All of its members were black. It emerged in opposition to a white organization, the Delano Edwards Eisner Foundation (hereafter referred to as DEE), which ran a Head Start program in the local community. The funds for the program came from the Office of Economic Opportunity and were allocated by an agency of the city, the Community Development Agency. The entire poverty program was administered by a board of citizens, the Council Against Poverty.

The confrontation between the Community Action Group and DEE developed out of local dissatifaction with the program of DEE, intensified by the black-white polarization of the period. The conflict was largely based on two issues: the way in which the director and his staff treated the parents, and the lack of parental involvement in the operation of the program.

In order for action to be taken, the parents had to be organized. This effort was undertaken primarily by one individual. She organized a core of people, they organized the rest of the parents, then recruited support from the residents of the immediate community. In attempting to replace DEE, the community residents appealed to the Community Development Agency and the Council Against Poverty, since they had the power to change the sponsorship of the program. Thus, at a public hearing convened by the local Council Against Poverty, it was decided that the Early Childhood Educational Program currently conducted by DEE be terminated and entrusted to the Community Action Group as a delegate agency of the city's Antipoverty Agency. The Community Development Agency and the Council Against Poverty are referred to collectively as the Central Office, the term that will be used in this paper.

For many of the local people, the successful seizure of the Child Development Center literally meant they controlled it. Thus, there was an early need to explain the structure of the group to local people (see table 5.1). One of the first documents written for internal circulation described the status of the delegate agency: "An organization which becomes a delegate agency of the Central Office means that the Central Office has delegated authority to the organization to operate an antipoverty program with funds granted by the Office of Economic Opportunity. The program is operated by the local organization in accordance with rules and regulations of the Central Office and OEO. The funds must be accounted for in accordance with the rules and regulations of the Central Office and OEO."

The organizers of the Action Group were a group of parents whose children attended the program while it was still administered by DEE. When the Action Group was awarded control over the program, these parents became the new board of directors, and the leaders of the organization. In addition to the parents involved in the program, the board also included people from the immediate community, among them six black professionals. At the local level, the board was the policymaking sector of the organization, but it could make and institute policies only within the framework of rules and guidelines imposed by the Central Office.

As seen from table 5.1, both the board and the parent organization occupied leadership positions in the organization. Parental involvement was an important aspect of Head Start guidelines. Each year the parents whose children attended each of the four classrooms of the center elected officials. These elected officials then constituted the leadership of the parents' organization. Thus, while the membership on the board remained stable from year to year, the parent leadership was selected annually by the parent population. The board held primary responsibility for the administration of the program, but was supposed to consult with parent leadership on major decisions.

The other section of the Action Group was the staff. The staff was divided among those who were educated professionals, such as the director, teachers, and social worker, and those who were not—the teachers' aides, family workers, cook, custodian, etc. The staff was involved in the daily operations of the center, providing educational, health, and welfare services to the parents and the community.

Personnel have been remarkably stable throughout the history of the

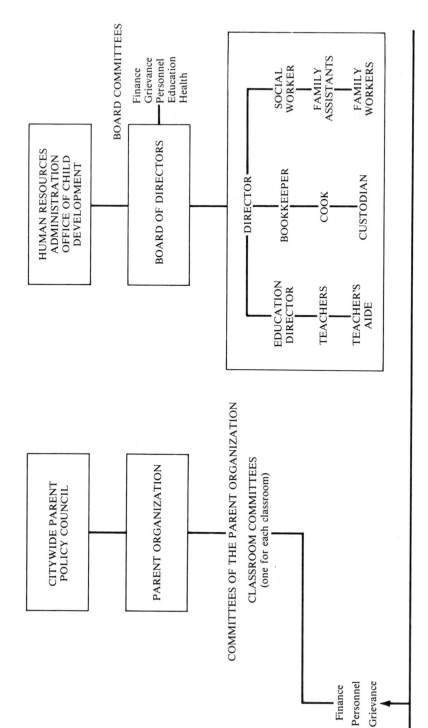

Table 5.1. The Action Group's Organization Chart

Action Group. In 1974, the board still contained individuals who were involved in the takeover, and a majority of the paraprofessional staff had worked in the center since its inception. Although a new set of parents entered the scene each school year, people who had been active in the parent organization often retained a degree of influence. Some parents became board members and a few sent younger children or grandchildren to the center, so that their involvement spanned the life of the organization. It was only among the professional staff that a complete turnover of personnel had occurred.

The First Stage: Advocate for the Community

The Action Group arose in response to a specific set of problems associated with the education of small children within the context of a specific educational center, and like most such groups wanted to have a positive impact. The organizer of the group saw the need to reconstruct the environment and concluded that this required organization and confrontation with those in control.

The group sought not merely to operate within the framework of the philosophy and guidelines handed down from the Central Office, but they decreed that "a positive identification with our racial and cultural heritage shall be a part and priority of our program." The development of a positive self-image was also declared to be a priority: "We shall use the community as a part of our classroom laboratory so that our children develop greater respect for the community in which they live."

The philosophy of the program emphasized more than the education of the children. Community action, in its widest sense, was a goal. In fact, Emery, the first director of the Action Group, believed that the education of the children was the least important activity that the center could perform. He believed that an organization such as the Community Action Group should not survive unless it was used as an instrument to do something political. "The talk about correcting the educational deprivation of the children is nonsense. If no child got much of an education, but the parents became politicized to the extent that they could deal with all the institutions which govern their lives, then that would have been well worth it." But, Emery went on to point out, "any group which is working toward a political goal will also be taking care of its children."

One reflection of the activist theme in the organization was the aggressive relationship that the group maintained with the Central Office. "We openly defied the Central Office," according to Emery. For Emery, the wishes of the parents were more important than the rules. Thus, he attempted to bend the rules in order to satisfy the parents. But as will be shown, rules were to have an ultimate impact.

The Transformation of Leadership

The Action Group began as a grass-roots organization and evolved into a quasi-bureaucracy. The transformation of the organization was reflected in changes in the nature of its leadership, and changes in the relationship between that leadership and the parents.

The shift in leadership styles can be demonstrated by contrasting the views of Emery, the first director of the center, and Colby, the person who followed Emery in that position. Emery viewed the staff, the parents, and the community in familistic terms, and his approach to leadership was personal and informal. Emery made a distinction between a leader of a program of this sort and an administrator. "A leader has to see himself as having responsibilities outside the strict administrative confines, so he cannot afford to say, 'It's five o'clock, the day is over, and it's time to go.' "

Colby's policy of leadership was almost the opposite of Emery's. His view was less political, with a strong emphasis on professionalism and a firm belief that his job was to help people. In contrast to Emery's family approach, Colby proclaimed: "I didn't believe in kinship. I think that a productive society is a working society and we could be friends, but we don't need to have a kinship society. I believe in working from nine to five. And after five go about my own way."

The differences between the views of Emery and Colby also reflected a different perspective on the role of the center in the community. For Emery, the problem of the center and its staff was not divorced from the problems faced by the local population. In contrast, for Colby, the center was an instrument to attack the problems of the community, and the intrusion of problems of individuals into the center disturbed him.

Accompanying this shift in leadership style was a decline in political activism directed at external institutions, an increase in conflict between the leadership and the parents, and a reduction in the interaction between the leadership of the organization and the larger community.

The data strongly indicate that Emery's informal and personal style of leadership was more compatible with the local setting than the formal approach advocated by Colby. On the other hand, it is equally clear that the approach advocated by Colby was more compatible with the expectations of the Central Office.

The Structure of Communication

Changes in the internal structure of the Action Group were significantly influenced by the organization's relationship to the Central Office. An inspection of the communication between the Action Group and the Central Office offered reinforcement for this conclusion.

Table 5.2. Topics of Communication Ranked by Frequencies

Rank	Topic	Frequency
1	Rules, guidelines, and regulations	84
2	Staff duties and performance	66
3	Meetings	32
4	Political conflict in the organization	29
5	Employment (firing, promotions, resignations)	27
6	Budget or financial matters	24
7	Complaints and grievances	18
8	General information	15
9	Etiquette	13
9	Health and educational information	13
9	Staff as workers (tax, insurance, etc.)	13
10	Training programs and workshops	11
11	The structure of the organization	9
12	Performance of board members	7
13	Social and recreational activities	6
14	Purchase of supplies	6
15	Recruitment of parents to serve on board	5
15	Staff salaries	5
16	Sociopolitical	4
16	Lunch program	4
17	Local community	4
18	Visitors	2
	TOTAL	397

An analysis of the documents in the files indicated that most of the letters and memos were from the director of the organization to the staff. The most frequent topic of these communications concerned staff performance (see tables 5.2 and 5.3). The second most frequent topic concerned

Table 5.3. Direction of Communication Ranked by Frequencies

Rank	*Direction*	*Frequency*
1	From the director of the organization to the staff	115
2	From the Central Office to the Action Group	62
3	Direction undeterminable	35
4	From the board to the staff	27
5	From the director to the board	21[a]
5	From the director to the parents	21
6	From the board to the parents	18
7	From the director to the Central Office	16
8	From the staff to the director	14
8	From outside agencies to the organization	14
9	From the board to the Central Office	10
10	From the group as a whole to the Central Office	7
11	From the Action Group to outside agencies	5
11	From parents and staff to the Central Office	5
11	From the staff to parents	5
11	From outside individuals to the Action Group	5
12	From parent to parent	4
12	From parents to the board	4
13	From the staff to the board	3
13	From parents to the director	3
13	From the Action Group to outside individuals	3
	TOTAL	397

[a]This number includes 14 reports from the director to the board.

rules, regulations, and guidelines. The second highest frequency of communication was memos and letters from the Central Office to the organization; the most frequent topic was rules, regulations, and guidelines.

The next stage in the analysis was to determine the degree to which internal communications reflected the concerns of the Central Office. Board meetings were key settings for this problem to be investigated. I attended a number of board meetings during the period of research. In addition, I studied minutes which extended back to the beginning of the organization.

The director was required to submit a written report to the board covering all of the major issues and events pertaining to the center's day-to-day operation. An analysis of discussions taking place at board meetings and the reports made by the center directors to the board reflected concerns of the Central Office. For example, at one board meeting, the following exchange occurred:

The board chairman asked the director to explain the status of the medical examinations. "How many medical examinations have been completed?" The director indicated that additional children had received medical examinations but that not all of the paperwork on them had been completed. "Is there anyone on the staff who has reviewed all the children's forms to make sure that everything that is supposed to be [on the forms] is there [a reference to the topic of staff performance]?" The answer was "No." The director was told, "One of the things that the Central Office people had to say was that our health files are inadequate. The records are important for the people downtown. They don't go by nothing we say—only the records. It's very important to have those forms filled out. Anybody from downtown can come and look at the files, and if they see blanks the center is in trouble. Even if every child has had a complete examination, if that's not on paper, it will not matter to the folks downtown. It's the same as no examination at all [a reference to the Central Office regulations]." The board then pointed an accusing finger at the staff: "If the forms of a child are not complete, it reflects on the worker responsible for that child's record. If they are not filled out properly, it means that that person is not doing her job."

The food service was also discussed during this meeting. The cook was then on a short leave of absence, and the director was asked if he had hired someone who met Board of Health requirements [another reference to rules and regulations]. "No, the replacement did not meet those standards, but she was someone that the parents liked and had highly recommended." A board member pointed out that the parents had little awareness or knowledge of the Board of Health rules. They only knew that the person is a "good cook" and is good with the children. The board member conceded that it was sometimes difficult to explain the rules in "communities such as this." But sometimes the rules make a lot of sense. They should know that some people may cook good enough but still be inadequate to cook for a large group of people.

Rules and regulations refer to the organization's operational procedures. Most of the documents on this topic originate from the Central Office. Letters and memos to parents and staff as well as verbal interaction often relayed information about operational procedures which came originally from the Central Office. Central Office communications either informed the group of new rules and regulations, changes in rules and regulations, or infractions of rules and regulations. These memos were often duplicated and circulated within the organization, becoming the topic of verbal interaction and stimulating the need for decisions and actions.

The above excerpt from a board meeting highlighted an important aspect of the relationships between the Central Office, the board, the staff, and the parents: the board and staff constantly explained rules of operation to parents, rules that had to be followed for the center to remain in operation. Parents, on the other hand, often did not see the logic of these rules. Strain between the parents and the board often arose from cases in which parents were told to follow rules they considered to be unreasonable. This produced a considerable amount of conflict between the parent leadership and the board. That conflict often focused on the role of parents who considered themselves to be the community, in the structure of a community organization.

The excerpt also makes repeated references to the staff and the performance of the staff. Emery's view was that the problems of the community and the problems of the staff were closely related. But this view gave way to one that stressed the role of the staff as *workers,* divorced from the environmental conditions under which they lived.

Staff Duties and Performance

As noted earlier, many memos from the director to the staff pertained to rules, regulations, and guidelines. Most of these sprang from a concern with the staff and their performance as workers. Head Start centers are charged to carry out a certain series of activities: health and dental examinations of every child in the program, a nutritious lunch for every child every day, a home visit to every family, etc. In addition to the activities themselves, a record must be kept of each activity. Thus, many of the tasks were never completed for every child, or the tasks were completed but unrecorded. These gaps were the source of much pressure on the staff by the director and the board.

When representatives from the Central Office visited the center they checked the records, observed the staff at work, and made comments. Their comments placed additional pressure on the staff, and because the director communicated the comments to the staff, he was the medium for the pressure. The criticisms of the staff by Central Office officials led the leadership to attempt to organize and detail tasks and duties, and to develop strict rules about activities that were thought to interfere with the ability of the staff to perform the job. Thus, when one director observed that the children of staff members came into the center after school to wait for the workday to end, he declared that this practice must stop because it interfered with the work schedule. When another director observed that people from the community came into the center to sell crafts, food, and even sometimes "the numbers," he decreed that these activities must be discontinued because they interfered with the work of the staff.

The preceding discussion suggests that the Action Group was a setting where formal and informal patterns of operation were in conflict. The tendency was to force the staff to operate under formal procedures. Yet the context was largely informal in nature. That is, parents tended to respond to informality and resisted formal treatment. Thus, to a large degree, the center was incompatible with its setting, following procedures in opposition to the prevailing values found in the local population. Although the organization emerged from the locality, as it developed, it was no more accountable to the locality than any other formal institution of the city. The close relationship between the center and the Central Office, in contrast to the growing distance between it and the local population, was dramatically highlighted during the teachers' strike in 1974.

The Strike of 1974

During the first stage of the organization's existence, when community action was a primary goal, the leadership of the Action Group was able to mobilize the community. The ability to mobilize is a kind of affirmation, or reaffirmation, of the relationship between a leadership and the people. When a leadership is unable to mobilize, it has lost its legitimacy. Mobilization requires interaction between the mobilizers and the people who are the object of that mobilization. The key dimension of the interaction is communication, and the task is to convince the members of a general population to take some action in order to achieve a specific set of goals. This interaction between a leadership and a population is one means whereby the goals of the leadership are brought in line with the desires and aspirations of the local population. While the Action Group initially acted on behalf of some community people, the leadership was never selected or controlled by either the parents or anyone else in the locality.

Throughout much of the center's history, conflict revolved around the attempt on the part of parents, with the support of local people, to resist the way the center was run—a battle that was always lost because of the relationship between the center and the Central Office. In these conflicts, the dominant lines of the division within the organization were drawn between "the community" or those claiming to embrace community practices and values, and "outsiders" or the agents of outsiders.

When I began my research on the Action Group in December of 1973, one of the first subjects that I heard discussed, was the period of Emery's leadership, as contrasted with the chaos that the center was undergoing at that time. I learned that the center had been without a director for almost a year. As discussed earlier, Colby had been the second director of the center. When the group came to select a replacement for Colby, a series of exchanges took place between the board and the Central Office that marked a major shift in the process of selecting a director.

The hiring of the director involved numerous meetings of the parent personnel committee and the board's personnel committee, at which there was considerable amount of discussion about the personality characteristics and experiences of the candidates. After this process, the board selected a director, based on their assessment of the needs of the center. However, a letter from the Central Office informed them: "In accordance with memorandum #448, we inform you that your candidate does not meet all the qualifications set forth in the 'Standard Job Description.'" Memorandum #448 had, in fact, changed the qualifications for delegate agency directors, and in effect placed the final decision in the hands of the Central Office staff. Thus, although the board had chosen a director, they were unable to implement the decision.

Things were still at a standstill a year later. This place, I was told, "is in trouble." The situation was so serious that the Central Office had called the board to a meeting to discuss the problem. I was invited to attend.

The meeting began with an explanation by a Central Office staff member that the Action Group would be defunded if they did not install a director by the following Monday. The Central Office claimed that they wanted to prevent this from happening. When the time came for the members of the board to speak, there was a long silence. As the discussion began, it became obvious that the board was angry and frustrated, and placed part of the blame for this situation on the Central Staff itself. One member of the board asked, "Why is it that you have rejected all of the people whom we have tried to hire?"

The discussion revealed that the process of appointing a director involved the approval of the parent group's personnel committee, and the board had been having difficulty in getting the parent group to approve a candidate. Candidates proposed by the board would not be approved by the parents and vice versa. This was followed by a long discussion of how the board could avoid having to deal with the parent group. The Central Office staff suggested that because this was an emergency situation, the board could appoint a temporary director without the certification process and parents' approval that would be required for a permanent director.

Much of the ensuing discussion of the center's problems focused primarily on the parents, the teachers, and the social service staff. The parents were described as obstructionists, the staff as inefficient. The discussion ended with the decision that the temporary director would be hired and given the task of firing the teachers and those staff judged to be incompetent. It was agreed that the board would stand united in support of the director's actions, against the expected opposition from the parents and staff. The parent group was to be left out of the picture with the explanation that an emergency existed and the program had to be saved. The Central Office would stand behind the board. The meeting ended with the admonition that the members of the board not discuss the plan with anyone.

The temporary director was hired the following week. Immediately rumors arose about his goals. The board wanted a whole new staff. But they especially wanted a new set of teachers. It was this task that the emergency director set out to accomplish.

The work of some of the teachers had been criticized from the very beginning of the organization. In 1973, a psychological consultant concluded that the overall educational functioning of the center was not satisfactory. "The teachers do not stimulate the children's learning, but are primarily concerned with discipline and control. They either sit passively or respond negatively to the children's curiosity. . . . They are," the report claimed, "rarely sensitive to the children's emotional and interpersonal needs. These problems," the consultant concluded, "are not due to lack of knowledge or training but to the lack of a serious commitment to the children's learning."

January 5, 1974: The new director moved quickly to accomplish the task of firing the teachers. First, he placed them on probation and informed them that their continuation would depend on evaluation by the psychological consultant, the social worker, and himself.

January 8, 1974: The teachers responded angrily to the probation. A memo was sent to the director with copies to the parent group, the board, and the Central Office. The teachers clearly implied that the criteria were "externally" derived. After all, the psychological consultant was not even black. What did he know about black children?

January 10, 1974: The board had committed themselves to stand behind the actions of the director. Immediately following the teachers' memo, they sent their own memo to the director with copies to the parent group and Central Office. The memo stated simply that the board was united in its support of the action of the director.

February 1974: After placing the teachers on probation, the director arranged for another evaluation of the teachers by the same consultant. In his second report the consultant concluded that "the overall educational functioning of the center continues to be unsatisfactory. There has been no significant positive shift in the teachers' performance, attitudes, moods, or modes of teaching since previous observations." The consultant concluded that there was little to warrant leaving these teachers in the position "where they may continue to adversely warp the children's development."

The acting director was not without ambivalence, aggravated by his daily interaction with the staff. His charge was to fire the staff, beginning with the teachers. However, as he began to develop personal relationships with some staff members, he realized that he would be depriving poor black people of their livelihood. "It's tough," he said once, "but it has to be done. Those teachers are terrible."

March 1, 1974: The director informed three teachers and one assistant teacher, in writing, that their employment as teachers at the Community Action Group Child Development Center was terminated upon the completion of the workday of Monday, March 4, 1974. The next day the teachers set up a picket line around the center which the parents refused to cross. The signs carried by the teachers dramatized the "community" versus "outsider" concerns, charging that poor black people were being deprived of their jobs and proclaiming that the board of directors was anticommunity. The teachers mobilized the support of the parents as well as others in the community.

During the strike a number of parents came to the center to support the teachers. The exchanges between the director and these parents revealed conflicting judgment about what constituted good teaching. One parent related her own experience with one of the teachers, proclaiming that Mrs. M had helped her child.

March 8, 1974: The teachers successfully closed the center, mobilized support in the locality, and captured the support of a public official. The issue was also covered in the press. An emergency meeting was called to discuss the dismissal of the teachers. The list of demands submitted by the parent group included the demands that the teachers be reinstated with no loss of pay, and that the present board of directors be removed.

The meeting was advertised as a closed meeting and I was not invited to attend. By all reports, it turned out to have been a very open meeting. One informant described the meeting in the following way:

I'm telling you, that meeting was scheduled for seven o'clock and do you know when the doors opened at seven o'clock, over seventy-five people walked in that door. There were a few local politicians there. The Board had planned this nice elaborate agenda and they didn't have a chance to take up any of that agenda. The Board sat and remained in a state of neutrality while everybody was jumping on RD [the acting director]. It was like he was on trial. He must have smoked a pack of cigarettes. They got so they were just gunning at him. No one on the Board spoke up for him. The Board didn't say anything. And then RD quit. He just jumped up and said, "Effective as of right now I quit. I do not have to sit here and take all this shit."

When I inquired why the Board members kept quiet during the meeting, I was informed that Board members were instructed by the chairman not to speak because the meeting was not planned as a public meeting, and the Board was not to conduct its business in public.

The Director was very angry that he had not been supported by the Board. After all, he was carrying out Board directives and had been promised their support. On the other hand, the firing of the teachers had occurred without consultation with parents and it was clear that other procedures had not been followed.

Thus, although the staff at the Central Office had promised their support at the November 20 meeting, they were unable to follow through. As one of the Central Office staff members explained in an interview, "We knew that we were walking on thin ice. But we decided that we would turn our heads to the guidelines. With the situation being public, we had no choice but to reinstate the teachers."

March 11, 1974: The teachers returned to work. And the center was once again without a director.

The teachers' strike did win the teachers back their jobs, but it resulted in no other changes in the situation. Although the parents again complained to the Central Office about the board, the board remained unchanged. However, the board was once again frustrated in its attempt to administer the center in the manner it believed best. Positions hardened. From the time of the reinstatement of the teachers to the demise of the group in 1985, the situation continued to deteriorate.

Conclusion

This paper has described the transformation of a local organization from a grass-roots group, which operated on behalf of the local population, to a component that served the ends of the Central Office. I examined the organization's relationships to the local population on the one hand, and to higher-level institutions on the other. Organizations of this type that link local populations to higher-level institutions embrace two environments that are often in conflict. From the external environment comes the organization's resources and its operational procedures. From its local environment comes a set of expectations and aspirations that are often in direct opposition to the organization as a component of an external institution. The situation was described by Holden in the following way: black organizations "operate on something approaching a hunger budget of skills, money, internal attention, and external recognition." Thus, the leaders of organizations often lose internal attention— the respect of local people—in the process of trying to achieve the recognition and support of external institutions (1973:16).

The history of the Action Group confirms Holden's conclusions. However, it is the consequences of this that most concern us. The local people viewed the director of the center and members of the board as leaders, and were very disappointed when the people they perceived as leaders acted like bureaucrats. But whatever the degree of dissatisfaction with the leadership, the parents were unable to alter the situation because membership on the board was decided by the board itself. This produced a state of permanent factionalism.

From 1970, the parents had continued to apply pressure on the board in order to gain a right to share in the selection of some of the board members. This pressure accounts for the frequency with which the topic of parents on the board was discussed at board meetings. Failing in this effort, the parents began to advocate the replacement of the whole board. The board's authority derived from its relationship with the Central Office and its control of resources, namely the twenty-two paid positions at the center.

A great deal of the conflict between the board and the parents revolved around the selection of the center director. The parents were mandated to play a role in the selection of the director. One of the reasons the center was without a director in 1973 was that the board and the parents could not agree on a choice: the board sought to select a director who could meet Central Office certification requirements and who would be firm with the staff, while the parents were more interested in someone with compatible social and ideological characteristics. The informal and personal style preferred by the parents was inconsistent with the bureaucratic requirements of the operation.

The case study of the Action Group has implications for the concept of community discussed at the outset of this paper. The concept of community denotes a situation where a network of social relations embraces a whole, and where the criterion of leadership is known and shared by members of a community who collectively select leaders. The mechanisms whereby leaders can be recalled are also known and shared. Given the situation as described, the retention of positions in the organization cannot be explained by using the popular conceptualization of community. It is best explained by using Leeds' notion of locality, where the very lack of a collective sharedness makes possible the development and survival of many kinds of groups, some serving the locality and others exploiting it.

However, the direction of current policies is to utilize local groups for the solution of urban problems (Levine 1984; Percy 1984; Warren 1984). For example, political decentralization, an experiment under way in New York City, defines a special role for local-level organizations (see Jones and Tumelty 1986). While the focus on local organizations as a means for dealing with a certain set of urban problems may turn out to be a positive policy, the use of these kinds of organizations for a type of administrative control at the local level is also a possible outcome.

The concept of "community" implies consensus. To say that someone is a leader of a community, or that an organization is a community group, implies compatibility and unity rather than adversity, conflict, and discontinuity. When higher-level institutions deal with community groups, the assumption of community characteristics allows them to ignore local opposition. Thus what began as an assumption, the community as a collective, becomes a distortion of social reality through the implementation of policies. The possiblity that a local group may lack legitimacy in the locality but still operate as though it represented a communal consensus highlights the possible control functions of organizations of this type.

The control functions of local organizations, even those that are concerned with social welfare, must be considered. The structural relationship between ghetto populations and larger institutions of the society is often characterized in terms of discontinuity. According to Lewis, "The disengagement, the non-integration, of the poor with respect to the major institutions of the society is a crucial element in the culture of poverty. . . . It is because of this that there is a certain potential for protest and political movements aimed against the social order to develop among the poor" (1966:5,7). Thus, urban poor populations are seen as a continuous social problem, and the social welfare programs aimed at the poor are historically attempts to deal with that problem. Thus, Schlossman argued that the "culture of poverty" concept first emerged in the nineteenth century when middle-class citizens "issued dire warnings that without vigorous public intervention into the lives of the youth of the foreign-born, unregulated immigration would wreck havoc on American cities" (1976:152). The primary mode of intervention was voluntary agencies organized for social welfare among immigrant groups. But such agencies did more than deliver services, they were instruments of socialization.

Similarly, the structure of the Action Group facilitated the penetration of formal rules into the locality. Unfamiliarity with formal rules is one dimension of the disengagement and one of the attributes that make the poor as a population hard to reach, especially through formal bureaucracies (Esman 1978). The role of reaching the poor, or hard-to-reach, is then allocated to already existing local organizations, or to organizations formed from the local setting specially for that purpose (Esman 1978:167).

The early history of the Action Group stands out as testimony to what can be accomplished by local organizations. Its later development demonstrates the way in which linkages with external institutions changed the structure of the organization, shifting its orientation. When this happened, a movement developed to oppose and replace the existing leadership. If successful, that effort may have maintained the community orientation of the organization. It was the external link between the group and the Central Office that prevented this from taking place.

A final conclusion is that the locality cannot be understood apart from its connections with higher-level institutions. A position that does not fully appreciate the inherently dependent status of the locality may be itself a part of a rationale for a policy that will end up making the locality more dependent rather than more independent. Thus, understanding the context of organizations and their relationships, their possible positive and negative role, is essential for political as well as theoretical reasons.

Acknowledgment

This paper is based on work done with support of a Research Scientist Development Award (MH 70524) and the Faculty Research Awards Program of the City University of New York. The conclusions, opinions, and other statements presented in this paper are those of the author and not necessarily those of the above agencies.

Notes

1. Emphasis was placed on analysis of written documents. The research involved an inspection of almost all of the letters, memos, reports, and minutes of meetings from the files of the Action Group. More than 1,200 items were inspected, and most of these were placed on Macabee keysort cards. Then 387 letters and memoranda were selected for detailed analysis.

2. Each document was coded by topic. Initially, I looked for recurrent topics or themes. These were arranged sequentially in order to show the historical unfolding of key situations. Thus, if a particular letter referred to a specific problem, the next step was to look for the occurrence of the same topic in another document, and to check for some reference in the second to the first document. In this manner, I constructed a picture of what transpired around a set of issues over a period of time.

References

Arnstein, S. R. 1972. "Maximum Feasible Manipulation." *Public Administration Review* 32:377–402.
Bahrdt, P. H. 1966. "Public Activity and Private Activity as Basic Forms of City Associa-

tions." In Roland L. Warren, ed., *Perspectives on the American Community* p. 78–85. Chicago: Rand McNally.

Buckley, Walter. 1968. "Society as a Complex Adaptive System." In Buckley, ed., *Modern Systems Research for the Behavioral Scientist,* p. 490–513. Chicago: Aldine.

Cadwallander, M. L. 1968. "The Cybernetic Analysis of Complex Social Organizations." In Buckley, ed., *Modern Systems Research for the Behavioral Scientist,* p. 437–440.

Elkins, Stephen L. 1974. "Comparative Urban Politics and Interorganizational Behavior." *Comparative Urban Research* 5:5–28.

Esman, M. J. 1978. "Development Administration and Constituency Organization." *Public Administration Review* 38:166–172.

Friedl, John and Noel Chrisman. 1975. *City Ways: A Selected Reader in Urban Anthropology.* New York: Crowell.

Gans, H. J. 1962. *The Urban Villagers.* New York: Free Press.

Goldfield, David R. and James B. Lane. 1973. *The Enduring Ghetto.* Philadelphia: Lippincott.

Gonzalez, Nancie L. 1970. "The Neoteric Society." *Comparative Studies in Society and History* 12:1–13.

Hammond, Dorothy. 1972. "Associations." Reading, Mass.: Addison-Wesley Modular Publications.

Hannerz, Ulf. 1969. *Soulside.* New York: Columbia University Press.

Holden, Matthew, Jr. 1973. *The Politics of the Black "Nation."* New York: Chandler.

Jones, Delmos J. 1972. "Incipient Organizations and Organizational Failures in an Urban Ghetto." *Urban Anthropology* 1:51–67.

Jones, Delmos J. and Susanne M. Tumelty. 1986. "Are There Really 10,000 Black Associations?" *Social Policy* 17(2):52–53.

Kochen, M. and K. W. Deutsch. 1977. "Delegation and Control in Organizations with Varying Degrees of Decentralization." *Behavioral Science* 22:258–269.

Kramer, R. M. 1969. *Participation of the Poor: Comparative Community Case Studies in the War on Poverty.* Englewood Cliffs, N.J.: Prentice-Hall.

Leeds, Anthony. 1973. "Locality Power in Relation to Supra-local Power Institutions." In Aidan Southall, ed., *Urban Anthropology: Cross-Cultural Studies of Urbanization,* pp. 15–51. New York: Oxford University Press.

Levine, C. H. 1984. "Citizenship and Service Delivery: The Promise of Coproduction." *Public Administration Review* (March), pp. 178–186.

Lewis, Oscar. 1966. "The Culture of Poverty." *Scientific American* 215:3–9.

Little, Kenneth. 1970. *West African Urbanization: A Study of Voluntary Associations in Social Change.* Cambridge: Cambridge University Press.

Mayer, Adrian C. 1966. "The Significance of Quasi-Groups in the Study of Complex Societies." In Michael Banton, ed., *The Social Anthropology of Complex Societies,* p. 97–122. London: Tavistock.

Percy, S. L. 1984. "Citizen Participation in the Coproduction of Urban Services." *Urban Affairs Quarterly* 19:431–446.

Portes, Alejandro. 1972. "Rationality in the Slum: An Essay in Interpretive Sociology." *Comparative Studies in Society and History* 14:268–286.

Rainwater, Lee. 1972. *Behind Ghetto Walls.* Chicago: Aldine. New York: Atherton Press.

Reismann, S. C. and Anantori Negandhi. 1977. "Strategies of Administrative Control and Organizational Effectiveness." *Human Relations* 28:475–486.

Schlossman, S. L. 1974. The 'Culture of Poverty' in Ante-Bellum Social Thought." *Science and Society* 38:150–166.

Walsh, A. H. 1972. "What Price Decentralization in New York?" *City Almanac* 7:1–11.

Warren, D. I. 1977. "The Functional Diversity of Urban Neighborhoods." *Urban Affairs Quarterly* 13(2):151–179.

——1978. "Explorations in Neighborhood Differentiation." *The Sociological Quarterly* 19:310–331.

Warren, R. L., ed. 1969. *Politics and the Ghettos*. New York: Atherton Press.

Warren, Robert. 1984. "Coproduction, Equity, and the Distribution of Safety." *Urban Affairs Quarterly* 19:447–464.

Weaver, Thomas and Douglas White. 1972. *The Anthropology of Urban Environments*. In the Society for Applied Anthropology Monograph Series, Monograph No. 11, pp. 21–38. Washington, D.C.: Society for Applied Anthropology.

6. Ethnoecology of Urban Schooling

John U. Ogbu

Prior to 1960, anthropologists wrote about schooling as a social problem among native populations in colonial and trust territories and among immigrants, ethnic minorities, and lower-class peoples of their own societies (Boas 1928; Malinowski 1936; Mead 1943; Redfield 1943), but few had actually carried out ethnographic studies of formal education (Henry 1963; Spindler 1963:xvii). In the 1960s, however, anthropologists began serious ethnographic study of schooling in the United States and elsewhere. There were perhaps two reasons for this. First, anthropologists, like other social scientists motivated by the sociopolitical ideology of the period, wanted to contribute to the government's war on poverty. An important aspect of that war was breaking the cycle of poverty through increasing the school success of the poor and minorities (Hughes and Hughes 1972:10; Little and Smith 1971; Marris and Rein 1967; Ogbu 1978). Second, anthropological ethnography was also intended as a refutation of cultural deprivation and other theories that purported to explain the educability problems of subordinate-group children in terms of inferior or deficient cultures. Anthropologists entered the field with a strong bias in favor of cultural differences, thus adding culture conflict to the prevailing theories of educability problems of minority children. The ethnoecological approach, which provides a framework for exploring the nature of this culture conflict, was employed in a study of the schooling of blacks and Chicanos in Stockton, California. A brief review of the prevailing theories will provide a perspective on this approach.

Theories of Urban Educability

Cultural deprivation was the dominant explanation which influenced educational policy regarding educability problems of subordinate groups in the 1960s. The central thesis of this theory is that subordinate-group parents do not function adequately as teachers, for example, in teaching their children to acquire proper language, cognitive, and other skills required for the white middle-class type of school success (Bloom, Davis, and Hess 1965; Deutsch 1967; Gottfried 1973; Hunt 1969). But the cultural deprivation theory errs in two important respects: first, it erroneously labels many aspects of minority-group childhood experiences as pathological, and second, it fails to explain how minority children are able to learn their culture so well if their parents are such poor teachers.

A second theory attributes the educability problems to a lack of equal educational opportunity. An older version of this theory defines inequality of educational opportunity as *inequality of access* to fundamental resources like curriculum, facilities, staffing, and funding which are available to white middle-class children. This lack of equal access continues to be documented in several studies and in school desegregation cases (see Aguila 1980; Ashmore 1954; Bond 1966; Bullock 1970; Clement et al. 1976; Guthrie et al. 1971; Ogbu 1974a; Sexton 1961; U.S. Commission on Civil Rights 1967; U.S. Senate Select Committee 1972; Weinberg 1977). One difficulty with this explanation is its reliance on correlational studies which frequently turn up contradictory evidence. In the mid-1960s, its validity was further challenged by the publication of Coleman's controversial study (1966) which found that differences between white middle-class schools and subordinate-group schools in these resources were not as large as generally believed and that where large differences existed they accounted only for a small part of the differences in school performance. This finding led Coleman to redefine equality of educational opportunity as *equality of results of schooling* as measured by tests, not merely of access to school resources. The new version has some affinity to the cultural deprivation theory insofar as it holds that subordinate-group children fail in school because schools are not able to overcome the deficiencies in values and skills children acquired from their cultural backgrounds (U.S. Senate Select Committee 1972:87).

Institutional deficiency is the third major theory. It asserts that the present organization of the public schools tends to suppress the aspirations of minority and lower-class children. More specifically, it criticizes traditional school organization for (a) ineffectiveness in dealing with the educational handicaps of minority and lower-class children; (b) not preparing black and other children to adapt successfully to the requirements of the fast-changing technological society of the year 2000; and (c) not promoting optimal development in children. The solution to these problems, according to the theory, lies in reorganizing the schools in the form of "free schools" and "open classrooms" (U.S. Senate Select Committee 1972:129; see also Kohl 1969; Kozol 1972; Stein 1971).

At least four problems of the institutional deficiency theory can be identified. First, while the critics and reformers import their ideas mainly from Britain, they fail to note that free schools and open classrooms have not solved similar educational problems among racial minorities and lower-class people in Britain (see Bernstein 1971; Inner London Educational Authority 1967; Newson Report 1963; Parliamentary Select Committee 1973). Second, these critics advocate a school reform to prepare children for an ideal type of society rather than for the social and economic realities which the children will face as adults (see Cohen 1971:21; Kluckhohn, quoted in Kneller 1965:64). Third, reformers often ignore the minority perspective, which urges that the schools teach their children the same skills that enable white middle-class people to obtain good jobs, good wages, and other educational benefits *today*. Finally, institutional deficiency theorists confuse two current problems in the American education system: the problem of the ability of the schools to prepare *all children* adequately for a changing economy and technological society, and the problem of teaching black and other minority children the same skills that it successfully teaches white middle-class children. The confusion arises from the inability to recognize the public schools as an agent of a castelike society that selectively assigns blacks and similar minorities on the one hand and whites on the other hand to different positions in adult life, requiring different skills and yielding different educational payoffs.

Complementing the institutional deficiency explanation is the culture conflict theory, a theory endorsed by most educational anthropologists. This theory attributes educability problems to the failure of the schools to educate children in their own cultures. Instead they are taught in an alien (white middle-class) culture. As Philips (1976:30) puts it, "Because they come from a different cultural environment, minority children do not acquire the content and style of learning which are presumed by the curriculum and teaching methods of the (public) schools." One difficulty with the culture conflict theory is that it does not go far enough to explain why conflict *persists* between mainstream and minority-group cultures. Cultural differences do not always result in persistent conflicts. For example, some minorities (e.g., Arabs, Chinese, Filipinos, Japanese) do well in American schools, although their cultures are no more similar to white middle-class cultures than are black, Chicano, and Indian cultures.

Finally, there is the genetic theory, which explains educability in terms of genetic differences. This theory claims that blacks and similar minorities do less well in school than whites because the former have inferior genetic endowments for the kinds of intellectual skills which underlie school learning (Jensen 1969). It also claims that lower-class whites do less well than middle-class whites for similar reasons (Herrnstein 1973; Jensen 1969). There are now several good critiques of the genetic theory of educability (see Alland 1973; Hunt 1969; Kamin 1974; Montagu 1975; Ogbu 1978). It is important to emphasize that this theory is based on an erroneous model of American society, especially a serious misreading of its principles of stratification and of its reward system (see Ogbu 1979).

All the above theories share two fundamental weaknesses. First, they do not consider the adaptive relationship between rewards for educational accomplishments and efforts expended for those accomplishments. American society does not accord all groups (e.g., blacks and whites) equal rewards for equal educational accomplishments, and this certainly affects the way different groups may respond to public school education. Herrnstein (1971:63) argues that people who occupy upper levels of society can generally be shown to have higher IQs than others because of their superior genes. It follows, he suggests, that even when all external social and legal barriers to upward mobility are removed, subordinate groups will continue to retain their inferior positions in the job hierarchy because "actual social mobility is blocked by innate human differences." But an equally plausible argument is that members of a group consistently experiencing unfair rewards for their achievement over a long period of time might have ceased to maximize their accomplishments and have probably adjusted their efforts to the level of expected rewards.

Second, and more important for this essay, these theories fail to consider the ethnoecology or epistemology of subordinate groups and usually proceed to explain their educability problems in terms of the ethnoecology of the white middle class. Ethnoecology of schooling refers to people's epistemology about schooling, to their "folk system" (Bohannon 1957) or the model of "social reality" (Berger and Luckman 1966) which forms the basis of their participation in and interpretation of educational events. However, although the study of people's perceptions, knowledge, and resulting behaviors forms the core of ethnoecology of schooling, this term also refers to the study of school, societal, and historical forces which influence the perceptions, knowledge, and responses to schooling among the group being studied.

When ethnic groups which make up a society or a community have different histories and occupy different social and economic positions, they also tend to have different experiential relationships with the societal institutions. Such ethnic groups may perceive these institutions differently, acquire different knowledge about them, and respond to them differently. The objective of the study described below is to show that we can gain a better understanding of the educability problems of subordinate-group children by studying their own perceptions and knowledge of schooling and their responses to schooling as well as the perceptions, knowledge, and behaviors of the dominant white middle class who control the minority schooling.

This chapter, then, is an analysis of one aspect of research I conducted in Stockton, California, between 1968 and 1970, with some occasional fieldwork up to 1980. This analysis is intended to contribute to the culture conflict theory of minority school failure. At the same time it is also intended to go beyond the limitations of that theory to explain why the conflict persists by examining the support factors outside the classroom—those historical and structural forces which generate and maintain minority and majority ethnoecological differences.

The Setting and the Problem

The research upon which this essay is based was carried out in Stockton, California, a city of over 120,000, located in the San Joaquin Valley, about eighty miles from the San Francisco Bay area. From its inception in 1848, Stockton's population has included American Indians, Chicanos, and blacks. Today it includes other minorities in addition, such as Burmese, Chinese, Filipinos, Hawaiians, Indian Sikhs, Japanese, Koreans, and Vietnamese (Litherland 1978; Ogbu 1974a). There are significant differences between the earlier "indigenous" minorities and the later "immigrant" minorities (Ogbu 1974a, 1977). For example, problems of educability are generally associated with the indigenous minorities whom I have elsewhere designated as castelike minorities (Ogbu 1978).

This study focuses on the educability problems of low-income blacks and Chicanos in a low-income South Stockton neighborhood, here called Burgherside. The majority of employed adults work as farm laborers, manual laborers, or domestic workers. Of the approximately 2,000 people who live in the neighborhood, 92 percent are black or Chicano.

Efforts to improve the school performance of Burgherside children have been based on the theories reviewed earlier, especially the theory of cultural deprivation. This study examines the reasons why Burgherside children are not doing well in school and why remedial educational programs, like Head Start and compensatory education, have not effectively improved their school success.

Because a large number of Burgherside adults appear to be first-generation urban in-migrants from the rural American South and rural Mexico, I initially formulated the research problem in terms of urban adjustment. Specifically, I wanted to answer two separate but related questions: first, what changes might have occurred in patterns of social relations and in beliefs, values, and behaviors of the urban in-migrants? Second, why have these new urbanites not attempted to raise their children to succeed in schools so that the children would adjust more easily than their parents to the demands of the urban social and economic environment?[1]

The fact that Burgherside children do so poorly in school would suggest that their parents either have not changed their child-rearing practices as they adjust to urban environments, or that the changes they have made are not those that help their children succeed in school. It was hypothesized that if the latter is the case, it is perhaps because these parents may have formed an inaccurate image of the urban school system and what is required to succeed in it. Alternatively it was hypothesized that there may be some external forces (e.g., forces beyond the control of Burghersiders) that discourage their children from doing well in school regardless of how hard their parents try to bring them up to succeed in school. Such factors could neutralize any deliberate efforts of the parents to train their children to do well in school. I therefore sought to discover whether there were any such external factors and how they affected formal schooling in Burgherside. One such factor that appeared to be particularly important is the way in which the wider society rewarded Burghersiders for their educational accomplishments, assuming that the way in which Burghersiders perceive and interpret these rewards would affect their responses to schooling. Consequently, after preliminary study my main hypothesis was reformulated. I hypothesized that barriers to educational payoffs among Burgherside adults discouraged Burgherside children from maximizing their school performance efforts, causing them to do relatively poorly in school. Thus the study came to be formulated in terms of ecological studies, particularly ethnoecology of schooling (Bronfenbrenner 1979).

The fieldwork approach was basically ethnographic and has been described elsewhere (Ogbu 1974a, 1974b). The "natural community" of the study was the entire neighborhood of Burgherside, viewed in its ecological context, i.e., the neighborhood as it is linked to the school system and to other institutions and other areas of the city. With regard to schooling, the range of data included not only objectively measurable behaviors but also the knowledge of schooling possessed by different groups (students, parents, school personnel, community leaders, middle-class Stocktonians in general, etc.) as this knowledge influenced the strategies of participation of the groups concerned. Gaining informants' perspectives was considered more important than random sampling. For some aspects of the study (e.g., patterns of school attendance), I collected data for all students in the neighborhood; for other aspects, a good rapport with key informants was more important. Rapport was important in interviews with approximately forty families conducted during the last three months of the study. Relevant objective data were also collected from school records and from the records of other community agencies.

Ethnoecologies of Schooling in Burgherside

Various groups involved in Burgherside education perceive and interpret the school system differently, and these differences influence their behavior. Here I focus only on two opposing ethnoecologies—those of "taxpayers" and "nontaxpayers." As used in this chapter, taxpayers and nontaxpayers are "emic" categories based on perceptions of middle-class Stocktonians who use these categories to order reality in dealing with low-income and minority peoples. Thus, those who classify themselves as taxpayers are generally middle- and upper-class whites, though they also include the more affluent minorities. To be a taxpayer a Stocktonian must not only pay taxes (e.g., property, income, sales, etc.), but must also receive public recognition as a taxpayer. To receive that honor the person must live in a neighborhood which does not have many welfare recipients, particularly of Aid to Families with Dependent Children (AFDC); should be middle-class or "working class"; and, preferably, should be white. People who do not have some combination of these attributes, particularly if they are welfare recipients are labeled nontaxpayers. By this categorization, Burghersiders are considered to be non-taxpayers (Ogbu 1974a:50–51).

Taxpayers control Burgherside education directly as school board members and school personnel, and indirectly as pressure groups exerting strong influences on local educational politics and policies. Taxpayers' perceptions of Stockton, of the functions of schooling, and of Burghersiders as nontaxpayers greatly influence their conception of Burgherside educability and their management of its schooling. They view their city as a microcosm of American society, a land of equal opportunity. They insist that formal education offers everyone the same opportunity to become taxpayers, i.e., to achieve middle-class status. By this they mean that blacks and Chicanos have equal opportunity to get more desirable jobs, earn higher wages and salaries, gain promotions on the job on the basis of training and ability, and move into desirable neighborhoods. Taxpayers believe that they are true representatives of Stockton's "mainstream culture" into which they were either born or have assimilated, and that anyone who desires to do so can assimilate into the mainstream culture. They see a relationship between nontaxpayer status like that of Burghersiders and a resistance to assimilation. Those who "resist" assimilation are viewed as people who are not willing to adopt the values that can transform them into "useful" and "responsible" citizens. A study commissioned by a coalition of local churches summarizes well taxpayers' perceptions of nontaxpayers: over 65 percent of those surveyed thought that low income people are "stupid, narrow in their views, intolerant, lacking in imagination, lacking in curiosity, and lacking in ambition"; that low-income people are immoral and dirty; and that such people do not want to get ahead. "Among those who said these things," the study points out, "are *teachers, professional* [people], housewives, secretaries, and young people" (Hutchinson 1965:4).

Taxpayers, including those working in the school system, see one of their primary responsibilities as transforming nontaxpayers like Burghersiders into taxpayers through public school education and job training. Their approach to this task, through their management of schooling and other training programs for Burghersiders, is guided by their perceptions and stereotypes. They achieve only a partial success, however, because many Burgherside children fail in school, and as adults some become marginally employed or unemployed; others become "wards" of the city, maintained through "public assistance." Those who become welfare recipients, and their children, are perceived as most resistant to education and retraining, thereby creating another major responsibility for taxpayers (Ogbu 1974a:57).

Let us look now at some examples of the way in which taxpayers explain the educability problems of Burgherside children and what is to be done about them. First, it is said that Burgherside children fail in school because their parents neither value education nor encourage them to succeed. For these reasons taxpayers place emphasis on getting Burgherside parents to "become more involved" in school programs. They establish programs to enable teachers and others to visit the parents at home and help them get more involved. They often assume that school failure in Burgherside is a "cultural trait" passed on from one generation to another. That is, Burgherside children are failing in school as their parents and grandparents did.

It is also said that Burgherside children fail in school because they come from homes without male models. When there is a man in the home as a husband-father, taxpayers believe that he usually does not perform adequately as the head of his family. To prove that a Burghersider is a responsible or adequate head of his family, the husband-father should attend various meetings and programs organized by the schools.

Finally, Burgherside children are said to fail in school because they are caught in a "welfare cycle." By this taxpayers mean that people receiving public assistance do not encourage their children to do well in school; consequently their children grow up unable or unwilling to work, and eventually they, like their parents, become welfare recipients. People caught in the welfare cycle are described as lacking interest in becoming responsible, taxpaying citizens through education and work; they prefer to depend on public assistance and thereby remain a burden to "hardworking taxpayers." Even some Burghersiders believe that there is something like a welfare cycle, although they point out that only actual welfare recipients are caught in the cycle. Taxpayers, however, make no such distinctions, preferring to lump all Burghersiders together as people caught in the welfare cycle because they are "hard core" unemployed or "the working poor."

How do Burghersiders view their city, their schooling, and the causes of their children's school failure? Burghersiders do not believe that Stockton is a land of equal opportunity. They point out that racial and ethnic discriminations have traditionally prevented them from obtaining the more desirable jobs, higher wages, and promotions on the job on the basis of education and ability, and from buying or renting homes in better parts of the city. Although there might be some exaggeration, several informants would recount instances in which minority-group persons "had degrees in their pockets" and yet could only find jobs in Stockton as manual laborers or farm workers.

Burghersiders believe that they cannot trust the school system—a white institution—to understand their children and give them "the right education." This belief is much stronger among blacks than among Chicanos, although it is increasingly shared by younger Mexican-Americans. For blacks the mistrust is an outgrowth of a long history of their struggle against discriminatory treatment in the school system. For example, blacks first "fought" against total exclusion when public school education began in Stockton in 1853; then they "fought" against separate and inferior schools until 1879, when they were admitted to the same schools attended by whites "amidst the protestation of many [white] citizens" (Martin 1959:155). Stockton blacks and Chicanos still maintain that their children attend segregated and inferior schools. This has led to protests, boycotts, and legal actions against the school district. In the latter case the court has ruled in their favor (Litherland 1978; see also Ogbu 1974a:235–241).

The theory of schooling—the conception of the teaching and learning process—held by Burghersiders differs markedly from that of the schools and taxpayers. Burghersiders believe that children learn to read and compute when they are taught basic skills in Head Start and other preschool programs and in kindergarten. They say that the preschools and early grades should emphasize the "three R's" rather than play; the children will acquire skills and learning habits they will need to do well in higher grades by learning how to write their names, letters, and numbers. Burghersiders criticize the schools for failing to do these things, for emphasizing play, and for "baby-sitting" in these crucial early years. They also maintain that schools do not treat taxpayers' children as they treat Burgherside children; that schools teach taxpayers' children the basic skills of reading, writing, and arithmetic as soon as those children begin school. Taxpayers' children are said to be able to "finish two or three books" by the time they complete first grade "because they learned their 'ABC' in the kindergarten" (Ogbu 1974a:154–57).

As this brief sketch shows, Burghersiders and taxpayers who control Burgherside education do not share the same knowledge, beliefs, and attitudes about Burgherside education. Their ethnoecologies are different. Consequently, they define the problem of educability and remedies for the problem differently. In the next section I will examine more closely the way in which these contrasting perceptions work to maintain a high rate of school failure in Burgherside.

Ethnoecologies and Maintenance of School Failure

When the knowledge and beliefs of taxpayers and Burghersiders are examined against other types of data, some do not correspond to reality, while others do. Nonetheless, all these folk conceptions and beliefs strongly affect school behaviors of both groups and thereby sustain school failure in Burgherside.

Let us begin with an examination of taxpayers' assertion that school failure in Burgherside is a cultural trait, against the educational backgrounds of three generations of Burghersides: grandparents, parents, and schoolchildren. (In many cases, data on the grandparents came from Burgherside parents because many of the grandparents either did not migrate to Stockton or have died.) For each generation the aspirations of its members, what they expected from their education, and how their aspirations in life and perceptions of opportunities affected their schooling behavior have been examined. Findings do not support the assertion that Burghersiders are indifferent to their children's education and that school failure is a cultural trait. Many Burghersiders of older generations did not finish high school partly because they grew up in rural communities where schools did not go beyond the sixth or eighth grade, and where jobs available for adults did not require high school education. Burghersiders do not seem to be indifferent to their children's education: those who can, assist their children with their lessons or supervise their homework when it is given. They often ask their children about their schoolwork and reward them with money and praise for good report cards and punish them with spanking for poor report cards. In general, they appear to stress the importance of education to a greater degree than school personnel and other taxpayers realize. However, these parents do not always exercise an effective influence over their children's behavior and attitudes toward schoolwork because of the "pull" of peer groups and other forces beyond the control of the parents (Ogbu 1974a:116–132).

From the grandparents to present-day schoolchildren there is a steady rise in both educational aspirations and educational attainment levels of Burghersiders. This increase is directly related to the availability of higher levels of schooling within the reach of each subsequent generation, and to raising the compulsory school-leaving age. The increase in educational aspirations also appears to be related to the perceived widening of social and economic opportunities to benefit from one's education. Before the civil rights revolution of the 1960s, Burghersiders felt that even though they would like to have more education, remaining in school did not generally solve their economic and other problems. Therefore they probably did not stress the importance of staying in school and of doing well as they appear to do now. The civil rights revolution which expanded opportunities for educated minorities to get good jobs, better wages, and even achieve coveted sociopolitical positions resulted in increased emphasis on education. An additional factor is the new and growing pride in ethnic identity. But as will be seen below, the attitudes and habits developed in response to the past and continuing restrictive opportunity structure linger on and work against their goals and whatever new opportunities that may be emerging.

Demographic data show that most Burgherside children do not grow up in households where there is no male model. Males as grandfathers, fathers, stepfathers, and resident boyfriends provide male role models as defined by Burghersiders, even though these may not be the same as for taxpayers. The latter, for example, do not understand that in Burgherside there is a definite division of labor in which school matters are delegated to the woman as the deputy for her husband. Furthermore, because they work as farm and manual laborers, Burgherside fathers are not able to attend school meetings and conferences which are frequently held during working hours. And my observations in home interviews and visits suggest that most laboring parents are too tired to attend meetings in the evenings.

The basic residential unit in Burgherside is the nuclear family, which sometimes includes other consanguineal and affinal kin. The nuclear family represents approximately 65 percent of the neighborhood households; households headed by women are about 20 percent of the total. The absence of a male spouse in the latter group may result from several causes: unwed motherhood, desertion, separation (including deportation of aliens), divorce, or widowhood. Such a household may include the woman's aged parents, her boyfriend, grandchildren, a son/daughter-in-law. Women heads of households vary in education and capability. Many of them do not fit the local stereotype of people caught in the "welfare cycle." Under scrutiny this stereotype, too, collapsed.

Local politics and economic conditions discourage people on welfare from seeking alternatives in employment. Stockton has a persistently high rate of unemployment which averaged more than 7 percent per annum between 1959 and 1969 for the total population, and nearly 14 percent for black and Chicano males, and for black and Chicano women it was 41 percent and 28 percent respectively (Ogbu 1974b:117). People go on welfare when they are unable to find employment, and local statistics show that there is a strong relationship between rates of unemployment in the city and the number of fathers on welfare (South Stockton Parish 1967; Ogbu 1974a:187). Furthermore, a study for the city a few years earlier showed that it was the "official policy regarding welfare payments, rather than the attitudes of welfare recipients, which discouraged persons with low earning power from rejoining the labor force once they become [welfare] recipients" (Little 1965:133–134). Until recently people on welfare who could earn no more than $200 a month had no financial incentives to seek employment because each dollar earned resulted in a dollar reduction in their welfare payments.

The average family income in Burgherside (1969) was $3,778. Burghersiders were not satisfied with merely meeting their subsistence needs but sought to achieve higher status, "to make it" in other ways, such as owning a house. Many who started by living in shacks or rentals saved enough money to build more desirable structures: over 60 percent of the households in my survey have built or are buying their own homes.

Taxpayers' perceptions and characterization of Burghersiders are thus far from accurate. Yet these are the major determinants of the way taxpayers try to educate Burgherside children. Publicly, and no doubt sincerely, taxpayers claim that their mission is to transform Burghersiders into taxpayers through education. But in reality their actions promote school failure and reinforce Burghersiders' subordinate status. For example, Burghersiders sometimes complain that their children actually do better in school than the grades on their report cards indicate. Further, they assert that teachers deliberately give Burgherside children lower grades than the same teachers would give taxpayers' children for the same accomplishments. Burghersiders' assessment of grading is illustrated by the reaction of one family whose son received the following marks in his music class in 1969: first quarter, C; second quarter, B; third quarter, B; final grade on report card, C. His parents said that his final grade should have been either B or B-. They pointed out that he did all his assignments and practiced his music at home. They concluded that the teacher was punishing their son with a lower grade because his mother took him out of class one day fifteen minutes early to keep a doctor's appointment.

I did not give the children an independent test by which to judge their true ability; it is therefore difficult to generalize about the extent to which teachers, perhaps unconsciously, underreward Burghersiders for their classroom efforts. However, my analysis of the letter grades received by all children in the neighborhood elementary school indicates that most children receive low marks (C or D) in the first grade and that they seem to continue receiving the same low grades throughout their elementary school career. For example, in 1964 there were seventeen children in the first grade who received the grade of C for their classwork during the year. By June of 1969, only one of the seventeen children had "improved," receiving a C+ to B− in one year. That is, approximately 94 percent of these children had shown no academic improvement over a period of four years, taught by more than four different teachers. This tendency for teachers to evaluate Burgherside children as previous teachers have done is due in part to the fact that when a teacher gets a new class she reads the children's past records and forms opinions about them before she meets them. Thus, although teachers say that they give letter grades on the basis of students' schoolwork and test results, after listening to their descriptions of two children in the same class it is often difficult to see why both should receive the same grade, or why two other children should receive different grades (Ogbu 1974a:111−113).

It is not suggested here that teachers deliberately give low marks to Burgherside children. Nevertheless, although teachers' behavior, i.e., lack of encouraging rewards for children's improvements, may be largely unconscious, it has some important and unfortunate educational consequences. On the basis of a preliminary analysis of data it can be hypothesized that one consequence of this pattern of classroom rewards is that Burgherside children soon learn that their classroom efforts have little bearing on how teachers grade them. Thus at the elementary school Burgherside children may fail to learn to work hard for maximum rewards. When they enter junior high school where teachers have no direct access to their previous records and may begin to grade them more or less according to their real performance, Burgherside children continue to fail.

Taxpayers' perceptions of Burghersiders also influence the way in which school counselors attempt to help children at the secondary school level. Based largely on preconceptions of Burghersiders as "culturally deprived," some counselors define their academic difficulties in clinical terms, as social and psychological problems resulting from their family situation. With this kind of definition, Burgherside children do not receive a much-needed academic and vocational guidance, but rather a sort of group or individual therapy focusing on their alleged personal problems (Ogbu 1974a:191–204).

Burghersiders' response to schooling is also influenced by their own ethnoecology and definition of the educability problems. For example, their perception of the schools as an unfriendly institution that cannot be trusted results in "fighting" against the schools rather than in working with them to educate their children. Mistrust also reduces the extent to which Burghersiders accept the goals, standards, and instructional approaches of the schools, i.e., the extent to which they genuinely follow school rules of behavior for achievement. It has already been noted that Burghersiders do not share the schools' theory and practice of teaching and learning. The schools often respond to this conflict and mistrust by stressing order and control, paternalism, and even "contest" in dealing with Burghersiders as parents and students. This, too, diverts attention from the educational needs of Burgherside children.

I should point out that the experiences and perceptions of Burghersiders contrasts with those of taxpayers. Taxpayers and their children tend to perceive school rules, school assignments, and school standards as necessary, desirable, and compatible with their own goals; Burghersiders may interpret the school demands differently, sometimes regarding them as deceptions or unnecessary impositions incompatible with their "real educational needs." Note, however, that the schools do not always present taxpayers and Burghersiders with the same rules of behavior for achievement, educational goals, standards, and approaches. I have already described above the way in which the marks teachers assign to elementary school students in Burgherside may not reflect their actual performance, with the result that at the crucial stage of elementary school education, the school may not be teaching Burgherside children to maximize their academic efforts in order to receive higher marks or grades. Further, analysis of the distribution of junior and senior high students in various curriculum areas shows that they are concentrated in what Burgherside parents and students consider "dead-end" courses. Some students complained that in higher grades they are often assigned courses that teach them nothing that they had not already covered in lower grades. This situation may partially explain Burghersiders' rejection of school requirements. But their interpretation and rejection of the school requirements make commitment to and perseverance at academic tasks difficult.

Burghersiders' perceptions of their opportunity structure in relation to their schooling may be responsible for their lack of "effort optimism" in school. There is a general belief in the neighborhood, which is undoubtedly learned by every child, that to compete successfully with a white person for a given job or other position in adult life a Burghersider has to be "twice as good" or "twice as qualified" as the white, a perception and an experiential reality not confined to Stockton minorities. The experience and perception of having to be "twice as qualified" as the white gives rise to a more generalized belief that a Burghersider cannot successfully compete openly with a white: it is hard enough to be as good as the white; it is much harder to be twice as good. Hence, there is no use trying to do well at all in open competition.

There is evidence that schooling has not traditionally enabled local blacks and Chicanos to secure employment or earning on equal footing with whites. I have used the concept of *job ceiling* to describe the employment experiences of these minorities. A job ceiling refers to the facts that as a result of discrimination these minorities are *not permitted to compete freely as individuals* for any jobs to which they aspire and for which they have the training and ability; they are not allowed to obtain their proportional share of the more desirable, higher-paying jobs because of their subordinate status; and as a result of these limitations, minorities are overrepresented in low-status jobs. The operation of the job ceiling in Stockton is well documented by an investigative committee appointed by the city council in 1969 and by the California State Fair Employment Practices Commission in a 1972 study (Ogbu 1974a, 1977).

One consequence of the job ceiling and concentration in low-status

Table 6.1. Schooling and Income of Blacks and the General Population in Census Tracts with 400 or More Blacks, 1969

Census Tract	Median Years of Schooling Completed		Median Family Income	
	Total	Black	Total	Black
*1	8.7	9.3	$4,732	$3,625
6	9.3	8.9	5,545	5,500
7	8.6	8.5	7,094	3,775
*8	7.7	8.3	4,708	3,917
**19	9.3	10.6	6,571	7,274
**20	10.0	11.3	7,784	8,588
*21	10.8	11.0	9,318	8,588
*22	9.6	10.3	5,363	4,633
*23	10.0	10.5	6,435	5,818
*24	8.3	9.3	6,404	5,818
*25	9.0	10.8	5,329	4,231
28	8.8	8.6	7,148	3,913
**38	10.8	11.2	6,077	6,643

Sources: City Planning Department and San Joaquin County Planning Department, 1973.

jobs is low wages that result in higher poverty among blacks and Chicanos in the city. Table 6.1 shows how higher average educational attainment for blacks, for instance, does not translate into higher average family income when compared with taxpayers or the general population. In seven of the thirteen census tracts (those with single asterisks) for which data are available by race, blacks have higher than median years of schooling completed in 1969, but substantially lower median family income when compared with the total population. In three other census tracts (those with double asterisks), where blacks completed higher median years of schooling, their median family income is only slightly higher than that of the general population. In the remaining three census tracts, where median years of schooling completed are lower for blacks, their median family income is usually below that of the general population (see Perlo 1975 for documentation of this phenomenon on a national level).

The reduced rewards for school accomplishments add weight to Burghersiders' belief that as minorities they have to work twice as hard as whites or be twice as qualified to get the same jobs or earn the same wages in an open competition. It is suggested that this may be a factor in Burghersiders' not maximizing their academic efforts though they still believe in the *potential* value of education. They seem to have reduced their efforts unconsciously in proportion to the societal rewards they expect for their educational accomplishments. Such a response is suggested by Shack's (1970) comparison of the historical experiences underlying black and white attitudes toward education and work in America. The absence of a job ceiling has enabled white Americans to receive adequate payoffs for their educational efforts and therefore to develop what he calls "effort optimism" toward work and education. That is, because white people have received social and occupational rewards proportionate to their educational accomplishments they have developed a maxim of "If at first you don't succeed, try, try again." The contrary experiences of black Americans have taught them that social and occupational rewards are not proportional to their educational accomplishments; consequently, many have developed a different maxim: "What's the use of trying?" (see also Dollard 1957; Frazier 1940; Ogbu 1974a, 1974b; Schulz 1969).

It is perhaps because of these experiences and perceptions that Burgherside parents appear to be teaching their children two contradictory attitudes and behaviors toward school. On the one hand, they emphasize the need for their children to work hard and do well in school in order to get more education than their parents. On the other hand, they also appear to teach them that it is not easy for blacks and Chicanos to make it in adult life in terms of good jobs, good wages, and other societal rewards even if they succeed in school. This latter powerful message is not necessarily taught deliberately to the children but is conveyed by the actual texture of parents' and other adults' lives in the neighborhood. By observing the employment experiences of adult members of their community, Burgherside children pick up the connection—or lack of it—between jobs and the value of doing well in school. And they acquire their ethnic communities' beliefs about opportunity structures which "blame the system" for the high rates of low-status jobs, unemployment, and poverty in the neighborhood. The result is that the children increasingly become disillusioned about their ability to succeed in adult life through education and about the value of schooling.

Detailed interviews with some seventy-five junior and senior high students produced responses that appear to support this interpretation, namely, that Burgherside children are discouraged from taking their schoolwork seriously partly by their knowledge and beliefs about the local opportunity structure. In the interview the students were first

Table 6.2. Placement in the "Track System" as Seen by Burghersiders

Track	*"Standard"*	*Region*	*Ethnic Groups*
Upper	"Above average"	Northside	Anglos of Northside, Orientals generally
Middle	"Average"	Burgherside, Southside neighborhoods	Anglos of Southside, mostly blacks and Chicanos
Low	"Below average"	Burgherside and Southside	Some Southside Anglos, blacks and Chicanos "who have not seen the light" (i.e., do not yet recognize changes taking place because of civil rights revolution)

Source: My interviews with Burgherside students (Ogbu 1974a:90).

asked to describe the academic achievement of different ethnic groups and areas served by the school system; they were then asked to give reasons for the differences in the school performance. Table 6.2 presents the way they see stratification of the school population by academic performance. These students place themselves in the middle ("average performance") and low ("below-average performance") tracks. More important is their explanation of the academic stratification, particularly their own placement in the average and below-average groups. These black and Chicano students explained that to get into the upper ("above-average performance") track required both hard work and serious attitudes about school, qualities which they attributed to taxpayers (i.e., Northside Anglos) and Orientals. They said that blacks and Chicanos do not exhibit these same qualities because they do not expect the same jobs and other opportunities open to whites when they finish school. They admitted that Orientals do not have the same employment and other opportunities as whites, but explained that the performance of Orientals is superior because they are "born smarter" and they also learn to take their education seriously and to work hard in school. Thus Burgherside children claim that it requires serious attitudes and hard work to do well in school and that they do not demonstrate these qualities because of pessimistic expectations about the future.

If junior and senior high school students do poorly in school because they anticipate dismal job and status prospects and/or infer the same from their parents' experiences, what causes low school performance among very young, elementary school children in Burgherside? The low school performance of these very young children appears to be related in part to conflicting demands of "survival strategies" on the one hand, and of the schools on the other. Burghersiders, like other blacks and Chicanos, have responded to the job ceiling and other barriers in the opportunity structure by developing a number of "survival strategies" or ways of "making it" in spite of these barriers. One type of response consists of strategies which are aimed at increasing their chances of getting better jobs, wages, and other benefits of education through conventional economic and social realms. Among these strategies are *collective struggle* or civil rights activities (Newman et al 1978; Scott 1976) and *clientship* or Uncle Tomming (Dollard 1957; Myrdal 1944; Farmer 1968). The other type of response involves partial or total withdrawal into a subeconomy or street economy by means of *hustling, pimping,* and related strategies (Bullock 1973; Foster 1974; Heard 1968; Milner 1970; Moore 1978; Valentine 1978; Wolfe 1970). Both types of survival strategies demand and encourage rules of behavior for achievement, as well as instrumental competencies which are incongruent with those required for taxpayers' type of school success. And because these survival strategies have become a part of the minority cultures, children of these minority communities begin to acquire them from preschool years. Thus when the children begin school they do so with rudimentary rules of behavior and competencies potentially in conflict with school demands. When this situation exists, as it often does, in the context of the misconceptions and mistreatment of minorities by the schools and the mistrust between the schools and minorities as described earlier, early academic difficulties may arise.

Clientship in Stockton illustrates how survival strategies may demand rules of behavior for achievement and instrumental competencies different from those which "work" for taxpayers. Historically, blacks and Chicanos have learned that one key to achievement in that part of the universe open to them is through white patronage (i.e., favoritism, not merit), and the way to gain that favoritism is by playing an Uncle Tom rôle, i.e., by being dependent, compliant, and manipulative.

The necessity for white patronage shows up in the experiences of minority-group members on the local school board. The general pattern before 1973 when district voting was introduced was that "safe" minority individuals were appointed or elected to the school board through white sponsorship. The person so appointed or elected remained an effective school board member as long as his clientship was considered in good standing. The experiences of two minority members who took opposite sides on a plan to integrate local public schools in 1969 illustrate this very well. The prointegration member had been "sponsored" for an election in 1965 and was the first minority member to be elected to the school board. By 1969 he had, however, become "too outspoken" on racial matters, and furthermore, he was the only school board member in 1969 to vote to integrate the schools "by busing." His outspokenness and his vote for integration increased his support within minority communities, but cost him his white patronage, forcing him to "retire" from the board because he could not be reelected.

In contrast, the other minority member who had also been sponsored to the board by appointment the year before rarely spoke out on racial issues, and he voted against the integration plan. His vote against the integration plan cost him the support of minority communities, but it simultaneously increased his white patronage. Prior to the integration vote by the school board, a coalition of sixteen organizations of his own ethnic community sent a delegation to request that he vote for the plan. He refused, and he justified his decision by saying that he could do more for minority peoples by remaining on the board. This strategy was not accepted by his ethnic community, whose organizations publicly challenged his claim to represent the community. Just before the school board election which took place after the board voted down the integration plan, a local chapter of his ethnic statewide political organization passed a vote of no confidence in him at a public meeting at which he was present. Yet with white patronage he entered the election and received the highest number of votes in a field of nine candidates, including seven whites.

Sponsored leadership and social mobility are sources of tension and animosity in Burgherside and in minority communities in general. However, although minorities publicly condemn Uncle Tomming or clientship, it appears to be a widespread practice, or at least it is believed to be so. In both formal interviews and casual conversations, minorities as well as whites often describe successful local blacks and Chicanos as Uncle Toms or *tio tacos* (Ogbu 1977). The significance of Uncle Tomming or clientship for the Burgherside educability problem is that Uncle Toms cannot serve as effective models for either taxpayers' type of school success or taxpayers' type of success in adult life, both of which are based on "open contest" (Turner 1961). The rules of behavior for achievement in taxpayers' education and adult status system are supposed to be designed to give everyone an equal opportunity to win by their own efforts, as is the case in sports.

Conclusion

The United States adopted a policy in the 1960s to improve the school performance of poor and minority populations in the belief that this would enable them to become middle-class Americans. To this end, schools have been encouraged to develop and implement remedial programs like Head Start, compensatory education, follow-through, bilingual education, school integration, and the like. These laudable efforts are almost all based on the dominant group's (i.e., middle class, but not necessarily all white) assumptions about the causes of school failures and of poverty among the poor and subordinate minorities. These assumptions about educability and poverty, reflecting only the knowledge and perceptions—the ethnoecology of schooling—of the dominant-group members, are not necessarily accurate or congruent with reality. More important, the ethnoecologies of the poor and subordinate minorities have neither been systematically studied nor seriously taken into consideration in formulating and implementing policies and programs dealing with the educability issues. Nor have these theories, policies, and programs taken into account the structural reality—the castelike stratification system—which generates and maintains the differential knowledge and perceptions.

The case study described here—that of Burgherside, a minority neighborhood in Stockton, California—demonstrates the need to study the ethnoecologies of both the dominant-group members who control minority schools and of the minorities who have to respond to that schooling and programs for change, as well as the need to study the structural basis of these differential ethnoecologies. The contrasting ethnoecologies function in Burgherside, as they probably do in similar urban communities, to maintain a high rate of school failure among the minorities, thereby reinforcing existing urban inequality. It is hoped that studies such as this can provide insights for designing and implementing policies for effective social change—that of reducing urban inequality through schooling.

Note

1. Studies by Clignet (1967), Inkeles (1955), and LeVine et al. (1967) indicate that environmental changes—whether caused by changes in technology, economy, migration, or urbanization—tend to affect the way parents bring up their children. According to these studies, parents who have experienced social change try, more or less purposively, to prepare their children to adjust more effectively as adults to the new environment. In contrast, other studies by Boggs (1958) and Kluckhohn and Leighton (1947) suggest that no such purposive changes take place in child-rearing practices of some groups when their environments change.

References

Aguila, Frank D., ed. 1980. *Race Equity in Education: The History of School Desegregation, 1849–1979*. Bloomington: Indiana University School of Education.

Alland, Alexander, Jr. 1973. *Human Diversity*. Garden City, N.Y.: Anchor Press.

Ashmore, Harry S. 1954. *The Negro and the Schools*. Chapel Hill: University of North Carolina Press.

Berger, Peter L. and Thomas Luckman. 1966. *The Social Construction of Reality: A Treatise in the Sociology of Knowledge*. Garden City, N.Y.: Doubleday.

Bernstein, Basil. 1971. "Education Cannot Compensate for Society." In B. R. Cosin et al., eds., *School and Society: A Sociological Reader*, pp. 61–67. Cambridge: MIT Press.

Bloom, Benjamin S., Allison Davis, and Robert Hess. 1965. *Compensatory Education for Cultural Deprivation*. New York: Holt, Rinehart and Winston.

Boas, Franz. 1928. "Education, Conformity, and Cultural Change." In *Anthropology and Modern Life*, pp. 164–197. New York: Norton.

Boggs, Stephen T. 1958. "Culture Change and Personality." *American Anthropologist* 60:47–58.

Bohannon, Paul. 1957. *Justice and Judgment Among the Tiv*. London: Oxford University Press.

Bond, Horace Mann. 1966. *The Education of the Negro in the American Social Order*. New York: Octagon.

Bronfenbrenner, Urie. 1979. *The Ecology of Human Development: Experiments by Nature and Design*. Cambridge, Mass.: Harvard University Press.

Bullock, Henry Allen. 1970. *A History of Negro Education in the South: From 1619 to the Present*. New York: Praeger.

Bullock, Paul. 1973. *Aspiration vs. Opportunity: "Careers" in the Inner City*. Ann Arbor: University of Michigan Institute of Labor.

City Planning Department. 1974. *Education Study Profile No. 5*. Stockton.

Clement, Dorothy C., Margaret Eisenhart, and John W. Wood. 1976. "School Desegregation and Educational Inequality: Trends in the Literature, 1960–1975." In *The Desegregation Literature: A Critical Appraisal*, pp. 1–77. Washington, D.C.: National Institute of Education.

Clignet, Remi. 1967. "Environmental Change, Type of Descent, and Child-Rearing Practices." In Miner, ed., *The City in Modern Africa*, pp. 257–296.

Cohen, Yehudi A. 1971. "The Shaping of Men's Minds: Adaptations to the Imperatives of

Culture." In Murray L. Wax, Stanley Diamond, and Fred O. Gearing, eds., *Anthropological Perspectives on Education*, pp. 19–50. New York: Basic.

Coleman, James S., Ernest R. Campbell, Carol J. Hobson, James McPartland, Alexander M. Mood, Frederic D. Wernfield, and Robert L. York. 1966. *Equality of Educational Opportunity*. Washington, D.C.: GPO.

Deutsch, Martin. 1967. *The Disadvantaged Child*. New York: Basic.

Dollard, John. 1957. *Caste and Class in a Southern Town*. 3d ed. Garden City, N.Y.: Doubleday.

Farmer, James. 1968. "Stereotypes of the Negro and Their Relationship to His Self-Image." In Herbert C. Rudman and Richard L. Featherstone, eds., *Urban Schooling*, pp. 135–149. New York: Harcourt Brace Jovanovich.

Foster, Herbert L. 1974. *Ribbin', Jivin', and Playin' the Dozens: The Unrecognized Dilemma of Inner City Schools*. Cambridge, Mass.: Ballinger.

Frazier, E. Franklin. 1940. *Negro Youth at the Crossways: Their Personality Development in the Middle States*. Washington, D.C.: American Council on Education.

Gottfried, Nathan W. 1973. "Effects of Early Intervention Programs." In Kent S. Miller and Ralph Mason Dreger, eds., *Comparative Studies of Blacks and Whites in the United States*, pp. 274–293. New York: Seminar Press.

Guthrie, James W., George B. Kleindorfer, Henry M. Levin, and Robert T. Stout. 1971. *Schools and Inequality*. Cambridge: MIT Press.

Heard, Nathan C. 1968. *Howard Street*. New York: Dial Press.

Henry, Jules. 1963. "Attitude Organization in Elementary School Classrooms." In George D. Spindler, ed., *Education and Culture: Anthropological Approaches*, pp. 192–214. New York: Holt, Rinehart and Winston.

Herrnstein, Richard J. 1971. "I.Q." *The Atlantic Monthly*, September, pp. 43–64.

——1973. *The I.Q. in the Meritocracy*. Boston: Little, Brown.

Hughes, John F. and Anne O. Hughes. 1972. *Equal Education: A New National Strategy*. Bloomington: Indiana University Press.

Hunt, J. McV. 1969. "Has Compensatory Education Failed? Has It Been Attempted?" In *Harvard Educational Review*, Reprint Series No. 2, *Environment, Heredity, and Intelligence*, pp. 130–152.

Hutchinson, Edward W. 1965. *Stockton Church Metropolitan Strategies: Parish Studies Report 1*. Appendix A: Characteristics of the Stockton Metropolitan Area. Mimeo.

Inkeles, Alex. 1955. "Social Change and Social Character: The Role of Parental Mediation." *Journal of Social Issues* 11:12–23.

Inner London Education Authority. 1967. *The Education of Immigrant Pupils in Primary School*. The ILEA Report. London.

Jensen, Arthur R. 1969. "How Much Can We Boost I.Q. and Scholastic Achievement?" *Harvard Educational Review*, Reprint Series No. 2, *Environment, Heredity, and Intelligence*, pp. 1–123.

Kamin, Leon J. 1974. *The Science and Politics of I.Q.* New York: Wiley.

Kluckhohn, Clyde and Dorothy Leighton. 1947. *Children of the People*. Cambridge: Harvard University Press.

Kneller, George F. 1965. *Educational Anthropology: An Introduction*. New York: Wiley.

Kohl, Herbert. 1969. *The Open Classroom*. New York: Random House.

Kozol, Jonathan. 1972. *Free Schools*. Boston: Houghton Mifflin.

LeVine, Robert A. et al. 1967. "Father-Child Relationships and Changing Life-Styles in Ibadan, Nigeria." In Miner, ed., *The City in Modern Africa*, pp. 215–255.

Litherland, Richard Hughes. 1978. *The Role of the Church in Educational Change: A Case History of a Feasible Strategy*. D.Min. dissertation, San Francisco Theological Seminary.

Little, Alan and George Smith. 1971. *Strategies of Compensatory Education: A Review of Educa-

tional Projects for the Disadvantaged in the United States. Paris: Center for Educational Research and Innovation, Organization of Economic Cooperation for Development.

Little, Arthur D. 1965. *Stockton Community: Renewal Policies and Programs*. Stockton: Department of City Planning.

Malinowski, Bronislaw. 1936. "Native Education and Culture Contact." In *International Review of Missions*, 25:480–515.

Marris, Peter and M. Rein. 1967. *Dilemmas of Social Reform: Poverty and Community Action in the United States*. London: Routledge and Kegan Paul.

Martin, V. Covert. 1959. *Stockton Album Through the Years*. Stockton: Stockton Record.

Mead, Margaret. 1943. "Our Educational Emphasis in Primitive Perspective." *American Journal of Sociology* 48(6):633–639.

Milner, Christina Andrea. 1970. *Black Pimps and Their Prostitutes: Social Organization and Values Systems of a Ghetto Occupational Subculture*. Ph.D. diss., University of California, Berkeley.

Miner, Horace, ed. 1967. *The City in Modern Africa*. New York: Praeger.

Montagu, Ashley, ed. 1975. *Race and IQ*. New York: Oxford University Press.

Moore, Joan W. 1978. *Homeboys: Gangs, Drugs, and Prison in the Barrios of Los Angeles*. Philadelphia: Temple University Press.

Murayama, Magoroh. 1969. "Epistemology of Social Science Research: Explorations in Inculture Researchers." *Dialectica* 23:229–280.

Myrdal, Gunnar. 1944. *An American Dilemma: The Negro Problem and Modern Democracy*. New York: Harper.

Newman, Dorothy K. et al. 1978. *Protest, Politics, and Prosperity: Black Americans and White Institutions, 1940–1975*. New York: Pantheon.

Newson Report. 1963. *Half Our Future*. London: H.M.S.O.

Ogbu, John U. 1974a. *The Next Generation: An Ethnography of Education in an Urban Neighborhood*. New York: Academic Press.

——1974b. "Learning in Burgherside: The Ethnography of Education." In George M. Foster and Robert V. Kemper, eds., *Anthropologists in the City*, pp. 93–122. Boston: Little, Brown.

——1977. "Racial Stratification and Education: The Case of Stockton, California." *ICRD Bulletin* 12(3):1–26.

——1978. *Minority Education and Caste: The American System in Cross-Cultural Perspective*. New York: Academic Press.

——1979. "Social Stratification and Education: Toward a Theoretical Synthesis." Paper read at the 78th Annual Meeting of the American Anthropological Association, Cincinnati, Ohio, November.

Parliamentary Select Committee on Immigration and Race Relations, Sessions 1972–73. 1973. *Education, vol. 1: Report*. London: H.M.S.O.

Perlo, Victor. 1975. *The Economics of Racism, U.S.A.: Roots of Black Inequality*. New York: International.

Philips, Susan U. 1976. "Commentary: Access to Power and Maintenance of Ethnic Identity as Goals of Multi-cultural Education." In Margaret A. Gibson, ed., *Anthropological Perspectives on Multi-cultural Education*, Anthropology and Education Quarterly, 7(4): 30–32.

Redfield, Robert. 1943. "Culture and Education in the Midwestern Highlands of Guatemala." *American Journal of Sociology* 48:640–648.

San Joaquin County Planning Department. 1973. *Median Family Income, 1970: By Race and Census Tract*. Stockton: Mimeo.

Schulz, David A. 1969. *Coming Up Black: Patterns of Ghetto Socialization*. Englewood Cliffs, N.J.: Prentice-Hall.

Scott, Joseph W. 1976. *The Black Revolts: Racial Stratification in the USA.* Cambridge, Mass.: Schenkman.

Sexton, Patricia Cayo. 1961. *Education and Income: Inequalities in Our Public Schools.* New York: Viking Press.

——1968. "City Schools." In Louis A. Ferman et al., eds., *Negroes and Jobs: A Book of Readings,* pp. 222–236. Ann Arbor: University of Michigan Press.

Shack, William A. 1970. *On Black American Values in White America: Some Perspectives on the Cultural Aspects of Learning Behavior and Compensatory Education.* Paper prepared for the Social Science Research Council, Subcommittee on Values and Compensatory Education, 1970–71.

South Stockton Parish. 1967. *A Statistical Study of South and East Stockton.* Mimeo.

Spindler, George D. 1963. *Education and Culture: Anthropological Approaches.* New York: Holt, Rinehart and Winston.

Stein, Annie. 1971. "Strategies for Failures." In *Harvard Educational Review,* Reprint Series No. 5, *Challenging the Myths: The Schools, the Blacks, and the Poor,* pp. 133–179.

Stockton, City of. 1974. *Neighborhood Analysis Program, Profile No. 5: Education Study.* Department of City Planning.

Turner, Ralph H. 1961. "Modes of Social Ascent Through Education: Sponsored and Contest Mobility." In A. H. Halsey, Jean Floud, and C. Arnold Anderson, eds., *Education, Economy, and Society: A Reader in the Sociology of Education.* pp. 121–138. New York: Free Press.

U.S. Commission on Civil Rights. 1967. *Racial Isolation in the Public Schools: A Report.* Vol. 1 Washington, D.C.: GPO.

U.S. Senate Select Committee. 1972. *Toward Equal Educational Opportunity.* Washington, D.C.: GPO.

Valentine, Bettylou. 1978. *Hustling and Other Hard Work: Life Styles in the Ghetto.* New York: Free Press.

Weinberg, Meyer. 1977. *A Chance to Learn: A History of Race and Education in the United States.* Cambridge: Cambridge University Press.

Wolfe, Tom. 1970. *Radical Chic and Mau-Mauing the Flack Catchers.* New York: Farrai, Straus and Giroux.

7. Anthropological Work at a Gray Panther Health Clinic: Academic, Applied, and Advocacy Goals

Roger Sanjek

In recent years there has been an increasing fascination among anthropologists with the surface symbols and settings of American urban life. We see this in Spradley and Rynkiewich's *The Nacirema: Readings on American Culture* (1975)—Nacirema is 'American" spelled backward—which features anthropological analyses of encyclopedia salesmen, college dormitory life, and dispute settlements in an American supermarket. In Arens and Montague's *The American Dimension: Cultural Myths and Social Realities* (1976), we find articles on astrology, bagels, and rock concerts. Anthropologists writing in popular magazines like *Psychology Today* and *Natural History* offer interpretations of the movie *Star Wars*, college football games, and the symbolism of the "golden arches" of McDonald's. I find some of this work interesting, even entertaining. But as a model for coming to grips with the "realities" of urban America, these anthropological tidbits are insufficient.

Nacirema or America?

America certainly does have a surface culture that anthropology has some justification in examining. But beneath that surface there are political and economic "realities." Urban America is more than "baseball, hot dogs, apple pie, and Chevrolet." It is the advertising firm and the television networks which bring this jingle—or "symbolic text"—into American homes. It is the General Motors Corporation which pays for the jingle. It is the United Automobile Workers, whose members' labor provides G.M. with the profits, which pay the advertising firm, which buys the commercial audience from the television network.

In the 1950s, C. Wright Mills warned students of American urban society against an overattention to narrow social settings, and a corresponding neglect of such questions as "What is the structure of this particular society as a whole? What are its essential components, and how are they related to one another? Where does this society stand in human history? What are the mechanics by which it is changing?" (1959:6–7). (See Plotke 1978 for a searching attempt to answer these questions with respect to contemporary America.)

In the 1960s, Eric Wolf reminded anthropologists that "the period of the present is marked by the extension into all spheres of public life of a set of civil and military bureaucracies connected through contracts to private concerns" (1969:3–4). Noting that throughout its history American anthropology has neglected "the phenomenon of power," Wolf called for a new anthropological focus upon "the processes by which an organization of power is equipped with economic resources as central to the organic constellation to be explained" (1969:7).

In the early 1970s, Dell Hymes emphasized that anthropologists grapple not only with methodological and theoretical problems, but also with a "moral problem, a problem of one's commitments in, and to, the world. Anthropologists have indeed commonly thought of themselves as belonging to the 'party of humanity' " (1972:14). In Hymes' view this implies both an interest in the human past, *and* "a concern with the outcome" (*ibid.*).

Today many view alternative concepts of what society can be as essential. The threat of totalitarian control in the name of a conception of the future is to be answered by open participation in formulation and criticism of what goals constitute genuine progress, what conditions for the realization of goals are acceptable costs. To scorn conceptions of this sort (especially among scholars and movements for change) is to play into the hands of those who are already busy shaping our future by their power to implement their own. . . . The difference between science, practical affairs, and efforts to comprehend and make our own history is a difference of degree, not of kind. (1972:16–17)

From this perspective, the future can be made by self-aware men and women, and *is* being made by *some* men and women; it is more than merely "cultural premises," "structures," or "the material conditions of life" playing themselves out. Anthropologists may be participants as well as participant-observers. Hymes identifies for anthropologists three "relationships to such work—that of critic and scholar in the academic world; that of working for communities, movements, operational institutions; that of direct action as a member of a community or movement. There is need for all three" (1972:56).

I agree. I accept the conception of anthropology and anthropological work set out by Mills, Wolf, and Hymes. It is within this frame of reference that I will discuss my participation in the work of a free community health clinic for older people, and the prospects for what Kay (1977) has disparagingly termed "nonacademic employment."

The American Health Care Scene

There can be no doubt that the health sector is one of the "essential components," as Mills put it, of American society. In the health sector we see the complex interplay of profit-making business corporations, nationally organized professional and provider interest groups, governmental bodies at every level, community organizations of every stripe, and individual citizens—you and me—the "consumers" of health and sickness care. By 1974, health expenditures accounted for $104 billion, or 7.7 percent of the Gross National Product (Kotelchuck 1976:17). In 1983, $355.4 billion, or 10.8 percent of the Gross National Product, was spent on health (Statistical Abstract of the U.S. 1985:96).

As Navarro (1976) so carefully demonstrates, the distribution and delivery of health services is closely related to the class structure of the United States. Poor and working-class communities are disadvantaged with respect to available health resources, and appear at the high ends of such measures of health status as infant mortality, prevalence of chronic conditions, and disability (Kotelchuck 1976:5–16). Because of poverty, because of language and other cultural differences, but also because of the medical profession's relative lack of interest in everyday health concerns (Engel 1973; White 1973), large segments of urban America—the poor, American minority communities, the elderly, the disabled, and women, including many middle-class women—find themselves "medically underserved."

Most of the goods and services which comprise health care are purchased by individual consumers in the marketplace. Here the desperate and relatively powerless individual patient confronts well-organized and powerful provider coalitions and national corporations. "The supply of physicians is sharply limited. . . . The American Medical Association consistently has opposed the federal financial assistance necessary for the establishment of new medical schools and for expanding the number of available positions for students" (Waitzkin and Waterman 1974:11). And despite the limited numbers of doctors, the distribution of medical specialties is skewed away from the major primary care and chronic illness needs which prompt individuals to decide "I'm sick," and to seek health care (Bunker 1970; Ebert 1973; White 1973). Profit-making enterprise in the health sector is shared by the medical profession with five major types of business firms—"pharmaceutical companies, insurance corporations, health equipment industries, proprietary hospitals, and nursing homes" (Waitzkin and Waterman 1974:14; see also Goddard 1973; Kotelchuck 1976).

Increasingly, the payments to health sector profit-making enterprises are made indirectly by consumers, through "third parties"—private health insurance plans, and Medicare and Medicaid. Most Americans, 95 percent or more, have some form of health insurance coverage, even if much of it is shallow, covering only a portion of actual hospital, doctor, or drug bills (Feldstein 1973). The third-party payment system has operated to institutionalize the capitalist structure of health care at levels of profit controlled by the providers: with the shift to third-party payment, hospital costs rose by more than 500 percent between 1950 and 1972 (Feldstein 1973). Critics of National Health *Insurance,* the next most likely change in the economic relations among patients, government, and providers, see this step as one which will further entrench the existing health care system, with power to be retained and expanded in the hands of profit-making health care interests (Kotelchuck 1976).

Within this political-economic framework, several points of unease and dissatisfaction with the prevailing situation appear.

1. Government officials, organized labor, and liberal consumer groups are moving to "contain" if not directly control costs for hospitalization and other medical procedures. The paramount position of physicians in health policymaking is under challenge (Starkweather 1975).

2. Public health specialists, epidemiologists, and other researchers question whether the key problems of sickness and illness in the United States are amenable to medical intervention. They see major improvement in health status arising from environmental regulation, political

action, and an increased understanding and involvement on the part of consumers in the control of their own health (Blum 1976; Burkitt 1971; Waitzkin 1978; Winkelstein 1972).

3. Political and health activists call for a socialized health care system to provide non-profit-making care as a right of all citizens, regardless of ability to pay or location of residence (Blum 1976; Waitzkin 1978). Congressman Ron Dellums of California in 1977 introduced such a bill in the U.S. House of Representatives, outlining the structure and transition process for a National Health *Service*. In evolutionary and comparative terms, such a late date for raising this issue at the national level (passage is unlikely soon) must be seen as a consequence of the distribution of economic and political power in the American health sector. National health services in other industrial democracies are, of course, well established.

4. A variety of groups are working to expand the definition of health care to include a continuum of steps between walk-in (or "ambulatory") medical and clinic office visits on the one hand, and hospitalization on the other. Home health care, adult day health centers, community health outreach programs, and efforts to increase the independence and mobility of several million disabled Americans are key elements in this movement. Key participants, like the Center for Independent Living in Berkeley, California, frequently combine political activism, research, and the provision of services. But, as with earlier advances in health care, profit-making firms are moving into many of these services, and co-opting a progressive movement.

5. Medically underserved communities have taken matters into their own hands and organized free or low-cost clinics to provide models for primary care at the local level (Hayes-Bautista 1976; Jacobs 1974a, 1974b, 1979; Kleiber and Light 1978).

Enter the Anthropologist

There is a place for anthropology in each of the areas I have just outlined, areas in which research can be directed to what Mills called "the mechanics by which society is changing," what Wolf spoke of as "the means by which an organization of power is equipped with economic resources," and what Hymes termed "alternative concepts of what society can be" and "a concern with the outcome."

A distinctive contribution anthropologists can make is ethnography:

"to employ our ethnographic tradition of work, and such ethnological insight as informs it, in the study of the emergence of cultural form in concrete settings and in relation to a world society" (Hymes 1972:35, 56). Similar positions on the importance of urban ethnography in relation to social issues are taken by the Valentines (1970:91–92) and Nader (1972). Accessible and available ethnographic descriptions of arenas of change, and of new models of health care, both failures and successes, are desirable as part of the ethnography of urban America, and as tools for social transformation.

Ethnography in these research contexts, however, must take on an expanded meaning, to include academic, applied, and advocacy goals— the three "relations to work" Hymes identified as "critic and scholar in the academic world," "working for communities, movements, operational institutions," and "direct action as a member of community movement." Furthermore, I agree with Szwed that in arguing for the place of "commitment and political partisanship in social science . . . the links between advocacy and research [need to] be clearly articulated, related, and executed" (1972:172). To this end:

First, *academic* research goals have their origin in theoretical debates in the social sciences rather than in the stated needs and values of the actors in the ethnographic setting. The medical sociologist Freidson (1970) distinguishes the applied concerns of "sociology *in* medicine" from what I would call the academic concerns of the "sociology *of* medicine." Freidson calls for research, that is ethnography, "in the concrete settings of medical care—offices, clinics, and hospitals located in actual communities—[where] we find coming together medical knowledge, the ideology of illness, the layman and his complaints, the physician and other workers" (1970:31). In terms of the perspectives on change I have outlined, the arena for the ethnography of health in urban America would also include day health care centers, home health care, nursing homes, community interest groups, environmental protection agencies, health action committees of labor organizations and other consumer (e.g., feminist, disabled, elderly, ethnically based) groups, government legislative and judicial proceedings and hearings, the homes and workplaces of health care consumers, and to document alternatives, health care settings in socialist countries. Theoretical interests and concepts from political and legal anthropology, urban anthropology, social organization, network analysis, and cognitive anthropology, as well as medical anthropology, would all be relevant.

Second, *applied* ethnographic goals address the stated needs and values of the actors in the research setting, or clarify such needs for them on the basis of the ethnographer's analysis. In undertaking applied work, the anthropologist accepts the needs and values of her or his sponsors in the research setting, if not explicitly, then certainly in the eyes of onlookers. Like "pure" scientific research, applied social science tasks—gathering and processing information and recommending ways in which the setting can function more effectively—are value-free in themselves, but once work is begun, the values of those under whose auspices it is carried out inevitably become the values of the anthropologist. Those who find applied anthropology distasteful must ask themselves whether it is not the values of the sponsors to which they object rather than the idea of committed research. While I find little I wish to claim as a heritage in the applied work of anthropologists in colonial territories or American Relocation Camps, I have no qualms about the applied work of Cohen (1976) for the American Indian Movement patrols in Minneapolis, of Schensul (1974) for a Latino community organization in Chicago, or of Jacobs (1974a, 1974b, 1979) for a black community clinic in Illinois. Academics who object even to this research are clearly the ones of whom Mills, Wolf, and Hymes are critical.

Third, *advocacy* for the ethnographer involves participation with or on behalf of the actors in the research setting to obtain needed resources, or to challenge concentrations of power within the society. Advocacy can span a range of activities—some time-consuming and quiet, like preparing funding proposals for a health clinic (Jacobs 1974a) or community group (Schensul 1974), others dramatic and difficult, like testifying about the distortions in public statements by the U.S. Department of Defense concerning a bomb testing program in Micronesia (Kiste 1976), or supplying the press with damaging and personally risky information about public treatment of alcoholics (Spradley 1976), or joining demonstrations with urban ghetto residents (Valentine and Valentine 1970). While advocacy may mesh with academic research interests (Kiste 1976), the critical difference is that the needs of the people rather than the academic values of the scholar are paramount. When opportunities to speak out and protest interfere with chances to record and observe, an advocate forgoes academic values.

In any particular research setting, academic, applied, and advocacy goals may be in conflict. However, there can also be considerable compatibility among them. It is to this aspect of my own research work at a community clinic that I will now turn. The discussion concentrates on the period of February 1977 to May 1978. After Proposition 13 was passed in California in June 1978, major changes in the clinic's organization and structure were undertaken.

The Over 60 Clinic: Social Process, Ideology, and Social Structure. Opened in January 1976 after a year of planning by the Berkeley, California, Gray Panthers, the Over 60 Clinic provided services designed to fill what an Alameda County study had shown to be a clear gap in the health needs of elderly residents. The clinic emphasized prevention and health maintenance by offering a variety of screening tests and assessments for common chronic diseases and health problems, including hypertension (high blood pressure), arthritis, diabetes, heart problems, peripheral vascular diseases, skin problems, bladder and kidney infections, prostate problems, foot problems, hearing and ear conditions, vision problems, glaucoma, mobility limitations, dietary needs, constipation, and multiple medication use.

After an initial visit, clinic users were encouraged to return to monitor chronic conditions, to participate in arthritis exercise groups, to have foot care treatments, to report on results of self-care plans made in conjunction with Over 60 nurses, and to prepare for and evaluate experiences with other health care providers—doctors, dentists, hospitals, other clinics—to which the patient might be referred by the clinic staff.

As with other community clinics, it was part of the ideology of the Over 60 Clinic to "attempt to demystify the medical care encounter so that the patient has a significant amount of decision making power in the choice and evaluation of an appropriate treatment" (Hayes-Bautista 1976:7). Accordingly, many clinic visits were long in comparison with established medical norms, averaging almost two hours for a first visit, and almost one hour on return visits. Most visits were with the nurses who had found such time commitments essential to achieving the health education and empowerment goals of the clinic. Health education was seen as a two-way process involving the building of trust, the transfer of knowledge from the staff to clinic users, and the transfer from users to the staff of information on self-care practices and philosophies. "If a patient holds notions of health and medical care which are quite at odds with those held by standard medical care, it should not be expected that the patient unilaterally drop his or her views and adopt those of medical care" (Hayes-Bautista 1976:11).

The clinic staff consisted of a nurse practitioner/director, two registered nurses, a community health worker, a part-time health educator, a secretary-receptionist, and a score of volunteers who worked in several phases of clinic operations. As with other free community clinics, "financial backing is pieced together from a number of sources" (Hayes-Bautista 1976:11); during the January-May 1978 period, funding sources included Revenue Sharing through Alameda County, Older Americans Act funds, CETA, City of Berkeley monies, and a grant from the county property-tax based General Fund. Much of the funding came on short-term three- and six-month contracts, requiring a constant administrative burden of paperwork and proposal preparation. "A minimax game must be played with outside resources. Funding must be sought such that the clinic's autonomy is maximized while outside interference occasioned by the funding sources is minimized" (*ibid.*).

More than 1,000 older people, from age sixty to ninety-six, used the clinic in its first two years. They were a diverse group, including retired factory, dockyard, and clerical workers, railwaymen, domestics, and professionals; housewives, many of them widows; self-employed small businessmen; and a few skid row chronic alcoholics. Many were homeowners in the outer city and suburban residential neighborhoods which made up the bulk of the Berkeley-North and downtown Oakland-Albany-Emeryville catchment area, but some were apartment renters, some lived in senior citizen congregate housing, and some were central city single-room-occupancy hotel dwellers. The median and mean age of clinic users was seventy-two; 67 percent were women. About 40 percent were white, many of them European born; 40 percent black, with large contingents from Texas and Louisiana; 15 percent Asian (Japanese, Chinese, Filipino); and 3 percent Latino, mostly Mexican-American. Two-thirds of the users lived in low-income census tracts—the flatlands which stretch out to meet San Francisco Bay from the edge of the high-income Berkeley and Oakland hills.

The founders and nucleus of the governing board of the Over 60 Clinic were members of the Berkeley Gray Panthers. The Gray Panthers are a national organization made up of several dozen local groups, or networks, working toward social change in the quality of life for older people. While each local network defines its own set of issues and projects, the Gray Panthers all recognize a common target—ageism.

As Robert Butler, head of the National Institute on Aging, phrases it:

Ageism can be seen as a process of systematic stereotyping of and discrimination against people because they are old, just as racism and sexism accomplish this with skin color and gender. Old people are categorized as senile, rigid in thought and manner, old-fashioned in morality and skills. . . . Ageism allows the younger generations to see older people as different from themselves; thus they subtly cease to identify with their elders as human beings.

Ageism makes it easier to ignore the frequently poor social and economic plight of older people. We can avoid dealing with the reality that our productivity-minded society has little use for nonproducers—in this case those who have reached an arbitrarily defined retirement age. . . . Ageism is manifested in a wide range of phenomena, both on individual and institutional levels—stereotypes and myths, outright disdain and dislike, or simple subtle avoidance of contact; discriminatory practices in housing, employment and services of all kinds; epithets, cartoons and jokes. At times ageism becomes an expedient method by which society promotes viewpoints about the aged in order to relieve itself of responsibility toward them. (Butler 1975:12)

Health care for older people was an area of special concern for the Berkeley Gray Panthers. The establishment of the Over 60 Clinic, in which they enlisted the help of the Berkeley Public Health Department and the Alameda County Department on Aging, was only one of their health-related activities. The Berkeley network had a membership of 150, with an active core of 40–50. The core group included several younger members, in their twenties and thirties, who worked in social service occupations dealing with the elderly. The older members, the majority, numbered many who had retired from social service work, and who had long been active in political groups and causes. The membership was predominantly white and middle class.

It is a central belief of the Gray Panther movement that in programs serving the elderly, "old people . . . should be determining the policy that prevails in the program, and should be monitoring the performance of the staff in providing the kinds of services that they need and desire" (Kuhn 1974:4–6). "Consumer control"—that "the patient should be involved in the organization, governance and evaluation of the clinic as well as in the therapeutic encounter" (Hayes-Bautista 1976:10)—is also a distinctive tenet Over 60 shared with other community clinics. From this value position, the Over 60 Clinic in early 1978 began the process of expanding the governing board to include non-Gray Panther users, and to represent more fully the class and ethnic background of the user population.

The Over 60 Clinic: Social Field and Political Arena. Like any health care setting, the Over 60 Clinic existed within a social field made up of individuals and groups with whom it interacted, and a political arena in which it competed for resources and attempted to win support for its ideology of health care. The principal components of the social field were the current and potential user population, the senior citizen programs and organizations within its catchment area, community organizations and individual neighbors within its immediate neighborhood, volunteer recruiting bases, referral locations, and doctors and other health care providers. The political arena extended from governmental agencies, health interest groups and coalitions, and key actors at the local City of Berkeley and Alameda County level to include similar actors and groups at the state level in Sacramento, and at the national level, in Washington and throughout the country, through ties to the national Gray Panthers.

At this highest level, the Over 60 Clinic had a direct relationship with Maggie Kuhn, founder and principal spokesperson of the Gray Panthers at such national-level operations as public appearances and lobbying in Washington, and on television guest spots and interviews. Ms. Kuhn visited the clinic in November 1977, and had discussions with the director and other Gray Panthers. She saw the clinic as a model component of how health care might be provided under a comprehensive National Health Service. The Gray Panthers were the first national organization to endorse Congressman Dellums' National Health Service legislation, and are in active cooperation with him to build support for the bill. (Congressman Dellums, it may be added, represented the congressional district in which the Over 60 Clinic is located, and was a guest speaker at the clinic's 1978 December community meeting/Christmas party.)

At the local level, the principal political tie of the Over 60 Clinic was its membership in the Alameda Health Consortium. The consortium is a coalition of twelve community clinics, most of which operated in the lowest-income Health Planning Areas of Alameda County. Like Over 60 with its focus on the elderly, the other consortium clinics developed to serve the needs of particular medically underserved groups—blacks, Chicanos and Latinos, Asians, Native Americans, women, gays, and counterculture youth. The directors of the consortium clinics met monthly to exchange information, coordinate activities, and develop common positions in negotiations with Alameda County over funding and programs.

Most of the consortium clinics received federal Revenue Sharing funds through individual contracts with Alameda County, but in 1977 the consortium clinics were successful in jointly obtaining an additional allocation of $250,000 (for January-June 1978) from the county. This represented the first grant of locally raised property tax funds for any Alameda County community clinic, and demonstrated the strength of the consortium coalition. It was achieved with the active support of one of the five county supervisors, John George, a politician with close ties to Congressman Dellums.

As an alliance across the American ethnic spectrum, and one bringing together such interests as Gray Panthers, inner city blacks and Chicanos, and radical feminists, the consortium represents a people's health coalition which is rare in America. It is also probably a unique situation that in Alameda County, community clinics provided primary health care to more people each year than the county's own primary care facilities. How this fact was discovered brings us to a discussion of academic, applied, and advocacy values in my role as anthropologist at the Over 60 Clinic.

An Anthropologist's Role

I began working as a volunteer at the Over 60 Clinic in February 1977, when it had already been in operation for one year, but just a few weeks after the new nurse practitioner/director (Lani Morioka Sanjek, my wife) had begun work. I was asked to prepare a profile of the clinic users from existing records.

Over the next four months I completed a study of 639 user charts, representing the first fourteen months of the clinic's life. I wrote a thirty-eight-page report which included recommendations on record management, on guidelines for the composition of an expanded community board of directors, and on outreach goals in terms of underserved areas and social categories within the catchment area. I was able to use the computer facilities at the University of California in Berkeley, where I held a 1976–77 postdoctoral fellowship in the Department of Anthropology. I also had help in coding data for the analysis from three Berkeley undergraduates working at the clinic as part of a field placement course. My report was warmly received by the clinic staff and the Gray Panthers. It proved useful in planning and evaluation, in preparing funding proposals, in representing the clinic to interested outsiders, and in relations with local government agencies having administrative power over the clinic.

During this period I also joined the Gray Panthers, attending general membership and health committee meetings, and I participated as a Gray Panther with other senior citizen interest groups in a statewide demonstration and lobbying effort at the California legislature building in Sacramento. I began reading the social gerontology literature, and put together a research proposal, later accepted, to fund another year's work at the clinic. (This was for a 1977–78 postdoctoral fellowship in gerontological anthropology in the Program in Medical Anthropology, University of California, San Francisco.)

From July 1977 my role at the clinic expanded. I accompanied the community health worker in outreach and follow-up activities at senior centers, on street corners where older people shop, and in home visits. I worked at the clinic as a screening and office volunteer, and attended weekly staff meetings. I implemented recommendations on record keeping, which included assigning the tasks of typing a client mailing list and making operational a rotating user card file to the one staff member whose schedule could accommodate this extra work—the anthropologist. I read and made recommendations on letters and proposals from individuals and colleges who wished to use the Over 60 Clinic and its users for projects. I worked with the director on analyzing clinic operations in order to formulate procedures for planning. I served as secretary to the Gray Panther Clinic governing board. I prepared a monthly column on the clinic for the Gray Panther newsletter. And I maintained a liaison role between the clinic and the Gray Panther network following my election by the membership to a seat on the Gray Panther executive committee.

This work served academic, applied, and advocacy goals in a variety of ways, some obvious, some subtle. To discuss this in more detail, I will describe two phases of my work at Over 60: (a) representing the clinic in a county-sponsored study of publicly funded primary care settings, and (b) planning interviews with nineteenth-century-born Over 60 users.

Academic, Applied, and Advocacy Goals: (a) The Primary Care Study. During 1977, the Alameda County Board of Supervisors commissioned a County Hospitals Project team to study the role of the county public hospitals, and to make recommendations about their future. This step was brought on by the concern of public officials over mounting hospital costs. Between 1970–71 and 1976–77, the appropriation of Alameda County property-tax dollars for health services had grown from $17.4 million to

$49.3 million, a figure which represented 30 percent of all 1977 General Fund expenditures. During the same period, county expenditures on the two county hospitals alone had grown from $2.2 million to $10.1 million. Overall, Alameda County health services supported by county, state, and federal funds totaled $320 million in 1976–77, or roughly $300 per county resident.

During the summer of 1977, the County Hospitals Project team asked the consortium clinics to participate in the study. The project's aims were to determine the demographic characteristics of the community clinic users, to identify their pattern of health services use beyond the clinics, to assess their attitudes to county and private hospitals, to study clinic referral practices, and to profile each clinic's current and potential role in the total delivery of primary health care to Alameda County residents. Similar data were to be collected at the four county-run primary care facilities.

Although most consortium clinics already received Revenue Sharing funds through the county, and all stood to benefit from the $250,000 appropriated by the supervisors for 1978, the relationship between the county and the clinics was highly charged. The clinics had considerable trepidation, given their general "minimax" strategy with respect to outside control by funding agents, in providing the county with so much key information. Plans to "rationalize" primary health care in Alameda County—with the community clinics more firmly under county control—were a potential outcome of the project study. An immediate problem was the difficulty which already overworked clinic staffs would face in devoting work time to the project research.

At the same time, the clinics realized they must continue to rely upon county funding, and they saw the value to themselves of some of the project data gathering. After negotiations over client and record confidentiality and over the methodology and wording of each component of the study, the consortium members agreed to participate. At the consortium's insistence, money was allocated by the project for the extensive research tasks each clinic staff would undertake. It was recognized by all, however, that this compensation was only token in terms of the time required.

In my applied role I agreed to do the project work at Over 60. (The funds I thereby "earned" were contributed to the clinic.) I also recognized that advocacy for the clinic might well be involved in the form of supporting Over 60's case for funding from the county. My academic interests were not well served by some parts of the work, which were of little ethnographic value or which repeated work I had done for my earlier report. Having similar data on other primary care settings—both consortium and county—however, would certainly be useful in describing the social field of the Over 60 Clinic. As it turned out the entire project episode revealed much to me about the political arena.

Following project training sessions, and hours of reading background documents, in October 1977 I completed the first component of the study—the transfer of demographic information from clinic charts to project forms on a sample of fifty Over 60 users. During November and December, I interviewed seventeen clients about attitudes to health clinics, doctors, and hospitals, using the project interview form. The next two phases were a questionnaire on referrals and a week's referral tally, each completed by the nurses. My role here was simply explaining the tasks, collating the results, and returning this to the project staff.

The final component in January 1978 was a week's tally of all telephone and drop-in requests for service, appointments, or information. This was intended by the project to be kept by the clinics' receptionists. At that time, the Over 60 receptionist-secretary position was unfilled, and several volunteers were sharing the work. I decided to do this piece of the project research myself, but to expand this opportunity and record the flow of behavior at the clinic for a one-week period. I subsequently transcribed a log of all people who came to the clinic, and all telephone calls, and extracted from it the information required for the county study. The scale of Over 60 was such that it was possible for me to sit at the secretary-receptionist's desk and observe all entrances and exits over the day; in addition, I could monitor all incoming and outgoing telephone calls, and check later with other staff members to see who was called about what.

In terms of the three intersecting values in my role, this was the most significant portion of the project study. Basic ethnographic data for a sample week were collected on numbers of users and requests for appointments and information, duration of visits, the pattern of previous user-clinic contacts (which I obtained from the charts), and the social field of the clinic as revealed in its week "network" (Sanjek 1978) of telephone and in-person contacts. This all met academic values involved in my commitment to make a contribution to what Friedson calls "the sociology *of* medicine."

Managing the project research for the clinic met the applied goal of, in

Hymes' words, "work for" the clinic. But so did the presentation of the results of my one-week observational log to the staff. Information on the duration of visits and the time which screening volunteers spent with new users was useful in clarifying scheduling procedures and rethinking volunteer roles. The data I provided to the nurses showing patterns of client visits and the profile of past clinic contacts among the week's returning users offered a new perspective on their work.

Having such a record of its operations was also useful to the clinic for advocacy—in building support within the political arena and in strengthening its case for funding. I published the results of my analysis of the week in the Gray Panther newsletter and made copies available for the clinic to use in providing the public with information about itself.

As the County Hospital Project began to release tabulations in January 1978, my role in this work expanded beyond the clinic. In early January, I prepared a short analysis of the first figures on the numbers of patients seen by all consortium and county clinics over the twenty-two-month period covered in the project study. This showed that ten consortium clinics had provided primary care to 44,000 users, while the county primary care facilities had seen 33,000. The consortium's share of publicly funded primary care amounted to 51 percent, and the county's to 39 percent. Another clinic, a Neighborhood Health Center in Oakland funded by HEW, but not a consortium member, accounted for the remaining 10 percent.

I circulated my analysis to the consortium members and published the information in the Gray Panther newsletter. This put in sharp relief what was a major surprise, and the key finding of the whole project study: that the growth of community clinics in Alameda County had reached the point where more people used them than used the county-run primary care facilities. As an advocate for community-based health care, I was pleased.

During February 1978, I participated in a series of work sessions with representatives from three other consortium clinics and a member of the project staff to analyze computer printouts of the chart review data. While academic and applied values were served, I viewed my primary role in this work as advocacy—to focus the analysis on the role of the community clinics in reaching medically underserved social categories and neighborhoods.

Our work highlighted the facts that the community clinics were serving the working poor, whom the county barely reached, as well as the below-poverty-level Medicaid population; that the clinics were serving the vast majority of Latino and Asian users, by offering services in Spanish, Chinese, and Filipino languages; that among the thirty-three Health Planning Areas making up Alameda County, in those seven with the greatest percentage of families below the poverty level, the community clinics saw 61 percent of those seeking health care at a publicly funded setting.

In March, our group met at the county health department building with the director of the project and a health department program specialist. We learned that the report we had developed with the project staff member was now to be rewritten by the program specialist. It became clear during the meeting that this was intended to produce a report more favorable to the county facilities, and would "cover up" or abandon much of the analysis we had done.

The program specialist told us that the county hospitals were in fact seeing far more Latinos than their own figures indicated—there was "reason to believe" their records had coded some Latinos as "Caucasian," but to an indeterminable extent. So our findings that the majority of Latinos used the community clinics could not be a conclusion of the project report. The program specialist did not think it was significant that the community clinics saw the majority of users in the poverty areas because "if there was a county facility there, they might use it instead of a community clinic." The program specialist's comments indicated little knowledge of the reasons why medically underserved groups might prefer the personally-oriented and community-based care the clinics offered. Other reports the program specialist had prepared contained conclusions and assumptions with no basis in the project data, but which revealed a clear bias against the consortium clinics. It was evident the program specialist was being brought in to defend the county.

As I found myself arguing across the table in the county health department with a county-employed adversary, I realized more fully than before the importance of my advocacy role as an anthropologist. The next steps in this political struggle were clear: to help present the facts from the community clinic point of view, and to see that the information became public and available to supporters and other actors in the political arena. In May, I prepared a three-page summary for the consortium of what our work group saw as the principal conclusions to be drawn from the sample of consortium and county user records. After further negotiations, this presentation of the community clinic point of view was included in the final report of the County Hospitals Project.

Academic, Applied, and Advocacy Goals: (b) User Interviews. The final portion of the work at Over 60 I will discuss is a set of interviews I had planned to carry out between June and September 1978. On June 6, 1978, these plans were abruptly abandoned when the voters of California passed Proposition 13, a referendum item limiting property taxes. Over 60, like all other social services in California, was plunged into a survival crisis. During the next three months, the clinic underwent a series of internal changes which established it as an independent nonprofit corporation with an expanded governing board of older persons, two-thirds of whom were users of the clinic's services. Everyone at the clinic, including the anthropologist, mobilized to meet the crisis of Proposition 13, a political drama too intricate to describe here. As a consequence I was unable to conduct the projected interviews. (The clinic survived the Proposition 13 crisis, and in January 1985 celebrated its ninth anniversary.)

In my original plan I can see now that I was operating primarily from academic values and research models—looking for "a people" to study. My earlier fieldwork in Brazil and Ghana had dealt with theoretical issues and had no applied or advocacy components. And neither the Brazilian nor the Ghanaian research had an organization as its focus; in both cases I defined my unit of study locationally—the residents of a Brazilian fishing village, or a Ghanian urban neighborhood, people who had no common link to any organizational center. At Over 60, where applied and advocacy values were coordinated with academic ones, I gradually came to see the organizational center as the core of my research—the place where the action began. The interviews with older people, which I had originally seen as the focus of my research, became only one element in ethnographic investigation of the clinic's social field.

I was also influenced in my original research plan by Townsend's study (1957) of old people in Bethnal Green, a working-class section of London, and by Spradley's research among Seattle alcoholics. Advocacy was involved in each case—in policy recommendations in Townsend's book, and in action as well as recommendations on the part of Spradley (1970, 1976). As in my earlier fieldwork, Townsend's unit of study consisted of the residents of a locale. Spradley began from an organizational base, but left it as his own values came more and more into conflict with those of the alcoholic treatment program.

Clearly there is no single "correct" unit of analysis in urban anthropological research. While there is always something to be learned anywhere—on a street corner, in a church, in homes, in a formal organization, or among the dispersed population which shares a common ethnic identity, life cycle position, or occupation—a choice of where to begin, where the anchor point for the research will be, must be made early on. There has been all too little discussion among urban anthropologists of how, and why, they choose their units of analysis. What discussion there has been, or what suggestions theorists and synthesizers give to prospective fieldworkers, usually avoids the question of political values in research choices. Rather, advice is presented about which units of analysis are appropriate to theoretical issues in academic writing.

In contemporary urban America it will do nobody any good to pretend there is not a diversity of political values within arenas of research, and that anthropologists do not have, or should not discuss, political values of their own. There needs to be open discussion—in academia and in urban communities—of the political values which determine units of analysis and frame issues for research.

By March 1978, I had been at the clinic for just over one year. By then I had decided to limit the interviews to users in their eighties and nineties, and to people who were relatively active, those living in their own homes or rented apartments. During April and May 1978, I compiled a list of the clinic's users born before 1900 (about 225 people) and discussed potential subjects with clinic staff members. I hoped to interview ten women and ten men. The results were intended to have academic, applied, and advocacy uses. My year at Over 60, and many hours of contact with its users, underlay the selection of interview topics I considered significant and productive. The research, as I presented it to the Over 60 staff, would cover the following areas: views of the clinic;[1] ideas about longevity and health;[2] transportation;[3] food shopping;[4] how people spend time.[5]

Prior academic interests of my own in network analysis and kinship and friendship patterns are reflected in the last of these topics (Sanjek 1978). Other research interests in cognitive outlooks (Sanjek 1971, 1977; cf. Spradley 1970) emerge in the areas of transportation and food shopping. And new interests I developed during my postdoctoral tenure as a result of course work and reading in medical anthropology, public health, and social gerontology appear in the concern with personal definitions of health, and philosophies of longevity and self-care.

But applied and advocacy values were also on my mind in determining what purposes interviews could serve. Client views of clinic operations, and ideas about change, new services, and effectiveness, were to be probed in hopes of improving the Over 60 program. Findings about transportation and food shopping might have implications for health education at the clinic, and also for advocacy with the Gray Panthers around emerging discoveries of how older people in their eighties and nineties see the situation and define problems of access, security, comfort, and availability. An understanding of why those in their eighties and nineties believe they have lived as long as they have and their ideas about work experiences, exercise, mobility, food and diet, self-care, attitudes toward life, and experience with health care providers could produce ideas to be shared with clinic users in their sixties and seventies. And a determination of the qualities people find desirable and interesting in those settings of everyday life in which they in fact do spend time might prove useful to the clinic and other service programs in planning the use of space and the content of group activities.

Overall, the interview materials would have added to an ethnographic description of the social field of the Over 60 Clinic, and served compatible academic, applied, and advocacy goals. Once Proposition 13 passed, however, full-time advocacy and applied commitments squeezed out the academic concerns. While the decision to forgo the interviews illustrates the primacy of applied and advocacy values over academic ones in a crisis situation, I hope that the content and planning process of the interviews illustrates as well that academic values did have a strong and positive influence on my role at the clinic.

Nonacademic Employment and Nonacademic Engagement

In presenting a value position (based on Mills, Wolf, and Hymes) which provides an intellectual and moral foundation for applied and advocacy roles for anthropologists, in mentioning such research by others, and in discussing my own work at length, I have attempted to build a case for what I wish to call "nonacademic engagement." In undertaking urban research from the point of view of "the party of humanity"—research concerned with the direction of social change, with power, with "the outcome"—anthropologists will increasingly be called upon to work for and to speak out with the groups and movements which their academic or other values bring them to study. The issue has a practical as well as moral side. As Native Americans in Minneapolis made clear to Cohen (1976), as the Enewetak Islanders made clear to Kiste (1976), as black ghetto dwellers made clear to the

Valentines (1970), in the absence of such applied and advocacy commitments, there will be no research.

Without the mutuality and reciprocity applied and advocacy roles necessitate, "pure" academic values will increasingly lead American urban ethnography into the safety and triviality of Naciremaland. The question is not one of abandoning academic values. As Hymes (1972) affirms, the contribution anthropology makes to understanding *past* human history and cultural diversity is essential. Rather, it is the stance anthropology adopts with respect to *ongoing* and *future* human history—to the realities of life in our own society—which is at stake. When scholarly values become scholasticism, when they stand only for retreat and narrow, self-interested "professionalism," then critics inside the universities must join those outside in rejecting such values.

It is these narrow professionalist values which I detect as underlying the influential attack by Kay (1977) on "the myth of nonacademic employment." I find Kay's assumptions, and all but one of his conclusions, to be inaccurate and uninformed. Only to the extent that Kay's professionalist ivory tower values bring him to criticize academic opportunists using the "applied anthropology" banner—those "established members of established departments" who are finding it "a profitable enterprise" to run programs "training PhD students for nonacademic employment"—do I agree with him. But I refuse to define the issues as a choice between a conservative professionalism (an ideology well analyzed by Plotke [1978:21–22]), and an "applied anthropology" willing to train students as have-gun-will-travel social science mercenaries. A pox on both their houses.

Kay's first assumption is that "enthusiasm among anthropologists for the future of nonacademic employment [is] widespread." My own contacts at several universities, including many with graduate students who see nonacademic jobs as their only choice, suggest to me the situation is rather one of unease and uncertainty. Any realistic appraisal of nonacademic work opportunities must recognize that a struggle is involved. As Thompson (1977), in reply to Kay, points out, new anthropology graduates will have to "carve out new careers" and "open up unexplored fields" just as those already employed outside the university have done.

In historical terms, such a struggle should be seen as continuous with the past struggles to establish and maintain anthropology in museums and in government in the nineteenth century, and in academic departments and undergraduate curricula in the twentieth. Such efforts were no doubt pooh-poohed by the Kays of Boas' day. These successes, from which we all benefit, should not be forgotten. But neither should we insist that the academic department be anthropology's final resting place (see Hymes 1972:6–7, 10–11).

Kay's second assumption is that future expansion of anthropology into nonacademic roles is "without serious empirical content. . . . Anthropologists who have spoken about expanding nonacademic job opportunities for holders of the Ph.D. in anthropology have not looked realistically at the finite nature of the U.S. labor market." In this classic presentation of an ideology of "limited good," Kay contends that nonacademic jobs for anthropologists only rob other Americans of their jobs. But Kay does not offer his own "realistic look" at the U.S. labor market. His assumptions are dubious. As Thompson (1977) and Angrosino et al. (1977) point out, anthropologists *are* getting nonacademic jobs, the labor market is not finite, and the distribution of types of occupation is constantly changing.

In fact, the number of "professional and technical workers" in the United States has been steadily increasing since 1900. Between 1960 and 1970, this broad category grew from 7.5 million (11.1 percent of the labor force) to 11.3 million (14.4 percent) (Plotke 1978). In such a fluid situation, the relatively small number of nonacademic anthropologists are hardly putting other workers on welfare. Kay's sanctimonious pleas for fair play aside, what is at issue is, more appropriately, the values and kinds of training which may equip anthropologists to obtain nonacademic work.

Kay's third assumption is that whether or not nonacademic jobs materialize, an emphasis on nonacademic training programs is primarily "advantageous to those who hold power in the profession, i.e., tenured academics." I believe the opposite is true. *Under current conditions*, an emphasis on training anthropology students for jobs outside the university will be dangerous to tenured academics.

A few careerist professors may benefit from such new training programs, as Kay points out. But to the extent that such benefits accrue and the training programs are successful, it is the other tenured professors who will confront shrinking enrollments, those academics who like Kay disparage nonacademic work. In a purely instrumental sense, they will have nothing or little to contribute to prepare *any* of their students for *any* job opportunities, academic or nonacademic.

Administrators and politicians who see these highly paid academics holding positions in such departments will be tempted to eliminate lines or entire anthropology programs, leaving perhaps a few anthropologists in new departments of "applied social science" or institutes of "policy research." Consolidation has ended independent departments of classics and foreign languages, and such can be the case with anthropology. (See Silverman 1976 on threats to anthropology from administrators.) Despite its centrality to the anthropological vision, the study of pan-human history and contemporary non-Western peoples will wither in the absence of new anthropologists who can pass that vision on to future generations of students. I do not want this to happen. There is room enough for us all. I believe, however, that Kay's purist call for retreat to "the traditional scholarly roles within the academy" is a call to doom. (For an example of what lies along this road, see Kay 1971:881–885.)

If any salvation for academic anthropology exists through developing training programs for nonacademic work, the entire content and ethos of graduate education must change. This will require more than adding a few new courses. It will mean changing what we all do every day in our work: new respect for applied and advocacy goals, new acceptance of urban American ethnography, new policies in journals, new relationships outside academia in the communities in which we are employed, new commitments within our academic research lifetimes, and new admissions goals and recruiting efforts. If anthropologists begin such changes only for the professionalist and careerist objectives of keeping lines and getting jobs, then the jobs they get will probably be the establishment administrator and facilitator roles which have given "applied anthropology" a bad taste in the mouths of many. I for one have no interest in training program specialist hatchetmen, or the 1980s equivalent of colonial and relocation camp anthropologists. This is the "nonacademic employment" strategy.

On the other hand, if a policy of "nonacademic engagement" is pursued—on the intellectual and political grounds that anthropology in America belongs "in the world" and "in the party of humanity"—then different consequences are involved. To spell out only one:

Community clinics and many other groups struggling for self-determination and empowerment in the United States have work which needs to be done; the sorts of work I have described. Health clinics like Over 60 recognize the need to employ people in broadly defined positions which include research, information management, administration, preparing funding proposals, assessing needs, conducting or responding to evaluations, appearing at public hearings and in government agencies, locating potential users of services and supporters in their communities, publishing newsletters, and so on. Skills in interpreting statistics, preparing budgets, handling census data, using computers (at least to the level of SPSS), and abilities to work and write quickly are critical. Such skills, of course, are not unique to anthropologists, nor even to academics. People with a variety of backgrounds can and do hold such positions. Since 1979, the Over 60 Health Clinic has employed a "community coordinator" in such a role.

In filling these jobs, anthropologists do bring our own special ethnographic techniques and a comparatively based view of the "social field." But a degree in anthropology, or academic credentials of any sort, is not sufficient to satisfy a community group that a job candidate is suitable. Political commitments and personal qualities are paramount. People with no academic credentials, but with years of community experience, or with a willingness to develop new skills, are often preferable to graduates of university training programs. Anthropologists working for community-based organizations should be prepared to find themselves among nonanthropologists and community residents who are as capable, or more so, at the very ethnographic, applied, and advocacy tasks the anthropologist is doing.

These jobs will not pay at the same rate as tenured professorships or upper-level government positions. And these jobs will probably not be listed as "Wanted: Urban Anthropologist" in the *Anthropology Newsletter* or through the American Anthropological Association placement service. These jobs will not be easy to find. In many cases a person will have to begin as a volunteer, take on applied and advocacy roles, and negotiate research opportunities which will not only satisfy academic urges (which is perfectly proper), but perhaps more important, prove valuable enough that the group will fight for funds to maintain such a position.

The decision to follow the course of nonacademic engagement grows out of our intellectual, moral, and political values. Above all, it is values that we and our students must be clear about. It is questions about values on which urban anthropologists will be tested in these settings, not questions about research interests, field-work opportunities, or scholarly publications. Although it may be no solace to students, I believe that the question "What do I think is important in life and human relationships?" is prior to "What kind of job can I get?"

Acknowledgments

I was fortunate to have the example and advice of many talented and experienced people in California. I am especially grateful to Lillian Rabinowitz, Helene London, Isabel van Frank, Charlotte Knight, Eugenia Hickman, Lorna Brangwin, Rose Dellamonica, Leslie Kwass, Ann Squires, and Rick Smith of the Gray Panthers; Lani Morioka Sanjek, Sylvia Brown, Janet Peoples, Nancy Mackowsky, Maria Calderon, Ray Greene, and Rae Wahrhaftig of the Over 60 Clinic; Leatha Phillips, proprietor of the Bustop Restaurant, and a South Berkeley neighbor of Over 60; Joel Garcia and Yolanda Baldovinos of La Clinica de la Raza; Sarah Walker of the West Berkeley Health Center; Sherry Hirota and Geri Mitsunaga of Asian Health Services; Harvey Smith of the Berkeley Free Clinic and the Alameda Health Consortium; Dani Taylor of the consortium; Dorothy Graham; Judy Heumann of the Center for Independent Living; Florence Stroud of the Berkeley Public Health Department; David Hayes-Bautista of the School of Public Health, University of California, Berkeley; and Margaret Clark, Program in Medical Anthropology, University of California, San Francisco. Earlier versions of this paper were presented at the Anthropology Colloquium of the CUNY Graduate Program in Anthropology, the Southwestern Anthropological Association, the New School for Social Research, the CUNY Gerontology Seminar, and the Queens College Anthropology Club. I thank all who offered their views, especially Nancy Geilhufe, Joan Ablon, John Cole, Dan Gross, Peter Schnall, Jane and Peter Schneider, Sydel Silverman, Anne Okongwu, Shirley Lindenbaum, Leith Mullings, Bert Pelto, and Bob Paynter.

Notes

1. Do you think the care you received at the Over 60 Clinic is different in any way from other health care experiences you have had? In what ways? Did you find out anything helpful to you from the Over 60 Clinic? Did it enable you to make changes in how you take care of your health? There are lots of ways to spend the clinic's funds: what improvements do *you* think should be made? What do you think should be done differently at the clinic? Are there any new additional services you would like to see? Is there anything the clinic staff could do to make it easier or more comfortable for you to use the clinic?

2. What do you think has helped you to live as long as you have—into your eighties (or nineties)? (After people say what they think is important, then ask about some specific areas: work they did when they were younger, exercise and mobility, food and diet, self-care, attitudes toward life and people around them, health care from doctors and other providers.)

3. How do you travel around Berkeley or Oakland—do you drive or use buses or other means of transportation? Do you walk a lot; where to and how much? (Then ask about advantages and disadvantages of different means of transportation in cost, time, comfort, availability, security and safety, personal accessibility or ease.) Does lack of transportation present any problems in going places you would like to go?

4. Where do you do your food shopping? Are there any problems in getting there? In using the store? In going only at certain times of day? In how you are treated? In bringing food home? Do you have people to help you in shopping? Do you ever use delivery services? What do they charge? Is there anything that the stores you use, or would like to use, could do to make things easier or more comfortable for you?

5. What did you do yesterday? (Then go through the day.) When did you get up? What did you do then? (and so on, finding out what people did, where they went, and who they saw. Also ask about important friends and relatives who might not turn up in a sample day. Repeat for total of four days, two weekdays and a weekend).

References

Angrosino, Michael, Erve Chambers, Stephen Gluckman, Gilbert Kushner, Curtis Wienker, and Alvin Wolfe. 1977. " 'Myth of Nonacademic Anthropology' Criticized." *Anthropology Newsletter* 18(10):18.

Arens, W. and Susan Montague, eds. 1976. *The American Dimension: Cultural Myths and Social Realities.* Sherman Oaks, Calif.: Alfred.

Blum, Henrik. 1976. *Expanding Health Care Horizons: From a General Systems Concept of Health to a National Health Policy.* Oakland, Calif.: Third Party Associates.

Bunker, John. 1970. "Surgical Manpower: A Comparison of Operations and Surgeons in the United States and in England and Wales." *New England Journal of Medicine* 282:135–144.

Burkitt, Denis. 1971. "Epidemiology of Cancer of the Colon and Rectum." *Cancer* 28(3):3–13.

Butler, Robert N. 1975. *Why Survive? Being Old in America.* New York: Harper and Row.

Cohen, Fay. 1976. "The American Indian Movement and the Anthropologists: Issues and Implications of Consent." In Rynkiewich and Spradley, eds., *Ethics and Anthropology*, pp. 81–94.

Ebert, Robert. 1973. "The Medical School." In *Life and Death and Medicine*, pp. 103–109.

Engel, George. 1973. " 'The Best and the Brightest': The Missing Dimension in Medical Education." *The Pharos*, October, pp. 129–133.

Feldstein, Martin. 1973. "The Medical Economy." In *Life and Death and Medicine*, pp. 112–118.

Freidson, Eliot. 1970. *Professional Dominance: The Social Structure of Medical Care.* Chicago: Aldine.

Goddard, James. 1973. "The Medical Business." In *Life and Death and Medicine*, pp. 120–125.

Hayes-Bautista, David. 1976. "Deviant Delivery Systems." Presented at the Western Health Consortium, February 12–13, San Francisco, mimeographed.

Hymes, Dell. 1972. "The Use of Anthropology: Critical, Political, Personal." In Hymes, ed., *Reinventing Anthropology*, pp. 3–79. New York: Vintage.

Jacobs, Sue-Ellen. 1974a. "Action and Advocacy Anthropology." *Human Organization* 33:209–215.

——1974b. "Doing It Our Way and Mostly for Our Own." *Human Organization* 33:380–382.

——. 1979. " 'Our Babies Shall Not Die': A Community's Response to Medical Neglect." *Human Organization* 38:120–133.

Kay, Paul. 1971. Taxonomy and Semantic Contrast. *Language* 47:866–887.

——. 1977. "The Myth of Nonacademic Employment: Observations on the Growth of an Ideology." *Anthropology Newsletter* 18(8):11–12.

Kiste, Robert. 1976. The People of Enewetak Atoll versus the U.S. Department of Defense." In Michael Rynkiewich and James Spradley, eds., *Ethics and Anthropology: Dilemmas in Fieldwork*. Pp. 61–80. New York: Wiley.

Kleiber, Nancy and Linda Light. 1978. *Caring for Ourselves: An Alternative Structure for Health Care*. Report on the Vancouver Women's Health Collective. Vancouver: University of British Columbia.

Kotelchuck, David, ed. 1976. *Prognosis Negative: Crisis in the Health Care System*. A Health-PAC Book. New York: Vintage.

Kuhn, Maggie. 1974. "Grass-Roots Gray Power." Gray Panther reprint from *Prime Time*, June 5, pp. 4–6.

Life and Death and Medicine: A Scientific American Book. 1973. San Francisco: W. H. Freeman.

Mills, C. Wright. 1959. *The Sociological Imagination*. New York: Evergreen.

Nader, Laura. 1972. "Up the Anthropologist—Perspectives Gained from Studying Up." In Dell Hymes, ed. *Reinventing Anthropology*, pp. 284–311. New York: Vintage.

Navarro, Vicente. 1976. *Medicine Under Capitalism*. New York: Prodist.

Plotke, David. 1978. "American Political and Class Forces in the 1970s." *Socialist Review* 8:11–39.

Rynkiewich, Michael and James Spradley, eds. 1976. *Ethics and Anthropology: Dilemmas in Fieldwork*. New York: Wiley.

Sanjek, Roger. 1971. "Brazilian Racial Terms: Some Aspects of Meaning and Learning." *American Anthropologist* 73:1126–1143.

—— 1977. "Cognitive Maps of the Ethnic Domain in Urban Ghana: Reflections on Variability and Change." *American Ethnologist* 4:603–622.

—— 1978. "A Network Method and Its Uses in Urban Ethnography." *Human Organization* 37:257–268.

Schensul, Stephen. 1974. "Skills Needed in Action Anthropology: Lessons from El Centro de la Causa." *Human Organization* 33:203–209.

Silverman, Sydel. 1976. "Anthropology and the Crisis at CUNY." *Anthropology Newsletter* 17(10):7–10.

Spradley, James. 1970. *You Owe Yourself a Drunk: An Ethnography of Urban Nomads*. Boston: Little, Brown.

——. 1976. "Trouble in the Tank." In Rynkiewich and Spradley, eds., *Ethics and Anthropology*, pp. 17–31.

Spradley, James and Michael Rynkiewich, eds. 1975. *The Nacirema: Readings on American Culture*. Boston: Little, Brown.

Starkweather, David. 1975. "Hospitals: From Physician Dominance to Public Control." *Public Affairs Report* 16(5):1–6.

Statistical Abstract of the U.S. 1985. Washington, D.C.: G.P.O.

Szwed, John. 1972. "An American Anthropological Dilemma: The Politics of Afro-American Culture." In Hymes, ed., *Reinventing Anthropology*, pp. 153–181.

Thompson, Laura. 1977. " 'Myth of Nonacademic Anthropology' Criticized." *Anthropology Newsletter* 18(10):17.

Townsend, Peter. 1957. *The Family Life of Old People*. Baltimore: Penguin.

Valentine, Charles and Bettylou Valentine. 1970. "Making the Scene, Digging the Action, and Telling It Like It Is: Anthropologists at Work in a Dark Ghetto." In Norman Whitten and John Szwed, eds., *Afro-American Anthropology*, pp. 403–418. New York: Free Press.

Waitzkin, Howard. 1978. "A Marxist View of Medical Care." *Annals of Internal Medicine* 89:264–278.

Waitzkin, Howard and Barbara Waterman. 1974. *The Exploitation of Illness in Capitalist Society*. Indianapolis: Bobbs-Merrill.

White, Kerr. 1973. "Life and Death and Medicine." In *Life and Death and Medicine,* pp. 3–13.

Winkelstein, Warren. 1972. "Epidemiological Considerations Underlying the Allocation of Health and Disease Care Resources." *International Journal of Epidemiology* 1:69–74.

Wolf, Eric. 1969. "American Anthropologists and American Society." In Stephen Tyler, ed., *Concepts and Assumptions in Contemporary Anthropology,* pp. 3–11. Southern Anthropological Society Proceedings, No. 3. Athens: University of Georgia Press.

8. The Foundations and Genesis of a Mexican-American Community: A Sociohistorical Perspective

Robert R. Alvarez

Contemporary Mexican migration is characterized by migrants searching for economic opportunity in the growing urban centers throughout the United States. However, Mexicans are often seen as a single immigrant type (primarily believed to be undocumented or "illegal"), unified by a single culture and language, and typified by their single economic relationship to the United States. These broad generalizations hide a number of important sociohistoric and regional characteristics of Mexican migration that are germane to understanding not only the present communities of Mexican immigrants and Chicanos in the United States, but the migration process itself.

This chapter describes the rise of Lemon Grove, a Mexican-American community along the U.S.-Mexican border in southern California. Today, Lemon Grove is a typical southern California suburb with a population of 20,000, nine miles from the city of San Diego. This community was settled by families from the Mexican peninsula of Baja California just after the turn of the century and illustrates the sociocultural process that was instrumental in the successful settlement and adaptation of settlers who began arriving in the 1900s.

The story of this Mexican community begins just after the turn of the century, but in 1931 a dramatic event occurred which highlights not only the cohesion of the pioneers who came from the south, but also their successful adaptation to life in the United States.

On January 5, 1931, the Mexican children of Lemon Grove returned to school after the Christmas recess. The principal, Jerome Green, stood at the door of the school and prohibited their entrance. He announced that all desks and other possessions of the Mexican children had been moved to a new two-room structure. They were instructed to attend a new school built in the Mexican section of Lemon Grove. However, the principal and the school board were not prepared for the response of the community, nor the court battle that ensued in the Superior Court of the County of San Diego during the next six months (Alvarez 1986a).[1] The parents rallied, forced a school attendance strike of their children, and organized themselves into the Lemon Grove Neighbors' Committee (El Comite de Vecinos de Lemon Grove). They sought assistance from the Mexican consulate in San Diego, and wrote for help through the Spanish language press, *La Opinión*, in Los Angeles and papers across the U.S.-Mexican border in Tijuana. Articles appeared in local county newspapers announcing "Mexican Students Go on Strike" (*San Diego Evening Tribune* 1931). The parents sought a legal injunction and through a writ of mandate from the Superior Court of San Diego charged the school board (composed of civic leaders) with segregation, and demanded the reinstatement of their children. The injustice of the segregation was exacerbated by the fact that the majority of the "Mexican" children were natural-born citizens of the United States. Before their lawyers went to court, the actions of the school board were approved by the local chamber of commerce. The community, however, persisted, and in a final ruling won the right of entrance and equal instruction for their children. This little-known court battle, now beginning to take its place in the history of U.S. civil rights, dramatized the level of organization and mutual help that characterized the community.

The Lemon Grove case was the first successful desegregation court battle in the history of the United States, over twenty years before the Supreme Court took up the landmark case of *Brown v. the Topeka School Board* in 1954. The surprising outcome was an isolated incident during the Depression, a period when the Mexican population in the United States was viewed by the public and government as a primary contributor to the nation's economic trouble (Alvarez 1984; Cardenas 1975; Divine 1957; Hoffman 1974; Romo 1975; Scott 1971). Mexicans were blamed for taking jobs from Americans, and for burdening the public welfare system. Public reports claimed that Mexicans were uninterested in becoming "Americans," because they held strong ties to Mexico and spoke Spanish rather than English. Journalists and scholars accused Mexicans of being lustful and immoral (see Divine 1957; Hoffman 1974; Romo 1975; Scott 1971). In this atmosphere of contempt and fear, the United States began a policy of repatriation that saw some 400,000 Mexicans and Mexican-Americans returned through force and social pressure to Mexico (Balderrama 1982; Bogardus 1934; Cardoso 1980; Divine 1957; Hoffman 1974; Romo 1975; Scott 1971). It was at the height of this anti-Mexican period that the Lemon Grove community successfully defended their right to equal education and reinstated their children in the local school.[2]

Why was it that the Lemon Grove community was successful in challenging the established structure? What made their solidarity and action so effective? The answers to these and other questions lie, at least in part, in the history of the Mexican settlers of Lemon Grove.

For the people of Lemon Grove, as for other urban immigrant communities, there were a number of antecedent events and processes that provided the foundations for the development of a community. These individuals and their families lived through events that were instrumental in forming a kin-based network that became the basis of support in both the migration and settlement process. Long before the segregation incident occurred, ancestors of these families were trekking through a mining labor circuit that eventually brought them to the United States. These migrations occurred over long periods of time; it was often decades before the migrants turned immigrants and crossed the international border. Even before the migration, Baja California had been tied to the north through the political and economic development of the Spanish and Mexican frontier in which the northern sector, Alta California, was the region best suited for settlement and development (Alvarez 1984; 1986b). This larger context influenced a migration cycle that would eventually end in the United States and lead to the development of the Mexican-American community in the United States. Each phase—leaving the towns of Baja California, entering a mining labor circuit, crossing the international border, and settling in the United States—coincides with political-economic patterns at national and international levels that affected the region of the Californias. Economic and political conditions formed the context for individual and group behavior. At the same time, the migrant made specific choices about kin ties and economic security, interpreting and acting upon the changing socioeconomic context.

Social scientists have begun to focus on the explanation of behavior through the combined analysis of both macro- and microlevel influences (see, for example, Davis 1985; Fischer 1977; Ortner 1984). Central to this view are the macrohistorical contexts that condition "on the ground" behavior. The "constraint-choice" model is used to examine the larger socioeconomic circumstances and the resultant individual and group behavior (Davis 1985; Fischer 1977). The concept, simply put, is that people find themselves in socioeconomic circumstances that are particular to geographic regions, conditioned by political and economic events. These circumstances provide limited alternatives for survival. Within these limits, people select alternatives and create the social relationships that offer support and social continuity. As this paper will show, different socioeconomic contexts at differing historical periods were instrumental in the settlement of the Lemon Grove community.

Mexican immigration and settlement into the United States is intimately linked to the political economy of the border and the U.S. demand for labor. The immediate causes of the mass movements that began during the 1920s seem obvious: Mexico was undergoing a revolution; people were freed from land bondage and were escaping the chaotic environment of the revolution; and in the United States, labor was needed to fill gaps in industry and a growing agribusiness (see Cardoso 1980). However, limiting the analysis to this level has created a number of stereotypes about the Mexican immigrant and the rise of new communities in the United States, obscuring the interrelationships on individual and community levels between Mexico and the United States.[3]

Methodology

The primary research for the study was done from September 1975 through 1977. Working principally in San Diego County, California, I contacted and interviewed pioneer migrants and their offspring who had crossed the border around the turn of the century. As principal individuals identified kin and friends, I followed a natural pattern of genealogical and friendship connections that led me to other individuals within the county and various peninsular towns in Baja California. In a "snowball" process, one individual led to another, and slowly I came to realize that these individuals were tied together in a distinguishable kinship network. The fifty families settled in Lemon Grove had genealogical roots in the Mexican peninsula.

In addition to interviewing pioneer migrants and their children, I collected genealogical material on births and deaths, marriages and baptisms, from family records, mission archives recorded in Baja California, and personal documents and photographs of families on both sides of the U.S.-Mexican border. Once individuals had collectively identified the historical episodes important in the migration north, and the establishment of a supportive network, I reconstructed the migration experience and the context in which these individuals found themselves.

At the beginning of this reconstruction, I was impressed with the numerous human dimensions in this migration. People were indeed coming for jobs and economic reasons, but they did so within the context of a history of traditional movements along the border, of strong sentiments and affiliation to their hometowns and regions. Tight kin connections were established through migration. The result was a regional network of kin and friends that extends over five generations of time and reaches across the U.S.-Mexican border some 1,000 miles into the peninsula of Baja California (Alvarez 1986b).

The Migration Process

The history of the Lemon Grove community begins when nineteenth-century migrants left their homes in the peninsula of Baja California and entered a migratory stream that had been developed long before. At first only a handful of settlers came to Lemon Grove, but this was to be a continuous process as more and more people came to know Lemon Grove as a place where hometown folk and other Baja Californios congregated. By 1930, Lemon Grove had grown to a sizable neighborhood of Mexican immigrants, primarily from Baja California, who continued to receive newcomers from the south. Today Lemon Grove, like many of the Mexican communities that sprang up throughout California, Texas, and Arizona during the twenties and thirties, has been absorbed by urban growth.

The pattern of movement through the peninsula took different forms as economic transformations required different types of labor. Most significant were the rise of a mining economy and the economic development of the border region in the twentieth century, and a Mexican economic policy that allowed foreign development to capitalize natural resources throughout the Mexican nation.

The Baja California Mining Circuit. The development of mines in the peninsula of Baja California came on the coattails of the largest gold strike in modern times: the California Gold Rush of 1849. As the gold craze in upper California subsided, American and British investors were stirred by news of new gold strikes in the Mexican peninsula that promised mineral wealth akin to that found in northern California. One year after the strike, the territory of California became a state and the gold fever quickly spread to the peninsula which was viewed by many Americans as a natural extension of the new state. Mexico, emerging from a series of devastating internal and external political conflicts (the United States–Mexican War, 1846–48, the War of the Reform, 1858–1861, and the French Occupation, 1861–67), permitted the use of foreign capital to help back political reform and economic development. Mexico began granting large concessions for mining throughout the nation. In Baja, as in all of Mexico, foreign exploitation in the name of investment and development became a principal pattern. Americans, British, and French competed for control of Mexico's natural resources, and Baja California became a haven for foreign investment, particularly from the United States (see Alvarez 1986b; Bernstein 1964).

The Mexican policy of granting mining concessions soon allowed American companies a free reign to exploit the sectors of northern and central Baja California where ores were discovered. This activity was based on placer mining, which required a sophisticated stamp-mill process developed during the forty-niner rush. American companies imported the necessary technology, skilled personnel and equipment into unpopulated sectors. This activity not only resulted in new towns but also established a new system of roads linking both Pacific coast ports as well as ports along the Gulf of California. These regions required labor as well as the primary necessities for supporting the mining activity. Goods, mules, machinery, and building materials were transported into the peninsula by way of company ships.

The developing mining labor circuit was dependent on the company towns that appeared and disappeared as the mines experienced booms and busts. This circuit was sporadic because the placers of even the principal mines were short-lived. As mines gave out and were no longer productive, mining companies pulled up stakes, virtually dismantled towns, and traveled to new sites where activity was initiated in full earnest again.

The circuit companies depended on a labor pool of migrants that moved from mine to mine as booms came and went. At first this labor came from the mainland, but southern peninsulars soon joined the labor circuit. Californios slowly began moving out of small hometowns in family groups. The Mesa-Smiths are a typical example.[4]

Family Migration. In 1894, the year of their marriage, Manuel Smith Mesa and his wife, Apolonia Mesa Smith, left the small mission pueblo of Comondú for the mines of Las Flores. Their decision to migrate was primarily economic, but it was also sanctioned by an extensive kin base that had been fostered by the early settlers of Comondú.

Comondú, a desert oasis, was typical of the towns from which those entering the mining circuit originated. Horticulture and small-scale farming were primary economic activities. The size of the town has varied only slightly since the turn of the century. In 1910, the population was 1,050; in 1920, 852 (Departamento de la Estadística Nacional 1926); and in 1960, 755 (Secretaría de Industría y Comercio 1963). Limited land and water allowed no real expansion, and as families grew, people began leaving. The mines provided, however, an alternative to which people could turn without the risk of leaving the home region.

In addition to economic motives to migrate, the security provided by friends and kin were factors influencing northward migration. Manuel Smith had also been in communication with a sister, Ramona Smith de Howard, who married an American and traveled with him in the mining circuit. The decision to move north was not only a result of better economic opportunities in the north, but was also based on the presence of close kin in the mines who had migrated before.

The family ties within the mining circuit and in the north offered security and knowledge of the area the Smith family was about to enter. Further security came in the actual move out of Comondú as an extended family unit. The couple embarked with Manuel's grandfather Antonio Smith (who had brothers living in San Diego County), his wife and family, and a maternal aunt of Apolonia, Encarnación Smith.

The extended family unit traveled up the gulf coast about 300 miles to the San Juan mining district. Here in Las Flores, Manuel soon established himself as a *leñador* (wood collector) who cut, collected, and delivered wood for fuel used in the processing boilers of the mines. This was to be his vocation for the next decade as he and the family traveled from mine to mine until they crossed the border into the United States. Sometime during this period Antonio and Manuel took separate routes. Antonio Smith went north and crossed the border to San Diego County to the homes of his brothers. Encarnación, Apolonia's aunt, went north as well, but stayed in the Pacific coast port of Ensenada. Manuel and Apolonia remained in Las Flores (where two children were born) until just after the turn of the century. When the San Juan mines gave out, they moved south to a new boom area.

Like the Smiths, there were other families that entered the mines of San Juan in the valley of Las Flores. Two other families that would also settle Lemon Grove were the Castellanos and the Sotelos. Narcisso and Cleofas Castellanos were wed in La Paz but soon migrated north. Their first daughter, Ramona, was born in Comondú in 1886 and spent her early adolescence in the mining towns of the mid-peninsula. The Castellanos moved north into Las Flores where they met other families and began establishing social relations that led to strong social and kin ties in later years. Such relations were begun with the Sotelos, a family who two generations later would be united through marriage to the Castellanos in Lemon Grove.

In Las Flores, the Castellanos and the Sotelos struck up a close relationship that continued through the shared residences in the mines and in the United States. In Lemon Grove, Francisco Sotelo often reminisced about their joint experiences in the mining towns. "Yo era el Juez y el vale Chicho [Narcisso] la autoridad" (I was the judge and my buddy Narcisso the sheriff).

Like the children of the Castellanos, Smiths, and others, each of the Sotelos' eight children were born in various mining towns of the peninsula. The birth dates of the children coincide with those of other migrant families' offspring in the same towns, and indicate the period of residence in particular places as well as the acquaintances that were begun during the mining migration. The first two children were born in Las Flores (Teodora around 1898 and Prudencio in 1901). A third child (Guillermo) was born in San Fernando on the Pacific coast in 1903. The family moved south again to El Marmol (an onyx mine) where another son (Federico) was born in 1905, and back to San Fernando where Refugio, a daughter, was born in 1907. The family remained in the northern peninsula after this period. The youngest son (Francisco) was born in El Rosario (1912) and a daughter, Amalia, was born on the border in Mexicali in 1917.

There are no clear records of when the Castellanos and Sotelos left Las Flores, but like the Smiths their next stop was Calmallí. They trekked south, crossed the Sierra de la Gigante, and arrived in the area of the most productive gold mines known in the peninsula.

Calmallí: The Social Nexus. The Calmallí gold mine was the nexus of the relationships that ultimately led to the community of Lemon Grove in the United States. Some families had met in Las Flores or Santa Rosalía before arriving in Calmallí; others became friends later in El Marmol and El Alamo in the northern district, but Calmallí was the site at which a core of the Lemon Grove settlers met and began to establish social relations. Compared with other desert mines of the peninsula, the placers of Calmallí had a long production period requiring a long-term working population. Here pioneer settlers of Lemon Grove had their longest contact before entering the United States.

Calmallí lies deep in the central desert almost at midpoint between the gulf and the Pacific, and between the tip of the cape and the U.S. border (about 450 miles north). During the late 1880s, a San Francisco–based firm transformed crude diggings into a company operation that produced over $3 million in gold (valued at more than $60 million by today's standards) and operated into the first quarter of the twentieth century (Goldbaum 1971:29).

Calmallí was a company town, with a population of company laborers and some gold seekers. It, too, fluctuated with the production boom cycles of the placers. When there was no production the town was abandoned. But during the booms the town was a center of activity. In the late 1800s, during its heyday, there were hundreds or possibly thousands of miners living in the vicinity (*ibid.*). In 1905, a report indicated that the area was deserted (Nelson 1922:31). By 1912, the mines were not being worked, and in 1921 the Mexican census reported forty-four inhabitants for Calmallí (Departamento de la Estadística Nacional 1926). Today there are only mining remnants, old cars, and dilapidated buildings. However, the migrant families on which I am focusing began arriving in Calmallí in the late 1880s and 1890s and left during the down cycle after the turn of the century. During their stay there, Calmallí experienced the greatest population fluctuation.

Calmallí is important not only because numerous families met there for the first time, but because it also provided a long-standing base of residence and employment for migrants, allowing social relations to flourish and expand. The families that later formed the foundation of the Lemon Grove community came together as a group in Calmallí. The Castellanos and the Sotelos, who had met in Las Flores, arrived in this period. The Smiths also joined family members who were in Calmallí. The Becerras, originally from El Triunfo, the Gonzales from the southern cape, the Alvarezes from San Jose del Cabo, the Villavicencios from the Loreto area, the Bolumes from the cape, the Simpsons from San Antonio, and the Vasquez and Marquez families also arrived during this period. These and other families formed the basis for a kin network that would endure into the latter half of the twentieth century along the border in the United States.

Calmallí, like other mining circuit towns, was a self-contained community. It was surrounded by a natural boundary of open desert and was distant from other towns and population centers. All social relations took place within the immediate community. There were no other outlets or possibilities for social interaction. It was a neighborhood within a geographically confined territory. As a result, individuals and families saw each other daily, worked together, and socialized after working hours. The families shared significant life cycle experiences—births, child rearing, adolescent development, and death—and created social environments that revolved around the work and life-style of Calmallí (and other mining sites). The long production of Calmallí provided the economic security that allowed long, continuous contacts among mining families who were now not small pueblo dwellers or migrants, but a permanent part of the mining economy. The mining economy was the landscape of their social environment and the foundation for a life-style that became permanent in family lore. In this mining context, families shared work and social experiences and developed the trust which was elaborated into a system of reciprocity along the mining circuit to the north, as well as later in San Diego and Lemon Grove.

Along with the formation of friendships and close ties with nonkin, families also maintained hometown kin ties throughout their stay in Calmallí and the other mining circuit towns. The Smiths, for example, received news from Manuel's sister, Ramona Howard, who received them in Calmallí. Similarly, the Smiths also aided and kept close contact with kin in Comondú. Letters to Apolonia's parents and sisters kept hometown kin in constant communication, and allowed for the support of kin who were on their way north (as well as of kin who came north later in the century).

One family that was welcomed by Apolonia and Manuel in Calmallí was that of Salvador and Juana Mesa (Apolonia's maternal aunt). Paula, a daughter, recounted to me the migrant trail north and their arrival in Calmallí. They, like others before, left Comondú in search of better economic possibilities, but a major impetus was the fact that her eldest brother had migrated north and their mother wanted to be close to him. Her father, Salvador, had picked grapes and figs in Comondú, and in San Ignacio he had managed some fruit orchards. With six children, Salvador and Juana went north into the central desert and to Calmallí. There they stayed with Apolonia and Manuel Smith for several days, resting, visiting, and exchanging news with Apolonia. The Mesas moved on to the north, passed Julio César (another mine in the circuit), and arrived in San Quintín where they, in turn, received the Smiths when Calmallí ended production. These instances of reciprocity became more numerous once families were in the border region of the north.

In Calmallí, then, the families settled as permanent workers. But as the mines fluctuated, they were forced to seek jobs and settlement elsewhere. In many ways these individuals were locked into the mines. Narcisso Castellanos as a crew captain had developed, like others, a skill specific to the mining economy. He built his and his family's life around this security. All his children were born (and the eldest raised) in this environment, as were the children of the Sotelos, Smiths, and others. When Calmallí eventually failed and could no longer support the families of workers, people moved out again. Many were encouraged to head north because El Marmol, Julio César, El Alamo, and other small mines were producing and employing mine laborers.

North to the International Border. In the early twentieth century, the border region, which had been virtually unpopulated, began to develop as a result of new capitalist enterprise based primarily in San Diego. Northern Baja California of 1900–1920 was still a frontier territory, but San Diego and Calexico (on the California-Arizona border) became bustling economic centers. This development occurred at a time when the mines of the peninsula were in their last boom cycles. People left the mines and entered this economic boom area where jobs were plentiful. Many families were separated at this time as some went to San Diego and others went to Calexico. By 1925, a nucleus of mining families were in San Diego and Lemon Grove.

At the turn of the century, San Diego was a metropolis of 30,000 people, characterized by economic growth and a booming population. Activity on the port, the construction of a new town by a local developer, road building, and agricultural development were evident throughout the county (MacPhail 1979; Mills 1976). On the other side of the border, the Mexican towns were also experiencing economic growth. Mexicali became a major producer of cotton, with American investment directed from Calexico. Tijuana grew from a small rancho to tourist center, with gambling, horse racing, and cabarets.

All these cities experienced population growth. By 1930, the population of Mexicali had reached 30,000 people. Tijuana had grown from a *pueblo* of less than 2,000 in 1920 to a township of 11,000, and within three decades it surpassed 165,000 (Departamento de la Estadística Nacional 1926; Secretaría de Industría y Comercio 1963). San Diego continued its geometric growth begun in the 1880s (McWilliams 1973:113–37). The city's 1910 population of 39,500 almost doubled in the next decade, and by 1930 it was 148,000 (U.S. Department of Commerce 1931).

The development along the border was the context in which the Mexican founders of Lemon Grove moved to San Diego. In a process that had become familiar, the mining circuit migrants packed their belongings and moved on to the next place of employment, which in this case required the crossing of the border. Some families crossed after boarding mining company steamers at small Pacific ports (used to ship ore and materials out of the peninsula), and went directly from the mines to San Diego. Others moved overland, by foot and wagon, to the small mines of the northern peninsula and then into the Mexicali Valley before moving to San Diego. Still others crossed at Tijuana and Tecate (Mesas, Alvarezes, and Simpsons, c. 1905). Once on the border, these overland travelers also went directly into the United States because in Mexicali there was little commerce and virtually no housing facilities. But Calexico in the United States offered housing, stores, and markets of all types.[5]

Migration of Baja Californios into the United States after 1900 can be viewed as an extension of the former mining circuit. Decisions continued to be based on both economic and family considerations. Again, most families initiated this move because of the talk of good jobs and because friends and kin were already across the border. But this episode differed from previous ones because it involved entering the United States, where the majority population were Euro-Americans, spoke English, and had an alien culture. Once in the United States, migrants strengthened relations among themselves in the face of the new and often discriminatory sociocultural conditions. Marriage and godparent ties that existed before were intensified.

In this new environment, individuals and families extended reciprocal support, including assistance with employment and housing, all along the northward route. Many, if not most, initial adjustments to the United States were done through the sharing among households. As new settlers arrived, they lived with friends from the mining circuit and kin from hometowns. People got jobs through the assistance of those who had immigrated earlier.

The pattern of reciprocity among migrants is exemplified in the case of the Castellanos. The Castellanos arrived in San Diego harbor on a steamer, the *St. Denise,* that made regular trips between San Diego and southern Pacific ports. Here they were welcomed by the family of Guillermo Simpson (from San Antonio on the cape), whom they had met in Calmallí. The Simpsons housed them and helped Narcisso Castellanos find employment in construction. Later, the Castellanos and Sotelos became united through godparenthood and marriages between offspring of both families. Subsequently, the Castellanos also helped the Marquez family whom they had met in Calmallí to settle in San Diego. These relations of support were common and continued as a new wave of migrants in a second stream came north directly from the southern peninsula. During this period (1910–1925), Lemon Grove grew slowly as the news of plentiful work and the presence of Baja families drew other migrant families.

The Second Stream

A second stream of immigrants from the hometowns of Santa Rosalia, Loreta, La Paz, Comondú, and other gulf coast and interior peninsular towns arrived after 1920. For these peninsulars of the second stream, news of the cotton boom, improved gulf travel, cotton labor contracts, and the relative success of kin in the border region combined to favor decisions to migrate northward.

The pattern of second-stream migration was very similar to that of the mining circuit, except it usually entailed a direct crossing into the United States. Like the movement out of hometowns at the turn of the century, this, too, was a family movement and was similarly induced by the lack of economic alternatives in hometowns and sporadic fighting and turmoil of the revolution. The decisions of families to leave, however, were again sanctioned by kin in the north, and almost as a rule, they traveled either as nuclear families or family groups.

In the 1920s the major migration of Mexicans to the United States began. Although the second stream I am describing here can be seen as part of this migration, there are important distinctions within the Baja migration that illustrate the ties of peninsular migrants to the California region.

During the 1920s, Mexicali became a major crossing point for the thousands of mainland Mexicans who labored in the fields of California. In 1910, cotton was planted in the Imperial Valley and growers contracted Mexicans to pick the crop. By 1920, cotton production expanded and shifted to the San Joaquin Valley, and by 1930 an average of 58,000 Mexicans entered the valley yearly (McWilliams 1968:174). These people were a cheap source of labor and provided the basic means to foment the cotton industry in California.

At this time, Mexican migrants did hard, menial labor in the United States. In agriculture, unsanitary and poor living conditions were the rule, and American discrimination and prejudice in commerce, education, and public services was common (see Taylor 1928, 1929, 1931, 1932, 1933, 1934; Weinberg 1977; Camarillo 1979; Daniel 1981). After entering California, many of these people from the mainland continued north following the farm labor routes that scattered them throughout the United States. But the peninsular families of this wave entered and remained in the border area. Emigration for mainland Mexicans meant journeys to the distant states of the interior, while for peninsular families, a return to home and family in Mexico often meant simply a change of residence from Calexico to Mexicali, or from San Diego to Tijuana, where family members had settled.

This second stream is illustrated by the migration of two sisters of the Mesa family. Martina Mesa de Romero and her sister Berta Mesa de Bareno and their families left the town of Loreto for the United States in 1920. Berta and her husband had decided to go in search of work, but Martina's main objective was to be with her sister Berta, and to find her elder sister, Apolonia, who had left Comondú before the turn of the century.

Again, the move out of Loreto was a joint family venture. Martina and her husband, Olayo, their two children, along with Berta, her husband, Miguel, and their six children, boarded one of the many steamers that was headed toward the northern gulf with contracted laborers for the Mexicali cotton fields. When the two families arrived, they were met in Mexicali by a younger brother (Levorio Mesa) who had contracted to work in a Mexicali cotton ranch. He took the sisters and their families directly across the border to Calexico where Apolonia lived. There the two families resided until they found work and housing of their own. By 1925, they (Martina, Berta, Apolonia, their families, and the younger brother Levorio) had all moved to San Diego.

Social and familial relations were maintained and further developed among the new settlers. The old friends of the south were now pulled together in stronger relationships based on the mutual experiences of their migration north, settlement in the new environment, and the extension of aid and assistance offered to both family members and friends. The common tie of regional identity and the extended period of contact through the mines, along with the added impetus of a second stream of kin and hometown folk, became natural inducements in forming new communities and initiating formal family extensions through marriage and godparenthood.

The second-stream migrants also helped regenerate the sentiment and communication with hometown regions and kin in the south. As kin, they were readily accepted into households and offered the mutual support that had become common among the earlier immigrants. For many families, it was a time of reunion. In some cases, brothers and sisters who had been separated because of the migration north were now together, and kin of all degrees sought refuge with the settled, experienced migrants. News of loved ones and change in the south rekindled the regional bonds felt by earlier migrants. Not only were kin seeking relatives in the north, but those in the border began sending for kin as well. Soon aunts, uncles, and parents of immigrants were coming to the border to be with their kin.

Once across the border in Calexico, Baja Californios, like other Mexicans, worked primarily in the fields picking cotton, or on large ranches doing field maintenance. Some initially worked on the Mexicali canal system. Working conditions were difficult, and some peninsulars found the pay poorer than in the mines.

People were attracted to San Diego, because work opportunities were more numerous. A number of migrant families settled in eastern San Diego, and about ten extended families moved to Lemon Grove. These families were, for the most part, mining circuit families, and although many of the heads of households had died, their offspring born or raised in the trek north came together and continued to extend the support and ties that had become common. In Lemon Grove, citrus groves and a citrus packing house employed both men and women. A local railroad, agriculture, and a nearby rock quarry provided principal sources for permanent employment. Many early miners were drawn to the quarry because of their previous work in the mines of Baja California.

When migrants arrived in Lemon Grove, it had a small population of growers and small commercial entrepreneurs, living on the outskirts of the citrus groves. The Baja migrants that moved into the area were like other Mexican immigrants who settled in the United States. First small numbers of individuals and families came to the community, and were later joined by family, friends, and other Mexicans who sought life and community similar to that they had known in the south. They came north from small rural villages seeking better jobs and ended up working in a variety of unskilled and semiskilled labor. They worked on road construction gangs as railroad loaders, and in seasonal labor in Lemon Grove and the county of San Diego. Although never a visible force in the economy or politics of San Diego, they contributed to all conceivable developments of the growing city.

Despite the historical presence and settlement of peninsular and other Mexican immigrants in San Diego (and the southwestern United States), Americans continued to view "the Mexican" derogatorily. Segregation of Mexican laborers throughout the Southwest was common. Most Mexicans were to be found in small communities such as Lemon Grove or in agricultural regions, shanty towns, and labor camps that were kept isolated by growers. As in the mines, Mexicans in U.S. agriculture were not allowed in managerial positions and were maintained as a working-class population. Only during the Depression, when Euro-American labor was suffering from high unemployment and competition for public welfare was high, was the benefit of Mexican labor challenged (see Cardoso 1980; Hoffman 1974; Romo 1975).

These hostile conditions and minority-group status further served to unite the people of Lemon Grove. In addition to familial ties, the community helped people maintain a strong cultural identity and provided political and economic support in times of heightened aggression from society at large. This was the case when the Lemon Grove School Board sought to segregate the Lemon Grove children from the local school.

The following decades were marked by collective social gatherings in which early peninsular family members formed the core. Marriages, birthdays, baptisms, funerals, and holidays were large social gatherings of kindred in which children, like adults, came together, reinforcing family ties and a cultural community based on antecedent processes.

Tijuana and the town of Tecate on the border (about midway between Tijuana and Mexicali) were also becoming important attractions. As these towns grew, some migrants moved to resettle in Mexico. Before long, peninsular migrants were established on both sides of the international border, with a principal nucleus in San Diego and Lemon Grove. By the mid-fifties, three generations of peninsular migrants had arrived in San Diego, and numerous offspring had been born and raised in this border environment.

By the 1960s, Lemon Grove was no longer attracting immigrants. Marriages between peninsular families continued to occur, and some individuals, especially offspring of the second stream, maintained ties to peninsular hometowns. However, most families have since moved out of Lemon Grove into other areas of the city and county of San Diego. As the city of San Diego grew and as the young people were exposed to ways of American life, education, and middle-class values, people moved away from Lemon Grove. But then as today, these individuals maintain a close affinity to the region of Baja California and to the history of the families that originally came to Lemon Grove from the south.

Conclusion

This chapter presents a socio-history of the development of a Mexican-American community along the California-Mexico border. The history of Lemon Grove adds to contemporary perspectives about the formation of border communities, the cities of the U.S.-Mexican border, and the processes of Mexican immigration to the United States. Unlike studies in which the city is seen as a central locus of activity and regulator of behavior, this case reveals the city (San Diego) as part of a socioeconomic context which developed as a result of successive economic and political processes in the California region as a whole. Further, this case suggests that decisions to migrate, although induced by economic conditions, are also conditioned by kin relations.[6]

The perspective presented here stems from that of the early pioneer migrants, settlers, and their offspring who settled Lemon Grove. Lemon Grove settlers identified the southern peninsular towns, the mining labor circuit, and the activities that led to their crossing the international border and their settlement in the United States. Like the mobilization of the community in the desegregation court case, these historical episodes were undocumented, but were important factors in forming lasting relationships that not only endured, but were the basis of community in San Diego. Regional affiliation, kinship extensions, the migration experience itself, and the kinship network that formed the basis for settlement were all part of the sociocultural process in which these settlers, like Mexicans from other regions, adapted and survived in the new environment of the United States.

The implications of Lemon Grove go beyond documenting the history that led to the rise of a Mexican-American community. Today it is not uncommon for Mexican immigrants, settlers, and Chicanos to seek out and support other individuals from hometown regions. People continue to recognize regional and hometown affinity and often return to visit relatives even after generations of settlement in the United States. The study of these regional ties and networks is of great importance in understanding the process of migration, settlement, and the nature of the regions within which Mexicans have immigrated and settled. Although a few studies have indicated such regionality and use of regional networks, especially along the U.S.-Mexican border (Camara and Van Kemper 1979; Camara 1979; Cornelius 1978; Mines 1982; Whiteford 1979), more studies that delineate these sociocultural processes are urgently needed.[7]

Notes

1. This case is the basis of a current PBS television production that focuses on the events that led to the case and the community of Lemon Grove.

2. However unique this case appears to be, segregation of Mexican children was not uncommon (Carter 1970; Moore 1970; Taylor 1928; Weinberg 1977). New schools were constructed throughout the Southwest specifically for Mexican immigrant children. These were Americanization schools where "backward and deficient" children would receive English language and "Americanization" instruction while separating them from, and protecting, Euro-American children.

3. Anthropologists have not focused on urban social history for a number of reasons.

This has not been out of lack of interest, but rather because of an attempt to understand the immediate problems associated with urbanization. Urban studies were done primarily in the developing nations of the world examining the rise of communities in the face of rapidly advancing urbanization (e.g., Banton 1957, 1973; Eisenstadt 1955; Epstein 1967; Friedl 1959, 1964; Little 1957, 1965; Mitchell 1969b). Immigrants and migrants to the cities became a topic of considerable interest because of the problem of overpopulation and stressfully overcrowded cities. In the case of Latin America, the cities were ill prepared for the influx of large numbers of people, and a variety of serious problems developed in housing, health, and unemployment. The concern of social scientists was to explore the immediate problem and to provide some understanding about the adaptation and plight of rural-urban migrants (e.g., Butterworth 1970; Doughty 1970; Lewis 1952, 1959, 1973; Lomnitz 1977; Mangin 1973; Matosmar 1961; Pearse 1961). Unlike the prevalent notion proposed by some that migrants were carriers of social problems, were uprooted and unorganized, these studies (like those in Africa and elsewhere) illustrated a remarkably adaptive syle based on traditional values and institutions (Graves and Graves 1974). In fact, new institutions were created out of interaction with the new social environment. Migrants maintained links with hometowns through family organization, settled in clusters often creating mirrorlike images of home communities, and, once established, provided support and encouragement to new migrants from respective hometowns and areas.

4. European family names are very common in the southern peninsula of Baja California. They originated primarily through the marriage of peninsular women with traders and seamen who stayed in the peninsula during the early part of the eighteenth century. Comondú is known as the home of the original Smith who had come from New York on a Yankee clipper in 1808 (Alvarez 1987).

5. The actual crossing of the border was an easy process at this time. Immigration laws of the period were very loosely interpreted by border officials, and only in rare cases of sickness were incoming Mexicans turned away. In fact, some individuals crossed into the United States and then returned to pay quota fees later. Restrictions were virtually unknown at this time (Alvarez 1984; Cardoso 1980).

6. The importance of family and kin in migration has begun to receive more attention. In a recent study of health service usage in San Diego, 2,043 Mexican migrants indicated that one of two primary reasons for entering the United States was family unification; the other reason was economic (Cornelius, Chavez, and Castro 1982).

7. I would like to thank Karen H. Alvarez, Leo R. Chavez, and William Demarest for their valuable comments on earlier drafts of this paper.

References

Alvarez, Robert R. 1984. "The Border as Social System: The California Case." *The New Scholar* 9(1–2):119–134.

—— 1986a. "The Lemon Grove Incident: The Nation's First Successful Desegregation Court Case." *Journal of San Diego History* 32:116–136.

——1987. *Familia: Migration and Adaptation in Alta and Baja California, 1800–1980.* Berkeley and Los Angeles: University of California Press.

Balderrama, Francisco. 1982. *In Defense of La Raza: The Los Angeles Mexican Consulate and the Mexican Community, 1929–1936.* Tucson: University of Arizona Press.

Banton, Michael. 1957. *West African City*. London: Oxford University Press.

—— 1973. "Urbanization and Role Analysis." In Southall, ed., *Urban Anthropology*, pp. 43–70.

Bernstein, Marvin O. 1964. *The Mexican Mining Industry, 1890–1950*. New York: State University of New York.

Bogardus, Emory. 1934. *Mexicans in the United States*. Los Angeles: University of Southern California Press.

Butterworth, Douglas. 1970. "A Study of the Urbanization Process Among Mixtec Migrants from Tilantongo in Mexico City." In William Mangin, ed., *Peasants in Cities*, pp. 98–113. Boston: Houghton Mifflin.

Camara, Fernando. 1979. "Differential Migration Streams, Economic Growth, and Socio-Cultural Changes in Mexican Border Cities." In Camara and Van Kemper, eds., *Migration Across Frontiers*, pp. 101–126.

Camara, Fernando and Robert Van Kemper, eds. 1979. *Migration Across Frontiers: Mexico and the United States*. Contributions of the Latin American Anthropology Group, vol. 3. Institute for Mesoamerican Studies. Albany: State University of New York.

Camarillo, Albert. 1979. *Chicanos in a Changing Society*. Cambridge: Harvard University Press.

Cardenas, Gilbert. 1975. "United States Immigration Policy Towards Mexico: An Historical Perspective." *Chicano Law Review* 2:66–91.

Cardoso, Lawrence. 1980. *Mexican Emigration to the United States, 1897–1931*. Tucson: University of Arizona Press.

Carter, Thomas. 1970. *Mexican Americans in Schools: A History of Educational Neglect*. New York: College Entrance Examination Board.

Cornelius, Wayne. 1978. *Mexican Migration to the United States: Causes, Consequences, and U.S. Responses*. Cambridge: MIT Press.

Cornelius, Wayne, Leo R. Chavez, and Jorge G. Castro. 1982. *Mexican Immigrants and Southern California: A Summary of Current Knowledge*. Research Report Series No. 36, Center for U.S.-Mexican Studies. San Diego: University of California.

Daniel, Cletus E. 1981. *Bitter Harvest: A History of California Farmworkers, 1870–1941*. Berkeley and Los Angeles: University of California Press.

Davis, William G. 1985. "Class, Political Constraints, and Entrepreneurial Strategies: Elites and Petty Market Traders in Northern Luzon." In Sidney Greenfield and Arnold Stricken, eds., *Entrepreneurs and Social Change*, pp. 166–194. New York: University Press of America.

Departamento de la Estadística Nacional. 1926. *Censo General de Habitantes, 1921*. Baja California Sur. Mexico D.F.

Divine, Robert A. 1957. *American Immigration Policy, 1924–1952*. New Haven: Yale University Press.

Doughty, Paul. 1970. "Behind the Back of the City: Provincial Life in Lima, Peru." In William Mangin, ed., *Peasants in Cities*, pp. 30–46. Boston: Houghton Mifflin.

Eisenstadt, S. N. 1955. *The Absorption of Immigrants*. New York: Free Press.

—— 1956. "Sociological Aspects of the Economic Adaptation of Oriental Immigrants in Israel: A Case Study of the Problem of Modernization." *Economic Development and Cultural Change* 4:269–295.

Epstein, A. L. 1967. "Urbanization and Social Change in Africa." *Current Anthropology* 8(4):275–295.

Fischer, Claude S. et al. 1977. *Networks and Places*. New York: Free Press.

Friedl, Ernestine. 1959. "The Role of Kinship in the Transmission of National Culture to Rural Villages in Mainland Greece." *American Anthropologist* 61:30–38.

—— 1964. "Lagging Emulation in Post-Peasant Society." *American Anthropologist* 66:569–587.

Galarza, Ernesto. 1964. *Merchants of Labor: An Account of the Managed Migration of Mexican Farm Workers in California, 1942–1960.* Santa Barbara: McNally and Loftin.

Gamio, Manuel. 1930. *Mexican Immigration to the United States.* Chicago: University of Chicago Press.

Goldbaum, David. 1971. *The Towns of Baja California, a 1918 Report.* Glendale: La Siesta Press.

Graves, Nancy B. and Theodore D. Graves. 1974. "Adaptive Strategies in Urban Migration." *Annual Review of Anthropology* 3:117–151.

Grebler, Leo. 1966. *Mexican Immigration to the United States: The Record and Its Implications.* Mexican-American Study Project, Advance Report. Berkeley and Los Angeles: University of California Press.

Hauser, P. M., ed. 1961. *Urbanization in Latin America.* New York: Columbia University Press.

Heath, D. and R. Adams, eds. 1965. *Contemporary Cultures and Societies of Latin America.* New York: Random House.

Hoffman, Abraham. 1974. *Unwanted Mexicans in the Great Depression.* Tucson: University of Arizona Press.

Jordan, Fernando. 1951. "El Otro Mexico: Biografía de Baja California." Mexico, D.F.: Biografías Banders.

La Opinion. 1931. "No Admiten a Los Niños." January 25, Los Angeles.

Lewis, Oscar. 1965. "Urbanization Without Breakdown: A Case Study." In Heath and Adams, eds., *Contemporary Cultures and Societies of Latin America,* pp. 469–479.

—— 1973. "Some Perspectives on Urbanization with Special Reference to Mexico City." In Southall, ed., *Urban Anthropology,* pp. 125–138.

Little, Kenneth. 1957. "The Role of Voluntary Associations in West African Urbanization." *American Anthropologist* 59(4):579–596.

—— 1965. *West African Urbanization: A Study of Voluntary Associations in Change.* London: Cambridge University Press.

Lomnitz, Larissa Adler. 1977. *Networks and Marginality: Life in a Mexican Shantytown.* New York: Academic Press.

MacPhail, Elizabeth. 1979. *The Story of New San Diego and of Its Founder, Alonzo E. Horton.* San Diego: San Diego Historical Society.

Mangin, William. 1965. "Mental Health and Migration to Cities: A Peruvian Case." In Heath and Adams, eds., *Contemporary Cultures and Societies of Latin America.* pp. 340–365.

—— 1973. "Sociological, Cultural, and Political Characteristics of Some Urban Migrants in Peru." In Southall, ed., *Urban Anthropology,* pp. 315–350.

Matosmar, Jose. 1961. "Migration and Urbanization: The Barriadas of Lima." In Hauser, ed., *Urbanization in Latin America,* pp. 170–191.

McWilliams, Carey. 1968. *North from Mexico: The Spanish Speaking People of the United States.* Connecticut: Greenwood Press.

—— 1973. *Southern California: An Island in the Sun.* Santa Barbara: Peregrine and Smith.

Mills, James R. 1976. *San Diego: Where California Began.* San Diego: San Diego Historical Society.

Mines, Richard. 1982. *The Evolution of Mexican Migration to the United States: A Case Study.* Division of Agricultural Sciences, Bulletin 1902. Berkeley and Los Angeles: University of California Press.

Mitchell, J. Clyde. 1969a. "The Concept and Use of Social Networks." In J. Clyde Mitchell, ed., *Social Networks in Urban Situations,* pp. 1–50. London: Manchester University Press.

—— 1969b. "Structural Plurality, Urbanization, and Labour Circulation in Southern Rhodesia." In J. A. Jackson, ed., *Migration,* pp. 156–180. London: Cambridge University Press.

Moore, J. W. and A. Cuellar. 1970. *The Mexican-Americans.* Englewood Cliffs, N.J.: Prentice-Hall.

Nelson, Edward W. 1922. "Lower California and Its Natural Resources." *National Academy of Sciences,* vol. 16, First Memoir.

Ortner, Sherry B. 1984. "Theory in Anthropology Since the Sixties." *Comparative Studies in Society and History* 4:126–166.

Pearse, Andrew. 1961. "Some Characteristics of Urbanization in the City of Rio de Janeiro." In Hauser, ed., *Urbanization of Latin America,* pp. 191–205.

Portes, Alejandro. 1974. "Return of the Wetback." *Society* 3:40–46.

Price, John. 1973. *Tijuana: Urbanization in a Border Culture.* Notre Dame: University of Notre Dame Press.

Romo, Ricardo. 1975. *Mexican Workers in the City: Los Angeles, 1915–1930. Ph.D. dissertation.* University of California, Los Angeles.

Samora, Julian. 1971. *Los Mojados: The Wetback Story.* Notre Dame: University of Notre Dame Press.

San Diego Evening Tribune. 1931. "75 Mexican Students Go on Strike." January 8.

Scott, Robin F. 1971. *The Mexican in the Los Angeles Area, 1920–1950: From Acquiescence to Activity.* Ph.D. dissertation. University of Southern California.

Secretaría de Industría y Comercio, Direccion General de Estadistica. 1963. *Censo General de Poblacion.* Mexico, D.F.: Estado de Baja California.

Southall, Aidan, ed. 1973. *Urban Anthropology: Cross-Cultural Studies of Urbanization.* New York: Oxford University Press.

Taylor, Paul. 1928. *Mexican Labor in the United States: Imperial Valley, California.* University of California Publications in Economics, vol. 6, no. 1. Berkeley and Los Angeles: University of California Press.

—— 1929. *Mexican Labor in the United States Valley of the South Platte, Colorado.* University of California Publications in Economics, vol. 6, no. 2. Berkeley and Los Angeles: University of California Press.

—— 1931. *Mexican Labor in the United States: Bethlehem, Pennsylvania.* University of California Publications in Economics, vol. 7, no. 1. Berkeley and Los Angeles: University of California Press.

—— 1932. *Mexican Labor in the United States: Chicago and the Calumet Region.* University of California Publications in Economics, vol. 3, no. 2. Berkeley and Los Angeles: University of California Press.

—— 1934. *An American-Mexican Frontier: Nueces County, Texas.* Chapel Hill: University of North Carolina.

United States Department of Commerce. 1931. *15th Census of the United States, 1930.* Vol. 1. Washington, D.C.: GPO.

Villalpando, M. et al. 1977. *A Study of the Socioeconomic Impact of Illegal Aliens on the County of San Diego.* San Diego: Human Resources Agency.

Weinberg, Meyer. 1977. *A Chance to Learn.* Boston: Cambridge University Press.

Whiteford, Linda. 1979. "The Borderlands as an Extended Community." In F. Camara and R. Van Kemper, eds. *Migration Across Frontiers: Mexico and the United States,* pp. 127–137. Contributions of the Latin American Anthropology Group, Vol. 3. Institute for Mesoamerican Studies, Albany: State University of New York.

9. The Colonial Polo Club: An Examination of Class Processes in the Suburban-Rural Fringe

Benjamin Miller

Much of the upper class in the United States lives, at least part of the time, in the suburban-rural fringes that ring the country's major cities. There, in splendid isolation, those who control the processes of extraction, production, distribution, consumption, and destruction—the processes that determine the overall structure of American society—are able to escape the social and ecological effects of those processes. Commuting by day into the metropolis, they return at night to an environment as self-consciously and artfully "pristine" as was the Romantic English garden, an environment, in fact, that bears much the same relationship to the contemporary degradation of our cities that the English garden bore to industrializing England.

Access to these greenbelts is restricted. They function, therefore, as barriers that separate the immobile urban poor from the commuting suburban rich. This exclusive access is created through a pattern of private ownership in which elaborate homes are interspersed among tracts of open land. This open land, commonly owned by private associations such as country clubs, is often strategically located to prevent industrial and residential development, and to shield the homes of the rich from the expressways that link suburb and city.

Ethnographers are faced with the same difficulties in obtaining access to the private clubs and residential areas of the upper class as others are. The study of the processes of upper-class social and economic domination, therefore, demands that the ethnographer take advantage of whatever opportunities he or she can find to penetrate this barrier of purchased privacy. I discovered such an opportunity in the exclusively upper-class, suburban-rural-fringe sport of polo.

This paper is based on three months of fieldwork in 1976 at one of the major polo clubs in the Eastern megalopolis (Miller 1977).[1] The Colonial Polo Club (a pseudonym) is located in the suburban-rural fringe of a relatively small industrial city. This city is overwhelmingly dominated by a single corporation that is in turn controlled by a single family. This company employs about 20 percent of the work force of the entire region, and generates well over 20 percent of the area's gross product. The dominant family, with the rest of the upper-class network of which it is the center, exerts control over most of the economic and political processes in the area.

The principal forms of urban renewal in this deteriorating city are malls near the buildings of the dominant corporation, and new highways to get the corporate executives in and out quickly. Meanwhile, the greenbelt is controlled by the corporate family's related residential and club landholdings. "The consequences of this greenbelt," according to a group of researchers who studied the area, "include grievous misallocation of land resources and recreational facilities, overcrowding in sectors beyond the greenbelt, diminished property tax revenues, and rigid stratification of social classes into their respective ghettos—poor and rich alike."

The members of the Colonial Polo Club include upper-level executives of the major corporation and its subsidiaries, individuals belonging to the family which controls this corporation, and real estate agents, bankers, and businessmen who share residence in the greenbelt and financial ties to the metropolis. They share a common enjoyment in the sport of polo, and they also derive similar benefits from their participation in this extravagant pastime.

Polo requires a substantial expenditure that offers no direct financial return for its participants. The sport offers non-monetary benefits, however, which serve the interests of these members of the upper class. The anthropologist, therefore, need have no temptation to relegate its rationality strictly to the world of play. On the contrary, the Colonial Polo Club has a distinct impact on its local environment, an impact which strengthens the disproportionate access to local resources enjoyed by its members. And as a node in a national/international network, the Colonial Polo Club plays a role in enhancing the supralocal advantages enjoyed by the generalized upper class which it represents. For these reasons, the present examination of the Colonial Polo Club in particular, and of the sport of polo in general, may offer insights into several processes related to upper-class dominance throughout the United States.

Polo is a dangerously fast-moving game played on horseback by a small segment of the international upper class. Its history spans more than a thousand years and most of the globe, but its contemporary incarnation in the United States is distinctively and ingeniously suited to the status needs of a particular segment of the American upper class. So well suited, in fact, that participation in the sport has almost doubled in the last decade and, according to a popular magazine, "has suddenly become the glamorous new power game of the Eighties" (de Suze and Waller 1986).

In what follows, polo in the United States will be examined in terms of four processes which, it will be argued, are necessary for the persistence of a stable and dominant upper class: social closure; status marking; network maintenance; and the incorporation of new members in order to maintain maximal class control over relevant resources over time.

Polo as a Means of Establishing Social Closure

Parkin (1974), drawing on Weber's concept of social closure (1968: 362ff.), argues that a strategy of exclusion is an essential element in the formation of upper-class dominance. This exclusion, which does not require intensive collaboration on the part of the dominant group, is directed downward against subordinates. It can be based on virtually any criteria; such factors as dialect, education, and occupation are among those most commonly used. In the uppermost strata in any given society, it could be argued, these exclusionary criteria are increasingly finely drawn.

Prestigious social clubs often contribute to strategies of exclusion at the highest social levels (Domhoff 1974, 1975; Baltzell 1958:355–363, 1964: 353–380; Mills 1956:61–62; Lynd and Lynd 1929:296–312; Warner and Lunt 1941:301–355). Polo clubs (every U.S. polo player must belong to at least one club in order to participate in official games) are the basis of a very distinctive exclusionary criterion: an individual is either a polo player and therefore can be safely recognized as possessing all the other qualities that are believed to pertain to polo players as a group, or he is not.[2] "Polo," according to the *New York Times,* "goes beyond the old notion of amateur-sports purists that 'it matters not who wins or loses, but how you play the game.' . . . What counts is *whether* you play" (Cady 1979). Polo players as a group are generally considered—by players and non-players alike—to possess a variety of attributes, including wealth, leisure, skill, ownership of country estates, daring aristocratic taste, a love of extravagance. Wealth is certainly the basic prerequisite for gaining access to a polo club, but almost as important is having the knowledge and inclination to spend wealth in this particular, socially significant, "well-bred" way.

The slightest familiarity with the game makes it apparent why wealth, and the willingness to spend it, should be so important an exclusionary aspect of polo. Polo is played by two teams of four players each, on a field the size of ten football fields. The game is divided into six seven-and-one-half-minute periods called "chukkers." Few horses can tolerate the strain of playing more than one such period in a day; serious play therefore requires at least six horses per player. Most of the approximately 2,300 players in this country pay their own expenses. There are, however, slightly over 100 players in the country who make at least part of their living from playing polo; their expenses and salaries are paid by other polo players in return for playing with them on their teams. (These paid players are called "pros" to distinguish them from the "owners.") In addition to the pros, hired labor is required for the maintenance and training of the horses, and for the maintenance of the fields and grounds. Polo is played in the United States year-round. In the summer months, it is played in the northern half of the country; it is played in the South during the winter. Many players play during both seasons, and many players also ship their strings of ponies and their stable crews around the country (and, more rarely, abroad) in order to participate in regional and national tournaments.

As an illustration of the level of financial commitment that can be involved, one player at the Colonial Polo Club managed to spend nearly $1 million on polo and related activities during the winter and summer seasons of 1976. This is a somewhat extreme example, but a well-documented one. This player had been playing polo for some years previous to 1976, on a more modest scale. Dissatisfied with this level of involvement, he suddenly "came into some money" and became something of an overnight polo celebrity. The pressures that this man felt to increase his polo spending were apparent when, shortly after the fieldwork period ended, his employer discovered that this money had been embezzled.

The following categories of polo expenditures, unless otherwise noted, were typical in 1976. It can be assumed that these expenses have increased significantly since then.

Horses. Horses suitable for playing polo ranged in price from about $1,000 to around $10,000 per horse. At the Colonial Polo Club, the amount that individual owners had invested in their strings of horses ranged from about $2,500 for a novice who had only two meager "ponies" to around $250,000 for the man mentioned above who "mounted" two pros in addition to himself, and who owned almost forty horses. In 1986, polo ponies cost up to $40,000; horses suitable for high-level play began at $15,000 (de Suze and Waller 1986).

Stabling costs depend on whether the horses are stabled in club facilities or at the owner's estate. At the Colonial Polo Club, stables rented for $100 per horse per season. The cost of feeding a polo pony is about the same as that of feeding a racehorse at the track. The average price for keeping each pony shod was about $100 per season. Veterinary bills averaged several hundred dollars a year per horse. Tack for each horse cost around $600. A player must also outfit himself with all the necessary personal riding accessories, which at the time averaged around $600.

Labor. Virtually all players at the Colonial Polo Club had at least one full-time groom to care for their horses, at least during the summer season. Grooms were paid between $85 and $125 a week, and were usually provided with lodging. Five professional players were regular members of the Colonial Polo Club (which included twenty-six members in all). The pros were paid a base salary that started at around $200 a week; this was supplemented by free lodging, the free use of a vehicle (usually), profits from the sale of horses they had trained, special payments for tournament games (the very best pros—not at the Colonial Polo Club—sometimes received up to $1,000 per tournament), and other bonuses, in addition to most expenses related to playing and traveling with the team. In 1986, the top-rated pros in the country command six-figure salaries (de Suze and Waller 1986).

Physical Plant. Polo fields are expensive to build and maintain because of their size, the requirement that they be perfectly level and evenly covered with closely mown grass, and because they are subjected to the regular abuse of being torn up by crashing horses. The Colonial Polo Club used three "outdoor fields" and one arena (a smaller, walled-in playing area, which is lighted for night play). In addition to the fields and stables, polo clubs provide a clubhouse with locker and shower rooms, and with facilities for serving refreshments and drinks after matches. The cost of maintaining these facilities was defrayed by the seasonal dues of $1,200 paid by each member. The capital to buy the land and build the club, as is the case with most polo clubs, had been provided by a small core of players who continued to own these facilities. (I was unable to discover the extent to which these "angels" may also have subsidized the club's ongoing expenses.) In addition to these public facilities, there are the additional costs of private facilities. Two of the players at the Colonial Polo Club also maintained their own private polo fields, which they used for their own practice and for special tournaments. Most players also had their own stable facilities and land for their horses.

Transportation. The final major category of expenses stems from the necessity of transporting a string of horses from one's estate to the local club, or from the local club to regional and national tournaments. Most serious players own at least one "gooseneck" truck-and-trailer rig for hauling their ponies. These cost upward of $35,000. With the associated expenses of supporting a crew during travel, transportation expenses alone represent a considerable expenditure.

These substantial expenses play a significant role in making polo a strategy for social closure: any player in the polo network can be secure in the knowledge that fellow players possess the minimal financial prerequisites and share the values associated with this type of expenditure. A man who had tried without success to join the Colonial Polo Club (this occurred during a period of especially active recruitment by the club) told me afterward:

Nobody would bother with you to try to teach you polo, or rent you a horse, or let you ride, or do anything. And B—— [the manager] told me if I didn't have two thousand dollars for a horse, and if I couldn't buy six horses—from him—forget it. The point, I guess, was that if I had to ask how much it cost, I couldn't afford it. The financial commitment was just an insurmountable problem. . . . So I said the hell with it, these people are not for me, they're not human . . . they have their own closed club.

From the opposite perspective, however, this basis of exclusion is one of the primary attractions of the game. A player told me:

Well, I tell you what—and this is very true, and a bit harsh to say— but polo players throughout the world, of one's own social stratum, tend to be very wealthy. And wealthy people tend to be doing more interesting things because they are able to travel freely, and really pick the plums of life. And I think that . . . that's the reason that people who say, "We're drawn together because of polo"—that's only true to a certain extent. So many of my friends who are involved in polo are also involved in racing, and for the same reason, or the same reasoning applies. And I think that part of it's the glamour, part of it's the affluence that comes with the stratum of society that plays polo.

Polo as a Status Marker

Status marking is an essential element in the development and maintenance of self-conscious, elite groups. Status marks in medieval society were obvious: certain types of cloth, certain colors, certain objects (e.g., swords) could only be worn by the nobility. In advanced industrialized societies, however, status-marking needs are more complex. Since consumer commodities are more readily available to larger segments of the population and the scale of the society is vastly magnified, it is far more difficult to distinguish fellow elites in a large and geographically dispersed population. Polo is well-suited to the status needs of elites in large-scale societies because of its highly distinctive image, an image which is widely recognized as denoting a secure position in an exotic and glamorous social set.

The use of polo imagery by the advertising media demonstates this. Polo has been associated with a myriad of expensive consumer products, ranging from perfumes to lawn furniture. Ralph Lauren, the designer of a well-known line of expensive clothing called "Polo," has perhaps created the product with the most widely recognized polo image. Lauren's use of the stereotype not only typifies the way it is exploited by advertisers; it also reflects the way polo players themselves make use of this identity, and points to a fundamental reason for the contemporary persistence of the sport in the United States. According to Charles Hix, a writer on male fashions, "The name of his firm, 'Polo by Ralph Lauren,' was selected frankly because the word 'polo' conjures up an image of refined elegance and cosmopolitan wealth" (1976:20).[3]

The most significant change that has taken place in the game over the last decade, in fact, is based on the exploitation of polo by corporate sponsors for advertising purposes. In 1976, the first cash prize ever offered in this country for a polo match was sponsored by Gould, Inc. Now, "image-conscious corporations" like Cartier, Black, Starr & Frost, Corrigan's Jewelers, Piaget and Rolex (watches and jewels); The Glenlivet, Pimms, Taittinger, Piper-Heidsieck, Schweppes, Perrier, Michelob, Coca-Cola, Pepsi, St. Pauli Girl, Bolla (beverages); Gucci, Boehm (leather and porcelains); Mercedes-Benz, Cadillac and BMW; Royal Viking Line, Paine Weber and Shearson Lehman Brothers, Inc. pay for 98 percent of the high-level polo played in the United States, sponsoring "trophies, tournaments, and high-goal teams that march into battle with signature shirts and logo saddle blankets." (quotation from de Suze and Waller 1986:57 [see also p. 77]; *The New Yorker* 1979).

It is evident that the referent of this advertising symbology is not simply the specific activity itself, but an entire personal identity. One of the Colonial Club players, who was featured in the society pages of a metropolitan newspaper, chose to identify himself as a "physician and polo player." Janey Ylvisaker, wife of William Ylvisaker, the chairman of Gould Inc., and the former president of the U.S. Polo Association, wrote an article for *Town and Country* magazine which focused on the clothes and makeup she wears to polo games. Similarly Jerzy Kosinski, the novelist, publicizes (Kosinski 1979; *The New Yorker* 1979) his identity as a polo player.[4]

This media use of the polo identity for status purposes is only the most public of the game's status-marking aspects. There are other key status markers associated with polo.

Land. As has been already noted, a country estate is of crucial significance to a polo player's identity. He needs an estate on which to put his horses (with a paddock near the house, so that they are easily visible when he is entertaining). Though polo players often work in the metropolis, living in the suburban-rural fringe seems to be one of the principal elements of polo status. Among the first steps that one new player at the Colonial Club took after joining the club was to purchase a suitable place in the country. Polo teams mounted by a single individual or family are usually named after the owner's estate; in some cases, the name of the estate itself clearly identifies the owner as a polo player (e.g., "Chukker Springs"). The image of "landed gentry," with all that it connotes in terms of wealth, taste, and family ties, is a fundamental status attribute.

Retainers. The grooms, trainers, and pros whose labor actually produces the game are also an important status marker for the players for whom they work. As Veblen wrote (1899:60–61; see also pp. 42–49), retainers dressed in the distinctive livery of the master (pros wear the owner's team uniform; sometimes grooms also dress in an owner's uniform-shirt on game days), who are engaged in the public performance of nonproductive activities (polo is, after all, a spectator sport), represent a particularly significant form of conspicuous consumption. From Veblen's perspective, it is not at all coincidental that most polo employees (grooms and their helpers) are female, and that the richest owners, as a mark of superior status, hire men (as trainers, pros, and grooms) (1899:42–44). These servants are particularly useful for the status purposes of the players because of their public displays of servility. Between chukkers, for example, as the spectators look on, a groom will help her owner dismount, take his helmet, whip, and mallet while handing him a towel and a drink, then hand him his fresh horse and pick up the towel and empty beverage container from where he has thrown it on the ground. Pros, for their part (though they may chafe about it in private), realize that part of their job while on the field is to "feed the man the ball," i.e., to make the owner look good whenever possible, rather than scoring the goal themselves.

Another status advantage of these servants is that since polo is played within a relatively closed social orbit, they form an excluded underclass within the system itself. In the words of a pro's wife,

Polo people are a world unto themselves, and then you break it up into subdivisions of the world. There are the grooms, the pros, the owners, the wives—and *don't* let anybody tell you that there isn't a caste system. . . . Up until two years ago, Bill and I never went to the clubhouse, *never!* . . . Because the royal high mucky-mucks were in there, and they looked down their noses at you as if to say your feet smell.

Family. Polo, though until recently nearly unique among American ama-
teur sports in that it was played only by adult males, is almost always
treated as a family activity. The primary family linkage is between a
father and his sons: the father may have begun playing polo himself after
he made his fortune, but his sons will have the opportunity of playing
polo from the time, in their early teens, when they are first capable of
joining the men. Polo thus legitimizes family wealth by providing a polo
pedigree for the sons, and through them, legitimization is reflected back
on the head of the family. Many polo players play on teams with other
male relatives, and most of the better-known players in the country
belong to "polo families." A man who can say, as a player at the Colonial Club did, "My grandfather died on the playing fields of Oakbrook"
lays claim to a securely legitimated status identity.

But female family members are also integrally involved. Wives, girl-
friends, daughters, and mothers usually attend a player's games (often
carrying a camera), but though this is one of the more public means of
identifying themselves with the game and of enhancing the player's
status image (see Veblen 1899:63–65, 139–42; Rapp, in this volume, on
this female function), it is by far the least demanding. Daughters are
often expected to help with the horses, at least to the extent of handing
the father a fresh mount between chukkers. Wives are expected to give
cocktail and dinner parties for visiting teams, to participate in the highly
ritualized ceremony of awarding trophies, and to follow the player
around the country on his tournamental peregrinations.[5] The most demanding role entails adapting one's life to the north-south seasonal
migrations that the most serious players make. One wife at the Colonial
Polo Club moves to Florida every fall, taking her children out of their
northern schools and enrolling them in Florida for the winter months,
then moving them back in the spring. Meanwhile, her husband con-
ducts his business in the north, and flies south to join them and play
polo on the weekends.[6]

Polo as the Basis of an Upper-Class Network

Many writers have stressed the importance of upper-class clubs for the
development and maintenance of a self-conscious sense of class and of
group cohesiveness. It has also been noted that such clubs serve as networks that offer practical advantages, such as business connections and

favorable marriage opportunities, to their members. Conversely, such networks serve to monopolize access to scarce resources, and thus function as kinship ties, ethnic groups, corporations, etc., do in other contexts. Baltzell writes, "At the upper-class level in America . . . the club (a private voluntary association) lies at the very core of the social organization of the accesses to power and authority" (1964:354). Domhoff suggests that this control over social power networks is the ultimate end of such clubs (1974, 1975). Mills emphasizes the role of these clubs in linking the power elite (and *only* the power elite) of different regions. "These clubs of the various cities are truly exclusive in that they are not widely known to the middle and lower classes in general. They are above those better-known arenas where upper-class status is more widely recognized. They are of and by and for the upper circles, and no other. But they are known and visited by the upper circles of more than one city" (1956:61).

All of these functions are clearly fulfilled by polo. The polo network provides a means of producing, maintaining, and displaying a sense of the shared interests of the upper class; of producing and maintaining bonds of affiliation and kinship between far-flung members of this class; and of enhancing their business relationships.

The most obvious sense, perhaps, in which polo serves to create and maintain a network of upper-class participants is the geographical one. On a local level, polo clubs bring together wealthy families and individuals from the suburban-rural estate fringes that ring the major metropolises.[7] On a national level, polo players are brought together through tournament competition, and through the seasonal migrations from north to south.[8] On an international level, polo players have a ready-made network available to them whenever they travel.

One of the inevitable consequences of this kind of contact is a heightened sense of class consciousness and cohesion. As a player at the Colonial Polo Club, explaining his reasons for playing polo, said:

I like the people that do it . . . like the people that I've met in other parts of the world that do it. I have friends that play polo in England, a few in South America . . . Africa . . . Australia, South Africa, Malaysia—places like that that I've seen and have kept contacts with through polo that have made traveling in other parts of the world more interesting—going to see people that you know. I suspect there's a taste of glamour connected with it, too—that you enjoy being part of, if the truth were known. I don't know how many people would *tell* you that, but I think that's part of the formula.

Janey Ylvisaker ("Around the World in Eighty Chukkers") described a trip she took with her husband, during which he played polo in Manila, Singapore, and Sydney. The account is replete with the names of the corporate heads, the governmental officials, the titled nobility, and the socially prominent with whom Ylvisaker played polo and discussed business. These people entertained the Ylvisakers and facilitated their travel by arranging visas, circumventing customs delays, and providing local guides, accommodations, transportation, and introductions. In addition to Asians and Australians, the Ylvisakers also encountered a significant number of other Americans who, like Ylvisaker, were corporate heads traveling within the polo network; polo also serves the needs of the modern multinational corporation.

Town & Country recently published a "Guide to International Polo," which offers another illustration:

Europe's polo scene . . . lur[es] the polo-playing tycoons of the Eighties from Dubai, Singapore, Athens, and Brazil, who mingle with European aristocrats and hired professional players. [The] former president of the Argentine Polo Association[:] "It's a very friendly sport. If you're anywhere in the world on a business trip and you're a good rider with a reasonable handicap, other players will invariably welcome you. Polo is a great passport." [A pro:] "Even though competition is serious on the field, after hours we're all essentially friends. Polo is really one big global family. The French are treating us like movie stars, and there's always a table at good restaurants." (de Suze and Waller 1986:57, 62, 68)

Business advantages, then, while almost never a motive elicited from the participants, are nonetheless apparent to an observer. An article in the *Wall Street Journal* (1979:1), for example, described a custom home builder who tried to deduct his polo expenses from his federal taxes as a business deduction. The builder argued "that several jobs resulted from his polo-playing contacts, publicity about his play helped business, and polo 'enabled him to meet wealthy people' who might become customers." His argument would surely not have been appreciated by his fellow players, who would have found it crassly petty bourgeois (a contention supported by the low level of his self-described expenses). It was also rejected by the tax court. But in spite of the breach of etiquette and the illegality of the deductions, the logic of the builder's claim is apparent. During my fieldwork I found other examples of polo "investments" being taken as tax deductions. These deductions are usually ascribed to losses resulting from a more gentlemanly "horse farm" operation. But since few polo estates are actually in the business of selling horses, fear of IRS audits in the polo world is not altogether unjustified. My fieldwork also revealed other cases, such as mergers, new clients, and new partnerships, in which significant financial benefits were directly the result of membership in the polo network.

In addition to financial advantages, other pragmatic benefits often accrue to members of the polo network. Cooperation between players is a distinct component of the polo ethos, as is apparent in informants' statements. A trainer told me, for example, that his boss had once offered, as a favor, to transport another player's horses a considerable distance. The trainer, driving his boss' truck and trailer with the other man's horses, was arrested in Florida; not having the proper ownership papers for the horses, his explanation that he was transporting the horses hundreds of miles merely as a favor was considered wildly implausible. The judge, on hearing the trainer's story, revealed that he was also a polo player, released the trainer simply on the basis of his claim to be carrying out a favor for another player, and admonished the arresting officer never again to doubt an excuse related to cooperation between polo players, no matter how implausible, since their generosity toward one another knew no bounds.

Another aspect of this network is its role in developing kinship ties between elites from different regions. Marriages between the families of polo players are a relatively common phenomenon. Insofar as the continuity of family status is an integral aspect of class, the marriage of sons and daughters within the polo network may be as important to the perpetuation of class status as is the tradition of father and son polo teams.

An example of the type of exclusive control over resources which the polo network helps to maintain can be found in the patterns of land use in the areas where polo clubs are located. Polo and real estate values are closely linked. In the South, where polo clubs are located in resort areas frequented in the winter by wealthy Northern industrialists, enormous real estate profits are being made by polo players (and the corporations that they head) through their ownership of land around their new polo clubs. According to one of my informants, for example, the original owner of the Gulf Stream Polo Club in Florida sold his land adjacent to the club for several million dollars. Gould, Inc., headed by polo player William Ylvisaker, invested 8,800 acres around its 1,650-acre Palm Beach Polo Club (Nemy 1980; *The New Yorker* 1979). Gulf and Western invested heavily in its Casa de Campo polo club/resort in the Dominican Republic (where its sugar and livestock operations are the island's major industries) (Shinitzky 1976). Player Peter N. Brant bought 1,500 acres of Connecticut woods and meadows, built polo fields on it, and subdivided the remainder into ten-acre parcels selling at prices that start at $1 million (de Suze and Waller 1986).

In the North, polo clubs are located in isolated pockets of rural estates situated near major metropolises. The networks formed by these clubs can be used by the area's affluent residents to resist the pressures of suburban encroachment. In the Colonial Polo Club case, members of the club shared a common concern about local real estate values, and about the exclusive use of surrounding land for farm estates. Several players were, or were closely related to, the major real estate agents in the area, who, naturally, specialized in the sale of "horse farms" and estates. (The class of their clientele is indicated by the fact that one of these men offered helicopter service in his advertisements.)

Others had major financial interests in local businesses that depended on the rural character of the area—selling thoroughbred horses and specialized agricultural products typical of the suburban-rural fringe. Several were members of the family that dominated the major corporation in the nearby metropolis, or were executives of this corporation. These men shared a common interest in preserving the family châteaus which greatly influenced the character of the region. One player who was related to the dominant family devoted his full-time efforts to preserving the aesthetic and ecological characteristics of the region through a major local institution which he founded. The common involvement of these men in polo helps to create a solidarity of interest and to strengthen the normative value placed on the "horse culture" and all that it represents in terms of exclusive access to a rural way of life.

In addition to this generalized concern for maintaining the high-amenity life-style associated with a low-density settlement pattern, the Colonial Club polo network also facilitated a pattern of exclusive control over a more specific environmental resource—water. The scarce surface water resources in the area are critical to the operation of the major corporation in the downstream metropolis. These scarce water resources are also crucial for the agricultural production within the area itself, which at once provides a significant source of income and a form of land use which blends harmoniously with the estates. The "horse farms" owned by polo players are a perfect support for these water uses, since they neither draw much water from the system for their own needs nor allow room for an influx of industrial or residential settlement which would divert water from these existing, exclusively controlled uses. Through its highlighting of horse farms and the common economic and status interests which they represent, the polo network, it could be argued, has contributed to the blocking of past attempts to create residential and industrial development in the area.[9]

Polo as a Means of Facilitating Upward Social Mobility

All exclusive social clubs, to a greater or lesser degree, allow individuals with certain qualifications to enhance their social status and, conversely, allow upper-status groups to assimilate suitable new personnel who will be an asset to the group. Mills has called these clubs "status elevators" for the new "merely rich" into the "old upper classes" (1956:61). Baltzell (1958:335–363) has plotted the gradient of these clubs, from the least exclusive (generally suburban country clubs) to the most exclusive (the metropolitan clubs which, as opposed to such associations as the college clubs and the clubs in which membership is based on professional, scholarly, or artistic achievement, base their membership qualifications primarily on family background). Polo's position within this continuum is somewhat anomalous: while it is certainly more exclusive than most suburban country clubs by virtue of its extremely high cost and its "old money" membership and image, it welcomes precisely those "merely rich" (provided only that they are merely rich enough) whom the most exclusive clubs are designed to keep out. Unlike, for example, such other horse sports of the upper class as the fox hunt and the steeplechase—in which participation is largely limited by family background—polo is open to almost anyone who can afford it.[10] The reason for this is that the financial burdens of the game can be so great for the existing members of a club that they encourage the acceptance of new members in order to lessen the per capita cost of maintaining the club's facilities, as well as to improve the level of competition.

This also explains, of course, the eagerness with which corporate sponsors have been welcomed into the game. Such corporate sponsorship is a very good deal for everyone involved. The polo players not only have their level of play enhanced and their costs reduced, they also gain glamorous public attention. For professional players, salaries and perquisites have significantly increased. And for the corporations, they find that the same upwardly mobile new-money clientele are attracted to their products as are attracted to the sport and their advertising dollar is effectively spent.[11] The only loser in the arrangement, if any, is the IRS—these polo costs, presumably, are legitimate business expenses.

In addition to offering an incentive for polo clubs to accept new recruits, polo also offers unique opportunities for new members to obtain favorable recognition within the polo network—and from polo spectators—strictly on the basis of their financial resources: championship polo requires, above all else, money. Common parlance has it that "90 percent of the game is the horse." While the numerical proportions could be disputed, it is unquestionably true that the outcome of a game is determined at least as much by the quality of the horses as by the quality of the players. The horses are not the only ingredient of high-level polo that can be purchased by the highest bidder: professional players are another. With good horses and professional teammates (as well as trainers and grooms), with a bit of practice (the availability of leisure time for this is also a function of financial resources), almost anyone could manage to play polo at the highest and most conspicuous level. Because money is unquestionably the prime requisite for high-quality polo, social mobility within this elite network can be purchased almost like any other luxury commodity.

For this reason, polo clubs are virtually unique among exclusive upper-class social organizations: almost anyone, providing he is willling and able to spend more money than the average player, is able to climb to the top of polo society, and from that vantage point, to facilitate his access to other upper-class networks and opportunities. Established players, on the other hand, can thus enjoy contact with newly rising wealth, and have privileged access to the opportunities this contact can offer. Patterns of upper-class dominance are thus maintained through the continued coincidence of financial resources and upper-class status.

As economic power is concentrated in the largest cities, so are the members of the upper class. However, unlike members of the urban lower classes, the rich are not confined to the cities, and can move at will from townhouse to country estate to resort. The family fortune may well have originated in the city, or be dependent on a metropolitan market, but, over time, some of this capital almost invariably flows to the countryside, where it is crystallized in protectively isolated real estate. It is in these contexts where "old," "landed" money meets "new" money, and where polo is played. Polo not only functions as a mechanism to consolidate upper-class control over the econo-ecology of these isolated locales, but also plays a general role in linking these local nodes into an upper class that is adapted to the scale of modern American society.

Notes

1. In 1976, there were approximately 125 polo clubs in the U.S. Polo Association, with an additional 12 clubs at schools and colleges. There were approximately 1,200 players with official USPA handicaps. The Colonial Club had 26 active members. In 1986, there were 170 clubs (of which 17 are college clubs, with another 15 in formative stages) and 2,300 registered players (de Suze and Waller, 1986).

2. Until recently, all members of the USPA were male; there are now 225 women members (de Suze and Waller 1986).

3. *Polo News*, an official publication of the U.S. Polo Association, also provides an interesting characterization of the use which Ralph Lauren makes of the polo image. Lauren "is a romantic novelist who uses cloth instead of pen and paper. He creates stories in wonderful settings of yesterday and today and centers the plot around you and me. He then lovingly dresses up the characters . . . from polo—the game and the people during the good days of the twenties and thirties. It's a mood and an anti-style style. It's a discreet and elegant expression of individualism and at-homeness with the good life. With the hustle and mass production of our time, such a flare is diminishing—Ralph Lauren wants to bring it back. . . . Polo and horses represented a class of people who knew how to live—people who weren't ashamed of being wealthy, but who didn't flaunt it either. Take the Duke of Windsor for example. He was as comfortable at a formal dinner as he was in the stable. At ease in his world he was probably very conscious of his clothes and style, but one wouldn't have suspected this because his attire was so much a part of his world—a comfortable tweed look perhaps a bit worn at the elbows, a seemingly casually-placed handkerchief in his pocket and an air of masculinity as if saying without boasting, "I know what it's all about." . . . Polo Fashion tries to combine the extremes—elegance and functional informality, rugged earthiness and class. Such a world may never exist again, but fragments of it can" (1975:28–30).

This statement is too rich to begin to plumb here, but it is clear that this realm of high male fashion is a perfect reflection of what polo might do for its participants. This "native" statement indicates that polo players themselves may be aware of, and may consciously manipulate, the image of upper-class insouciance which their behavior conveys. This brief statement also highlights several of the key symbolic elements that are associated with polo as a status marker: a linkage with an idealized past; a connection to England—particularly to its nobility; and a masculinity "combining the extremes of rugged earthiness and class."

4. Kosinski married the widow of an American steel magnate, Mary Hayward Weir. She died in 1968 (*Current Biography* 1974).

5. Rapp discusses middle-class households in which marriages are thought to be "egalitarian." Actually, she says, " 'egalitarian marriage' may be a biased gloss for a communication pattern in which the husband's career is in part reflected in the presentation of his wife. . . . [These wives] represent the private credentials of family to the public world" (1978:296). In the case of the upper-class wife, including Princess Diana and Queen

Elizabeth (de Suze and Waller 1986), this role, and subordination, is equally apparent, though the "public world" is narrowed to the interactions of the upper class. The wife of the president of the Colonial Polo Club, for instance, was the hostess for several polo functions at the club and at their home, and was very visible around the club. When I mentioned her involvement to her husband, he explained, "Well, my wife's very supportive of endeavors that I have, whether it be my law practice, or my interest in her family stable, or in the polo. . . . She feels that this club is a reflection, in a sense, of me. . . . But I think that when the time comes that I'm no longer president, neither she nor I will take a particularly strong interest in any of the extra activities that go on here."

6. In the ten years since this fieldwork was conducted, women have entered the game. In 1986, there were about 225 women rated by the U.S. Polo Association (de Suze and Waller 1986). Given the role women have long played in other equestrian sports, it is surprising that women did not enter the game sooner. Some of these women entered the game through college play. Some women, as part of the general expansion of women's economic roles in business, have joined the sport for the social and economic benefits of upward mobility that their male counterparts have found over the years. But many of the women who now play polo, like the men, come from polo families.

7. Polo players derive much of their economic power from cities, but invest much of it in the suburban-rural fringe, in real estate, etc. Polo players represent, therefore, what might be termed a "provincial" element of the upper class. Because their attention is directed away from the cities, rather than toward them, these people tend not to be members of the "power elite" in the sense that they influence foreign policy decisions or the fiscal policy of New York City; this subset of the upper class is more concerned with tasteful consumption in a relatively isolated context.

8. Polo clubs in the North are located outside the major financial, industrial, and governmental centers, e.g., Myopia outside Boston; Meadowbrook and Greenwich outside New York; Brandywine between Philadelphia and Wilmington; Potomac outside Washington, D.C.; Oakbrook outside Chicago. The main Southern clubs are located near major resort areas, primarily in Florida, but also in South Carolina, California, and the Dominican Republic and, starting with the oil boom of the seventies, in Texas.

9. Dan Rose (personal communication) provided my information on local water usage and management.

10. However, since polo is nonetheless played in private clubs, some exclusionary practices do persist. When fieldwork was conducted, there were no black polo players in the country, and only a very few Jewish players.

11. "In essence," a *Time* cover story notes, "the Lauren approach dangles old-money prestige in front of a new-money clientele" (Koepp 1986). "During Cadillac's first season of zipping Argentine high-goalers and VIPs about in luxurious white Sevilles, sales in its southern region rose 80 percent" (de Suze and Waller 1986).

References

Baltzell, E. Digby, 1958. *Philadelphia Gentlemen*. Glencoe, Ill.: Free Press.
—— 1964. *The Protestant Establishment*. New York: Random House.
Cady, Steve. 1979. "Where Ponies Do the Playing." *New York Times*, August 16, p. C20.
Current Biography. 1974. *Yearbook*. New York: H. W. Wilson Company, pp. 212–215.

de Suze, Brenda and Kim Waller, eds. 1986. "Town and Country's Guide to International Polo." *Town and Country* (January), pp. 55–94.

Domhoff, G. William. 1974. *The Bohemian Grove.* New York: Harper and Row.

—— 1975. "Social Clubs, Policy-Planning Groups, and Corporations: A Network Study of Ruling-Class Cohesiveness." *The Insurgent Sociologist* 5(3):173–184.

Hix, Charles. 1976. "The Polo World of Menswear: A Sense of Style." *Holiday Inn Companion* (September), 2(6):20–24.

Koepp, Stephen. 1986. "Selling A Dream of Elegance and the Good Life." *Time,* September 1, 1986, pp. 54–61.

Kosinski, Jerzy. 1979. *Passion Play.* New York: St. Martin's Press.

Lynd, Robert S. and Helen Merrell Lynd. 1929(1956). *Middletown.* New York: Harcourt Brace Jovanovich.

Miller, Benjamin. 1977. "An American Polo Club: A Study of a Leisure Activity as a Process of Production and Consumption, and as a Mechanism for the Maintenance and Enhancement of Elite Status." Master's thesis, Temple University, Philadelphia.

Mills, C. Wright. 1956. *The Power Elite.* New York: Oxford University Press.

Nemy, Enid. 1980. "In West Palm Beach, Polo Packs Them In, Plebians as Well as Patricians." *New York Times,* March 24, pp. C14.

New Yorker, The. "Talk of the Town." November 19, 1979, p. 40.

Parkin, Frank. 1974. "Strategies of Social Closure in Class Formation." In F. Parkin, ed., *The Social Analysis of Class Structure. London: Tavistock.*

Polo New S. 1975. "Ralph Lauren-Polo Fashion," 1(6):28–31.

Rapp, Rayna. 1978. "Family and Class in Contemporary America: Notes Toward an Understanding of Ideology." *Science and Society* 42(3):278–300.

Shinitzky, Ami. 1976. "Polo Anyone?" [*Colonial*] *Polo Club,* Annual Program.

Veblen, Thorstein. 1899. *The Theory of the Leisure Class.* New York: Funk and Wagnalls.

Wall Street Journal. "Tax Report." January 24, 1979, pp. 1.

Warner, William Lloyd and Paul S. Lunt. 1941. *The Social Life of a Modern Community.* New Haven: Yale University Press.

Warner, W. Lloyd, Marcia Meeker, and Kenneth Eells. 1949. *Social Class in America.* New York: American Books-Stratford Press.

Weber, Max. 1968. *Economy and Society.* Vol. 1. Berkeley and Los Angeles: University of California Press.

III

URBAN KINSHIP: GENERATION AND GENDER

The results of the 1980 census tell us that the family in the United States is undergoing radical change. Particularly significant is the massive increase in the number of women working outside the home and female-headed households. Researchers have noted the marked decline in the family form traditionally considered to be the ideal American family: a husband who goes out to work and a wife who stays at home with the children.

But as Rapp demonstrates, this image of the family has largely been an illusion. Households, she tells us, in responding to access to resources, take on different forms and functions. Thus, what we call family is "a cultural construction that reflects and distorts urban segregation between class and genders." Rapp's chapter is particularly illuminating in putting forward a specific theoretical approach and demonstrating its utility for the study of the family in urban society.

Two of the topics raised by Rapp—working women and fertility control—are examined in the next two chapters. Safa, in one of the few studies that take the occupational group as the unit of analysis, looks at the attitudes of women working in a garment factory in New Jersey. She describes women who work outside the home "for the sake of the family," but who also continue to be responsible for the organization of the household. However, she draws a picture of the working-class household that is not as authoritarian and male-dominated as often depicted in the literature. Further, unlike many other scholars, she finds that Afro-American working-class families are very similar to those of Euro-Americans of the same class.

Lopez's study of Puerto Rican women in Brooklyn, New York, examines the conditions under which they exercise fertility decisions, demonstrating that individual choices are limited by social, economic, and historical circumstances. Her discussion of the limitations of participant observation in the urban context and the supplemental methodological techniques she utilized is particularly informative for urban anthropologists.

It is appropriate to end this section with Smith's critique of the "Chicago School," which for many years dominated U.S. urban kinship studies. This article will give the reader insight into the way in which theoretical and methodological divergences among researchers may lead to contrasting conclusions, as Smith clarifies his own differences with David Schneider's emphasis on "integrated meaningful symbols" divorced from social context. To a great extent, Rapp's analysis may be seen as an answer to Smith's critique of the Chicago School.

10. Urban Kinship in Contemporary America: Families, Classes, and Ideology

Rayna Rapp

When urban anthropologists approach the study of contemporary kinship patterns in America, we discover ourselves to be recent migrants in an old and densely inhabited research domain: methodologies and ideologies of other branches of urban studies occupy the conceptual space we seek to explore. The Chicago school's litany of crisis, decay, and succession echoes through received notions of family breakdown. Parsonian analyses of reduced family functions reverberate in the extended, or truncated, kinship networks we map out (see Smith, in this volume). Such images are more than academic: popular American culture, too, has inherited an idealized notion of "traditional family life," now threatened by its loss of functions and the crisis of social disorganization cities supposedly evoke. Best-selling books entitled *The Fractured Family* and *The Death of the Family*, social services aimed at "patching up" or "creatively separating" family relations, courses at every level from high school through graduate studies on "the family in crisis," have become objects of national passion and consumption. The fear of "family breakdown" animates right-wing political movements and influences electoral results. Urban anthropologists should be able to sort out both the changing aspects of the family and the mythologies surrounding it. But we often lack a specific analysis of exactly how the recent growth of capitalist industrial cities affects the transformation of family life.

In attempting to transcend the malaise and alarmism that has beleaguered the discussion of American family life, urban anthropologists can turn for help to other fields of inquiry. In the last decade, the studies of city life on the one hand and family relations on the other have been the objects of vigorous intellectual movements of critique and renewal. Fields as diverse as urban political economy and history, literary criticism and semiotics, and family history and women's studies have produced fresh perspectives on terrains that border urban anthropology. We would do well to explore their resources as we analyze urban kinship patterns.

Advances in political economy and in urban sociology and history have allowed us to grasp what is specific to capitalist industrial cities. To sum up such a vast and growing literature briefly presents a challenge beyond the scope of this paper, but crucial boundary markers can be pointed out. Urban places in the West became sites of capital accumulation in the early modern period, and attracted the migration of cheap labor. By the nineteenth century, growing urban populations generated social movements to reform the quality of jobs, housing, and social services available in cities. They also challenged social control. The growth of regulatory state bureaucracies by the late nineteenth century in Western Europe, and the early twentieth century in the United States, is in large part a response to the social needs and the challenges that urban populations called forth. Cities, then, can be seen as spatial precipitates of the social reproduction of the class relations of capitalism. Their growth affects family life directly, through the provision of urban-based public services like education, sanitation, and health, and less directly (but no less profoundly) through political movements and policies whose aims include the redistribution of wealth. Investments in employment-producing industries, neighborhoods and housing, and social services all affect the lives of urban families and the possibilities for labor migration. In capitalist industrial cities, production and consumption are intimately linked, even as the two processes become spatially more and more segregated. The segregation of urban space occurs by land use—productive sites like factory zones and commercial districts are separated from tenement neighborhoods and suburbs, where consumption takes place. Spatial segregation also increases dramatically by class: recent urban migrants inhabit transitory areas, while working-class and bourgeois families are housed in their own "appropriate" urban and suburban spaces.[1]

Of course, the transformation of urban life is not simply political and economic; it is cultural as well. A rich neighborhood street life and a culture of work both flourish in cities. So does the development of consumption patterns to which new cultural images become attached—the "consumer palaces" of early department stores, supermarkets, and later educational and medical complexes, for example. Urban consumption includes the development of commercial recreation in pubs and amusement parks, in theaters and red-light districts, in expositions, and later in movie houses, all of which generate dense social meanings. Urban culture is also expressed in movements to reform city life—in waves of evangelical religion, temperance movements, and child-saving associations like the Boy Scouts, Girl Scouts, and some of the activities of the settlement houses. Urban cultural patterns are often class-specific—workingmen's bars and gentlemen's clubs provide very different locales for men's social networks, for example. Yet new cultural fantasies and images arise in cities which are based on the piercing of class boundaries. Gentlemen rakes "slumming" in red-light districts and the popularity of gothic novels which produce romance for a female, middle-class readership by mingling aristocracy, danger, and property are illustrations that readily come to mind. Urban life provides a context for the growth of mass media, first on the printed page and later in electronic form. Urbanites learn to read the language of pastoralism and urbanism as representing good and evil, as in the moral tales of Dickens and Horatio Alger, and the messages of tabloids, movies, and psyche-shaping advertisements.[2]

The political economy of cities and the analysis of urban culture—both elite and mass-based—provide windows into the changing nature of family life. For the same forces that generate spatial segregation, the regulatory state, and new forms of urban culture also segregate genders and generations as well. In capitalist industrial cities, the radical separation of workplace and home signals also the increasing segregation of the worlds of women and children from that of men. The actual separation between the sexes and the generations varies considerably by class. Wives and children of the immigrant poor participated in a dense street life and work culture at the turn of the twentieth century in New York, for example, while middle-class women conformed more closely to the image of "the angel of the hearth." But normative notions of sex roles and life cycles develop and are transmitted by the institutions of urban life. The home, increasingly seen as private and separated from work life, is symbolically attached to women and to children. Its activities are associated with consumption, and women become, symbolically, America's consumers. Work life and politics are seen as male domains and assigned the cultural values of productivity. Cultural distinctions between domestic and public life are thus linked to family organization. This is true internally, in the segregation of male and female symbolic domains, and externally, in the cultural notions of the family as a unit apart from the "larger world."[3]

Three forms of spatial segregation thus characterize the capitalist industrial city: segregation by land use of function, by class-based neighborhoods and services, and by gender-based activities and images. These multiple segregations mark off a cultural domain within which the antinomies of bourgeois life develop to their fullest. We experience the separation of workplace and home, of domestic and public, of production and reproduction, of labor and leisure, of male and female, *as if* they were separate "worlds," rather than the ideological images of one continuous (albeit very complex) set of social relationships.[4] It is that set of continuous social relations that actually contextualizes differences and changes in urban American family life, highly structured by class.

In order to see how such social processes generate differences in family experiences in urban America, we need to make a distinction between families and households. When we do so, the reproduction of class relations in the heart of family life is sharply revealed. Methodologically, we can best analyze the entities in which people actually live not as families, but as households (as any census taker, demographer, or fieldworking anthropologist will tell you). Households are the empirically measurable units within which people pool resources and perform certain tasks. They are residential units within which personnel and resources get distributed and connected. Households may vary in their membership composition and in their relation to resource allocation, especially in a system such as our own. That is, they vary systematically in their ability to hook into, accumulate, and transmit wealth, wages, or welfare. This seems a simple unit to define.

Families, on the other hand, are a bit more slippery to discuss. In English we tend to gloss "family" to mean household. But analytically, the concept means something else. For all classes of Americans, the word has at least two levels of meaning. One is normative: husbands, wives, and children as a set of relatives who should live together (that is, the nuclear family). The other meaning includes a more extended network of kin relations that people may activate selectively. That is, the American family includes the narrower and broader webs of kin ties that are "the nuclear family" and all relations by blood and marriage (Goody 1972; Schneider and Smith 1973). The concept of family is presumed in America to carry a heavy load of affect. We say "Blood is thicker than water," "till death do us part," "you can choose your friends, but not your relatives," and so on. What I will argue in this essay is that the concept of family also carries a heavy load of ideology.

The reason for this is that the family is the normative, correct way in which people get recruited into households. It is through families that people enter into productive, reproductive, and consumption relations. The two genders enter them differently. Families organize households, and it is within families that people experience the absence or presence, the sharing or withholding, of basic poolable resources. "Family" (as a normative concept in our culture) reflects those material relations; it also distorts them. As such, the concept of family is a socially necessary illusion which simultaneously expresses and masks recruitment to relations of production, reproduction, and consumption—relations that condition different kinds of household resource bases in different class sectors. Our notions of family absorb the conflicts, contradictions, and tensions actually generated by those material, class-structured relations that households hold to resources in advanced capitalism. "Family," as we understand (and misunderstand) the term, is conditioned by the exigencies of household formation, and serves as a shock absorber to keep households functioning. People are recruited and kept in households by families in all classes, yet the families they have (or don't have) are not the same.

Having asserted that households and families vary by class, we now need to consider that third concept, class. If ever a concept carried a heavy weight of ideology, it is the concept of class in American social science. We have a huge and muddled literature that attempts to reconcile objective and subjective criteria, to sort people into lowers, uppers, and middles, to argue about the relation of consciousness to material reality.[5] "Social class" is a shorthand for a process, not a thing. That process is the one by which different social relations to the means and meanings of production are inherited and reproduced under capitalism. As the concept is developed by Marx, the process of capital accumulation generates and constantly deepens relations between two categories of people: those who are both available and forced to work for wages because they own no means of production, and those who control those means of production.

The concept of class expresses a historical process of expanding capital. In the process, categories of people get swept up at different times and places and deposited into different relations to the means of production and to one another. People then get labeled blue collar or white collar; they may experience their social existence as mediated by ethnicity or the virulent legacy of slavery and racism. Yet all these categories must be viewed in the light of the historic process of capitalist accumulation in the United States. To a large extent, what are actually being accumulated are changing categories of proletarians. Class formation and composition is always in flux; what gets accumulated in it are relationships. Under advanced capitalism, there are shifting frontiers which separate poverty, stable wage earning, affluent salaries, and inherited wealth. The frontiers may be crossed by individuals, and in either direction. That is, both upward and downward mobility are real processes. The point is, "class" is not a static place that individuals inhabit. It is a process set up by capital accumulation.

Returning to the initial distinction between family and household, I want to explore how these two vary among differing class sectors in contemporary America and to draw a composite picture of the households formed around material relations by class, and the families which organize those households. I will argue that those families mean different things by class and by gender as well, because classes and genders stand in differing material relations to one another. I will further argue that their meanings are highly ideological.

I would like to begin with a review and interpretation of the studies done on the urban working-class family. Studies span the postwar decades from the late 1940s to the present. They are regionally diverse, and report on both cities and suburbs. The data provided by researchers such as Berger (1968), Gans (1962, 1967), Komarovsky (1962), Howell (1973), Rubin (1976), and others reveal a composite portrait.[6] The most salient characteristic of urban household organization in the working class is dependency on hourly wages. Stable working-class households participate in relations of production, reproduction, and consumption by sending out their labor power in exchange for wages. "Sending out" is important: there is a radical split between household and workplace, yet the resources upon which the household depends come from participation in production outside of itself. How much labor power a working-class household needs to send out is determined by many things: the cost of reproducing (or maintaining) the household, the work careers and earning trajectories of individual members, and the domestic cycle (that is, the relations between the genders and the generations, which specify when and if wives and adolescent children are available to work outside the home). Braverman estimated that the average working-class household sent out 1.7 full-time equivalent workers in 1974. That figure tells us that a high percentage of married women and teenaged children are contributing their wages to the household, despite the symbolic importance Americans attach to male economic responsibility (see Safa, in this volume).

What the working class sends out in exchange for basic resources is labor power. Labor power is the only commodity without which there can be no capitalism. Labor power is also a commodity over which working-class families appear to exercise some control—that is, they make their own fertility decisions. But, of course, family size itself is the product of economic, political, and social forces: availability or lack of birth control, abortion, and healthy environments in which to give birth to and raise children form the context within which reproductive "choice" is exercised (see Lopez, in this volume). Such contexts have varied historically and affected family relations by class and by sex.[7] In the early stages of industrialization, it appeared that working-class households literally produced a lot of babies (future labor power) as part of their strategy for dealing with a wage-labor economy (Tilly and Scott 1978). Now workers produce fewer children, but the work of servicing them (part of social reproduction) is still a major process that goes on in the household. Households are the basic units in which labor power is reproduced and maintained. This takes place in a location radically removed from the workplace. Such relations therefore appear as autonomous from capital, but of course they are not; without wages, households are hard to form and keep functioning; without the production of a disciplined labor force, factories cannot produce and profit.

The work that gets done in households (primarily by women) is not simply about babies. Housework itself has recently been rediscovered as work, and its contribution to arenas beyond the household is clear (e.g., Fee 1976; Fox 1980; Hartmann 1981; Malos 1980). At the least, housework cuts the reproduction costs of wage workers. Imagine if all those meals had to be bought at restaurants, those clothes cleaned at laundry rates, those beds made by hotel employees! Housework is also what women do in exchange for access to resources that are bought by their husband's wages. As such, it is a coin of exchange between men and women. As housework is wageless, it keeps its workers dependent on others for access to commodities bought with wages. It makes them extremely vulnerable to the work conditions of their men. When women work for wages (as increasingly they do), their primary definition as houseworker contributes to the problems they encounter in entering the paid labor force (see Safa, in this volume). They are available for part-time (or full-time) work in the lowest-paid sectors of the labor market, in jobs which leave them less economically secure than men. Participation in the "sexregated" labor market then reinforces dependency upon the earnings of other household members and the continued importance of women's domestic labor (Reagan and Blaxall 1976; U.S. Bureau of Census 1974).

Of course, these rather abstract notions of "household participation" in the labor market or in housework are experienced concretely by family members. Working-class families are normatively nuclear. They are formed via marriage, which links men and women "for love" and not "for money" (Schneider and Smith 1973:63). This relation is, of course, both real and a socially necessary illusion. As such, it is central to the ideology of the family. The cultural distinction between love and money corresponds to the distinction between private family life in the home and work life outside the home. The two are experienced as opposite; in fact they are interpenetrating. The seeming autonomy to exchange love at home expresses something ideological about the relations between home and work: one must work for the sake of the family, and having a family is the "payoff" for leading a good life. Founding a family is what people do for personal gratification, for love, and for autonomy. The working-class family literature is full of life histories in which young women saw "love" as a way to get out of their own often difficult families. Rubin's interviews, for example, are full of teenaged girls who said, "When I grow up, I'll marry for love, and it will be better than my parents' marriage." You may marry for love, but what you mainly get is babies. From 40 to 60 percent of teenaged pregnancies are conceived premaritally, and approximately 50 percent of working-class women marry in their teen years (Rubin 1976:49–68). It's a common experience to go from being someone's child to having someone's child in under a year. This is not exactly a situation that leads to autonomy.

For men, the situation is complementary. As one of the young working-class men in Rubin's study puts it:

I had to work from the time I was thirteen and turn over most of my pay to my mother to help pay the bills. By the time I was nineteen, I had been working for all those years and I didn't have anything—not a thing. I used to think alot about how when I got married, I would finally get to keep my money for myself. I guess that sounds a little crazy when I think about it now because I have to support a wife and kids. I don't know *what* I was thinking about, but I never thought about that then. (1976:56)

What you get from the romance of love and marriage is in fact not simply a family but a household, and that's quite another matter, economically speaking.

The romance which masks household formation through the appeal of marriage and family life is deeply implicated in gender identity and ideology. We are all aware of the cultural distinction Americans make between the sexual identity of a good and a bad girl. A good girl accumulates her sexual resources for later investment; a bad girl does not. For young men, gender ideology works somewhat differently; the cultural repertoire includes the role of a wild boy—one who "sows some wild oats," hangs out on street corners, perhaps gets in trouble with the police, and drinks (e.g., Shostack 1969; Howell 1973). Ideally, the cultural script reads like this: the good girl domesticates the wild boy. She gives him love, and he settles down and goes out to work. Autonomous adulthood means founding your own nuclear family as an escape. But, of course, autonomy is illusive. The family is culturally viewed as an escape from the harsh world of production, but it sends people into relations of production, for they need to work to support their families. The meaning of production is simultaneously denied and experienced through family relations. Working-class wives say of a good husband that he works steadily, provides for the kids, and never harms anyone in the family. The complementary statement is uttered by working-class husbands, who define a good wife as one who keeps the kids under control when he comes home from a hard day's work, and who runs the household well (e.g., Rubin 1976; Sennet and Cobb 1972; Terkel 1972). To exchange love is also to underwrite both the necessity and the ability to keep on working. *This* is the heritage that working-class families pass on, in lieu of property, to their children.

The family expresses ideology in another sense as well—the distinction between norms and realities. The norms concerning families are that people should be loving and sharing within them and they should be protective. The reality is too often otherwise, as the recent rising consciousness of domestic violence indicates. Even without domestic violence, there are more commonplace stresses to which families are often subjected. Rubin found in her study that 40 percent of the adults she interviewed had an alcoholic parent (1976:221–222); 50 percent had experienced parental desertion or divorce in their childhood. National statistics confirm these figures (1976:224–225). About half the adults in her study had seriously destabilizing experiences within their families. The tension generated by relations to resource base can often tear households apart. Under these conditions, to label the working-class personality "authoritarian" seems a cruel hoax. When the household is working, it expresses work discipline.

Families express the ideology of urbanism in their gender roles. Throughout the urban kinship literature, across classes and ethnic groups, the work of reproducing families is in part undertaken by larger kinship groups (the family in the broader sense of relatives). Family networks in this larger sense reflect the gender arrangements of urban segregation, for they are woman-centered. Connections through female relatives are stressed, and women expend a lot of time and energy servicing their extended kinship networks. In the urban kinship literature, it is usually assumed that women minister to their extended families because they are extensions of their nuclear families. Sylvia Yanagisako suggests that there is more to women's kinship behavior than meets the eye. Symbolically, women are assigned to "inside, home, private" domains, while men are seen to represent the outside world (1977). Nuclear families are under cultural constraints to appear as autonomous and private. Yet they are never as private in reality as such values might indicate. The ideal autonomy of an independent nuclear family is constantly being contradicted by the realities of social need, in which resources must be pooled, borrowed, shared.

It is women who bridge the gap between what a household's resources really are and what a family's position is supposed to be. Women exchange babysitting, share meals, lend small amounts of money. When a married child is out of work, his (or her) nuclear family turns to the mother, and often moves in for a while. The working-class family literature is filled with examples of such pooling (Yanagisako 1977; Wilmott and Young 1957; Bott 1971). To the extent that women "represent" the family, they facilitate the pooling needed at various points in the domestic cycle. Men maintain, at least symbolically, the autonomy of their families. Pooling is a norm in family behavior, but it's a hard norm to live with, to either meet or ignore. To comply with the demands of the extended family completely is to lose control over material and emotional resources; to refuse is very dangerous, as people know they will need one another. The tightrope act that ensures is well characterized in the classic mother-in-law story in which two women must figure out a way to share the services, material benefits, and emotional satisfactions one man brings to them both in their separate roles of mother and wife. The autonomy of the younger woman is often compromised by the elder's needs; the authority of the mother is sometimes undermined by the demands of the wife. Women must constantly test, strain, and repair the fibers of their kinship networks.

Such women-centered networks are implicated in a process that has not yet been discussed. I have spoken of production and reproduction as they affect the working-class household and family. I ought briefly to mention consumption as well. As a household function, consumption includes turning an amount of wages into commodities so that labor power may be reproduced. This is often women's work. And work it really is. Weinbaum and Bridges tell us that the centralization and rationalization of services and industry under advanced capitalism may be most efficient from the point of view of capital, but it leaves a lot of unrewarding, technical work to be done by women in supermarkets, in paying bills, in dealing with huge bureaucracies (1976). Women experience the pay packet in terms of the use values it will buy. Yet their consumption work is done in the world of exchange value. They mediate the tension between use and exchange, as exemplified in the classic tales concerning domestic quarrels over money in which the man blames the woman for not making his paycheck stretch far enough. In stable working-class neighborhoods, the consumption work is in part done by women united by family ties who exchange services, recipes, sales information, and general life-style skills. Kinship networks are part of "community control" for women. As Nancy Seifer notes, working-class women become involved in political issues that threaten the stability of their neighborhoods (1973, 1976). Perhaps one reason is that their neighborhoods are the locus of extended families within which both work needs and emotional needs are so often met.

When everyone submits to the conditions described here "for the sake of the family," we see the pattern that Howell labels "settled living" (1973). Its opposite, in his words, is "hard living," a family life-style that includes a lot of domestic instability, alcohol, and rootlessness. I want to stress that I am here departing from a "culture of poverty" approach. The value of a label like "hard living" is that it stresses a continuum made up of many attributes. It is composed of many processes with which the working class has a lot of experience. Given the national statistics on alcoholism, desertion, divorce, premarital pregnancy, and the like, everyone's family has included such experiences, either in its own domestic cycle or in the wider family network (Rubin 1976:223). Everyone had a wild brother, or was a bad girl, or had an uncle who drank too much or cousins who got divorced. In each of such cases, everyone experienced the pooling of resources (or the lack of pooling) as families attempted to cope with difficult, destabilizing situations. In a sense, the hard livers kept the settled livers more settled: the consequences of leaving the normative path are well known and are not appealing. This, too, is part of the working-class heritage. In studies by Seifer, Howell, and Rubin, young women express their hopes of leaving a difficult family situation by finding the right man to marry. They therefore marry young, with little formal education, possibly about to become parents, and the cycle begins again.

Of course, hard living is most consistently associated with poverty in the urban family literature. For essentially political reasons, black poverty has more frequently been the subject of social science analysis than has white poverty, but the pattern is found across races. Black Americans have survived under extremely difficult conditions; many of their household and family patterns have evolved to deal with their specific history, while others are shared with Americans of similar class and regional backgrounds. The problems of household formation under poverty conditions are not unique to any group of people; some of the specific, resilient solutions to those problems may be. Because we know far more about urban black families in poverty than we do about whites, I will draw a composite picture of households and families using studies that are primarily about blacks.[8] Even when talking about very poor people, analysts such as Liebow (1967), Hannerz (1969), Valentine (1968), and Stack (1974) note that there are multiple household types, based on domestic cycles and the relative ability to draw on resources. Hannerz, for example, divides his black sample into four categories.

Mainstreamers live in stable households composed of husband, wife, and children. The adults are employed, and either own their own homes or aspire to do so. Their households do not look very different from the rest of the working class. Swingers (Hannerz's second type) are younger, single persons who may be on their way into mainstream life, or they may be tending toward street families (type three), whose households are headed by women. This type is most important for our study. The fourth category is composed of street men who are peer-oriented, and predominantly hard-core unemployed or underemployed. They are similar to the men of *Tally's Corner*. While Hannerz and Liebow both give us a wealth of information about what men are doing, they do not analyze their domestic arrangements in detail. Carol Stack, who did her field-work from the perspective of female-centered households, most clearly analyzes household formation of the urban poor. She presents us with domestic networks: extremely flexible and fluctuating groups of people committed to resource pooling, to sharing, to mutual aid, who move in and out from under one another's roofs.

Given the state of the job market, welfare legislation, and segregated slum housing, households are unstable. These are people essentially living below socially necessary reproduction costs. They therefore reproduce themselves by spreading out the aid and the risks involved in daily life.[9] For the disproportionately high numbers who are prevented from obtaining steady employment, being part of what Marx called the floating surplus population is a perilous endeavor. What this means in human terms is not only that the poor pay more (as Caplovitz tells us [1963]) but that the poor share more as well. Stack's monograph contains richly textured descriptions of the way that food, furniture, clothing, appliances, kids, and money make the rounds between individuals and households. She subtitles one chapter "What Goes Round Comes Round" and describes the velocity with which pooling takes place. People try to give what they can and take what they need. Meeting consumption requirements is hard work under these conditions, and domestic networks get the task done. The pleasures and pressures of such survival networks are predominantly organized around the notion of family.

The families that organize domestic networks are responsible for the survival of children. As Ladner and Stack remind us, poverty, low levels of formal education, and early age for first pregnancy are highly correlated; a lot of young girls have children while they are not fully adults.

Under these circumstances, at least among black families, there is a tremendous sharing of the children themselves. On the whole, these are not kids who grow up in "isolated nuclear families." Stack, for example, found that 20 percent of the AFDC (Aid to Families with Dependent Children) children in her study were being raised in a household other than that which contained the biological mother. In the vast majority of cases, the household was related through the biological mother's family. Organizing kinship networks so that children are cared for is a primary function of families. While women form the nodes of survival networks, men, too, contribute by sharing out bits and pieces of whatever resources they have. A man may be sleeping in one household, but bringing groceries, money, and affection to several others where he has a sister or an aunt, a mother, a wife or a lover. Both Stack and Ladner analyze the importance of a father's recognition of his children, by which act he links the baby to his own kinship network. It is family in the broader sense of the term that organizes social reproduction.

Family may be a conscious construction of its participants. Liebow, Stack, Ladner, and others describe fictive kinship, by which friends are turned into family. Since family is supposed to be more reliable than friendship, "going for brothers," "for sisters," "for cousins," increases the commitment of a relationship, and makes people ideally more responsible for one another. Fictive kinship is a serious relationship. Stack (who is white) describes her own experience with Ruby, a black woman with whom she "went for sisters." When Ruby's child was seriously ill, Stack became deeply involved in the crisis. When the baby was admitted to the hospital, she and Ruby rushed over for visiting hours. They were stopped by a nurse, who insisted that only the immediate family could enter. Ruby responded, "Caroline here is my sister, and nothing's stopping her from visiting this baby." And they entered, unchallenged. Ruby was correct; under the circumstances, white Caroline was her sister (1974:21).

Liebow notes that fictive kinship increases the intensity of relationships to the point where they occasionally explode: the demands of brothers and sisters for constant emotional and material aid may lead to situations that shatter the bonds. Fictive kinship is a prime example of family-as-ideology. In this process, reality is inverted. "Everybody" gets a continuous family, even though the strains and mobility associated with poverty may consipre to keep biological families apart. The idiom of kinship brings people together despite centrifugal circumstances.

It is important not to romanticize this pattern. It has enormous benefits, but its participants also pay high costs. One of the most obvious costs is leveling. Resources must be available for all and none may get ahead. Variations in chances for survival are smoothed out in domestic networks via sharing. Stack tells the story of a central couple, Calvin and Magnolia, who unexpectedly inherit a sum of money. While the money might have enabled them to ensure their own security, it is gone within a few months. It disappears into the network to pay off bills, buy clothing for children, allow people to eat better (1974:105–107). Similar stories are told by Hannerz, Liebow, and Howell. No one gets ahead, because individual upward mobility can be bought only at the price of cutting off the very people who have contributed to one's survival. Upward mobility becomes a terribly scarring experience under these circumstances. To get out, a person must stop sharing, which is unfamilial, unfriendly, and quite dangerous. It also requires exceptional circumstances that rarely are available to the very poor—upward mobility through the "discovery" of talents in school, sports, or performing arts, for example. And even for that extraordinary person who entertains the possibilities of upward mobility, grasping the chance may simply be too costly. The pressures to stay in a supportive and constraining network and to level out differences may be immense. They contribute to the instability of marriages and normative nuclear families, for the old networks compete with new units for the same resources.

The family as an ideological construction is extremely important to poor people. Many studies show how the poor do not aspire to less "stable families," if that term is understood as nuclear families. They are simply much more realistic about their life chances. Ties to family, including fictive family, are the lifelines that simultaneously bind and sustain individuals. My guess is that among the poor, families do not exhibit the radical split between "private, at home" and "public, at work" found in families of the stable working class. Neither work relations nor household relations are as continuous or as distinct. What is continuous is the sharing of reproduction costs throughout a network whose resources are known to all. There can be no privatization when survival may depend on rapid circulation of limited resources. In this process, women do not "represent" kinship to the outside world. They become the nodal points in family nets which span whatever control very poor people have over domestic and resource-getting arrangments. Families are what make the huge gap between norm and reality survivable.

It is particularly ironic that the ideology of family, so important to poor people, is used to blame the poor for their own condition. In a society in which all Americans subscribe to some version of the normative nuclear family, it is cruelty to attack "the black family" as pathological. Mainstream culture, seeing the family as "what you work for" (and what works for you), uses "family language" to stigmatize those who are structurally prevented from accumulating stable resources. The very poor have used their families to cement and patch tenuous relations to survival; out of their belief in "family" they have invented networks capable of making next-to-nothing go a long way. In response, they are told that their notion of family is inadequate. It is not their notion of family that is deficient, but the relationship between household and productive resources.

Having considered the meaning of family and household among urban classes with regular or unstable relations to wages, we should now consider those sectors for whom resource bases are more affluent. Analyzing the family and household life of the middle class is a tricky business. The term "middle class" is ambiguous; a majority of Americans identify themselves as part of it whenever they answer questionnaires, and the category obviously carries positive connotations. Historically, we take the notion from the Marxian definition of the petty bourgeoisie: that category of people who own small amounts of productive resources and have control over their working conditions in ways that proletarians do not. The term signifies a stage in proletarianization in which small-scale entrepreneurs, tradesfolk, artisans, and professionals essentially stand outside the wage-labor/capital relation. That stage is virtually over: there are fewer small-scale proprietors or artisans working on their own account in post–World War II America. We now use the term to refer to a different sector—employees in corporate management, government and organizational bureaucrats of various kinds, and professionals, many of whom work directly or indirectly for big business, the state, and semipublic institutions. On the whole, this "new middle class" is dependent on wages; as such, it bears the mark of proletarianization. Yet the group lives at a level that is quite different from the wage levels of workers (Braverman 1974: ch. 18). Such a category is obviously hard to define; like all class sectors, it must be historically situated, for the middle class of early twentieth-century America differs markedly from that of our own times. To understand what middle class means for the different groups, we need to know not only their present status but also the ethnic and regional variations in class structure within which their families entered America.

The middle class is a highly ideological construction that pervades American culture; it is, among other things, the perspective from which mainstream social scientists approach the experiences of all the other sectors they attempt to analyze. To analyze the middle class' household formations and family patterns, we have to examine not only the data available on all the people who claim to be middle class, but also explore the biases inherent in much of social science. This is a task beyond the scope of the present essay. Here, I can only suggest some ideas toward research on the urban middle class.

Households among the middle class are obviously based on a stable resource base that allows for some amount of luxury and discretionary spending. When exceptional economic resources are called for, nonfamilial institutions usually are available in the form of better medical coverage, expense accounts, pension plans, credit at banks, and so on. Such households may maintain their economic stability at the cost of geographical instability; male career choices may move households around like pieces on a chessboard. When far from family support networks, such households may get transitional aid from professional moving specialists, or institutions like the Welcome Wagon. Middle-class households probably are able to rely on commodity forms rather than kinship processes to ease both economic and geographic transitions.

The families that organize such households are commonly thought to be characterized by egalitarian marriages (Schneider and Smith 1973: ch. 4). Rubin comments that "egalitarian marriage" may be a biased gloss for a communication pattern in which the husband's career is in part reflected in the presentation of his wife. To entertain intelligently, and instill the proper educational and social values in the children, women may need to know more about the male world. They represent the private credentials of family to the public world of their men at work. If this is the case, then "instrumental communication" might be a more appropriate term (Rubin 1976:97–99).

I am not prepared at this point to offer an analysis of middle-class kinship patterns, but I have a few hunches to present:

1. At this level, kinship probably shifts from the lateral toward the lineal. That is, resources (material and economic) are invested lineally,

between parents, children, and grandchildren, and not dispersed into larger networks, as happens with working-class and poor families. Such a pattern would, of course, vary with geographical mobility, and possibly with ethnicity. There is usually a greater investment across generations, and a careful accumulation within them. This kind of pattern can be seen, for example, in the sums invested in children's educations, setting up professional practices, wedding gifts (in which major development of property may occur), and so forth.

2. Perhaps friendship, rather than kinship, is the nexus within which the middle class invests its psychic and "familial" energies. Friendship allows for a great deal of affective support and exchange but usually does not include major resource pooling. It is a relation consistent with resource accumulation rather than dispersal. If the poor convert friendship into kinship to equalize pooling, it seems to me that the middle class does the converse: it reduces extended kinship exchanges and replaces them with friendship, which protects them from pooling and leveling.

There is one last sector of the American class system whose household and family patterns would be interesting to examine—the upper class, sometimes identified as the ruling class or the very rich. Once again, I have only a few tentative observations to make. As one sociologist (either naive or sardonic) commented, "We know so little about the very wealthy because they don't answer our questionnaires." Indeed! They fund them rather than answer them. The few classic studies we do have (by authors such as Domhoff, Amory, Baltzell, Veblen) are highly suggestive. The upper class, they tell us, seems to hang together as a cultural phenomenon. They defend their own interests corporately, and have tremendous ideological importance.

We know very little about the household structure of the very rich. They are described as having multiple households that are recomposed seasonally and filled with service workers rather than exclusively with kin and friends (Hoffman 1971; Baltzell 1958). While there is a general tendency toward "conspicuous consumption," we have no basic information on the relation of their resource bases to domestic arrangements.

When we turn to the family structure of the very rich, some interesting bits and pieces emerge (which may possibly be out-of-date). Families treasure and trace their lineal and lateral connections; geneaology matters a great deal, for people are identified by who they are rather than what they do. People have access to one another through their control of neighborhoods, schools, universities, clubs, churches, and ritual events (see Miller, in this volume). They are ancestor-oriented and conscious of the boundaries that separate the "best" families from all others. Families are obviously the units within which wealth is accumulated and transmitted. Yet the link between wealth and class is not so simple; some of the "best" families lose fortunes but remain in the upper class. Mobility is also possible. According to Baltzell, under certain circumstances it is possible for nonmembers to enter the class via educational and work-related contacts. What emerges from the literature is a sketch of a group that is perhaps the only face-to-face subculture that America contains.

Women serve as gatekeepers to many of the institutions of the very rich (Domhoff 1971). They launch children, serve as board members at private schools, run clubs, and facilitate marriage pools through events like debuts and charity balls. Men also preside over exclusive clubs and schools, but different ones. The upper class appears to live in a world that is very sex-segregated. Domhoff mentions several other functions that very rich women fulfill. These include (a) setting social and cultural standards and (b) softening the rough edges of capitalism by doing charity and cultural work. While he trivializes the cultural standards that women set to things like dress and high art, I think he has alerted us to something more important. In the upper class, women again "represent" the family to the outside world. But here, it is an outside world that is in many senses created by their own class (in the form of high cultural institutions, education, social welfare, and charity). Their public presence is an inversion of reality; they appear as wives and mothers, but it is not really their family roles but their class roles that dictate those appearances. To the extent that "everyone else" either has a wife/mother or is a wife/mother, upper-class women are available to be perceived as something both true and false. What they can do because of their families (and, ultimately, for their families) is utterly, radically different from what other women who "represent" their families can do. Yet what everyone sees is their womanness as family members rather than class members. They influence our cultural notions of what feminine and familial behavior should be. They simultaneously become symbols of domesticity and public service to which others may aspire. The very tiny percentage of very wealthy women who live in a sex-segregated world and have no need to work are thus perceived as benevolent and admirable by a much larger group of women whose relations to sex-role segregation and work is not nearly so benign. "Everybody" can yearn for a family in which sex-role segregation is valued; nobody else can have a family in which it is valued as highly as theirs. In upper-class families, at least as they present themselves to "the public," we see a systematic confusion of cultural values with the values of family fortunes.

In this essay, I've tried to analyze American family life not as a "world apart," but as a cultural construction that reflects and distorts urban segregation between classes and genders. Urban households clearly vary in their resources, and their ability to tap wealth, wages, and welfare. Yet these class differences are to a great extent smoothed over by cultural ideologies that give American life shared meanings, despite deep political, economic, and social cleavages. Others have suggested a range of cultural ideologies that contribute to normative concensus—myths of personal achievement, mobility, and perfectibility that shift the abstract burdens of class differences onto the concrete shoulders of individuals, for example. I would like to suggest that notions of "the family" contain a key ideological construction through which the shared meaning of American culture may be viewed. Because "the family" represents normative recruitment to household relations, it both reveals and masks class and gender stratification so central to capitalist urban life. It is a concept which is simultaneously shared by all levels of American society, yet which is reshaped to fit household exigencies to the lived reality of different social strata.

The flexibility of family ideology is also highly political. Recent social movements have challenged American life, in part by laying siege to political resources in familial language. Black Americans rejected notions of "family pathology" in the civil rights and black power movements, legitimizing alternative and resilient (rather than "inferior") family forms.[10] And in the women's movement, patriarchal power was challenged in part by revealing conflicting interests within middle-class family life.[11] These challenges were met by right-wing movements mobilized for electoral success under the banner of "saving the family." Using familial language, they have sought to dismantle the political rights and social services generated by both the civil rights and women's movements.[12] The definition of normative family life is once again a contested domain. It provides the cultural arena in which urban anthropologists may map the stratigraphy of class, race, and gender as they meet, are reproduced, or challenged in the meaning of family life.

Acknowledgments

The University of Michigan's Women's Studies Program called this paper into being, gave it a first airing, and contributed a stimulating set of discussions. Subsequent presentations of these ideas evolved through a URPE spring conference on public policy, a paper presented at the University of Northern Colorado, and conversations with students in urban anthropology and gender studies, all of which provided invaluable feedback. Special thanks are due to Jil Cherneff, Ingelore Fritsch, Susan Harding, Mike Hooper, Janet Siskind, Deborah Jay Stearns, Batya Weinbaum, Marilyn Young, and the women of Marxist-Feminist Group II. Above all, Gayle Rubin deserves thanks for her editorial ability to turn my primary process into a set of written ideas. Versions of this paper appeared first in a special issue of University of Michigan Papers in Women's Studies, and then in *Science and Society* (1978), 42:278–300, reprinted by permission of both the journal and the author.

Notes

1. An excellent introduction to Marxian urban political economy is provided by Zukin (1980). See also Gordon (1976), Harvey (1973), Castells (1979), and Tabb and Sawers (1978).

2. The cultural implications of rapid capitalist urbanization are discussed in Jones (1974), Kasson (1978), Ewin (1976), and *The Spatial Dimension of History* (1980). Urban reform movements are discussed in Marcus (1974), Ryan (1979), Ehrenreich and English (1978), and Stansell (1982). The semiotics of urban space figure in the works of Williams (1973) and Mounin (1980).

3. The sexual segregation of urbanism is a focus of Hayden (1981a,b), Pleck (1976), and *Women and the American City* (1980).

4. The connectedness of seemingly disconnected aspects of contemporary urban life is central to feminist analysis of gender and family relations, e.g., Kelly (1979), Rapp, Ross, and Bridenthal (1979), Rapp and Ross (n.d.), and Ross (1982).

5. For examples, see Otto (1975), Anderson (1974), Szymanski (1972), and Braverman (1974).

6. See also Howe (1970), J. Ryan (1973), Seifer (1973, 1976), Shostack (1969), Sennett and Cobb (1972), Sexton and Sexton (1971), and Terkel (1972).

7. See Gordon (1976), Petchesky (1980, 1984), and CARASA (1979).

8. Howell (1973) provides sensitive field data on the domestic lives of poverty whites. Black poverty domestic organization is discussed in Hannerz (1969), Ladner (1971), Liebow (1967), Rainwater (1970), Scanzoni (1971), Stack (1974), Valentine (1968).

9. Haley (1976) underlined this point in popular culture; Gutman (1976) provided scholarly confirmation of the importance of family life among black Americans in slavery and freedom.

10. See Gilkes (1983) for an important insight into this process. See also Staples (1971).

11. Domestic violence, including battering and marital rape, male dominance in intimate arenas ranging from sexuality to economic decision making, as well as psychological structuring of male/female antagonism, were all subjects of women's movement critiques of family life.

12. See Petchesky (1981), Oliker (1981), and Hunter (1981) for analyses of the New Right's use of family issues for political mobilization.

References

Amory, Cleveland. 1947. *The Proper Bostonians*. New York: Dutton.

Anderson, Charles. 1974. *The Political Economy of Social Class*. Englewood Cliffs, N.J.: Prentice-Hall.

Baltzell, E. Digby. 1958. *Philadelphia Gentlemen: The Making of a National Upper Class*. Glencoe, Ill.: Free Press.

Berger, Bennett. 1968. *Working Class Suburb: A Study of Auto Workers in Suburbia*. Berkeley and Los Angeles: University of California Press.

Bott, Elizabeth. 1971. *Family and Social Network*. 2d ed. New York: Free Press.

Braverman, Harry. 1974. *Labor and Monopoly Capitalism*. New York: Monthly Review Press.

Caplovitz, David. 1963. *The Poor Pay More*. New York: Free Press.

CARASA (Committee for Abortion Rights and Against Sterilization Abuse). 1979. *Women Under Attack*. Available from CARASA, 17 Murray St., New York, N.Y. 10007.

Castells, Manuell. 1979. *The Urban Question*. Cambridge: MIT Press.

Domhoff, G. William. 1971. *The Higher Circles*. New York: Vintage.

Ehrenreich, Barbara and Deirdre English. 1978. *For Her Own Good*. Garden City, N.Y.: Doubleday.

Ewin, Stewart. 1976. "Captains of Consciousness." New York: McGraw-Hill.

Fee, Terry. 1976. "Domestic Labor: An Analysis of Housework and Its Relation to the Production Process." *Review of Radical Political Economics* 8(1):1–8.

Fox, Bonnie, ed. 1980. *Hidden in the Household*. Toronto: Women's Press.

Gans, Herbert J. 1962. *The Urban Villagers*. New York: Free Press. 1967. *The Levittowners*. New York: Vintage.

Gilkes, Cheryl. 1983. "From Slavery to Social Welfare: Racism and the Control of Black Women." In Hanna Lessinger and Amy Swerdlow, eds., *Class, Race, and Sex*, pp. 288–300. Boston: Hall.

Goody, Jack. 1972. *The Evolution of the Family*. In Peter Laslett and Richard Wall, eds., *Household and Family in Past Time*, pp. 103–124. Cambridge: Cambridge University Press.

Gordon, David. 1977. "Capitalism and the Roots of the Urban Crisis." In Roger E. Alcaly and David Mermelstein, eds., *The Fiscal Crisis of American Cities*, pp. 82–112. New York: Vintage.

Gordon, Linda. 1976. *Woman's Body, Woman's Rights*. New York: Grossman.

Gutman, Herbert. 1976. *The Black Family in Slavery and Freedom, 1750–1925*. New York: Pantheon.

Haley, Alex. 1976. *Roots*. Garden City, N.Y.: Doubleday.

Hannerz, Ulf. 1969. *Soulside: Inquiries Into Ghetto Life and Culture*. New York: Columbia University Press.

Hartmann, Heidi. 1981. "The Family as the Locus of Gender, Class, and Political Struggle: The Example of Housework." *Signs* 6(3):366–394.

Harvey, David. 1973. *Social Justice and the City*. Baltimore: Johns Hopkins University Press.

Hayden, Dolores. 1981a. *The Grand Domestic Revolution*. Cambridge: MIT Press.

—— 1981b. "Domestic Work and Women's Neighborhood Cooperatives in the United States and Europe, 1870–1930." Paper presented at the Fifth Berkshire Conference on the History of Women, Vassar College, June.

Hoffman, William. 1971. *David: Report on a Rockefeller*. Secaucus, N.J.: Lyle Stuart.

Howe, Louise Kapp, ed. 1970. *The White Majority: Between Power and Affluence*. New York: Random House.

Howell, Joseph T. 1973. *Hard Living on Clay Street*. Garden City, N.Y.: Anchor/Doubleday.

Hunter, Allen. 1981. "In the Wings: New Right Organization and Ideology." *Radical America* 15(½):113–140.

Jones, Gareth Stedman. 1974. "Working-Class Culture and Working-Class Politics in London, 1870–1900." *Journal of Social History* 8:460–508.

Kasson, John F. 1978. *Amusing the Millions: Coney Island at the Turn of the Century.* New York: Hill and Wang.

Kelly, Joan. 1979. "The Doubled Vision of Feminist Theory." *Feminist Studies* 5(1):216–227.

Komarovsky, Mirra. 1962. *Blue Collar Marriage.* New York: Vintage.

Ladner, Joyce. 1971. *Tomorrow's Tomorrow.* Garden City, N.Y.: Anchor/Doubleday.

Liebow, Elliot. 1967. *Tally's Corner.* Boston: Little, Brown.

Malos, Ellen, ed. 1980. *The Politics of Housework.* London: Allison and Busby.

Marcus, Steven. 1974. *Engels, Manchester, and the Working Class.* New York: Vintage.

Mounin, Georges. 1980. "The Semiology of Orientation in Urban Space." *Current Anthropology* 21(4):491–501.

Oliker, Stacey. 1981. "Abortion and the Left: The Limits of "Pro-Family" Politics." *Socialist Review* 56:71–96.

Otto, Luther B. 1975. "Class and Status in Family Research." *Journal of Marriage and the Family* 37:315–332.

Petchesky, Rosalind. 1980. "Reproductive Freedom: Beyond 'A Woman's Right to Choose.' " *Signs* 5(4):661–685.

—— 1981. "Antiabortion, Antifeminism, and the Rise of the New Right." *Feminist Studies* 7(2):206–246.

—— 1984. *Abortion and Women's Choice.* New York: Longman.

Pleck, Elizabeth. 1976. "Two Worlds in One." *Journal of Social History* 10:178–195.

Rainwater, Lee. 1970. *Behind Ghetto Walls: Black Families in a Federal Slum.* Chicago: Aldine.

Rapp, Rayna, Ellen Ross, and Renate Bridenthal. 1979. "Examining Family History." *Feminist Studies* 5(1):174–200.

Rapp, Rayna and Ellen Ross. N.d. "Private Families, Public Problems" (manuscript).

Reagan, Barbara B. and Martha Blaxall, eds. 1976. "Women and the Workplace." *Signs,* vol. 1, no. 3, part 2.

Ross, Ellen. 1982. " 'Fierce Questions and Taunts': Married Life in Working Class London, 1870–1914." *Feminist Studies* 8(3):575–602.

Rubin, Lillian Breslow. 1976. *Worlds of Pain: Life in the Working Class Family.* New York: Basic.

Ryan, Joseph, ed. 1973. *White Ethnics: Life in Working Class America.* Englewood Cliffs, N.J.: Prentice-Hall.

Ryan, Mary P. 1979. "The Power of Women's Networks: A Case Study of Female Moral Reform in Antebellum America." *Feminist Studies* 5(1):66–86.

Schneider, David M. and Raymond T. Smith. 1973. *Class Differences and Sex Roles in American Kinship and Family Structure.* Englewood Cliffs, N.J.: Prentice-Hall.

Seifer, Nancy. 1973. *Absent from the Majority: Working Class Women in America.* Middle America Pamphlet Series, National Project on Ethnic America, American Jewish Committee, New York.

—— 1976. *Nobody Speaks for Me: Self-Portraits of American Working Class Women.* New York: Simon and Schuster.

Sennett, Richard and Jonathan Cobb. 1972. *The Hidden Injuries of Class.* New York: Knopf.

Sexton, Patricia Cayo and Brendan Sexton. 1971. *Blue Collars and Hard Hats.* New York: Vintage.

Scanzoni, John. 1971. *The Black Family in Modern Society.* Boston: Allyn and Bacon.

Shostack, Arthur B. 1969. *Blue Collar Life*. New York: Random House.

Spatial Dimension of History, The. 1980. *Radical History Review*, Special Issue (March), no. 21.

Stack, Carol. 1974. *All Our Kin: Strategies for Survival in a Black Community*. New York: Harper and Row.

Stansell, Christine. 1982. "Women, Children, and the Uses of the Streets—Class and Gender Conflict in New York City, 1850–1860." *Feminist Studies* 8(2):309–335.

Staples, Robert, ed. 1971. *The Black Family: Essays and Studies*. Belmont, Calif.: Wadsworth.

Szymanski, Alfred. 1972. "Trends in the American Class Structure." *Socialist Revolution* (July–August), no. 10.

Tabb, William and Larry Sawers, eds. 1978. *Marxism and the Metropolis*. New York: Oxford University Press.

Terkel, Studs. 1972. *Working*. New York: Pantheon.

Tilly, Louise A. and Joan W. Scott. 1978. *Women, Work, and Family*. New York: Holt, Rinehart, and Winston.

U.S. Bureau of the Census. 1974. *Statistical Abstract of the U.S.*, pp. 221f.

Valentine, Charles. 1968. *Culture and Poverty: Critique and Counter-Proposals*. Chicago: University of Chicago Press.

Veblen, Thorstein. 1953. *The Theory of the Leisure Class*. New York: New American Library.

Weinbaum, Batya and Amy Bridges. 1976. "The Other Side of the Paycheck: Monopoly Capital and the Structure of Consumption" *Monthly Review* 28, No. 3, 88–103.

Williams, Raymond. 1973. *The Country and the City*. New York: Oxford University Press.

Wilmott, Peter and Michael Young. 1957. *Family and Kinship in East London*. London: Tavistock.

"Women and the American City." 1980. Special Supplement, *Signs*, vol. 5, no. 3.

Yanagisako, Sylvia J. 1977. "Women-Centered Kin Networks in Urban, Bilateral Kinship." *American Ethnologist* 4(2):207–226.

Zukin, Sharon. 1980. "A Decade of the New Urban Sociology." *Theory and Society* 9:575–601.

11. Work and Women's Liberation: A Case Study of Garment Workers

Helen I. Safa

As increasing numbers of women enter the labor force in the United States, a substantial amount of research has been directed toward the impact of women's work on family life and the status of women generally. Although most of the research in this area has been conducted by sociologists, anthropologists can make an important contribution by questioning some of the major assumptions on which this research is based. By bringing to their material the comparative and holistic framework on which anthropology is based, anthropologists tend to be far more skeptical of universalistic norms regarding the "liberating" effects of wage labor on women in the United States or elsewhere.

There are at least two principal and contradictory theories regarding the "liberating" effects of wage labor on women, both of which will be examined here. The first stems from the modernization theory propounded by structural-functionalists who argue that incorporation into wage labor brings women greater self-fulfillment, economic independence, and authority within the home. Modernists postulate that working wives contribute to a more egalitarian form of family life, with decreased dependence on the man's income earning capacity (e.g., Blood and Wolfe 1960; Goode 1970; Shorter 1973). However, most of these suppositions are based on studies of middle-class women, who are relatively free to choose whether they wish to be employed or not and who also have a wider range of jobs open to them than working-class women, who continue to be confined to poorly paid, dead-end jobs. This ignores the fact that the great majority of working women in the United States are still forced to seek employment out of economic need, either to supplement the inadequate wages of their husbands or, in the case of female-headed households, to support the family entirely. In 1976, for example, 84 percent of the women in the labor force either supported themselves or were married to men earning under $15,000 per year (Zaretsky 1978:215). Thus, it is not just whether women work or not, but the reasons why they work and the kind of jobs they have which condition the effect of employment on women's status within the home and in the larger society.

While the structural-functionalists emphasize the autonomy which women gain from wage labor, Marxists applaud the entrance of women into the labor force for another reason. Following Marx and Engels, some Marxists feel that wage labor is the best way of overcoming the isolation and alienation of the housewife, and of promoting class consciousness in women. Liberation through work is thus largely defined as increasing politicalization and integration of women into the class struggle.

How "liberating," in fact, is wage labor upon women, in either the Marxist or structural-functionalist framework? Do working women enhance their status or authority in the household and in the larger society as a result of paid employment? Do they become more conscious of their own subordinate status as women and as members of an exploited working class? How, in short, does long-term paid employment alter women's perceptions of inequality and subordination in the home, in the workplace, and in the larger society?

This paper will attempt to answer this question by examining data gathered in 1977 on one group of eighty women who represent approximately a 20 percent sample of production workers in a fairly large garment plant in New Jersey.[1] I concentrated on one group of women, all employed in the same industry, in order to demonstrate the importance for female employment of such factors as the kind of work women do, the reason they are employed, the length of time they are employed, and the class origin, race, age, marital status, and other characteristics of the women workers. I will suggest that the impact of wage labor on women cannot be studied in isolation from these factors, and that in certain cases, paid work may actually reinforce traditional patterns and values rather than "liberating" women.

The garment plant we studied is located in a small, industrial city then numbering 72,000 with a working-class history dating back to the start of large-scale industrialization and the concurrent increase in immigration at the end of the nineteenth century. At the time of this study, 42 percent of all jobs in the city were still in the manufacturing sector (Goodman 1978:32). However, the area was experiencing a marked economic decline, characteristic of the steady withdrawal of industry from the Northeast in the 1970's. As a result of this deindustrialization, due largely to relocation overseas and to the Sunbelt, 39 percent of the large, established manufacturing plants in the Northeast closed between 1970 and 1976 (Bluestone and Harrison 1982:32). As in the plant studied here, the loss of jobs for both men and women in the aging industrial belt of the Northeast is depriving these working-class communities of the economic base which has sustained their distinct life-style (see Nash 1985).

Deindustrialization also has a debilitating effect on class consciousness and worker solidarity. It places women and men workers in an extremely vulnerable position, and has led to increasing unemployment, lower wages, and a sharp drop in union membership in the manufacturing sector. Conditions in the garment industry have worsened in the 1980's, since this study was conducted. Nearly a quarter-million jobs have been lost in the garment industry since 1980, and in 1984, imports accounted for one-third of all apparel consumed in the United States (Gist 1986). Apparel was one of the first sectors to internationalize, but since then similar cutbacks are affecting many other industries in the United States, including heavy industries such as automobiles and steel.

In urban anthropology it is extremely important that we become more aware of these international and national level processes that have a decisive impact on the lives of urban communities. A focus on urban workers makes these linkages more readily apparent than the traditional anthropological technique of studying bounded residential communities. For example, it became clear early in the study that in order to understand the attitudes and behavior of garment workers, we had to become informed about the changing structure of production of the industry in the United States (size of firms, level of technology and capital investment, etc.) as well as the kinds of women recruited to work in this industry in different historical periods. Therefore, before proceeding with an analysis of the data collected, the structure of production and worker recruitment in this industry will be discussed.

The Garment Industry

The apparel industry, which includes women's and men's clothing, is the largest industrial employer of women in the United States. It has remained far more labor intensive than other types of manufacturing, because of frequent and rapid shifts in style which limit the degree of technological change, especially in the sewing process. Because of fierce competition and the need for flexibility, only large manufacturing plants such as the one studied here engage in the full range of production, which in other firms is divided between jobbers who design and sell and contractors who sew. In 1974, roughly half the plants in the industry employed fewer than twenty workers, who are generally small contractors (NACLA 1977:5–7). The extent of competition in the industry can be judged by the fact that in 1978, 18 percent of apparel firms in New York City were in their first year of operation, while 20 percent went out of business during the year (NACLA 1979:38).

One way of meeting competition in the apparel industry is by keeping wages down. The apparel industry pays lower wages than any other major industry group in the United States, and is also subject to periodic layoffs and slowdowns (NACLA 1977:8). Like the women studied here, most women are employed as semiskilled operators, with average wages of $3.86 an hour in New York City in 1979 which, in terms of real income, represents a decrease over the decade (Waldinger 1985:335). This wage, while higher than in other areas, is less than half of what the Bureau of Labor Statistics said was needed as a lower-level budget for a family of four to survive in New York (NACLA 1979:38). In our sample, weekly wages ranged from 100 to over $160, depending on piecework. Though some garment workers apparently support a family on this wage,[2] in our sample most nonmarried women either live alone or with grown children or another relative (most likely a sister) who is also employed. The wages in the garment industry, then, are designed to be supplemental and force the women to look to their husbands or other sources of income for support.

There is almost no possibility of advancement in the garment industry. Workers can increase their wages through the speed and skill of their piecework, and therefore prefer to stay on one operation, no matter how monotonous, rather than be switched from one job to another, as often happens during slack periods. All operators are paid the same base rates and all workers earn this rate, regardless of years of service. Naturally, this induces considerable turnover in the garment industry, particularly in the smaller, nonunionized shops which offer no security of employment (Waldinger 1985:341). However, in the garment plant studied here, which is larger and unionized, almost three-fourths of the women sampled had been working in the same plant since the 1950s, and for many, it was their first and only source of employment.

One of the reasons this plant contained a high percentage of stable, long-term (and also older) women workers is that it had not hired many production workers since the mid 1950s, when it opened branch plants in West Virginia and later in Puerto Rico. Rather than shutting down completely, as some plants have done, the company has been following a slow process of attrition leaving them with older, long-term employees. The remaining women have been shifted out of production into shipping and distribution so that today all production takes place in its branch plants, which have also been opened in other areas overseas. This insecurity of employment is a basic cause of concern and dissatisfaction among the women and reinforces their dependency on management, which could threaten them with total shutdown. It adds to the already paternalistic quality of most garment shops, with a largely female work force presided over by male management, thus replicating the authority pattern of the traditional patriarchal family.

The union, the ILGWU (International Ladies Garment Workers Union), is also male-dominated and maintains a highly paternalistic style toward its members, emphasizing services and benefits like medical care, paid vacations, etc., over higher wages and worker militancy (NACLA 1979:37). Though known for its former militancy and radicalism, the ILGWU appears to have adopted a more cautious, restrictive policy, particularly in regard to wages, in a desperate attempt to keep the garment industry in New York City (Hill 1974:388). The union has lost much of its power to negotiate, as union membership dropped 14 percent between 1968 and 1974, with a loss of 28,000 members in 1974–75 alone (NACLA 1977:17).

Though the apparel industry is still the largest manufacturing industry in New York City, the City's share in the industry nationwide has declined precipitously from 41 percent in 1940 to less than 15 percent in

1979 (NACLA 1979:35), principally as a result of the movement of production to cheaper wage areas in the South and West (e.g., Los Angeles)
and also abroad to Asia, Latin America, and the Caribbean. Imports
totaled $8 billion in 1978 and were expected to amount to 22 percent of
the United States market in 1979 (*ibid.:*37). The result has been a declining real wage rate, especially in relation to rapid inflation, and increasing insecurity of employment.

It would seem, then, that the conditions of work in the garment
industry reinforce the subordination of women in the workplace. The
garment industry pays poorly, offers no chance of advancement, and is
increasingly insecure as production is moved abroad. Management and
union relationships with workers are also highly paternalistic, in part
stemming from the history of recruitment into the garment industry,
which will be examined in the next section.

Types of Workers Recruited

The garment industry has traditionally provided a principal source of
employment for immigrant women, beginning with Jewish women in
the late nineteenth century and continuing with Italian, Polish, and
other East European women (cf. Stein 1977), while today Hispanic and
Asian women constitute the latest-growing proportion of the work
force, at least in New York City (NACLA 1977:7). Immigrant women
were attracted to the garment industry because it did not require a
knowledge of English and often permitted them to work at home, although they were paid at exploitative piecework rates (cf. Cohen 1977).
In addition, immigrant women often possessed the sewing skills necessary for work in the garment industry, which gives only minimal on-the-
job training, and in which wages largely depend on the skill and speed
of the operator.

In contrast to the newer immigrants, most of the women we interviewed were second-generation Europeans, whose parents came from
Italy, Poland, or other East European countries. They pride themselves
considerably on their sewing skills, which set them apart from most
routine factory work. Nearly three-fourths of the women interviewed
were white and most of them were Roman Catholic. Most of them (71.2
percent) have lived in the area all their lives or arrived as children, while
over two-thirds were born in New Jersey. Many immigrant families
were attracted to this area earlier in the century by the availability of

manual jobs for men on the docks or in the burgeoning oil and chemical industry (much of which has now shut down). Though surrounded by black and Hispanic communities, the town in which the plant is located has largely retained its white ethnic working-class character. Nearly all (95 percent) of our respondents had relatives living nearby, chiefly siblings whom they see almost daily. Most of their brothers and sisters were also in blue-collar jobs.

Over 80 percent of the white women were hired at this plant in the 1950s or earlier, before the reduction in production took place. Over half started working before they were eighteen, often before they completed high school. Some starting working during the Depression in the 1930s, and 70 percent were still working at the same job.

Nearly 70 percent of these white women were over fifty years of age. Most of them married, usually between the ages of twenty and twenty-five (earlier if they were not working), but a good number remained single, and some were widowed. Today the white women in this plant break down into two major groups: a younger, married group and an older group of single and formerly married women, or, in most cases, widows. Single and formerly married women constituted nearly half the entire sample, and either lived alone or with their children (if formerly married) or other relatives, usually a sister (if single). Thus, households of these workers tended to be very small, with a median household size of approximately 2.15 persons, and over half consisting of one or two persons. Even in the case of married or formerly married women, few had more than one or two children, many of whom were grown and living apart.

Marital status was an important determinant of total family income, since it coincided with an increased number of wage earners in the family. Thus, 73 percent of married couples had annual incomes of $8,000 or more, compared with 27 percent of single and formerly married women. Where there were two wage earners in the household, 55 percent had an annual income of over $10,000, whereas two-thirds of the households with a single wage earner had annual incomes below $8,000 (table 11.1). Only one-fifth of the households studied here had ever been on welfare, which is generally shunned as a mark of low status.

Annual incomes were almost identical in the white and nonwhite group sampled here (table 11.2), though median family size among blacks and Hispanics was somewhat larger (2.71), thus resulting in

Table 11.1. Annual Family Income by Number of Wage Earners in Household

Annual Family Income	Number of Wage Earners in Household			
	One	Two	Three or More	Row Total
Under $5,000	3	4	3	10
	30.0	40.0	30.0	15.2
	12.5	13.8	23.1	
$5,000–$7,999	13	4	3	20
	65.0	20.0	15.0	30.3
	54.2	13.8	23.1	
$8,000–$9,999	5	5	2	12
	41.7	41.7	16.7	18.2
	20.8	17.2	15.4	
$10,000– $15,999	2	10	2	14
	14.3	71.4	14.3	21.2
	8.3	34.5	15.4	
$16,000 and over	1	6	3	10
	10.0	60.0	30.0	15.2
	4.2	20.7	23.1	
Column total	24	29	13	66[a]
	36.4	43.9	19.7	100.0

Note: Figures in cells (here and in following tables) represent number, row percentage, and column percentage respectively.
[a] Total n refers to total number responding to question rather than to total number of women interviewed.

slightly lower per capital incomes. Their salaries were also lower, with 60 percent earning less than $120 weekly compared with 35 percent of the white workers, a good number of whom earned $160 or more a week. This statistic may be partially explained by the fact that they had not worked in the plant as long as the white women. Few black and Hispanic women were hired before the 1950s. They arrived in the area at this time, generally as adults over the age of twenty, in contrast to white workers who were generally lifelong residents. Because of the relative recency of their arrival, fewer black and Hispanic women had relatives living in the area. Fewer of them also owned their own homes, which represents a major investment in white working-class families, with some houses passing from parents to children, or relatives sharing a two-family house.

Table 11.2. Annual Family Income by Race

Annual Family Income	Race[a]		
	White	Black, Hispanic	Row Total
Under $5,000	8	2	10
	80.0	20.0	14.9
	14.8	15.4	
$5,000–$7,999	16	4	20
	80.0	20.0	29.9
	29.6	30.8	
$8,000–$9,999	10	2	12
	83.3	16.7	17.9
	18.5	15.4	
$10,000–$15,999	11	4	15
	73.3	26.7	22.4
	20.4	30.8	
$16,000 and over	9	1	10
	90.0	10.0	14.9
	16.7	7.7	
	54	13	67
Column total	80.6	19.4	100.0

[a]Hispanics are better referred to as an ethnic group, but have here been grouped with blacks as a racial group in order to distinguish the impact of minority-group status on attitudes and behavior.

The sharpest racial differences in this sample occur in terms of age and marital status, which may be more important determinants of attitudes and values than race, per se. The black and Hispanic women tended to be younger; 62 percent were under fifty, compared with half that percentage among whites. Almost all the black and Hispanic women had married, but one-third were divorced or widowed. Like white women, most black and Hispanic women had only one or two children, though many women came from much larger households (for a discussion of the fertility implications of female employment, see Safa 1983). All the single women in the garment factory were white, and most of them lived alone on very small incomes. Many of them had cared for their parents in their old age and continued to live in their parents' home, which they inherited after their parents' death.

While the parents of our white respondents were, for the most part,

European immigrants, most of the parents of blacks and Hispanics were born in the southern United States or the Caribbean. Most parents in both groups had a grade school education, but a number of the white European parents had no schooling. Fathers were primarily employed in blue-collar jobs, but a small group were self-employed, either as small retail store owners in the case of white Europeans or as small farmers in the case of blacks and Hispanics. Most women in both groups came from intact families, though a higher percentage of fathers of black and Hispanic women died when they were young.

Despite these differences, the socioeconomic status of the white and black and Hispanic women in our sample is similar. All work at the same occupation and have generally comparable educational levels, with the greatest number having attended high school or completed high school. In both cases, their husbands are also employed predominantly in blue-collar jobs, generally making over $200 a week, with the result that annual family income is almost identical (table 11.2). In terms of income, occupation, education, and residence, both groups belong to the stable working class.

The long-term stability of marriage, residence, and occupation for most of these women is an important determinant of their attitudes toward work, the family, and the larger society, as we shall see in the following pages. The study sample cannot be considered representative of the garment industry as a whole, since the number of black and Hispanic women is very small, and they come from higher educational and class backgrounds than most garment workers.[3] The total absence of households headed by women with younger children attests to this fact. Instead, the sample should be considered representative of an older, predominantly white generation of garment workers, who have worked in the industry for a long time. As such, they offer us a unique opportunity to examine the impact of long-term female employment on women's attitudes toward inequality in the home, in the workplace, and in the larger society.

Attitudes Toward Work

In examining attitudes toward work, it is important to remember that most of the women are older, white, and have worked in the industry a long time. Does long-term employment lead to increased worker solidarity? Or does the advanced age of long-term employees militate against a heightened sense of discrimination and subordination on the job? How does this relate to job commitment?

As might be expected, age and length of employment correlate strongly with a woman's future work plans. Nearly 80 percent of the women over fifty are planning to continue working until retirement, although most of these older women would stay home if they lost their present job. Looking at the total sample, however, 65 percent of the women would look for another job, indicating a very strong work commitment among these women. Ninety percent of the formerly married women indicate they would look for another job if they lost their present employment, reflecting a greater economic need among these women. Over 75 percent of them are also over fifty.

While 70 percent of the women interviewed expressed satisfaction with their present job, those dissatisfied tended to be among the short-term employees, nonwhite and with higher educational backgrounds. Thus, over half of the black and Hispanic women indicated dissatisfaction with their present job compared with 21.4 percent of the white women, no doubt relating in part to their lower wages. Half of those women who completed high school were dissatisfied compared with about one-fifth of those women with less education. As would be expected, there was a strong correlation between dissatisfaction with present job and negative perception of changes at the plant in the time they had been working there; 80 percent of those dissatisfied felt that the work situation had worsened, largely because of reduction in production and consequent layoffs, switches between jobs, and declining job security.

Dissatisfaction with garment work was expressed primarily in the desire to find another job, rather than in increased worker solidarity in their current employment. Thus, nearly half of the black and Hispanic women said they had thought of looking for another job compared with 28.8 percent of the white women. Seventy percent of black and Hispanic women expressed an interest in office work, reflecting higher educational levels and occupational aspirations in this group.[4] Whereas 63.2 percent of the white women thought that factory jobs were good for women, one-half the black and Hispanic women rejected this notion. It would appear that most white women, particularly the older, long-term employees, have resigned themselves to staying in their current job until they retire. As one older white garment worker who had been employed in the plant for the last thirty years complained: "The skills we have now, we can't use anywhere else. . . . Where do we go from here? . . .

The young girls who come to work here don't last. But we stay on for our pensions. What choice do we have?"

It might be thought that such traditional women would reject the notion of married women with children working. However, the work ethic is so strong in these women that over three-fourths of them feel that married women with children should work. This belief is even more prevalent among married women, many of whom themselves managed to raise children while they worked, usually with the aid of female relatives. Prior to the mid-1950s, when this factory was in full production, the management made various concessions to women with children, including early dismissals to allow them to be home when the children came home from school, and temporary layoffs during summer vacations and for illness, pregnancy, and other family problems. As one older white woman told me proudly: "My son never knew that I worked!" She was proud, not of her job, but of her ability to keep a job and still fulfill her obligations as a mother.

Women were asked if a woman with young children, whose husband had abandoned her, should work or go on welfare. Again, a majority of our respondents felt that the woman should work, reflecting the strong stigma against welfare, in both white and nonwhite groups. This sentiment was even more prevalent among older women because of their increased fear of welfare dependency. Work differentiates these older, often financially insecure women from the welfare underclass, and even if it conflicts with other strong values, such as a woman's concern for her children, the work ethic is generally paramount.

As we would expect, black and Hispanic women were somewhat more sensitive to sexual discrimination on the job than were white women, who had been less subject to other forms of discrimination. Over half of the black and Hispanic women felt that women had a harder time finding a job than men, while nearly 70 percent of the white women rejected this notion. Most women, especially blacks and Hispanics, also felt that men are better paid for the same work than women, whereas almost all women believed in equal pay for equal work.

While most of our respondents were in favor of the Equal Rights Amendment, especially the better educated, only 20 percent of these women felt that legislation was the most effective way for women to get ahead. Even fewer placed their faith in unions. In general, there was a rejection of strategies implying collective action, such as unions or legislation, in favor of more individualistic approaches, such as education. When asked whether education, unions, or legislation is the most effective way for women to get ahead, almost 60 percent of the women cited education, and most felt that they would have gone much further with more schooling. The strong belief in education is curious, because as we shall see, it appears to have had little impact on our respondents' socioeconomic status, as measured by income or class identification.

Family and Sex Roles

It would seem from the foregoing that paid wage labor has hardly been conducive to class consciousness and worker solidarity in these women. Their attitudes toward work demonstrate a strong traditionalism manifested in a firm belief in the value of hard work, education, and other individualistic values. Is this traditionalism also evident in their family life? Has their concept of gender roles within the family changed as a result of their long years of labor?[5]

It is clear that paid wage labor has had a positive effect on how these women think about themselves. Self-image had improved in nearly 70 percent of these working women, most noting that they felt more independent, were better informed, dressed better, etc. However, the sense of independence which employment conveys to women did not appear to have a strong impact on household authority patterns. Almost 80 percent of the married women interviewed rejected the notion that working had given them more authority, many noting that they had always shared decision making with their husbands and that work had made little difference.[6] In fact, less than one-fourth of the married women said that their husbands made most of the important decisions; the rest responded that decisions were shared or that they alone made them, suggesting that working-class family patterns are not as patriarchal as has been assumed. However, there were racial differences. Less than half the married white women noted that working generally gave women more authority, compared with 70 percent of black and Hispanic women, who evidently had a stronger sense of economic autonomy. Nevertheless, nearly all the married women felt that it was easier for a woman to leave her husband if she were working, so work at least strengthens women's feeling of financial independence. However, the small number of divorced women (four) suggests that most of these women are strongly committed to marriage, even though most reported that they argued frequently with their husbands, and some had even thought of separating.

Women generally earned much less than their husbands, most of whom made over $200 a week unless they had retired. Most women continued to regard their husbands as the primary breadwinners, but resented the notion that they only worked for "pin money." Their wages were considered essential to the family's well-being and were rarely spent on their own personal needs. Most of the women's wages were "pooled" with their husbands' to further family interests such as the children's education or buying a house, furnishings, or a car. In most cases husbands and wives shared the decision on how to spend their wages. Paid labor did not appear to be a major threat to the man's authority, as has been reported in other working-class families (see Rubin 1976: 174–184). Nearly three-fourths of the married women reported that their husbands did not object to their working because both realized that the family needed the extra income.

Most of these working women continued to carry a full load of household chores, including cooking, cleaning, shopping, laundry, and paying the bills. While nearly three-fourths of the husbands helped with housework, many married women still felt that the home was their primary responsibility, and denied the need for outside help from their husbands or anyone else.

The respondents' traditional view of gender equality is reflected in the fact that nearly 60 percent of the white women felt that education was more important for men, compared with 30 percent of blacks and Hispanics, half of whom felt that education was equally important for both sexes (table 11.3). If forced to make a choice on whom to send to college, most white women would send the boy, while black and Hispanic women showed no marked sexual preferences. While these racial and ethnic differences are not statistically significant, they are supported by other literature, which suggests greater gender equality in black families (cf. Ladner 1971; Stack 1974).

If one compares the actual educational attainment of sons and daughters in these working-class families, however, they are very similar, with a good number of both sexes having gone to college or graduate school. There is a strong correlation between educational and occupational attainment, particularly among daughters, where almost all those who went to college or graduate school are in white-collar jobs

Table 11.3. Importance of Education for Men and Women by Race

Education More Important	Race White	Black, Hispanic	Row Total
	35	6	41
For the man	85.4	14.6	51.9
	59.3	30.0	
	2	4	6
For the woman	33.3	66.7	7.6
	3.4	20.2	
	22	10	32
Equally important for both	68.8	31.3	40.5
	37.3	50.0	
Column total	59	20	79
	74.7	25.3	100.0

(table 11.4). Most of these women reject factory work for their sons and even more so for their daughters.

While these women remain quite traditional with respect to the household division of labor, they seem to be more egalitarian than most nonworking women. This is particularly true of younger black and Hispanic women. Women control their own salaries, most of which, however, is spent on the family. Husbands share their wages and decision-making authority with their wives, and do not appear very authoritarian or very threatened by their wives' working. More than anything else, the ability to earn a living seems to enable women to feel more financially independent and to be more willing to accept responsibility for important household decisions, and to feel they can leave if the marital situation becomes intolerable.

Social Mobility and Class Identification

Now that I have examined respondents' perceptions of inequality in the home and in the workplace, I shall look at how they perceive themselves in relation to the larger society. With what class group do they identify themselves and their children? What is their degree of class consciousness as measured by their view of and participation in the

Table 11.4. Educational and Occupational Levels of Daughters

| First Daughter's Education[a] | First Daughter's Occupation | | | |
	White collar	Blue collar	Unemployed	Row Total
	5	5	0	10
High school	50.0	50.0	0	43.5
	31.3		0	
	9	1	1	11
College	81.8	9.1	9.1	47.8
	56.3	16.7	100.0	
	2	0	0	2
Graduate work	100.0	0	0	8.7
	17.5	0	0	
Column total	16	6	1	23
	69.6	26.1	4.3	100.0

[a]Data was recorded for first-born daughter only.

political process and their attitude toward social problems such as inflation and unemployment?

Though most Americans describe themselves as middle class, one-half of our respondents identified as working class, with about one-third identifying as middle class and 10 percent as poor. The group that identified as middle class tended to be white (88.9 percent) married (59.3 percent), and have higher family incomes (table 11.5). The strong correlation with income is shown by the fact that 80 percent of the families with incomes of $16,000 or over identified as middle class, whereas almost all of those who identified as working class had incomes below this amount, while those who identified as poor generally fell below $8,000 annually.

As I have shown previously (table 11.1), income is highly dependent on the number of wage earners in the household, which helps explain the high percentage of married couples who identified as middle class. However, income does not explain the low percentage of blacks and Hispanics who identified as middle class (11 percent), since income among whites and nonwhites was almost identical (table 11.2). Instead it would seem that blacks and Hispanic women factory workers are more likely to identify as working class regardless of income level.[7]

Table 11.5. Respondents' Class Identification by Annual Family Income

Class Identification	Annual Family Income					
	Under $5,000	$5,000–$7,999	$8,000–$9,999	$10,000–$15,999	$16,000 +	Row Totals
Middle class	0	6	6	4	8	24
	0.0	25.0	25.0	16.7	33.3	36.4
	0.0	31.6	50.0	26.7	80.0	
Working class	9	9	6	10	2	36
	25.0	25.0	16.7	27.8	5.6	54.5
	90.0	47.4	50.0	66.7	20.0	
Very poor	1	4	0	1	0	6
	16.7	66.7	0.0	16.7	0.0	9.1
	10.0	21.1	0.0	6.7	0.0	
Column totals	10	19	12	15	10	66
	15.2	28.8	18.2	22.7	15.2	100.0

In general, occupation or education does not appear to be as significant an indicator of class status for these working-class women as income. For example, the husband's occupation bears little relationship to perceived class identification. The husbands of our respondents were predominantly blue-collar workers, yet respondents' class identification in these cases is evenly divided between middle class and working class and a few poor. Of course, a large variety of jobs can be classified as blue collar, and status may vary by salary and skill level. Yet clearly the husband's occupation is not the status determinant in working-class, blue-collar families which it is thought to be in middle-class, white-collar families.

There is no significant evidence of upward mobility between respondents and their parents, as judged by the high correlation between perceived class levels of the two generations. Most women perceived themselves as the same class level as their parents, with the highest percentage identifying themselves and their parents as working class (table 11.6). Even most of those who identified as middle class saw their parents at the same class level.

There is some evidence of perceived upward mobility for the children of our respondents. Although parents' and childrens' class level were again strongly correlated, 62.2 percent of the mothers perceived their children as being middle class. Where sons and daughters were in

Table 11.6. Respondents' Class Identification of Self and Parents

Respondents' Class Identification	Parents' Class Identification				
	Upper class	*Middle class*	*Working class*	*Very poor*	*Row total*
Middle class	2	14	3	7	26
	7.7	53.8	11.5	26.9	33.3
	100.0	66.7	8.6	35.0	
Working class	0	6	31	7	44
	0.0	13.6	70.5	15.9	56.4
	0.0	28.6	88.6	35.0	
Very poor	0	1	1	6	8
	0.0	12.5	12.5	75.0	10.3
	0.0	4.8	2.9	30.0	
Column total	2	21	35	20	78
	2.6	26.9	44.9	25.6	100.0

white-collar occupations, they were primarily identified by their mothers as middle class, while blue-collar occupations were again evenly divided between middle class and working class.

Given the apparent upward mobility of most of our respondents' children, we might expect these women to be relatively optimistic regarding the possibilities of social mobility in the United States. However, nearly 70 percent of our respondents, regardless of race, rejected the idea that social mobility is easy in the United States. The minority who felt that mobility is easy usually were married (70 percent), identified as middle class (52 percent), and had annual family incomes of $10,000 or more (60 percent). See table 11.7.

While both racial groups were equally negative regarding mobility in the United States, the reasons given for their negativism were significantly different, with most whites citing the cost of living and most blacks and Hispanics blaming racial discrimination. In addition, whites tended to be divided as to whether it is easier or more difficult now than previously, while the majority of blacks and Hispanics saw it as easier. Undoubtedly, the previous socioeconomic situation of blacks and Hispanics were qualitatively worse, particularly for those migrating from the South and the Caribbean. The civil rights movement and equal opportunity legislation may also have contributed to their optimism.

Table 11.7. Respondents' Views of Mobility by Annual Family Income

View of Mobility	Annual Family Income					
	Under $5,000	$5,000– $7,999	$8,000– $9,999	10,000– $15,999	$16,000 +	Row Total
Mobility	0	5	3	7	5	20
easy in	0.0	25.0	15.0	35.0	25.0	29.9
U.S.	0.0	25.0	25.0	46.7	50.0	
Mobility	10	15	9	8	5	47
difficult	21.3	31.9	19.9	17.0	10.6	70.1
in U.S.	100.0	75.0	75.0	53.3	50.0	
Column	10	20	12	15	10	67
total	14.9	29.9	17.9	22.4	14.9	100.0

Nearly two-thirds of the women interviewed felt that the political parties in this country were not meeting the needs of working women. Even greater dissatisfaction was expressed by older, single, and formerly married women, and most especially by black and Hispanic women, 85 percent of whom expressed their dissatisfaction (table 11.8). Thus, it was generally the most disadvantaged who expressed the greatest dissatisfaction with political parties. Certainly the scant attention paid by political parties to working women in this country in the past decade has not addressed the needs of these disadvantaged groups, but appears to have been more directed toward the needs of the vocal middle class.

The working class is traditionally Democratic, and most women voted for Carter in the 1976 presidential election. Most were quite knowledgeable about local political figures such as the mayor and governor. However, most of these working women felt that they had no time to be involved in extradomestic activities, including politics and labor unions. Although almost all our respondents were members of the ILGWU at the garment plant and most agreed that trade unions have helped working women, less than 40 percent regularly attended union meetings and only 10 percent had ever held a union office.

It appears that most of our respondents had little faith in collective action, through the union or political parties. Though they identified as working class and came out of a classic working-class tradition, their primary goal was to help their children move out of the working class. These goals are essentially individualistic and emphasize personal achieve-

Table 11.8. Respondents' Opinions as to Whether Political Parties Are Meeting Needs of Working Women by Race

Political Parties Helping Women	Race		Row Total
	White	Black, Hispanic	
Yes	21	3	24
	87.5	12.5	33.8
	40.4	15.8	
No	31	16	47
	66.0	34.0	66.2
	59.6	84.2	
Column total	52	19	71
	73.2	26.8	100.0

ments like hard work, a good education, and home ownership. At that time, there was still optimism regarding these goals among our respondents, perhaps because a good number of their children had obtained a higher education and a white-collar job, which they equated with middle-class status. However, upward mobility is clearly not seen as easy in the United States, particularly with continuing problems such as inflation, unemployment, and for blacks and Hispanics, racial discrimination. Our respondents would like to see additional pressure put upon the government to solve these problems, and they certainly did not feel that the political parties were responsive to their needs as working women. However, it appears unlikely that agitation for change in the working conditions in this industry will come from these women, despite their dissatisfaction with the status quo.

In 1960 and again in 1966, the ILGWU local threatened to strike the plant against management's policy of reducing the number of production workers. However, each time the union conceded to more benefits for remaining workers rather than striking (Goodman 1978: 42). Thus, faced with the lack of support from the union, which feared the shutdown of the plant, and declining employment possibilities as production is moved elsewhere, most workers are resigned to the present situation or are looking for jobs elsewhere.

Conclusion

In summary: What has been the impact of the long-term employment of these women garment workers in terms of women's liberation? Is there any evidence that paid wage labor has heightened their sensitivity to subordination and inequality in the home, in the workplace, and in the larger society?

It is difficult to answer these questions conclusively on the basis of a small and limited sample, and in the absence of a sample of nonworking women with whom to compare our respondents. However, it appears that among our respondents, length of time employed has little impact on the variables examined here. It would seem that the possible effect of long-term employment is counteracted by the effects of generational differences regarding sex roles. That is, the long-term employed appear to be the most conservative, but that may simply be a function of their age.[8]

The literature on the working class in the United States generally portrays these families as strongly patriarchal and authoritarian (see Rubin 1976; Rainwater et al. 1959; Komarovsky 1962). Historical accounts of immigrant women in the United States, however, generally substantiate the important economic role played by these women as wage earners and contributors to the family income (Gordon 1978; Cantor and Laurie 1977, Yans McLaughlin 1977). The data presented here suggest that the ideology prevalent in historical accounts of immigrant families that women should work and contribute to the family income continues to be prevalent in these second-generation white ethnic women. There is little indication that these women experience role conflict over working. However, this commitment to work does not diminish their primary identification as wives and mothers. In fact, they are working to contribute to the family's welfare and, in particular, to enhance the life chances of their children through a better education, a better job, etc. Thus, there is little incompatibility between their domestic and wage-earning roles, since they are furthering their family's interests in both capacities (cf. Tilly and Scott 1978).

While not strictly authoritarian, these white working-class families also do not correspond to the egalitarian marriage patterns which modernization theory posited would evolve from wives engaging in paid wage labor. In these working-class families, men continue to be considered the chief breadwinners and women derive their status within the family primarily from their role as wives and mothers rather than as wage-earners. A woman is expected to contribute to the family income, if necessary, but this does not diminish the man's responsibility as bread-winner nor does it threaten his ability to carry out this role, as long as her wages are still considered supplementary. This is reinforced by the fact that these garment workers earn substantially less than their husbands and could not easily support a family on their wages if they tried. Nevertheless, as long as women contribute to the family income, they are likely to share in the authority and decisions of the home, as most of our respondents appear to. In short, despite some changes in decision-making and the household division of labor, most working-class families continue to adhere to a family ideology that emphasizes male authority (see Lamphere 1986).

Black and Hispanic women seem to place greater emphasis on the income-earning capacity of women, as evidenced by their strong belief in equality of education for the sexes, their emphasis on the authority which paid wage labor confers to women, and their greater sensitivity to sexual discrimination in employment. This would appear to indicate stronger cultural support for working women in the black community (Pleck 1978:491), where women have often been called upon to act as chief breadwinners.

It is interesting that as the younger, most recent recruits to the garment industry, black and Hispanic women seem the most dissatisfied, and the most disposed toward change. Thus, their shorter time on the job as well as their lack of integration into the neighborhood (where there appears to have been a conscious attempt to exclude them) would appear to make them less subject to the traditional norms of the white working-class community, in which they are still a distinct minority.

The most conservative of the white women workers in this plant appear to be the older single women, who are among the poorest and the most dependent on their wages for an income. These women have few if any alternatives to working in the garment industry, since for many it is the only work they have ever done and they are too old to learn a new trade. At the same time, they are strongly committed to work in order to maintain a minimum of economic security and in order to prevent becoming dependent on relatives or public welfare. Thus, they are the most threatened by the changes occurring in the garment industry, and the most committed to a maintenance of the status quo.

However, this should not lead us to conclude that paid wage labor has no impact on women's sense of class or sexual subordination. While we have no comparable sample of nonworking women, the women interviewed here appear to be very conscious of problems like inflation, unemployment, racial discrimination, the lack of responsiveness of political parties, and the increasing difficulties of social mobility in the United States. They are also aware of their low wages, declining employment, and worsening conditions in the plant, and some have participated in open protests backed by the ILGWU to support the union's campaign to reduce imports and "look for the union label."

The conditions which foster increased class consciousness and solidarity among working women are still poorly understood. The women studied here are clearly not the militant working-class women Susser (1986) describes who reacted to job instability by organizing their Brooklyn neighborhood to pressure the government to continue providing state-supported services such as daycare, nutrition and fire protection. In contrast, job instability among the women garment workers studied here appears to have weakened their resolve and their capacity for collective action. They reject welfare and other forms of state services which might identify them with the lower class (usually thought of as black). It is clear from this comparison that a great deal more attention needs to be paid to the potential for collective action among women workers, and how this is affected by the neighborhood in which they live, the conditions of the industries where they are employed, and the characteristics of workers recruited into these industries in terms of age, marital status, educational level, race, and class. As I have shown here, any discussion of the impact of wage labor on women must certainly take these factors into account.

Notes

1. Most of the data were collected in 1977 on the basis of one-hour structured interviews conducted in the plants and in the homes of our respondents. The sample was selected on the basis of the length of time employed, broken down by decades and emphasizing the long-term employees.

To increase the percentage of Hispanic and black workers, about 20 interviews were conducted among women employed in a small branch plant of this firm located in a neighboring community of New Jersey. For reasons of confidentiality, the names of the plants and the communities have not been identified.

Because certain groups (e.g., Hispanics and long-term employees) were overrepresented, this sample cannot be considered representative, even of the plants studied.

2. Sol Chaikin, president of the ILGWU, reported that 64 percent of their union workers "had to support or partly support their children, husbands, parents or other relatives in addition to supporting themselves" (1977:331).

3. Black and Hispanic women are actually overrepresented in our sample in terms of the total work force in this plant, since we deliberately interviewed as many of them as possible to see if race or ethnicity made a difference in their backgrounds and attitudes. The small number of black and Hispanic workers in this plant appears to be due largely to the recency of their arrival in the area, when there was no longer a strong demand for garment workers. However, Hill (1974) has also argued that black and Hispanic workers are consciously discriminated against by the ILGWU.

4. The clear preference of black and Hispanic garment workers for office work suggests that they have a more difficult time finding these jobs than white women, and are therefore relegated to lower-paying jobs in the garment industry. This helps explain their high level of dissatisfaction in contrast with older white women who, after many years of employment, prefer to stay in the garment industry, and only 27.6 percent of whom expressed an interest in office work.

5. Most of the responses in this section were taken only from married women, who constitute approximtely half the sample, and therefore only forty-one cases. It is unfortunate that we do not have a nonworking sample with which to compare these women. It is quite likely that in comparison with women who have never worked outside the home, these women would appear less conservative on issues such as ERA, sexual discrimination on the job, and even sex roles.

6. Mullings (personal communication) has suggested that working-class women may be unwilling to admit that work affects household decision-making or authority patterns, since it puts "the husband-wife relationship on an exchange contract rather than 'love-respect' basis" (Rapp 1978). This would tie in with their continued primary identification as wives and mothers, though they have worked much of their adult lives. Thus, these women may actually have more authority in the household than they perceive, or are willing to acknowledge.

7. National data indicate that, on the average, black Americans must have three to four years more education to earn the same median income of white Americans (Perlo 1975). This would help explain why black women with the same income are more likely to identify as working class than white women, and why occupation and education may be less directly related to perceived class identification.

8. Age and length of employment are also correlated with race, so that the youngest, most recently hired workers are also more likely to be black and Hispanic, whom we have seen are less conservative in many respects. This makes it very difficult to draw any adequate conclusions regarding the impact of long-term employment on the militancy of women from this sample. In a similar study of garment workers in Puerto Rico, we have found that older women are generally more militant than younger women (Safa 1985).

References

Bluestone, Barry and Bennett Harrison. 1982. *The Deindustrialization of America*. New York: Basic Books.

Blood, Robert and Donald Wolfe. 1960. *Husbands and Wives*. New York: Free Press.

Cantor, Milton and Bruce Laurie, eds. 1977. *Class, Sex, and the Woman Worker*. Westport, Conn.: Greenwood Press.

Chaikin, Sol. 1977. "Sweatshop: Item 807 Style." In L. Stein, ed., *Out of the Sweatshop*, pp. 329–332. New York: Quadrangle.

Cohen, Miriam, 1977. "Italian-American Women in New York City, 1900–1950: Work and School." In Cantor and Laurie, eds., *Class, Sex, and the Woman Worker*, pp. 120–143.

Gist, 1986. Textile Import Control Program. Washington, D.C.: Bureau of Public Affairs, Dept. of State.

Goode, William J. 1970. *World Revolution and Family Patterns*. New York: Free Press.

Goodman, Charity. 1978. "Growing Old in a Garment Factory: The Effects of Occupational Segregation and Runaway Shops on Working-Class Women." M.A. thesis, Rutgers University, Graduate Program in Anthropology.

Gordon, Michael, ed. 1978. *The American Family in Sociohistorical Perspective*. 2d ed. New York: St. Martin's Press.

Hill, Herbert. 1974. "Guardians of the Sweatshops: The Trade Unions, Racism, and the Garment Industry." In A. Lopez and J. Petras, eds., *Puerto Rico and Puerto Ricans: Studies in Society and History*, pp. 384–416. New York: Wiley.

Komarovsky, Mirra. 1962. *Blue-Collar Marriage*. New York: Vintage.

Ladner, Joyce. 1971. *Tomorrow's Tomorrow: The Black Woman*. Garden City, N.Y.: Anchor.

Lamphere, Louise. 1986. "From Working Daughters to Working Mothers: Production and Reproduction in an Industrial Community." *American Ethnologist* 13(1):118–130.

NACLA (North American Congress on Latin America). 1977. "Capitalist's Flight: The Apparel Industry Moves South." 11(3):2–33.

——1979. "Undocumented Immigrant Workers in New York City." 13(6):2–46.

Nash, June. 1985. "Segmentation of the Work Process in the International Division of Labor." In Steven E. Sanderson, ed., *The Americas in the International Division of Labor*, pp. 253–272. New York: Holmes and Meier.

Perlo, Victor. 1975. *The Economics of Racism*. New York: International Publishers.

Pleck, Elizabeth H. 1978. "A Mother's Wages: Income Earning Among Married Italian and Black Women, 1896–1911." In Nancy F. Cott and Elizabeth H. Pleck, eds. *A Heritage of Her Own: Toward a New Social History of American Women*, pp. 367–392. New York: Simon and Schuster.

Rainwater, Lee, Richard P. Coleman, and Gerald Handel. 1959. *Working-Man's Wife*. New York: MacFadden.

Rapp, Rayna. 1978. "Family and Class in Contemporary America: Notes Toward an Understanding of Ideology." *Science and Society* 42(3):278–300.

Rubin, Lillian Breslow. 1976. *Worlds of Pain: Life in the Working Class Family*. New York: Basic.

Safa, Helen Icken. 1983. "Women, Production, and Reproduction in Industrial Capitalism: A Comparison of Brazilian and U.S. Factory Workers." In June Nash and M. Patricia Fernandez-Kelly, eds., *Women, Men, and International Division of Labor*, pp. 95–116. Albany: State University of New York Press.

——1985. "Female Employment in the Puerto Rican Working Class." In June Nash and Helen Safa, eds., *Women and Change in Latin America*, pp. 84–106. South Hadley, Mass.: Bergin and Garvey.

Shorter, Edward. 1973. *The Making of the Modern Family*. New York: Basic.

Stack, Carol 1974. *All Our Kin*. New York: Harper and Row.

Stein, Leon, ed. 1977. *Out of the Sweatshops: The Struggle for Industrial Democracy*. New York: Quadrangle.

Susser, Ida. 1986. "Political Activity among Working Class Women in a U.S. City." *American Ethnologist* 13(1):108–117.

Tilly, Louise A. and Joan W. Scott. 1978. *Women, Work, and Family.* New York: Holt, Rinehart, and Winston.

Waldinger, Roger. 1985. "Immigration and Industrial Change in the New York City Apparel Industry." In George Borjas and Marta Tienda, eds., *Hispanics in the U.S. Economy,* pp. 323–350. Orlando, Fla.: Academic Press.

Yans-McLaughlin, Virginia. 1977. "Italian Women and Work: Experience and Perception." In Cantor and Laurie, eds., *Class, Sex, and the Woman Worker,* pp. 101–119.

Zaretsky, Eli. 1978. "The Effects of the Economic Crisis on the Family." *In U.S. Capitalism on Crisis,* pp. 209–218. New York: Union for Radical Political Economics.

12. Sterilization Among Puerto Rican Women in New York City: Public Policy and Social Constraints

Iris Lopez

Puerto Rican women have one of the highest rates of sterilization in the world.[1] By 1968, 35.5 percent of the island female population between the ages of fifteen and forty-five had been surgically sterilized (Vasquez-Calzada 1978). In New York City, where Puerto Ricans comprise 61 percent of the Spanish-origin female population, Hispanics have a rate of sterilization seven times greater than that of white women and almost twice that of Afro-American women (New York City Health and Hospital Corporation 1982). Although information is scarce for other cities where Puerto Ricans are concentrated, a recent study revealed that in Hartford, Connecticut, 51 percent of Puerto Rican females of reproductive age were sterilized (Gangalez et al. 1980). Even acknowledging that "contraceptive sterilization" is internationally becoming the most frequently used birth control method, the disproportionate rate of sterilization among Puerto Rican women demands closer examination.

Current trends indicate that all over the world fertility termination is on the rise as a family-planning method. Between 1970 and 1976, the number of couples using sterilization as birth control tripled from 20 to 75 million, surpassing other contraceptive techniques (Newman and Klein 1978). In the United States, where 2 million Puerto Ricans live, sterilization has also grown in popularity. According to a survey undertaken by the Allan Guttmacher Institute, one-third (11.6 million) of fertile women, eighteen to forty-four years of age, rely on the surgical termination of fertility to prevent pregnancy. Out of this proportion, 19 percent of these women were themselves sterilized, while the remainder had partners who were sterilized (*New York Times* 1983).

Unfortunately, these data do not allow us to assess ethnic affiliation and class status of these women—two crucial variables indispensable to a rigorous comparative analysis of the increasing incidence of sterilization among Puerto Rican women in the United States. It is revealing to note, however, that despite the paucity of reliable information, the vast majority of documented cases of sterilization abuse have been found among Hispanic (Rodriguez-Trias 1978), Afro-American (Davis 1981), Native American (CARASA 1979), Chicano (Velez 1978), and poor white (CARASA 1979) women. They, as women, share gender oppression and, as largely confined to the poor and working-class sectors of this country, share class-based discrimination.

These similarities are of key interest. It is undeniable that women in general have had their fertility options limited by the types of contraceptives developed and because they have had to accept much of the burden of population control programs. But while all women have to contend with the problem of birth control, the conditions which might prompt an upper-class woman to get sterilized are substantially different from those of a woman living under the poverty level. Therefore, when considering the factors that affect fertility decisions, class status must be taken into account, since it plays an influential role in determining the number of options available to an individual. In this regard, it appears that the most compelling context for fertility decisions for Puerto Rican females, as with other minority women, is socioeconomic status.

Nevertheless, many social scientists assume that fertile women, irrespective of social conditions, are free to choose whether they want to have children. Scholars who write about women, both here and on the island, argue that when Puerto Rican females opt for sterilization they are exercising free will (Stycos, Hill, and Back 1959). Following this line of thinking, others assert that sterilization is a culturally preferred method of birth control, evident in its "grass-roots demand" (Scrimshaw 1970; Presser 1973). While it is appropriate to consider both psychological and cultural factors surrounding fertility decisions, these authors choose to gloss over the general conditions of poverty, under- or unemployment, and lack of access to quality health services that other writers contend are more influential in determining birth control methods (Henderson 1976; Mass 1976; Ramirez de Arellano and Scheipp 1983; Ramos 1977).

In order to understand why Puerto Rican women have such a high rate of sterilization, this paper attempts to analyze the range of factors that operate simultaneously to actively guide fertility choices among Puerto Rican women in Brooklyn, New York. This approach entails the reinterpretation of the individual as unit of analysis; individual choice is examined within the context of societal pressures that constrain individual options.

Since most of the women studied were born in Puerto Rico and slightly more than 25 percent were sterilized there, a historical account of the sterilization policy on the island is pertinent to understanding present rates among Puerto Rican women living in New York City. In this respect, it is important to keep in view the prolonged migration experience and the long-term U.S. government population policy toward Puerto Ricans, particularly as they relate to the colonial status of Puerto Rico.

The Neo-Malthusian Legacy

The characterization of Puerto Rico as a country plagued by an acute and endemic "problem" of overpopulation has been repeatedly made since the United States began its colonial occupation of this Caribbean island in 1898. In 1901, when the population of the island was approximately one million, the first civilian governor declared that "Porto Rico has plenty of laborers and poor people generally. What the Island needs is men with capital, energy and enterprise." Governor Charles Allen, who prompted with determination the emigration of what he considered excess people, was followed by Governor Arthur Yager, who stated in 1915 that the only effective remedy to the "crowd of surplus population" was the "transfer of larger numbers of Porto Ricans to some other region." Moreover, inspired by Malthus' theory of population growth, Governor Yager justified his policy by invoking the powers of a "great biological law" that "we can neither alter nor repeal" (History Task Force 1982).

Hence, one of the most important chapters in the history of Puerto Rico during the twentieth century has been the constant emigration of its people, promoted by government agencies as a remedy to the alleged chronic population surplus of the island. Almost a quarter-million Puerto Ricans had been uprooted and displaced by this policy by the end of World War II, when a new economic development plan was designed to overcome the widespread poverty and joblessness resulting from an agricultural economy in which four North American corporations had control. By 1930, these four North American sugar corporations dominated Puerto Rico's sugar production. The new plan, "Operation Bootstrap," sought the industrialization of the colony through the investment of foreign capital. It rested, nonetheless, on emigration as an "escape valve" and the extension of other, more permanent methods of population control.

Much of the social analysis of Puerto Rico's population ignores the permanent cessation of reproductive functions as a solution developed to reduce the alleged excess of people. The major focus has been on the long-term and massive migration because it parallels similar experiences worldwide and is a less sensitive topic than the termination of women's fertility.

Sterilization legislation was introduced in Puerto Rico as early as 1937. An examination of the fundamental purpose and background of this legislation reveals a disturbingly close link with the eugenics movement that had emerged in the United States. Just as economic distress led to the passing of eugenics legislation in the United States, social unrest and chronic unemployment in Puerto Rico prompted the transfer of these laws to the island.

The widespread acceptance of sterilization among the medical establishment played a crucial role in its adoption and growth. Doctors, who considered lower-income women too ignorant to effectively use temporary methods of birth control, were instrumental in transforming legislation into practice.

The fact that the pill and IUD were not widely available until the decade of the 1950s further limited women's choices. Even after these mechanical and chemical forms of birth control were developed and tested, Puerto Rican women did not have adequate access to them. As a result of the lack of government support for these methods of family planning and opposition from the Catholic Church and established political groups, these birth control clinics opened and closed erratically.

In addition, abortions were illegal in Puerto Rico until 1973. Despite this, Puerto Rico had a reputation for being an "abortion haven," and through the seventies thousands of women, particularly women from the United States, had abortions in Puerto Rico (Ramirez de Arellano and Scheipp 1983). For local women, however, the lack of legal abortion services narrowed their options and induced large numbers to accept sterilization. Sterilization was legal and socially accepted while abortions were illegal and morally objectionable.

Further, federal funds did not become available for other methods of family planning in Puerto Rico until 1968. Therefore, Puerto Rican women accepted sterilization not through individual decisions based on a variety of choices but because of lack of alternatives. Fertility practices were constrained by the widespread acceptance of sterilization among the medical profession, the government's ambivalence toward other birth control methods, and the sexist orientation of policymakers, all within the context of a colonial economy that created an increasing number of landless people.

As a result of Operation Bootstrap, neo-Malthusian ideology and sterilization policy continued to dominate Puerto Rico's political and social landscape. When in the 1960s economic and social conditions worsened, it became obvious that Operation Bootstrap's industrialization program had not succeeded in producing enough jobs to accommodate all of the displaced agricultural workers. The neo-Malthusian argument of overpopulation was again invoked.

To further aggravate these difficult economic circumstances, adverse economic conditions in the United States caused a reverse migration trend (Hernandez Alvarez 1967). At the same time, large numbers of Dominicans and Cubans migrated to Puerto Rico. Government officials became concerned about this influx of people into an already glutted labor market and the increased demand for social services. It is no surprise that sterilization was seen as the solution for controlling the growth of the island population, and fertility termination programs were intensified (Mass 1976). The demographic effect has been impressive: the rate of natural increase has plummeted from 2.7 percent during the fifties to 1.7 percent in 1980. Equally outstanding is the nearly 40 percent female fertility reduction between 1960 and 1980 (Bonilla and Campos 1983).

In Puerto Rico, then, what appeared as individual choice about migration and sterilization was influenced by the development of capitalism on the island. The policies of the United States and colonial governments were such that migration and sterilization were used as alternate and reinforcing mechanisms of population control. Migration was seen as the temporary method—the escape valve—while sterilization, or "la operación" as it is known colloquially among Puerto Rican women, was considered the final solution. It is within this framework of political, economic, ideological, and social constraints that the nature of women's decisions to be sterilized must be examined.

After four decades of industrialization, massive migration, and large-scale sterilization, Puerto Rico continues to experience widespread poverty, dependency, and an "overpopulation problem." Compounding an official unemployment rate of over 20 percent, two-thirds of the population are considered poor by federal standards, while 60 percent depend on food stamps and other government subsidies for their daily sustenance (Bonilla and Campos 1981).

"La Operación" Continues: Class, Social Policies, and Economic Imperatives

Similarities to the social circumstances on the island are found among Puerto Ricans in New York City. The relocation of this population has not meant any substantial improvement in living or working conditions. Official unemployment levels for Puerto Ricans in New York City fluctuate around 14 percent and are currently rising (Stafford 1985), while 39 percent live under the official poverty level (Bonilla and Campos 1983). In the following section I intend to show how these conditions have contributed to the continued high rate of sterilization among Puerto Rican women.

In 1981, I did a survey of a poor neighborhood in Brooklyn, New York. Of the households with one or more Puerto Rican women over age twenty, 47 percent included one or more sterilized women. Ninety-three percent of the sterilized women were born on the island, but they were sterilized after they migrated to New York between the ages of seventeen and twenty-one. This raises the question, once again, of the extent to which these decisions were strictly voluntary or a response to societal pressure. In posing this issue, it is important to note that these categories are not mutually exclusive, since "individual preference" is influenced by the society in which an individual lives. Therefore, to address the issue of societal effects on fertility decisions, it is necessary to examine the context in which these decisions are made, specifically the social and economic conditions in which these women live.

Prior to examining the conditions that have influenced the fertility decisions of the women in this study, I will discuss both the methodology used to collect the data and some of the problems of doing urban anthropology.

Methodological Problems in Urban Anthropology. In undertaking this study, it was necessary to develop a methodology that would reveal the richness of experience captured by the ethnographic approach while making my findings more broadly generalizable in terms of class and ethnic comparisons. Therefore, several types of techniques were combined. These consisted of participant observation, oral histories, a systematic listing of the residents in the neighborhood, and an in-depth survey of a selected sample of the female population. Intensive interviews were conducted with 128 Puerto Rican women, 85 of whom were sterilized.[2] After spending approximately two months in the field doing participant observation, I developed an in-depth questionnaire which contained both open-ended and closed questions.

It was important to take a survey of this area because I suspected that the socioeconomic makeup of the population varied and I wanted to obtain as diversified a sample of Puerto Rican women as possible. Had I only used participant observation techniques in this investigation, the conclusions that emerged would have been applicable to a much smaller segment of the population. On the other hand, the ethnographic approach enhanced this work by allowing me to observe the context in which women make their reproductive decisions.

In the course of my fieldwork, specific problems related to the urban context arose. These concerned defining the neighborhood unit within a large metropolitan area, identifying my target population—Puerto Rican women—from hundreds of households, and gaining social entry into a neighborhood where people were suspicious of strangers.

A neighborhood in Brooklyn was selected because of the high percentage of Puerto Ricans residing there. There were several problems in defining the boundaries of the neighborhood itself to be surveyed. I was interested in investigating whether women in this area had a collective perception of the place in which they lived and how perceptions differed from the way the Census Bureau defined the boundaries of the area in which I worked. I elicited their perceptions by showing them a diagram of this census tract and questioning them about where the boundaries of their neighborhood began and ended. Because of the presence of conspicuous landmarks, there was a surprising lack of discrepancy in the responses of women in the neighborhood as to the placement of boundary lines.

Although the locale in which I worked is predominantly Puerto Rican, other ethnic and racial groups reside there as well. An immediate task was that of discovering where the Puerto Rican women lived in the neighborhood. This was accomplished by doing a systematic door-to-door canvasing of all the households, of which 66.7 percent (n = 587) were Puerto Rican. Of the 587 Puerto Rican households, women resided in 84 percent of them.[3] The remainder were either Puerto Rican all-male households or were unavailable for the initial canvasing. After compiling a master list of all residents, I was able to select a subsample of these women for the in-depth questionnaire.[4]

Numerous factors facilitated my entry and acceptance into the neighborhood. I had certain advantages as a Puerto Rican woman born in New York who grew up on the borders of this neighborhood. First of all, the fact that I speak Spanish fluently and am familiar with local colloquial speech and nonverbal expression was helpful. My acceptance by my female informants was aided by my ethnic identity and gender, as they felt they could be more comfortable discussing personal matters with someone of a similar background. This was demonstrated in the openness expressed during our discussions and interviews—even on such "private" subjects as birth control and sterilization. In addition, although I have not lived there for fourteen years, my parents still live on the periphery of the neighborhood, so that throughout the years I have kept abreast of the social, cultural, and economic changes occuring there.

One disadvantage I faced in working with this population was being single and not having children; marriage and parenthood are highly valued in Puerto Rican culture. Another problem partially related to my single status was avoiding situations where women with husbands or boyfriends could become jealous if their companions paid too much attention to me. I also faced the obstacle of assuring women that I was a legitimate researcher. On various occasions, women mistook me for a Jehovah's Witness, a salesperson, or a welfare investigator.

To allay their fears, I explained that I was a student doing a dissertation on the reasons why such a large number of Puerto Rican women were sterilized. I explained that I was not able to obtain this information from anyone else and that without their cooperation I could not carry out this research. In addition, I told them about my goal to use this material to help other women who might have questions or be misinformed about this operation.

In order to overcome women's inhibitions as much as possible, especially while I was doing the systematic listing of the neighborhood, I had an older woman from the neighborhood accompany me during the canvassing phase. This strategy not only made the women feel more comfortable but also made me feel more secure as I was knocking on the doors of strangers.

The majority of the women considered this a useful project and they participated either because they felt that their experiences might be helpful to other women or because their involvement with the project was a novelty. Moreover, some women may have participated because they wanted me to help them solve a problem related to work or the welfare system. In addition, some of the women thought that I would be a good role model for their children and encouraged me to talk to their older children about school and birth control.

Whenever possible I helped the women I worked with in any way that I could. This took the form of advocating for them in hospitals or city agencies, accompanying them to some place they had to go, or serving as an interpreter. Often I was able to obtain information on housing, education, sterilization, or employment not readily available to them. Whenever the opportunity arose, I counseled the women's older children about how to go back to school or how to stay in school using the few grants and scholarships. Occasionally I baby-sat for the women or helped them shop or clean their homes. Most of the time, however, I simply listened and shared my own experiences about my life.

The Setting. The women in this sample have been living in the neighborhood for five to fifteen years. During this time, the ethnic composition of the residents in the neighborhood has changed from predominantly working-class Italian to poor and working-class Puerto Rican. The area is primarily residential though interspersed with a few factories, *bodegas* (small grocery stores), *botanicas* (cultural centers where herbs, incense, candles, and an assortment of religious paraphernalia are sold). There is a park, police precinct, and large shopping area.

The section in which my informants reside is a low-income area characterized by abandoned buildings and a high rate of arson. In part, abandonment occurs because landlords inflate the rents on their property in order to reclaim their initial investment, at the same time spending as little money as possible in repairs. This means that many of the tenants are forced to leave; those who remain go without adequate heat and hot water through most of the year. Once the buildings become dilapidated, they are frequently set on fire by landlords eager to collect the fire insurance. According to a housing report prepared by the Department of City Planning, the fire department made 680 arson determinations between June 1977 and May 1979 in the district in which this neighborhood is located. Between 1965 and 1983, close to half of the buildings in the neighborhood were destroyed by fire (Department of City Planning 1981). As a result, parts of this neighborhood look like a "demolition site," as the residents call it.

Usually the streets are relatively quiet, with the exception of the summer months. Then the streets fill with the sounds of children playing in front of open hydrants and the sounds of people talking and laughing as they escape the heat of their homes by sitting on their "stoops" (the stairs in front of a building). One also hears subways and buses, Latin and disco music, from portable radios and the Latin rhythmic beat of a group of men playing their bongos in the street. At times the noise converges and sounds like a constant hum broken occasionally by a loud argument.

The Women. Although the women in this sample constitute only a fraction of the Puerto Rican population in New York, their social condition is similar to the overall situation of this population. For example, in 1981, more than three-quarters of the Puerto Rican women in this study were not working although 12.5 percent were actively looking for jobs, as compared with 14 percent of the Puerto Rican women in New York City (Stafford 1985). This high rate of unemployment is in part explained by the decline of blue-collar jobs in the city as a result of the suburbanization of capital (Rodriguez 1979).

The women in this study have a median of 6.3 years of education. Some of them, mostly those over forty years of age, can read and write only in Spanish, which is also their main language of everyday conversation. Among the younger women, English tends to be the dominant language.

Almost all of the women stated that they had been married at least once, though 53.1 percent said that they were now separated, divorced, or widowed. Sixty-six percent of the women in this study are heads of households. Almost three-quarters (70 percent) receive either supplementary or full assistance from Aid to Families with Dependent Children. The mean annual income in 1981 for all women in the study was $7,000 or less. This income supports a mean of 3.4 children and one or two adults. With this money, women are expected to support themselves and their children, buy food and clothing, and pay the rent. Most of the women and their companions attempt to supplement their income through odd jobs (see Susser and Kreniske, in this volume). Women baby-sit, clean offices, and occasionally cook Latin specialties to sell to neighbors on holidays. Men often do mechancial work or repairs. Both men and women work as janitors or supers (managers) of buildings, and both sexes are often involved in selling lottery tickets.

In 1981, more than three-quarters of the women in this study were not working outside the home, although 12.5 percent were actively looking for jobs. Of the women who have spouses, 31.3 percent had husbands who were employed and 15.6 percent had husbands who were not working at the time this study was undertaken.

The Puerto Rican women in this neighborhood are mostly employed as factory workers or in other low-paying jobs such as domestics, teachers' aides, baby-sitters, and cleaning women. Whereas a large proportion are unemployed because of the lack of employment opportunities, some are seasonably employed in a number of sweater factories and sweatshops.

The employed in this study are low-wage workers with little job stability, generally working in tedious jobs and often under difficult conditions. An important characteristic shared by the older women in this study is that many of them started to work at a young age. They have worked as migrant agricultural workers and as factory workers. The following oral history of a sixty-three-year-old woman illustrates these points.

I began to work when I was seven years old. We sewed handkerchiefs and gloves at home. There was no electric light. For light we used a small gas lamp. At times I sewed five-dozen handkerchiefs in one night. My first husband worked in the cane fields. He died of tuberculosis. I picked sugarcane and the cane flower.

I left Puerto Rico because our situation was so bad then, when it rained we would all get wet . . . our house was full of holes. Sometimes we could get a *pana* [tuber], and other times there wasn't even that. My second husband sent me twelve dollars every twelve days. He worked in a migrant camp in Florida. . . . By the time I received the twelve dollars I was already in debt in the store. The day least expected I . . . asked for money to complete my airfare to Florida. . . . I worked like a man in a migrant camp, I would have to lock up my children in the shack so that I could work.

I moved alone to New York with my four children. It was still very cold. We didn't have sweaters or anything. I came to live with my niece . . . but in three days her husband put me out. I moved to a furnished room. After paying the first week's rent I was broke. The neighbors got together and brought food to me every day. They also brought me clothes to wash and even lent me an iron and an ironing board so that I could earn a few dollars. After the first month I began to receive aid from welfare. Then I sent for my other five children in Puerto Rico, and there were ten of us in one room. We lived like sardines in a can.

I began to work in New York in 1957. My first job was in Astoria, Long Island, in a toy factory. I bought that job from an employment agency. . . . I worked in another factory in Brooklyn packing plastic curtains. I'd get up at 4:30 a.m. so that I could get to work by 7:30. In those days my eldest daughter and her husband took care of my children. After three years I had to stop working. . . . My daughter moved and there was no one who could care for my children and home. I suffered a lot and was forced to go back on welfare.

In addition to their wage labor, when these women leave their place of work they go home to start the second shift as mothers and housewives (see Safa 1976). Housework and child care frequently consume most, if not all, of their evenings and weekends. Some do not work outside the home, not only because of the difficulties of coordinating a job and domestic work but also because it does not make sense for them to work only to have the majority of their wages go to a baby-sitter. The lack of low-cost and quality child care services is yet another factor that has forced many to stay home. "Salaries are so low that all of a woman's money would go into the baby-sitting expenses. See, when someone takes care of your children not only do you have to pay them, but you have to buy them the food they will eat that day. After I had my third child, I stayed home so that I could rear them myself. If I had continued working, I would have worked just to pay the sitter. It didn't make sense."

Women's Attitudes Toward Sterilization. There are many reasons women give to explain why they get sterilized. Some are apparently directly related to women's socioeconomic circumstances, while for others the relationships are less obvious and give the impression that women exert control. At first glance, some of these explanations appear to be "individual" or "cultural" in nature; upon closer examination it becomes evident that most of these reasons for sterilization are ultimately a reflection of the larger socioeconomic context in which women make their reproductive decisions.

Those variables that are clearly related to women's class position include lack of access to quality health care services, under- and unemployment, and the lack of safe, effective, and convenient methods of birth control. Variables which appear to be more "individual" or "cultural" in nature are women's familiarity with sterilization, the early age at which they have their children, the degree of responsibility for their fertility, their aspirations for their lives in addition to bearing children, and their perception of the ideal number of children. In this section the reasons my informants cited for getting sterilized will be examined within the context of their class status and the parameters of a patriarchal society.

Socioeconomic Considerations. Eighty percent of my informants claimed that they had been sterilized because of their economic circumstances. Forty-four percent felt that if their economic condition had been better, they would not have undergone surgery. The following case illustrates this point:

If I had the necessary money to raise more children, I would not have been sterilized. When you can't afford it, you just can't afford it. Girl, I wish that I could have lived in a house where each of them had their own room, nice clothing, enough food, and everything else that they needed. But what's the sense of having a whole bunch of kids if when dinnertime rolls around all you can serve them is soup made of milk or cod fish because there is nothing else. Or when you are going to take them out, one wears a new pair of shoes while the other one has to wear hand-me-downs because you could only afford one pair of shoes. That's depressing. If I had another child, we would not have been able to survive.

Furthermore, the lack of safe and effective temporary methods of birth control prompted many women in this sample to get sterilized. Although 76 percent of the women used temporary methods of birth control before getting sterilized, they expressed dissatisfaction with the contraceptives available, especially the pill and the IUD. As one woman stated: "The pill made me swell up. After three years, I had an IUD inserted. It made me bleed a lot so I had it removed. I was sterilized at the age of twenty-five because I couldn't use the pill or the IUD. I tried using norforms and the withdrawal method before I was sterilized but neither method worked very well."

Once poor women have problems with the pill and IUD, their fertility options are more limited than that of middle-class women who, although they might not like the diaphragm, are evidently more prone to use it. Only 7.8 percent of the women in this sample had ever used the diaphragm. There are two reasons for this. First, few doctors or family planning counselors recommended it to them. Second, the overwhelming majority stated that they did not like it. Some believed that the diaphragm was unhygienic. They were uncomfortable with the manual manipulation necessary to use it properly, and the planning required. Unless a woman is a careful planner, the diaphragm requires a degree of male collaboration, while the condom requires total male cooperation. According to these women, many of their husbands and boyfriends were not cooperative about birth control. Therefore, although temporary methods of birth control are available today, if they have an adverse effect on women's health (Seaman and Seaman 1977) or if women are not familiar with the alternatives or dislike them, and if their companions will not use the condom, they have few options left but to accept sterilization.

Individual and Cultural Considerations. In addition to socioeconomic circumstances and lack of control over family planning methods, 56.7 percent of the women claimed that they were completely responsible for their fertility and child rearing. While in Puerto Rican and many other cultures there is an orientation that places this responsibility on women, this is explainable in part by the almost total lack of birth control methods available to men, and by the fact that historically birth control policy has been targeted solely toward women. Thus, while it may be tempting to explain women's responsibilities in terms of "Latin machismo," an understanding of the availability and marketing of birth control methods suggests that "culture" is not the final determinant of fertility decisions.

In conjunction with women's responsibility for their fertility, women's familiarity with sterilization serves as a catalyst to increase the rate at which they are operated on. High percentage rates among these women may give the impression that sterilization is a "cultural preference," but these statistics are generally taken out of historical context. After almost five decades of sterilization among Puerto Rican women and the increasing rate of sterilization among women in the United States, it seems clear that this is not a cultural trait but a decision women make when they have no other choice.

Concomitant with Puerto Rican women's responsibility for their fertility and predisposition toward sterilization, the tendency to either marry or have their children while they are still relatively young precipitates their decision to get sterilized at a younger age: 66 percent of these women were sterilized by the age of thirty. Statistics compiled by the New York City Department of Health in 1978 show that while white and black females were predominantly sterilized in the thirty-to-thirty-four age group, the largest number of Hispanic women were sterilized between the ages of twenty-five and twenty-nine (New York City Health and Hospital Corporation 1982). Moreover, most of the women in this study married and had their children before the age of twenty-five. Therefore, by their mid-twenties they had already achieved their desired family size but still had approximately twenty years of fecundity. Since the only method available to curtail fertility is sterilization, their choice was to accept it or continue using temporary methods of birth control for the next twenty years. In addition to the planning and precision required by temporary birth control methods, and the expense involved, some, such as the pill and the IUD, jeopardize women's health. This was of great concern to my informants.

The tendency of lower-income women to have their children in their early twenties is more a result of their socioeconomic circumstances than a cultural preference. Although to my knowledge this has not been documented, it appears that as Puerto Rican females achieve higher levels of education, like their North American counterparts, they, too, have children at an older age. The desire to do other things in addition to bearing children is not a cultural characteristic of Puerto Rican women but a legitimate aspiration shared by women of various classes and ethnic groups. However, unlike women who have more control over their economic resources and are able to delay childbearing, the narrow range of choices of fertility control open to Puerto Rican women reinforces the decision for sterilization.

In a similar manner, women's perceptions of the ideal number of children is not a unique attitude within this population but part of an urban society ideology that they share with the population at large.[5] A few in this study said they were sterilized because with fewer children they could be better mothers and have more energy to dedicate to each child. In most cases, in addition to caring for their children, women also have to summon energy to keep up with the domestic responsibilities and their husbands' needs. Although women cited this as a reason for sterilization, they qualified it by stating that this was only one factor among a host of other reasons, such as their low income and problems with access to birth control methods.

While these may appear as issues of individual choice, the reality of the nuclear family in a patriarchal society is such that the brunt of the responsibility of child rearing and birth control is relegated to women. Thus, because most women are cognizant of the constraints that their economic resources, domestic responsibility, and problems with contraceptives place on their fertility options, many of them feel that sterilization was the only feasible choice.

As we have seen, the tendency for women to have their children early, their familiarity with sterilization, the lack of safe and effective birth control, their responsibility for their fertility, their individual aspirations, and their perceptions of the ideal number of children affect Puerto Rican women's fertility decisions. Besides individual women's attitudes, the role of health policy and practitioners also conditions family planning outcomes.

The Role of Health Policy and Practitioners

Since the kind of health care a person can afford is very much a function of income, employment, and residence, women's general dissatisfaction with their health care experiences is largely a reflection of their low socioeconomic status.

Physicians' perceptions of lower-income Puerto Rican women are demonstrated by polls which showed that depending on the region of the United States, 30 to 52 percent of the doctors polled advocated accepting sterilization as a condition for being allowed to remain on public assistance. Another poll showed this attitude to be prevalent among U.S. citizens as well. According to a Gallup Poll taken in 1965, one out of every five Americans surveyed said that unwed mothers on welfare who continue to have children should be sterilized (Chase 1980). Thus, class and ethnicity play an important role in the interaction between physicians and Puerto Rican women. Similar to some Puerto Rican physicians on the island, male and female doctors in the United

States have recommended sterilization to my informants, giving as explanation that they would not understand how to use temporary methods of birth control effectively (Henderson 1976) or that women on welfare should limit their family size.

The negative health care experiences of the women in my sample are affected by problems with the English language and the shortage of interpreters in hospitals; the shortage of medical personnel, facilities, and equipment; overcrowded and uncomfortable reception areas; and the long period of time required to see a doctor in municipal hospitals.

Most women claimed that they did not trust doctors, and they felt that doctors had no concern for their personal health. After they wait for hours, doctors spend very little time with them. Moreover, women are rarely able to consult the same doctor. The two complaints most frequently articulated to me were that many doctors did not look at them when they were talking and that doctors began writing out prescriptions before they knew what was ailing them. As a result, close to half of the women do not trust doctors, and more than 50 percent feel that the doctors do not care about their health.

It is difficult to ascertain on an individual level the extent to which doctors influence women's decisions about sterilization. The role that health policy plays in narrowing women's fertility choices, however, is more apparent. Whereas federal funding initially covered the cost of abortion, by 1977 this was changed with the passing of the Hyde Amendment, which denied Medicaid funding for abortion except in restrictive cases. The refusal of the state to provide public funds for abortion services, except in narrowly defined therapeutic cases, while making sterilization readily available suggests a definite predilection for sterilization over temporary methods of birth control and abortion (CARASA 1979).

Health policy in the form of sterilization guidelines were implemented in New York City in 1975 to protect men and women from sterilization abuse. The guidelines state that a thirty-day waiting period must elapse from the day a woman signs a consent form to the day she is sterilized. Moreover, federal funds cannot be used to sterilize women under the age of twenty-one. The fact that all of the sterilized women in this study, with the exception of one, were sterilized before the guidelines were implemented suggests that these women may have been a vulnerable population because of their problems with the English language and their high rate of misinformation about the permanent nature of the operation.

The rate of misinformation among the women in this study is very high. Eighty-two percent of the women made a distinction between the "tying" and the "cutting" of the fallopian tubes, a distinction that does not exist. According to one woman: "I feel that if a woman is not sure if she wants any more kids, then she should have her tubes tied. Because of birth control pills women get cancer or veins on their legs. It's a different situation when you get your tubes tied. At least then you can feel relatively safe that you will not have any more children until you want to. If a woman really has decided she absolutely does not want to have more children, then she should have her tubes cut."

Although miniority and poor women are more likely to be misinformed about the permanent nature of sterilization, a study undertaken in 1977 found that regardless of ethnic group or class, most women are likely to be misinformed (Carlson and Vickers 1982). With the introduction of tuboplasty, a method used to try to reverse a tubal ligation, a new form of misinformation is developing among Puerto Rican women. Women claimed that if they underwent a tuboplasty, they could have a successful full-term pregnancy again. Almost two-thirds (63.8 percent) of the women in this study claimed that it was possible to have a child after undergoing an operation where a set of "plastic tubes" was inserted. Once again, this belief is inaccurate, since only a very small number of these reversal operations are successful. Despite this, most women are not being properly informed about the low rate of success of this operation and the high risk of ectopic pregnancy.

Some of the misinformation stems from language in both Spanish and English. For example, phrases such as "la operación," "Band-Aid sterilization," and the "bikini cut" serve to de-emphasize the serious and permanent nature of sterilization and create the illusion of simplicity. In many instances, this terminology may lead women to believe that the surgery is less complicated than it really is. Moreover, the fact that the Department of Health classifies sterilization, a permanent method of fertility control, as birth control can be misleading.[6] This is particularly true for those populations which already have a high rate of misinformation.

Women's Perceived Choices and Assessments

Here I will briefly examine women's ideas and beliefs about sterilization as well as how their religious attitudes may have affected their fertility decisions. In addition, I also consider the way in which these women assess their decisions, and how the high rate of sterilization among the respondents' female relatives has affected their views.

As noted earlier, Puerto Rican women are primarily responsible for birth control. Most men and some women agree that this is the way it should be. However, although the overall majority of women do not feel this way, they are powerless to change their situation, in part because most of the contraceptives available are made for women.

While 87 percent of women in this sample were raised as Catholics, only 32 percent felt that sterilization is against those beliefs. In comparison, 46.7 percent of the non-Catholics felt a conflict between their religious faith and undergoing sterilization. Therefore, in this sample, non-Catholics were actually more likely to be opposed to sterilization on religious grounds than were Catholics. Most women in this study were not aware of the position of the Catholic church on sterilization, or if they did know, their attitudes were very practical. For instance, in a number of cases women claimed that the church was not going to support their children, therefore they had to do something about controlling their own fertility. Although Catholicism may not appear to have a direct effect on women's decisions to be sterilized today, the fact that the Catholic church still forbids the use of other options, such as abortion, affects women's decisions by limiting their fertility choices.

Women's perceptions are also strongly influenced by the large number of females within their own families who have been sterilized. The effect that almost five decades of exposure to this operation has had on predisposing Puerto Rican women to sterilization cannot be underestimated. For example, a high rate of sterilization was found among the female relatives of the women surveyed. According to one woman:

When I decided to get sterilized, I didn't give it much thought. My mother is operated on, and so are two of my mother's sisters. My father has two sisters and one of them is operated on. My husband has three sisters and all three of them did it. My sister was operated on. On my father's side I have six brothers. Half of their wives are also operated on. Also the majority of the women where I work are sterilized. The doctor thought I should do it, too, so after my second child I was operated on.

The topic of assessment is complex because there are so many gray areas. Regret, among some of the women in this sample, is conditional upon their economic circumstances and marital status. From this study, it is feasible to conclude that 33 percent of the sterilized women regret they were sterilized, while 20 percent do not. The difficulty of assessing the issue of regret arises with the remainder of the sample (46 percent). As the following case illustrates, the early age at which some women get sterilized, the economic motives for this decision, and a change in their marital status all contribute to regretting their sterile condition. "If I could make that decision again today, I wouldn't do it. I was operated on when I was eighteen years old. I did it because in order to work, I couldn't take pregnancy leave. Now I've met a good man, and I'd like to give him a child, but I can't."

Some women regretted they were sterilized not only because of changes in their economic and/or marital status but also because they felt they had made a hasty decision. As the data indicates, before the New York City sterilization guidelines were issued, many women were sterilized shortly after making this decision. In this study, 49.4 percent of the women were operated upon between the same day that the operation was arranged and seven days later or less. Women who waited seven days or less had a higher percentage of regret than those who waited longer. Although the issue of regret is complicated, those women who deliberated longer over this decision tended to show less regret.

Conclusion

This study has demonstrated the numerous social and individual forces that reinforce the perpetuation of sterilization among Puerto Rican women in New York City. As I suggested at the outset, Puerto Rican women's fertility decisions must be examined within a broader socioeconomic context that includes population policy, neo-Malthusian ideology, economic incentives, and persistent poverty and job insecurity. On an individual level, familiarity with sterilization, the early age at which they have children, the high rate of misinformation, and responsibility for their fertility and child rearing must also be considered. Within this context, Puerto Ricans make a choice, but the choice is exercised under the most limited and constrained conditions. Their choice was either to get sterilized, or continue to have children under extremely difficult circumstances.

Therefore, to argue that Puerto Rican women's decisions to get sterilized are "voluntary," as Stycos et al. (1959), Scrimshaw (1970), and Presser (1973) insist, within the context of women's socio-historical, economic, and personal constraints, is not only simplistic, but misleading. Just as the "culture of poverty" thesis blames the values and behaviors of the poor for their poverty, these social scientists attribute the high rate of sterilization to cultural preference. But the social and economic conditions to which Puerto Ricans respond, both in Puerto Rico and in the United States, are not a product of their own making. It is the result of being constrained by social and economic forces which leave them little choice but to migrate and/or get sterilized. And these conditions form the real perimeters of "fertility choice"—migration or sterilization.

Notes

1. Sterilization consists of cutting and suturing the fallopian tubes in the female to permanently block the flow of the sperm to the egg cell and to prevent the egg cell from entering the uterus. In its broadest meaning, sterilization includes hysterectomies and vasectomies. The latter is the method used to sterilize men.

2. The discrepancy between the total number of sterilized women in the survey (eighty-five women) and the proportion of women sterilized in the neighborhood (47 percent) is a reflection of the different techniques used to elicit the data. Therefore, forty-seven percent is representative of the total number of Puerto Rican women sterilized in the entire neighborhood and not the survey sample.

3. Of the remaining households, 15.9 percent (n=140) were European immigrants or people of European descent, 10.3 percent were Latin American immigrants or people of Latin American origin, and 2.3 percent (n=20) were blacks from areas outside of Puerto Rico. The ethnicity of 4.8 percent (n=42) of the households was unknown.

4. Of the 496 households with women in them, 4.6 percent (n=23) refused to participate, making the total number of households 473.

5. The perception of the ideal number of children among the women in this study is slightly higher than the average that Puerto Rican families actually have. According to the 1980 census data, New York Puerto Ricans have an average of 2.1 children, as compared with 1.8 for non-Hispanic whites and 2.0 for non-Hispanic blacks. Obviously the number of children Puerto Rican women have is not that different from that of other women in the city, but it is very much in line with the conception of the "ideal family size" in large metropolitan cities.

6. Traditionally, sterilization has been represented as a method of "birth control." Contrary to this view, I believe that because sterilization is a permanent method of fertility control and birth control is the ability to determine one's fecundity, a distinction needs to be made between the two.

References

Bonilla, Frank and Ricardo Campos. 1981. "A Wealth of Poor: Puerto Ricans in the New Economic Order." *Daedalus* 110(2):133–176.
———. 1983. "Evolving Patterns of Puerto Rican Migration." In Steve Sanderson, ed., *The Americas in the New International Division of Labor*, pp. 172–205. New York: Holms and Meir.

CARASA (Committee for Abortion Rights and Against Sterilization Abuse). 1979. "Women Under Attack: Abortion, Sterilization Abuse, and Reproductive Freedom." New York: Committee Against Sterilization Abuse.

Carlson, Jody and George Vickers. 1982. "Voluntary Sterilization and Informed Consent: Are Guidelines Necessary?" New York: Women's Division of the United Methodist Church.

Chase, Allen. 1980. *The Legacy of Malthus: The Social Cost of the New Scientific Racism.* Urbana: University of Illinois Press.

Davis, Angela. 1981. *Women, Race, and Class.* New York: Random House.

Department of City Planning. 1981. "Proposed Seventh Year Community Development Program: Application and Budget." Report prepared for the City of New York, Office of Edward Koch, p. 211.

Gangalez, M., V. Barrera, P. Guanaccia, and S. Schensul. 1980. "The Impact of Sterilization on Puerto Rican Women, the Family, and the Community." Unpublished report. Connecticut: Hispanic Health Council.

Henderson, Peta. 1976. "Population Policy, Social Structure, and the Health System in Puerto Rico: The Case of Female Sterilization." Ph.D. dissertation, University of Connecticut.

Hernandez Alvarez, Jose. 1967. *Return Migration to Puerto Rico.* Berkeley: Institute of International Studies, University of California.

History Task Force. 1982. *Sources for the Study of Puerto Rican Migration—1879–1930.* New York: Centro de Estudios Puertorriqueños.

Mass, Bonnie. 1976. "Emigration and Sterilization in Puerto Rico." In Mass, ed., *Population Target: The Political Economy of Population in Latin America,* pp. 87–108. Ontario: Charters.

Newman, Sidney and Zanvel Klein. 1978. *Behavioral-Social Aspects of Contraceptive Sterilization.* Lexington, Mass.: Lexington Books.

New York City Health and Hospital Corporation. 1982. Sterilizations Reported in New York City. Unpublished data, Department of Biostatistics.

New York Times. 1983. "Birth Control: Sterilizing Relied On." December 21, section C, column 6, p. 10.

Presser, Harriet. 1973. *Sterilization and Fertility Decline in Puerto Rico.* Population Monograph No. 13. Berkeley: University of California.

Ramierez de Arellano, Annette and Conrad Scheipp. 1983. *Colonialism, Catholicism, and Birth Control in Puerto Rico: The History of Sterilization in Puerto Rico.* Chapel Hill: University of North Carolina Press.

Ramos, Carlos. 1977. "The Politics of Birth Control in Puerto Rico." Ph.D. dissertation. University of California, Berkeley.

Rodriguez, Clara. 1979. "Economic Factors Affecting Puerto Ricans in New York," *Labor Migration Under Capitalism,* pp. 197–221. New York: Monthly Review Press.

Rodriguez-Trias, Helen. 1978. *Women and the Health Care System: Sterilization Abuse.* New York: Barnard College.

Safa, Helen Icken. 1976. "Class Consciousness Among Working-Class Women in Latin America: Puerto Rico." In June Nash and Helen Safa, eds., *Sex and Class in Latin America,* pp. 69–85. New York: Praeger.

Scrimshaw, Susan. 1970. "The Demand for Female Sterilization in Spanish Harlem: Experiences of Puerto Ricans in New York City." Paper presented at the 69th annual meeting of the American Anthropological Association, San Diego, California.

Seaman, Barbara and Gideon Seaman. 1977. *Women and the Crisis in Sex Hormones.* New York: Bantam.

Stafford, Walter W. 1985. *Closed Labor Market: Underrepresentation of Blacks, Hispanics, and Women in New York Cities, Core Industries, and Jobs.* New York: Community Service Society.

Stycos, Mayone, Reuben Hill, and Kurt Back. 1959. *The Family and Population Control: A Puerto Rican Experiment in Social Change.* Chapel Hill: University of North Carolina Press.

Vasquez-Calzada, José. 1978. "La Población de Puerto Rico y su Trajectoria Historica." Escuela de Salud Púbica, Recinto de Ciencias Médicas. Puerto Rico: Universidad de Puerto Rico.

Velez, Carlos. 1978. "Se Me Acabo La Canción." Paper presented at the International Congress of Anthropological and Ethnological Sciences, New Delhi, India, December 10–18.

13. Kinship and Class in Chicago

Raymond T. Smith

If urban sociology was not invented in Chicago, it was certainly developed there to an unprecedented degree, and there is a rich legacy of both primary materials and secondary analysis. It is difficult to see what could be added to the total of our knowledge by new anthropological study, and yet such research is urged with the promise that it will bring a marked increment in our understanding of the dynamics of urban family life. For some anthropologists this deeper insight is to be obtained by looking very closely at a limited area, even if that involves sacrifice of representativeness; for others it will come from concentrating on the variety of "ethnic" traditions which crowd American cities. A more promising approach is emerging out of the current preoccupation with problems of meaning. As Clifford Geertz has written recently, "Many social scientists have turned away from a laws-and-instances ideal of explanation toward a cases-and-interpretations one, looking less for the sort of thing that connects planets and pendulums and more for the sort that connects chrysanthemums and swords" (Geertz 1980:165).

In this chapter I will discuss some of the results of anthropological research on kinship in Chicago, carried out first by David M. Schneider and his associates, and subsequently by Schneider and me, with the help of Joyce Aschenbrenner and various students at the University of Chicago. These studies would not be considered representative of the discipline by many anthropologists, but they provide an opportunity to consider the way in which anthropology differs most markedly from sociology and demography. A number of publications based on this work have already appeared (Schneider 1968,1969,1970,1972,1975, 1979,1980; Schneider and Smith 1978; Schneider and Cottrell 1975; Smith 1970; Aschenbrenner 1975). In previous publications I have argued against the uncritical amassing of quantitative information collected according to *a priori* assumptions about the nature of meaningful units (Smith 1970,1978). In this paper I shall focus more sharply upon some differences within the broad approach I am advocating. If this gives the impression of deep internal differences between anthropologists pursuing cultural analysis, it will not be inaccurate, but these are differences between people addressing a problem that is barely recognized by the majority of family researchers.

Background to the American Kinship Project

The first phase of the studies to be discussed here derived from the already established interests of Raymond Firth and David Schneider; my contribution was based upon many years of work in the Caribbean and West Africa, and it came much later. At the time Firth and Schneider first met at the London School of Economics in 1949, Firth had already organized a study of kinship in London. This study had grown out of the realization by members of his seminar that their knowledge of the most intimate aspects of their own social life was far from systematic. From 1947 to 1949, a group of staff and students engaged in sporadic interviewing in a borough south of the Thames. While recognizing the structural and functional prominence of the elementary family, the separation of the family from occupational specialization, the comparatively narrow range and shallow depth of kinship reckoning, and the variability in kinship behavior—all factors which had been described by Talcott Parsons in his seminal paper on "The Kinship System of the Contemporary United States" (1943)—Firth argued that "even in Western urban conditions" the elementary family is not an isolated unit, and the aim of his study would be to determine "what the range of extra-familial relations was, and how far it could be genealogically determined" (Firth 1956:23).

Schneider did not participate in these London studies, but when he returned to Harvard University in 1951 as a faculty member, he immediately began a collaborative study, with George C. Homans, of some aspects of American kinship (Schneider and Homans 1955:1194–1208).

The analytic framework of this study is highly functional, but certain themes appear which have been constant in Schneider's work and which reappear in the Chicago studies. Great stress is laid upon the central importance of the kinship system of the nuclear family, and kinship itself is seen as a socialization device which teaches the child "the fundamentals of his whole culture" (1955:1208), since it embodies the dominant values. One aspect of those values, individualism, is reflected in the language of American kinship, and this is seen most clearly in the elaboration of terms for husband and wife. "The marital relationship seems either to center on a highly individual definition of a presumably perpetual love affair . . . or it is a relationship defined by the presumption of children" (1955:1202). The paper also focuses on variability; there is a wide variety of terms for kinsmen, and which term is used depends to a large extent upon the relationship between the speaker and the person being referred to, and upon situational context. Other variations occur from subgroup to subgroup, but these are contained within one basic structure in which there is "bilateral descent, a strongly emphasized nuclear family, and a distinct but secondarily important kindred" (1955:1203–1204).

Schneider's shift of emphasis from structural-functional and psychological explanations to symbols and cultural analysis is difficult to chart, but in a draft article on kinship prepared for the *Encyclopedia Hebraica,* dated May 13, 1963, he was led into formulating a definition of kinship which established it as functionally diffuse, enduring solidarity which may be symbolized in various ways, most usually by consanguinity and affinity. The fact that the article was never actually published was, in retrospect, a matter of some gratification to its author, since he felt that the definition was premature and in some ways misguided. However, the core idea was to persist into the Chicago studies.

This brief summary of the background is important to an understanding of the way in which the Chicago study was designed and how it developed.

The Anglo-American Kinship Projects

In 1958–59, while Professor Raymond Firth was in the United States, he and David Schneider conceived the idea of a collaborative study of modern urban kinship with Firth working in London and Schneider in the United States (see Firth et al. 1970 and Schneider 1980 for details). Each study was to be separately executed, and actual collaboration was confined to the exchange of ideas, interview guides, and results. Although no joint publication appeared (probably because of diverging theoretical interests), Schneider used the opportunity to develop further a theory of culture, while Firth and his collaborators concentrated upon social relations. The theoretical divergence is embodied in their respective definitions of kinship. According to Firth: "Kinship is a set of ties socially recognised to exist between persons because of their genealogical connection, that is, in terms of the relationships thought to be created between them by marriage and/or procreation of children" (Firth et al. 1970:3). For Schneider: "This book is concerned with American kinship as a cultural system; that is, as a system of symbols. By symbol I mean something which stands for something else, or some things else, where there is no necessary or intrinsic relationship between the symbol and that which it symbolizes" (Schneider 1980:1).

The American Kinship Project actually began in the spring of 1961 when Schneider assembled a staff. With the active collaboration of a sociologist, Dr. Alice Rossi, a sample of 400 households was chosen from four neighborhoods thought to be predominantly inhabited by white middle-class Chicagoans. This questionnaire survey would both collect quantitative data and locate informants for more intensive study. In London, Firth and his associates worked in a housing estate in north London, and later in Highgate. Although the two studies used similar techniques, there was a fundamental difference in the assumptions about what was being collected. Both collected genealogies and interviewed intensively; neither used questionnaires after the initial locating survey. A clue to the differences is to be found in the way in which the genealogy was handled. Firth and his associates decided that the genealogy should be collected during the first interview and, "if it could be managed, before kin were discussed at all" (1970:33). The assumption was that a genealogy represents actual linkages, between individuals related by consanguinity and affinity, that are recognized for social purposes. Since the aim was to record all these linkages during the first interview, along with such "empirical" data as name, age, occupation, and residence of each relative, it is clear that the expectation was that genealogies would be small and nonproblematic.

While the Chicago study also aimed to collect the facts of names, ages, etc., Schneider's main interest was in the culture of kinship. The underlying theory was that behavior, including statements, contains and is influenced by a structure comparable to a grammar. Therefore the interviews were occasions on which the informant was encouraged to speak with as little interference as possible. The first interview was devoted to recording a "spontaneous kin listing" and to an exploration of the manner in which the informants thought about and defined "relatives." The interviewer was to begin the interview by asking, "List for me all the people you consider to be related to you," and was expressly forbidden to help the informant decide what "really" constitutes a relative (see Wolf 1964 for a full discussion of methods). The next step was to build a genealogy over a long series of interviews, by exploring systematically the informant's knowledge of the immediate relatives of every person mentioned at any stage. Some genealogies contained hundreds of individuals and took many sessions to record, but the dominant issue was, how does the informant think about this? What does it mean?

Just as the two studies differed in theoretical approach and in data collection, their results embody different views as to what anthropology can contribute to the study of urban social life. Firth and his associates chose to stress certain of anthropology's techniques of investigation while working in a broadly structural-functional mode familiar to any sociologist. They wanted to understand the nature of social relationships and the actual patterns of interaction among kin; their method of investigation was a variant, in practice, of the community study. The two areas of London chosen as the sites of the investigation are described in great detail. Their history is sketched and we are told what they look like, how their inhabitants live, what are the socioeconomic characteristics of the population, and so forth. The interviewers were charged to obtain as much "factual" information as possible, not only to check upon the veracity of the informants but also to situate them in the community for the benefit of the reader.

Schneider does nothing like this, and in fact *American Kinship: A Cultural Account* claims to be much more than an analysis of the interview data collected in the early 1960s. Apart from the "over six thousand pages of typed accounts of interviews . . . with 102 people," the genealogies, wedding invitation lists, interviews with children, and so on that constituted the results of the American Kinship Project, Schneider tells us:

But this book does not depend on these data alone. It has taken into account materials collected in an earlier study done among graduate students and faculty of the Department of Social Relations at Harvard University, materials collected informally from friends; neighbors; colleagues; acquaintances; newspaper accounts; newspaper columns; the literature in professional sociology, psychiatry, psychology, and anthropology journals; students' reports; and similar authentic but unsystematic sources. The final source of information is, of course, my own personal experience, since I was born and reared in America, am a native speaker of the language, and have lived in America almost all my life. . . .

Such a diverse array of sources can, of course, be regarded as a sample in the technical sense that every major segment of the population of the United States is represented in some way. (1980:13)

The fact that the core of these data comes from Chicago is irrelevant to the results, and no attempt is made to situate them in a specific social context. On the contrary, the aim is to "abstract" from all contexts.

Whereas Firth claims for anthropology only a special interest in kinship, a comparative perspective, and the method of intensive firsthand inquiry, Schneider tries to carve out a distinct subject matter—the study of culture as a system of symbols. He seeks to distinguish his problem from all others and sees it as the distinctive field of inquiry of anthropology:

This problem assumes that the cultural level of observation can be distinguished from all others; that cultural units and constructs can be described independently of all other levels of observation; and that the culture so isolated can be examined to see what its core symbols are (if there are core symbols); how meaning is systematically elaborated (if it is systematically elaborated) throughout its differentiated parts; and how the parts are differentiated and articulated as cultural units (if they are so articulated).

In the most general terms, then, the problem I have posed is that of describing and treating culture as an independent system and of analysing it in its own terms; that is, as a coherent system of symbols and meanings. (1980:8)

What the lasting theoretical value of this approach will be remains to be seen; so far it appears that the main contribution of his insistent stress upon the autonomy of culture has been to improve the quality of interviewing by demanding the revision, or abandonment, of the idea that kinship is a fact of nature used in different ways for social purposes. In *American Kinship* he showed how certain beliefs, or concepts, are accepted by all Americans, and how they play a part in structuring the most general values people hold in the domain of kinship. Thus, the belief that "blood" or unity of substance is shared by all consanguines; that marriage creates bonds of solidarity, not only between spouses, but more generally between those related through them; and that the combination of concepts of identity of substance and a code for conduct enjoining diffuse, enduring solidarity underlie all regularities of kinship in American culture. None of this will come as a complete surprise to the natives of North America, and it may be Schneider's greatest contribution to have alerted anthropologists to the fact that these ideas are particular to Euro-American culture; insofar as they have been embodied in kinship theory, they have distorted our very perception of other societies' beliefs and institutions.

However, there is another dimension to Schneider's work on American kinship which is relevant, and which also derives from his assertions about the conceptual unity of the culture of kinship and its generality among all Americans.

The central problem in the study of urban kinship in the United States is that of understanding variation, and it is here that cultural analysis faces its most severe test. Central to Schneider's analysis in *American Kinship* is the statement that variation occurs only in the social system and not at the cultural level. The social system is an integrated system of norms, which are rules for action in particular roles; thus to understand variation one must concentrate upon norms. Norms, apart from being rules for action (which are quite distinct from action itself, of course), are also a "conglomeration" of elements from various "pure" domains of culture. Thus a particular role, such as that of mother, would be governed by rules of behavior or norms, but such norms would from another point of view be compounded of elements from, say, the domains of kinship, sex role, age, class, and so forth (Schneider 1980: 113–114).

The implication of this view is that any particular role can be understood both as an element in a structural-functional whole—the social system—and as a conglomeration of elements derived from a series of "pure" cultural domains. The task of anthropology is to analyze the cultural elements and not to deal with the working of the social system. Although Schneider recognizes that the set of integrated symbols which constitute the cultural system is a creation of the analyst, an analytical abstraction from the flow of events which constitute social action, he nonetheless treats the cultural system so created as an entity, and attributes to it a determinative function in shaping social action. Historically derived presuppositions about the nature of the world and the limits of social action, which may be called cultural assumptions, are very important. However, the method of "abstraction" is highly problematic unless subject to the control made possible by careful, and frequent, reference back to the data of social action. Schneider does not specify what the relationship is between culture and social structure, though he has said repeatedly that the only purpose of cultural analysis is to contribute to the understanding of social action. "How is culture articulated in social action or how does culture affect social action? or, What role does culture play in social action? This is ultimately *the* question, of course; this is what social science is for. Without that question all the rest is empty" (Schneider 1980:127).

An opportunity to approach that question arose when we undertook a joint study of lower-class kinship in Chicago as part of a wider inquiry initiated by the Children's Bureau to throw light upon factors surrounding the increasing incidence of premarital pregnancy. This would involve focusing on class differences, it addressed directly the then salient issue of the supposed "problem of the Negro family," and it tied in with my own interest in a comparison of the United States and the Caribbean.

The Class Differences Study

Schneider's interest in class differences was of long standing, and in *American Kinship* he reported that "a volume on class and kinship is begun but not yet far along" (1968:13 n.3). However, sometime in the late 1960s this work was drawn together into a draft paper entitled "Middle Class and Lower Class American Kinship," a paper which was never published but circulated in Chicago. This paper, along with one of mine on "The Nuclear Family in Afro-American Kinship" (Smith 1970), constituted the starting point for the drafting of a report to the Children's Bureau, and was revised for publication as *Class Differences and Sex Roles in American Kinship and Family Structure* (1978).[1] As we explained in the preface to that volume, we started with differing viewpoints and did not always agree with each other, but we did attempt "to work out, in as systematic a manner as possible, the relationship among culture, normative or social system, and social action," and we observed that "the problem with treating culture at such high levels of generality as appear to be analytically necessary raises the problem of how such highly general symbols and meanings can be shown to relate to concrete patterns of behavior" (Schneider and Smith 1978:100). The attempt to establish that relationship was partially successful, but two matters remain problematical. The first is the treatment of class and the status of the class-linked familial norms; the second is the assumption that race, or ethnicity, is of no significance in the patterning of family behavior. Before dealing with these issues, I will outline briefly some of the main conclusions of the study.

The Reported Results. Just as Schneider had found in the middle-class studies, and Firth had discovered in London, our informants were firmly embedded in extensive networks of kin. The genealogies analyzed by Schneider and Cottrell ranged in size from 23 to 468, with a mean size of 159 for the middle-class whites. The lower class ranged in size from 30 to 806, but if one excludes the very small 30-person genealogy of a sixteen-year-old girl, which was probably incomplete, the mean size was 255. The range of variation is such that there is little significance in the class difference in mean size.[2] We may conclude that urban Americans know about and keep in touch with large numbers of kin. Although it cannot be discussed here, the initial spontaneous kin listing reveals no differences in the way in which informants list kin. If one alters names and incidental markers such as address and occupation, it is impossible to guess class position from the spontaneous listing (see Alexander 1976 for an example of such analysis).

Both lower- and middle-class informants keep in touch with relatives through reciprocal visiting, telephone calls, Christmas and Thanksgiving gatherings, and the like. They meet at weddings and funerals, and they provide each other with help when it is needed. Family reunions, organized by one person or several, for the sole purpose of bringing together scattered family members, seem to be an American phenomenon with no class boundaries. Such a reunion is described by Joyce Aschenbrenner (1975:118–134; see also Ayoub 1966:415–433).

Notwithstanding these similarities, we reported clear differences between those identified as lower and middle class. Some derived from obvious differences in economic situation. In one case in Schneider's middle-class sample, a married male informant worked in his father's business, and this resulted in close cooperation, indeed interdependence, between the two households, while at the same time it produced strain. Economic interests reinforced the ties of familial solidarity, but they also conflicted with the rule of nuclear family independence, and great care was taken to keep the affairs of the two households separate and to make explicit the son's prior commitment to his wife. The number of family firms in the United States is now so diminished that cases of this kind are much less common (Winch and Blumberg [1968] discuss kinship and economic activity in Chicago). A concern with individual and nuclear family autonomy seemed to be pronounced in the middle class, irrespective of economic cooperation. In the lower class, and particularly among blacks, we found equally interesting strains between linked households, but they arose from different causes. The case of Lucille Foster and Sylvester Charles described by Aschenbrenner is paradigmatic in many ways (1975:35–46).

Lucille is a practical nurse with her own income, her own apartment, and two children—one by her husband from whom she has been separated for many years, the other born as a result of one of her many short-term friendships with other men. Sylvester Charles is forty-two years old and has a steady job as a security guard. He is married, with two children, but separated from his wife and lives with his mother. Lucille and Sylvester have been friendly for some years and have considered each getting divorced so that they can marry, but something always seems to come up to make it seem less than a good idea. Gradually he begins to stay more and more at her apartment, moving his clothes in little by little. Periodically they quarrel, usually over his affairs with other women, and she puts him—and his clothes—out, whereupon he moves back to his mother's place. Her mother comes to stay with her periodically, which complicates matters, and her children go off periodically to stay with relatives. This couple, with their complex ties reaching into a number of other households, with relatives moving in and out all the time, and with frequent transfers of children as they spend time with separated parents, is quite unlike most of the middle-class households in Schneider's collection. (However, the increasing divorce rate among middle-class individuals is giving rise to cross-household relationships which may bear a superficial resemblance.)

Sylvester and Lucille have no agreed arrangement for contributions to housekeeping expenses; he frequently buys the groceries while she is at work—especially when he is on the night shift—and he often contributes to the utility expenses. However, there is no clear arrangement that he will always do so; everything is negotiable, and in that respect it reflects accurately her relative independence and the nature of their relationship. Both continue to have other friends of the opposite sex. By no stretch of the imagination could this couple be thought of as being desperately poor; she dresses well and looks after her children equally well, though at times she may speak of "poor people like me." She has a good and steady job and a lot of friends and relatives who help out if she is in trouble. Her various men friends and the fathers of her children contribute to expenses, and she in turn helps her parents and other relatives who descend on her looking for a place to stay until they get settled in the city.

It was case material such as this which reinforced the conclusion that one could abstract different patterns of priority of solidary emphasis in the internal relationships of primary kin in different classes. The distinction is drawn most clearly in Schneider's earlier paper on "Middle Class and Lower Class American Kinship," where he says:

In sum, the pattern of solidary emphasis for American middle class kinship is 1. spouse-spouse, 2. parent-child, 3. sibling-sibling. (1970:22)

[In lower-class American kinship] the pattern of solidary emphasis is: 1. mother-daughter 2. mother-son 3. sister-sister 4. sister-brother 5. brother-brother 6. husband-wife and 7. father-child. (1970:31)

In the book, we abandoned the numerical ranking of relationships while retaining the sense of difference of pattern, and we tried to relate it, as indeed Schneider had done previously, to class differences in the pattern of sex-role differentiation. It was pointed out that "sex" in American culture has two aspects. Sex can mean intercourse, or more generally, have an interactive meaning; at the same time it can mean difference, as when stress is laid upon physical difference or upon the supposed special attributes of each sex (see Schneider and Smith 1978:69–85).

These definitions, or cultural concepts, of sex are uniform throughout the society; what varies, we argued, is the manner in which social roles embody different aspects of the cultural array. Thus, in the middle class, primary stress is placed upon the interactive aspect of sex. Sex differences are stressed in many situations, of course, but sexual attributes are generally downplayed in favor of equality and cooperation. In the lower-class pattern, by contrast, it is the attributional aspect of sex that is stressed, so that the different characteristics of male and female are held to be intrinsic and largely beyond control. These differences of stress are associated with other concomitant features. In the middle class the normative differences between the sexes are subordinated to the values of reason, equality, and family independence such that the distribution of authority and tasks or the scheduling of activities is governed by norms which incorporate competence, impulse control, and independence. In the lower class, by contrast, the pattern of solidary emphasis within the body of close kin is highly dependent upon the sharp differences drawn between the sexes, and those differences are thought to be inherent.

Authority, tasks, and activities are based upon the apparently objective and unalterable—"traditional"—characteristics of men and women. In his earlier paper Schneider had been led to treat class itself at a very high level of abstraction when he said:

"Class" thus takes its structure from the evaluation placed on different modes of relating ends and means and the different kinds of ends which are selected. For the middle class, those which conform most closely to the systematic evaluation of means in terms of the rational appraisal of their relationship to stated ends are the values held in highest esteem, as are those ends which are held to be rationally selected. For the lower class as for the upper class, particularistic, traditional, attributive criteria are the most highly valued, as are these ends selected in terms of those criteria. (Schneider 1970:57)

In the book, we made an attempt to provide some context for this formulation by discussing the specific development of class relations in the United States and by outlining the different occupational milieu in which various groups in Chicago actually operate. We also warned that the distinctions we drew between class patterns should be thought of as distinctions between two contrasted models and not between empirical "subcultures" (Schneider and Smith 1978:42,78,79,118). However, having made that statement, we too frequently proceeded to write as if our data fell neatly into these patterns.

Class, Norms, and Cultural Analysis. The premature association of the contrasted models of family norms with "class" points up a definite weakness in our study. It derived partly from the inadequate specification of class, but also from the failure to move our models back into close conjunction with the data of observation. In this respect, it throws light upon the limitations of cultural analysis itself.

In the work that he has done subsequent to the class differences study, Schneider has concentrated upon much higher levels of abstracted cultural analysis, justifying this on the grounds that one must understand "grammar" before one can study speech, or discourse (Schneider 1980:127–136). Whether the abstract generalizations which have led him to conclude that kinship, nationality, religion, community, and ethnicity are all part of the same cultural domain can be sustained or not is really beside the point; they happen to be of little interest to anyone concerned with understanding social behavior. Schneider continues to insist upon the value, and indeed the logical priority, of a cultural account which will set out the perfectly integrated, meaningful system of cultural symbols, and galaxies of symbols, which has great stability over time (1976:218–220; 1980:128–136). I consider that an exclusive pre-occupation with the construction of abstract models which are not immediately set to use in analysis leads to reification.

It is interesting to compare the work of Basil Bernstein (1971) with Schneider's project of cultural analysis, and with the interpretations we attempted in *Class Differences*. Bernstein's central interest has been in the understanding of differences in speech and educational performance between children of different class background in London. He has concentrated upon trying to establish a relationship between speech codes, culture, and social context and starts from the following position.

> I shall take the view that the code which the linguist invents to explain the formal properties of the grammar is capable of generating any number of speech codes, and there is no reason for believing that any one language code is better than another in this respect. On this argument, language is a set of rules to which all speech codes must comply, but which speech codes are realised is a function of the culture acting through social relationships in specific contexts. (Bernstein 1971:173–174)

The argument is very similar to Schneider's view that "pure culture" is capable of varying specifications as it enters into the structure of norms appropriate to varying social contexts. However, Bernstein chooses *not* to follow Chomsky in severing competence, or the rule system of language, from performance, or the social use to which language rules are put—the direction in which Schneider deliberately heads. Bernstein focuses upon speech, much as we focused upon norms in our study of kinship, and the models he constructs of "elaborated" and "restricted" sociolinguistic codes, with their associated orders of meaning and social context, are remarkably similar to the general aspects of our models of kinship norms.

In brief, "restricted" speech codes arise, and are used, in social situations that are closely bounded, where meaning is context-specific and particularistic, and where communication is effected through condensed symbols. Elaborated codes are context-independent, they orient their users toward universalistic meanings, they make no assumptions about prior communal understanding but involve explicit rational elaboration by individual speakers, and are associated with "knowledge at the level of the meta-languages of control and innovation" (1971:175). Restricted codes are appropriate to situations where speakers know each other and the environment so well that explicit reference is not necessary in order to convey meaning; elaborated codes are used where the speech must make everything clear because nothing can be taken for granted. It is a very short step to see the lower class as being denied access to elaborated speech codes, and hence rendered incapable of filling roles where autonomy, rationality, abstract thinking, and innovation are required. Bernstein is careful to avoid making value judgments when comparing different speech codes, and indeed he is fulsome in his praise of the richness of metaphorical expression which is possible using condensed symbols in restricted codes. However, there is a definite tendency for all these models to assume an evolutionary progression from one type to the other, an assumption which derives from their common origin in such familiar dichotomies as gemeinschaft and gesellschaft, mechanical and organic solidarity, universalism and particularism. As we pointed out in *Class Differences*, there may be more similarity between the lower and the upper class than is allowed for in Bernstein's argument. Even so, two other considerations are as relevant to our work as to Bernstein's.

The first is that much of what appears to be universalistic, context-free rationality in the speech of the middle class or in their family norms may be nothing more than stylistic veneer. Labov makes a very telling analysis of the speech of a college-educated, middle-class person, and shows that its principal feature is verbosity rather than logical precision. By contrast, the speech of a fifteen-year-old gang member, despite its stylistic unacceptability in polite circles, is shown to be economical, logical, and precise (Labov 1972:214–221). The other fact is that the models capture contrasting modes of normative orientation *within* each "class" and not merely the differences between them. In the case of speech codes it is obvious that the use of restricted codes is appropriate in a great many situations of middle-class life, and Bernstein is clear about this. Elizabeth Bott, in her pioneering study of the relation between conjugal relations and external networks, was careful to assume no necessary association of conjugal role types and class position (Bott 1956). In our study it would have been preferable to label the contrasted models of norms by some neutral terms—such as A and B—rather than by class terms. Empirically there are no clear class boundaries in American cities, a fact which we tried to explain in a chapter on "Class and Ethnicity." In view of that fact, it would have been wise to leave open the use of normative models in exploring the degree of fit as one moves through different sectors of the society, or even as between different groups within the same sector.

An excellent study of a middle-class suburb of Toronto, carried out in the 1950s, pointed the way toward such caution. Seeley, Sim, and Loosley, in their book *Crestwood Heights: A Study of the Culture of Suburban Life* (1956), set out very convincingly the ideal structure of the love-based and lone nuclear family, with its internal life regulated by rationality, equality, and a firm belief in the progress of each and all. However, the Crestwood Heights investigators kept hearing of the contrast between the ideal way of doing things and that which their informants referred to as obtaining in "the Victorian era," which was authoritarian, male-dominated, and "traditional" in its orientation. What they discovered was that this contrast had little to do with historical sequence and everything to do with contrasted models for behavior which are of contemporary significance. The authors tell us that "the deepest cleavage in the belief system of Crestwood Heights—more basic and deeper (we feel) than differences in age, ethnic group, or status—is created by the striking divergences in the belief systems of men and women" (Seeley, Sim, and Loosley 1956:382). While women minimize the differences between the sexes and stress equality, rationality, and universalism, men exaggerate them and regard women as sentimental, nonlogical, incapable of real achievement, and needing to be handled like children. Men are more group-oriented; it is the organization, the business, the institution, the club, the rules, the law, that are more important than the individual and his self-expression, and they incline to the belief that swift physical punishment is better than reason in child rearing. One need not go on in order to make the point. It was a major failing of our study that we did not pay adequate attention to this aspect of sex-role differentiation, and part of the reason was the small number of men among our informants. However, there was also a tendency to ignore "submerged" elements in favor of what appeared to be the "encompassing" forms. The fact that sex-linked differences of this kind have appeared in the historical material analyzed by Sennett suggests that they may be very important (Sennett 1970).

Race and Ethnicity. Premature closure of the elements of the normative models and their association with an ideal form of class, rather than fitting them more closely to the action context, caused further problems in appreciating race and ethnic differences. We said unequivocally that the characteristics of the Afro-American family are not racially or ethnically specific, but reflect class background. To a very large extent this is true. In a new foreword to the reprint edition (1978:a–j), this position was shifted slightly. Further reflection on the material, and on the analytic procedures, suggests that a more careful examination of behavioral material would lead to a modification of the normative analysis. There appears to be a persistent difference between blacks and others in the pattern of conjugal relationships which is not simply a matter of "rate," or of exaggerated class position.

This difference can be inferred from the case material published by Joyce Aschenbrenner, which provides some feel for the particularity of what she calls "the Black experience" (Aschenbrenner 1975:7). Ethnicity is a characteristic feature of the structure of American society, and its meaning derives less from the content of "ethnic culture" than from the opposition between ethnic groups in an overall system of oppositions. But even when one allows for the fact that blackness in American culture is constituted in opposition to whiteness, and that each pole of the opposition may be transparent in relation to a more encompassing structure, there are aspects of "the Black experience" that are unique and which feed back into the cultural and normative systems. This cannot be discussed here, but it appears in Aschenbrenner's assertion that her data show "the concern to reach a compact satisfactory to both parties before they make any commitments. Here, marriage is viewed as the social recognition of a satisfactory resolution of differences, rather than as the beginning of a socially prescribed relationship. Such an agreement may be difficult to negotiate when consanguineal ties . . . are strong" (1975:46). Although one could argue that this is merely another expression of the low priority of solidary emphasis accorded the conjugal tie, a fine-grained analysis focused upon social action would, I believe, force a modification of the model of norms, and throw considerable doubt on the idea that coitus is the figure out of which all the symbols of American kinship are developed (see Wallace 1969 for a discussion of this issue).

Sylvia Yanagisako has make a similar, and most convincing, analysis of the cultural specificity of kinship—or some aspects of it—among Japanese Americans. In the process she has argued strongly for the recognition of "the interpenetration of cultural domains and the relationships among the levels of analysis we identify for heuristic purposes" (Yanagisako 1978:26). As she points out, Schneider's scheme entails a radical asymmetry between meaning and action, in that it appears that culture can affect behavior, but is itself insulated from any reciprocal effect.

Conclusion: Kinship, Class, and Urban Anthropology

At the beginning of this chapter it was pointed out that new anthropological study is being urged in fields of inquiry that one might well believe to be saturated. But for all the many surveys and censuses that exist, we know remarkably little about the connections between events and domains of life as they bear upon individual families. This is a constant complaint of scholars and policymakers alike, and almost any kind of anthropological research would be useful in remedying this situation. Anthropology typically seeks to understand action in its total social context. Social psychology is painfully struggling toward an understanding of the "ecology" of family life and child development (Bronfenbrenner 1979), and, of course, there has been a small but distinguished group of sociologists who have used an ethnographic approach to the study of urban society. The work of Bott (1956), Young and Wilmott (1957), Rosser and Harris (1965), and Firth, Hubert, and Forge (1970) shows the advantage of intensive firsthand study, while that of Gans (1962), Suttles (1968), and an increasing body of work on black families shows the marked increment of understanding that results from extended case studies (Rainwater 1970; Hill 1971; Liebow 1966; Stack 1974; Aschenbrenner 1975; Martin and Martin 1978). Studies such as this should, and will, continue.

American kinship studies are long overdue for theoretical innovation. The overwhelming majority of writers on urban kinship start from the assumption that the family is a natural unit of parents and children, rooted in the functions of reproduction and socialization, but shaped by social convention. The extension of ties generated in this way produce, so it is argued, the wider network of ties which constitute a genealogy. It is but a short step from this position to the conclusion that variations on this pattern are pathological. Of course, theory has a convenient way of responding to social pressure; witness the increasing body of writing that rationalizes mothers' participation in the labor force by suggesting that children really need to be free of maternal contact for a good deal of the time in order to develop independence and curiosity.

It has been the signal contribution of anthropology to disabuse us of the idea that kinship and the family is merely a social expression of a natural fact, though it has taken a long time and the process is not yet complete. The then radical views of Edmund Leach that "ethnographic facts will be much easier to understand if we approach them free of *all* . . . a priori assumptions" and try to understand the natives' own social categories—these views have steadily gained ground and encouraged new interpretations of familiar comparative problems (Leach 1961:27). Schneider and Needham, each in his own way, have been influential in developing this idea, and each has come to the conclusion that "kinship" is not a useful category for cross-cultural comparison, as it is too permeated by European assumptions. To put it more dramatically, each has declared that kinship does not really exist.

These considerations may not appear to be very relevant to the study of American kinship, except to alert us to the fact that many supposed "theoretical" categories in this field are really folk categories. However, they can provide new perspectives for kinship and family studies in Euro-American society.

The old beliefs that European families were once very large, because of the requirements of preindustrial production, and shrank in size and scope with the advent of industrial development has long been abandoned. One reason is that we can now see in European and American kinship certain structural principles which seem to have been remarkably constant over many centuries (Laslett 1965; Macfarlane 1979; Stone 1977). Schneider's work, along with that of other scholars, alerted us to these constancies and continuities, these structures of long duration, as they appear in modern American kinship. Most studies of urban kinship have focused upon disorder, social problems, or variation, and it is legitimate to ask what structural analysis, or the analysis of cultural systems, can contribute to this.

Practically all prior studies of variation in urban kinship have taken one of two positions: variation is produced by "subcultures" which have either persisted from a historical homeland, or are generated by the social conditions of the urban area, or are produced by a combination of the two; or variation arises with structured deviance from societal norms, those norms being either functionally necessary for healthy families, or rooted in nature.

The Chicago kinship studies tried to transcend the limitations of these approaches by asking how the core elements of a cultural tradition are differentially incorporated in the normative order of a highly differentiated society. Instead of trying to derive the logic of behavior from the actors' "adaptation," "adjustment," "coping strategies," or "exploitation" of the situation, it asked: how do the most general presuppositions embodied in a cultural tradition condition the behavior of actors by giving meaning to the situation? In its general conception, the project conforms to Marx's dictum that "men make their own history, but they do not make it just as they please; . . . but under circumstances directly encountered, given and transmitted from the past" (Marx 1963:15). If anything, it did not conform closely enough, since it slighted the possible effects of praxis upon structure. The points established by the research and the future directions which it suggests may be summarized as follows:

1. The research amply confirms the importance of extended kinship ties among all classes in Chicago. Although the number of informants is small, each one documents the existence of kinship networks which include many other people.

2. Schneider has shown that it is possible to construct abstract models which economically represent the most general characteristics of cultural symbolic systems. Following Dumont's pioneering work on Hindu culture (1970), he has used these formulations to suggest a radical reformulation of the comparative study of kinship, and an increasing number of studies demonstrate the potential of the project (see Inden and Nicholas 1977).

3. It has been more difficult to demonstrate how such abstract cultural symbols relate to norms and to the flow of social action, and various criticisms have focused on problems of replication and problems of understanding change (see Wallace 1969; Yanagisako 1978).

4. In *Class Differences* an attempt was made to bring together abstract cultural analysis and an understanding of the complexities of behavior in order to throw light upon variation between classes in Chicago. Although the study is suggestive, it could have been greatly improved by a modification of procedures as follows:

    a. avoid premature closure of the models of normative structure by fitting them to a wide range of social situations;

    b. avoid the identification of the models with "reality" by adopting neutral labels;

    c. recognize that meaning is both reproduced and modified in action.

5. The development of further studies along these lines will produce an urban anthropology that is both historically informed and empirically grounded, and will have the capacity to analyze generative structures as they operate and are reproduced in social practice.

Acknowledgments

The research on which this paper is based was supported by grants from the Children's Bureau (R328), the National Science Foundation, and the Lichtstern Fund.

Notes

1. Hereafter referred to as *Class Differences*. A reprint edition was published in 1978 with a new foreword.

2. We interviewed a total of 39 blacks, 11 whites, and 9 Spanish-Americans. Genealogies were complete enough to permit analyzing 21 blacks, 5 whites, and 2 Spanish-Americans. The informants for which genealogical analysis was possible had the following characteristics. The 21 blacks comprised 3 males and 18 females who ranged in age from 16 years to 62; 13 informants were under 30 years of age; 6 were between 30 and 49 years old; and 2 were over 50 years old. The whites included 4 females and one male ranging in age from 46 to 57 years of age. The Spanish-Americans comprised one male aged 48 years and one female aged 16 years. The genealogies varied considerably in size, ranging from 30 to 652 among the blacks, 77 to 806 among the whites, and 104 to 261 for the two Spanish-Americans. The vast majority were in the range of 150 to 250.

References

Alexander, Jack. 1976. "A Study of the Cultural Domain of 'Relations.' " *American Ethnologist* 3:17–38.

——1978. "The Cultural Domain of Marriage." *American Ethnologist* 5:5–14.

Aschenbrenner, Joyce. 1975. *Lifelines: Black Families in Chicago.* New York: Holt, Rinehart and Winston.

Ayoub, Millicent. 1966. "The Family Reunion." *Ethnology* 5:415–433.

Barnett, Steve and Martin D. Silverman. 1979. *Ideology and Everyday Life.* Ann Arbor: University of Michigan Press.

Bernstein, Basil, 1971. *Class, Codes, and Control.* Vol. 1. London: Routledge and Kegan Paul.

Bott, Elizabeth. 1956. *Family and Social Network.* London: Tavistock.

Bronfenbrenner, Urie. 1979. *The Ecology of Human Development.* Cambridge: Harvard University Press.

Dumont, Louis, 1970. *Homo Hierarchicus: An Essay on the Caste System.* Chicago: University of Chicago Press.

Firth, Raymond. 1956. *Two Studies of Kinship in London.* London: Athlone Press.

Firth, Raymond, Jane Hubert, and A. Forge. 1970. *Families and Their Relatives.* London: Routledge and Kegan Paul.

Gans, Herbert. 1962. *The Urban Villagers.* New York: Free Press.

Geertz, Clifford. 1980. "Blurred Genres: The Refiguration of Social Thought." *The American Scholar* 49:165–179.

Hill, Robert. 1971. *The Strengths of Black Families*. New York: Emerson Hall.

Inden, Ronald B, and Ralph W. Nicholas. 1977. *Kinship in Bengali Culture*. Chicago: University of Chicago Press.

Labov, William. 1972. *Language in the Inner City*. Philadelphia: University of Pennsylvania Press.

Laslett, Peter. 1965. *The World We Have Lost*. London: Methuen.

Leach, Edmund. 1961. *Rethinking Anthropology*. London: Athlone Press.

Liebow, Elliot. 1966. *Tally's Corner*. Boston: Little, Brown.

Macfarlane, Alan. 1979. *The Origins of English Individualism*. New York: Cambridge University Press.

Martin, Elmer P. and Joanne Mitchell Martin. 1978. *The Black Extended Family*. Chicago: University of Chicago Press.

Marx, Karl. 1963. *The Eighteenth Brumaire of Louis Bonaparte*. New York: International.

Needham, Rodney, ed. 1971. *Rethinking Kinship and Marriage*. London: Tavistock.

Parsons, Talcott. 1943. "The Kinship System of the Contemporary United States." *American Anthropologist* 45:22–38.

Rainwater, Lee. 1970. *Behind Ghetto Walls*. Chicago: Aldine.

Rosser, Colin and Christopher Harris. 1965. *The Family and Social Change*. London: Routledge and Kegan Paul.

Schneider, David M. 1963. "Kinship." Unpublished manuscript.

——1965. "American Kin Terms and Terms for Kinsmen: A Critique of Goodenough's Analysis of Yankee Kinship Terminology." In Eugene A. Hammell, ed., *Formal Semantic Analysis*, pp. 288–308. Washington, D.C.: American Anthropological Association.

——1968 *American Kinship: A Cultural Account*. Englewood Cliffs, N.J.: Prentice-Hall

——1969. "Kinship, Nationality, and Religion in American Culture." In Victor Turner, ed., *Forms of Symbolic Action*, pp. 116–125. Washington, D.C.: American Ethnological Society.

——1970. "Middle Class and Lower Class American Kinship." Unpublished manuscript, American Kinship Project, Department of Anthropology, University of Chicago.

——1972. "What Is Kinship All About?" In P. Reining, ed., *Kinship Studies in the Morgan Centennial Year*, pp. 32–63. Washington, D.C.: Washington Anthropological Society.

——1976. "Notes Toward a Theory of Culture." In K. Basso and H. Selby, eds., *Meaning in Anthropology*, pp. 197–220. Albuquerque: University of New Mexico Press.

——1979. "Kinship, Community, and Locality in American Culture." In A. J. Lichtman and J. R. Challinor, eds., *Kinship and Communities*, pp. 155–174. Washington, D.C.: Smithsonian Institution Press.

——1980. *American Kinship: A Cultural Account*. Chicago: University of Chicago Press.

Schneider, David and Calvert B. Cottrell. 1975. *The American Kin Universe: A Genealogical Study*. Chicago: University of Chicago Publications in Anthropology.

Schneider, David and George Homans. 1955. "Kinship Terminology and the American Kinship System." *American Anthropologist* 57:1194–1208.

Schneider, David and Raymond T. Smith. 1978 [1973]. *Class Difference in American Kinship*. Ann Arbor: University of Michigan Press. (Originally published as *Class Differences and Sex Roles in American Kinship and Family Structure*. Englewood Cliffs, N.J. Prentice-Hall.)

Seeley, John, Alexander Sim, and Elizabeth W. Loosley. 1956. *Crestwood Heights: A Study of the Culture of Suburban Life*. New York: Basic.

Sennett Richard. 1970. *Families Against the City*. Cambridge: Harvard University Press.

Smith, Raymond T. 1970. "The Nuclear Family in Afro-American Kinship." *Journal of Comparative Family Studies* 1:55–70.

——1978. "The Family and the Modern World System." *Journal of Family History* 3:337–360.

Stack, Carol. 1974. *All Our Kin*. New York: Harper and Row.

Stone, Lawrence. 1977. *The Family, Sex, and Marriage in England, 1500–1800*. New York: Harper and Row.

Suttles, Gerald D. 1968. *The Social Order of the Slum*. Chicago: University of Chicago Press.

Wallace, Anthony. 1969. "Review of American Kinship: A Cultural Account." *American Anthropologist* 71:100–106.

Winch, Robert F. and Rae L. Blumberg. 1968. "Societal Complexity and Family Organization." In Robert F. Winch and Louis Wolf Goodman, eds., *Selected Studies in Marriage and the Family*, pp. 70–92. New York: Holt, Rinehart and Winston.

Wolf, Linda. 1964. Anthropological interviewing in Chicago. Chicago: Department of Anthropolgy; University of Chicago.

Yanagisako, Sylvia Junko. 1978. "Variance in American Kinship: Implications for Cultural Analysis." *American Ethnologist* 5:15–29.

Young, Michael and Peter Wilmott. 1957. *Family and Kinship in East London*. London: Routledge and Kegan Paul.

——1973. *The Symmetrical Family*. London: Routledge and Kegan Paul.

IV

THE STUDY of the CITY:
THEORY, ETHICS, AND
ADVOCACY

In the final article Leacock discusses several issues that are raised in the volume. Based on thirty years of experience in research and teaching, she examines the way in which ethics and value orientation come into play in anthropological theorizing, as well as in applied urban research. Reviewing her own experience in doing academic, applied, and advocacy work in the public school system of New York City, she concludes that personal involvement is unavoidable and, indeed, desirable, in that it both clarifies issues for the researcher and produces data not otherwise obtainable.

14. Theory and Ethics in Applied Urban Anthropology

Eleanor Leacock

Two developments in anthropology have brought questions concerning professional ethics very much to the forefront. The first is the increasing involvement of anthropologists in urban applied work, either as engaged in policy-related research, or as employed in programs to do with health care delivery, drug or alcohol addiction, juvenile delinquency, community planning, bilingual and bicultural education, intergroup relations, labor-management relations, and so on. In such endeavors, ethical issues are commonly addressed in terms of defining and maintaining an "objective" professional stance. The second development has an opposite thrust. This is the angry criticism, primarily but not exclusively from Third World anthropologists, of the extent to which anthropologists, while professing neutrality, have in fact served as apologists for the colonial (or neocolonial) status quo. In such criticism, the whole concept of objectivity as possible or desirable is challenged. The two developments meet as anthropologists moving into urban applied work probe the implications of this challenge.

Meanwhile, the sharpening of debate on ethical issues tends to be viewed by academic anthropologists—when they bother to view it at all—as an annoyance which gets in the way of fieldwork and the theoretical development of the discipline. They continue to assume that personal commitments can and should be divorced from the scientific task of understanding human history and social-cultural processes. In opposing this view, I not only think personal commitment is unavoidable, but I see considered and humanistic commitment as often essential and at the very least beneficial for the development of effective theory. After a brief review of some issues concerning theory and ethics in "pure" and applied anthropology generally, I shall return to this point, and place particular emphasis on its implications for working with students who are interested in urban applied fields.

Theory and Ethics in Anthropology, "Pure" and "Applied"

It has been clear for some time that those who work in fields of anthropology dubbed "applied" are as much involved in theory development as "pure" academic anthropologists. Those whose research is directly focused on a recognized social problem with an aim to being useful to some planning program or popular organization, or who are working directly in the development and/or carrying out of some technological or social innovation, have the same choice as does the "pure" researcher to develop and report on theoretical explanations for their observations and recommendations. Nonetheless, purists continue to look askance at those working in practical areas, and students who wish to address their doctoral research to a practical economic or political problem may have difficulty getting their projects accepted by their faculty.

This state of affairs has been shifting as the academic job market has shrunk. The response is the right thing for the wrong reason. The same problems that are causing the academic job market to dry up also lead to programming related to social and economic problems, and jobs in such programs begin to look desirable. Nevertheless, applied anthropology is still not taken seriously enough, particularly when it comes to student training. It is acceptable for anthropologists who are already established to turn to applied fields, but a graduate student who wishes to become a medical or educational anthropologist may still face difficulties.

Some of the aloofness directed at applied anthropology arises not so much from ivory tower snobbery as from political considerations. Students who wish to take on projects with an "action anthropology" orientation or a frank position of advocacy with respect to the struggles of oppressed or colonized peoples meet conservative opposition. On the other hand, students with applied interests may meet with distrust from another direction, given the fact that anthropologists can acquire and abuse information that is dangerous to people being studied. The possibility of outright collusion with the CIA in its undeclared war against independence movements around the world was widely publicized in 1965 with the exposure of "Project Camelot," a multimillion-dollar U.S. Department of Defense project intended to draw social scientists into identifying ways of foreseeing and controlling "political unrest" in Latin America (Horowitz 1967). Five years later, the use of anthropologists in "large programs of counterinsurgency" in Thailand was brought before the business meeting of the American Anthropological Association for heated debate, after an unsuccessful attempt of the executive board of the association to hush the matter up (Weaver 1973:53–55; Wolf and Jorgensen 1970).

As dismaying as these revelations were, they did not deal with a far more prevalent and in the long run probably more pernicious form of collusion against the independence of people who are being studied. This is the indirect form whereby anthropologists become involved in programs of "modernization" or community development, whose formally stated purpose is to help solve problems for poor communities or countries, but whose effect (and often unstated purpose) is to adapt the program subjects to new forms of economic exploitation and political control (Huizer and Mannheim 1979).

Such programs have a long history. Onoge (1979:47) points out that the "practical anthropology" proposed by Malinowski in 1928 "advocated an anthropology 'mobilized for the task of assisting colonial control,' " as Malinowski put it, a task he elaborated upon in papers with titles such as "The Rationalization of Anthropology and Administration" and "Indirect Rule and Its Scientific Planning." The functionalist approach passed on by Malinowski to his students, with its downplaying of history and emphasis on equilibrium, has been amply criticized, Onoge goes on to say, but "what is not customarily emphasized is the grave *political* salience of these theoretical deficiencies in the research world of applied anthropology" (1979:49 italics in the original). The heritage of functionalism in the service of colonialism

has permeated the social science establishment within Africa itself. There we find the justification of social science in terms of its ability to *adapt* the masses to the program of our client neocolonial societies. In spite of the reflexive injection of a cultural nationalist sensibility at the level of theory, in practice the alleged ignorance of the masses is still held to be the primary obstacle to Africa's development. So the typical research design chases after "sociocultural" obstacles to all kinds of programs. The decisive character of the colonial experience—the incorporation of Africa into the capitalist/imperialist social order—is conveniently submerged. (1979:64 italics in the original)

I am in complete sympathy with the genre of skepticism about applied anthropology that arises from the growth of the discipline as "the child of imperialism," as Gough's (1968) now classic statement put it. However, to assume one can retreat into academic anthropology, or to advise students to try and do so, is unrealistic. As Onoge, Gough, and all other writers on the political relevance of anthropology (and science in general, for that matter) repeat, scientific neutrality is an illusion. For example, data on human biological variation always have social implications, and anthropologists are usually aware that these data must be handled with scientific rigor in order to avoid racist formulations that rationalize social inequality and injustice. The names of Franz Boas, Ruth Benedict, Gene Weltfish, Montague Cobb, and Sherwood Washburn head a long list of anthropologists who have exposed racist ideologies that are paraded as science.

Anthropologists collect data on many subjects that would appear to have no political significance, such as no longer functioning kinship systems, tool types from past archaeological horizons, and the like. However, as soon as such data are analyzed and related to comparable data in a theoretical statement, political implications become unavoidable. Theories about kinship do not develop far without entailing implications for male-female relations and the sources of women's oppression. Likewise, theories about tool sequences and the clues they afford for reconstructing social-economic relations in past societies inevitably involve assumptions about human nature, social inequality, political power, warfare, and so on. The impossibility of neutrality is well put by Polgar (1971:355). He writes, "To propound a theory about society is a political act," and "Even scientific facts are not 'objective' (since, if nothing else, their selection for ascertainment and dissemination is value-laden)."

In cultural anthropology, for example, a focus on "tribal culture" can, by avoiding political and economic realities and issues, play into the hands of colonialism. Onoge (1979:53) cites Audrey Richards' 1939 study *Land, Labour, and Diet in Northern Rhodesia* as a prime example. Onoge points out that Richards suggested all manner of cultural reasons why the Bemba diet was deteriorating, but failed to consider the fact that about half of the men had to leave their communities for work in European mines in order to pay colonial taxes.

Serious political issues continue to be avoided by many anthropologists who—along with psychologists, sociologists, and other social scientists—discuss contemporary change in Third World countries in terms of a "modern-traditional" continuum. A focus on "modernization" encourages the emphasis on relatively superficial culture traits and all too often masks the exploitative economic and political realities of neocolonialism (Gladwin 1971; Leacock 1980; Magubane 1971).

In sum, questions of political relevance, hence of ethics, are ever present. The ostrich pose, head in sand, may protect the would-be purist temporarily from self-criticism, but the ethical problems will not disappear. As part of an exchange of views on the subject, Delmos Jones points out that it was not only those who openly supported U.S. counter-insurgency efforts in southeast Asia who could be accused of unethical behavior; so also should "those who attempt to hide behind the idea of pure research while their activities aid the preservation of the status quo" (1971:350). Schoepf, who was advised as a student to avoid the policy-related dilemmas of applied research, writes:

But does avoiding applied research eliminate the hazards of involvement in social policy? Radcliffe-Brown pointed to the usefulness of basic studies of social structure for colonial policy. He mentioned, for example, that the African kinship studies indicated that "kinsmen speaking with the authority of the ancestors behind them" would serve as more effective agents of social control for the British colonial government than either the police or missionaries. It appeared that those who pose the issue as a choice between pure, value-free research and applied or "relevant" social science employ a false set of opposites. The real question is relevance on whose side? (1979:330)

Applied Anthropology and Personal Commitment

Students who wish to do something of immediate and practical use with their skills and knowledge find that arguments about "objectivity" are not limited to academic anthropologists. Applied anthropologists are also divided as to the possibility and desirability of taking a neutral stance. One line of reasoning runs that applied anthropologists should play the role of neutral mediators who, through recording and interpreting activities, and making relevant information available to the people in a given program, can contribute to the clarification of issues, the planning of effective action, and the prevention or resolution of unnecessary conflict.

In the case of conflict, however, true neutrality is only possible where

the parties involved have more or less equal access to power and resources. For example, an anthropologist who espouses neutrality can be
helpful in muting competition among community groups that have been
swayed by divide and rule politics and have factionalized rather than
united to achieve a common goal. However, programs of any magnitude,
whether they have to do with educational and occupational training,
with medical service, with the quality of community facilities, with problems of addiction, and so on, sooner or later involve conflicts of interest
between unequal constituencies. Any major change effort cannot bypass
the opposition that exists between business and administrative hierarchies on the one hand and working-class and minority populations on
the other (see Sharff, Susser and Kreniske, Mikell, Jones, Ogbu, Sanjek,
Lopez, in this volume). For poor people who are attempting to combat
exploitation and discrimination and gain a greater measure of control
over the course of their lives and those of their children, some confrontation with the structure of power is unavoidable. And, as Morton Fried
has put it, "When dealing with contending parties, one of which is in
power, 'neutrality' is support of the incumbent" (1972:45).

Whether anthropologists should attempt neutrality or take positions
of frank advocacy has been debated in the pages of *Human Organization*,
the journal of the Society for Applied Anthropology. In 1971, the
address before the society by the Mexican anthropologist Rodolfo Stavenhagen was published along with various supporting or dissenting
opinions. Titling his talk "Decolonizing Applied Social Sciences," Stavenhagen states that an applied social scientist "cannot remain true to
the ethical principles of his science and at the same time refuse to take
a stand on the wider ideological and ethical issues of the societal processes in which he is involved as a practitioner. . . . It is not a question
of science versus politics, but of one kind of science-in-politics versus
another" (1971:343).

Stavenhagen's point is important for students who are committed to
an advocacy role (see Sanjek, in this volume). Students commonly feel
embattled and isolated when they confront not only the enormous practical difficulties of initiating fieldwork, but also the nagging questions
about what they can realistically contribute to a given situation, and the
problem of presenting themselves honestly and acceptably to the group
with which they are working while also meeting the requirements of
academic mentors, funding agencies, and/or employers. It is hard
enough for them to interpret the conflicting demands upon them and

define the range of choices realistically open to them in an attempt to arrive at a reasonably satisfactory resolution or compromise. They should not also have to confront the false issue of whether they are primarily interested in science or in politics. By the decision to engage in advocacy anthropology, a student has already chosen to engage in what he or she sees as ethically acceptable *science-in-politics*.

The next question that suggests itself is, what are the scientific implications of taking a frank advocacy stance? Does not commitment blind researchers to realities they do not wish to recognize and distort their analyses and conclusions, as is commonly assumed? I would argue not of itself. Scientific rigor—conscientious attention to detail, careful consideration of the unexpected or seemingly contradictory, deliberate weighing of alternative explanations for behavior, and so forth—is not by itself a matter of politics. People on all sides of political fences can be either careful or sloppy in collecting and organizing data, and either intently thoughtful or casually superficial in drawing conclusions from them.

I would argue further that the more serious a person's commitment is to helping some group obtain the information or skills it needs to improve its situation, the greater the care and accuracy devoted to research and support service *should* be. I would submit that a student who is deeply concerned with assisting progressive change will find the level at which he or she can make an honest and scientifically valid contribution to a problem according to personal interests and abilities.

Yet there is a more cogent relation between advocacy and scientific validity. I contend that, given an able and conscientious researcher, advocacy leads to fuller and more accurate understanding than attempted neutrality. To attempt neutrality not only means to align oneself, by default, with the institutional structures that discriminate against and exploit poor and non-white people. It also means shielding oneself from the personal discomfort of being treated by institutional personnel with the same disrespect (if not worse) that the people one is studying may experience. In so doing, one can ignore the realities of power and skirt the touchy question of conflict, and thereby fail to deal with the total structure of relationships in which people are involved. One can fall back on a truncated version of "culture" as largely learned attitudes and values, and negate the holistic approach to which anthropological study is formally committed.

Laura Nader raises the question whether anthropological fieldwork "does not depend upon a certain power relationship in favor of the anthropologist," and she asks further whether "dominant-subordinate relationships may not be affecting the kinds of theories we are weaving." She stresses the urgency of anthropological studies that concern themselves with power (see Miller, in this volume), "for the quality of life and our lives themselves may depend upon the extent to which citizens understand those who shape attitudes and actually control institutional structures" (1972:284,289).

Stavenhagen asks how many studies we have "of the varied and multiple aspects of repression (physical, cultural, psychological, economic) that dominant groups use to maintain the status quo." He writes:

When describing the urban poor, what role do we attribute to real estate speculation and economic interest in the development of cities? When addressing ourselves to the rural migrant in the process of industrialization, how conscious are we of the role and function of the multinational corporation in determining levels of investment, technology and employment opportunities? When judging the effects of community development, health or nutrition programs at the local level, how much do we actually know of the bureaucratic and political processes involved? (1971:338)

To study "up" as well as "down" would lead to asking many questions in reverse, Nader points out; not why are people poor, but why others are so affluent; not why are peasants conservative, but why there is such a "fantastic resistance to change among the rich who have so many available options." After all, "the conservatism of . . . major institutions and bureaucratic organizations probably has wider implications for the species and for theories of change than does the conservatism of the peasantry" (1972:289).

In urban settings, the "culture of poverty" concept plays the same role as peasant "conservatism" or "traditionalism" does for rural people. Both concepts refer the difficulties of reforming poverty and oppression to supposed characteristics of the poor and oppressed themselves, and ignore the structure of oppression itself (Leacock 1971; Piven and Cloward 1971; Ryan 1972; B. Valentine 1978; C. Valentine 1968). Institutionalized oppression and discrimination confront people anew at each stage of their lives—from childhood discomforts of poor housing and the dreariness of limited recreational facilities (tied in with real estate interests) (see Sharff, Susser and Kreniske, Lopez, in this volume); through the double-track educational system with "good" college-bound schools in affluent neighborhoods and inadequate schools in poor and ghetto communities (see Ogbu, in this volume); to the myriad structural barriers to getting and holding a well-paid, steady job. However, the culture of poverty formulation assumes that early childhood experiences of themselves determine the course of later life, and has therefore become a socially acceptable form of expressing racism and class arrogance.

As originally formulated by Oscar Lewis, the culture of poverty "tends *to perpetuate itself* from generation to generation because of its effect on the children" (italics added). "Slum children . . . are not psychologically geared" to take full advantage of opportunities that occur in their lifetime. By the time they are six or seven years old, according to Lewis, they have internalized characteristic subcultural attitudes and values, including feelings of helplessness, dependence, and resignation; orality; a weak ego structure; "a lack of impulse control"; and "a strong present-time orientation with relatively little ability to defer gratification and plan for the future" (1966:xlv–xlviii).

Although it has been roundly criticized by anthropologists as well as other social scientists, the culture of poverty explanation for "failures" of the poor has been thoroughly institutionalized in education and the medical and social services. Affirming as it does complacent attitudes of superiority among the "successful," the concept serves "as a convenient ideological screen," as Schoepf puts it, for professionals who choose to discount "structural causes of worker alienation" and instead find "explanations in the characteristics of the people themselves" (1979:331–340). However, when one adopts "a view from below," and takes seriously the "concrete social knowledge of struggling poor people," alternate explanations for their failures are revealed.

Schoepf describes a research project pertaining to federally funded Neighborhood Health Centers, located mostly in ghetto communities. The federal program had provided for community participation, and local people sat on advisory councils and worked in the health centers. However, conflicts had arisen over health center programs, and the funding agency in Washington mandated research to ascertain the cause. The researchers found that neighborhood people had initially become involved with the centers in high hopes that their communities' serious health needs would finally in some part be met, but their enthusiasm had largely given away to alienation and demoralization. This discouragement was easily discounted by professionals attached to the centers; in the words of one high-level administrator, "What can you expect of those people? They never worked a day in their lives before they got here." The community workers themselves expressed bitter disillusionment over what they saw as the program's failure; said one, "When I came here I really thought we could change things. Now I'm only here because I need the job." Workers also expressed skepticism about the usefulness of the research. "One informant summarized the view of many," Schoepf writes, saying,

These programs are being used to divide working people, to set whites against blacks because the whites think we're getting something for nothing and their taxes are paying for it. We get a few crumbs, sure, but it doesn't change the conditions of our people. And even among us, the poor are set against the not-so-poor with steady jobs. If you can make people see *that,* then I guess there's a place for you. But don't think you're doing *us* any favors! (1979:333; italics in the original)

The researchers were unable to "study up," because of their limited access to information, but analyzing the functioning of the centers from the viewpoint of the community workers revealed a structure that could not be better designed to factionalize and alienate. First, inadequate funding and pressure not to antagonize local hospitals and practitioners meant only the poorest patients were eligible for care, thereby creating divisiveness and vitiating the neighborhood facility concept. Second, despite its official ideology, the Office of Economic Opportunity failed to support the concept of community control when conflicts in interest arose between the councils and local politicians or professionals (see Jones and Sanjek, in this volume). Third, the refusal of most professionals attached to the centers to involve poor and minority-group consumers in decisions made a mockery of council participation, and generated anger that was exacerbated by the fact that professionals freely used their personal networks to "find the best man for the job" but resisted council input, and saw the use of personal networks by community people as favoritism. Finally, the narrowly circumscribed role of the councils meant that they were being used as buffers between the professional staffs and dissatisfied community people—as scapegoats for a program that was not in the first place sufficiently funded to serve its stated purpose.

Schoepf writes that people who had originally been dedicated to the program found themselves being structured into "middle person roles . . . engaged in indirect rule. They were severely shaken when they discovered that, in effect, their job was to convey decisions down and news of unrest up the hierarchy, alerting the policymakers to trouble brewing in their communities." Schoepf raises the question "whether the citizen participation strategy is a deliberately designed policy of pacification or merely a serendipitous structural conjuncture, separate processes converging to produce a particular result." In my view, both alternatives are in a measure true, as policymakers manipulate functionally interlocked social processes in ways that reinforce the status quo. "In either case," Schoepf concludes, "the policy enables those who wield power in a society to stay in power by creating the appearance of change and flexibility on the part of the rulers, while assigning responsibility for failures to the social and personal characteristics of powerless people" (1979:336–337).

Personal Involvement and the Study of Schooling

In my own experience, advocacy work undertaken (on my own time) while I was conducting research on elementary schooling made it possible to observe the intricate intermeshing of the processes, some consciously manipulated by people in power, some seemingly serendipitous but in fact functionally interrelated, that combine in what is termed "institutionalized racism." In 1958, I began a comparative study of second and fifth grade classrooms in four schools, black middle income, black low income, white middle income, and white low income (Leacock 1969). Black parents and youth across the country were demanding an end to segregated and unequal schooling, and my research team and I were expecting to document the classroom effects of inequities in teacher experience, school plants, and the like, as well as the further difficulties for black children caused by a clash between their life-styles and the "white middle-class" values of the school.

Along with some members of the research team, I took full running records of classroom life, identifying individual children according to the seating plans given us by the teacher. One person interviewed teachers and did not discuss her material with people working on classroom observations until both had been analyzed. Children were interviewed briefly. Classroom protocols were analyzed for both the overt, or formal, and covert, or informal, ways in which teachers were conveying messages to children. That is, we looked at a teacher's formal directives, goal-setting statements, sanctions, and interchanges concerning curriculum content, and we also looked at the structuring of the learning situation in a classroom, at who and what were being rewarded or punished and how, at how children's experiences were being handled, and at the implications of the curriculum content itself for children from different backgrounds. Teacher interviews were examined in relation to a teacher's stated goals for her pupils and her unstated valuation of them, as well as for information about her training and experience, about the curriculum, and about the pupils. Child interviews were studied for clues as to how children were receiving and interpreting teacher messages.

Comparison of classroom analyses revealed some of the things we had expected, such as the higher goals set for middle-income children in better-equipped and less crowded schools. What we had not expected, however, was the sharpness with which our data refuted the generally accepted hypothesis that differences in school performance of middle- and low-income black and white children followed from differences in the children's home backgrounds rather than from differences in schooling. Instead, our data revealed that children were being systematically prepared by their schooling for a future that accorded with their class and caste background.

In what was seen as fitting teaching styles to children's needs and abilities, teachers were reinforcing unequal opportunities. The experiences of low-income black children, in particular, were not only absent from their texts but were ignored or denigrated by their teachers. In the low-income black fifth grade, the children's work was negatively evaluated far more than in any other classroom, even when correct. The learning situation was structured in authoritarian, or boss-worker, terms, in contrast to the "democratic" structure of the middle-income white fifth grade. There an elaborate system of student officers, discussion directors, and committee reports gave the children training in skills necessary for middle-income occupational roles. The main middle-class "value" the low-income children were being asked to accept was that they were unworthy of anything more than their low position in the status system. As I have written elsewhere: "As the socializing institution second only to the family in our society, the school differentiates in its treatment of children according to the position of their parents in the social status system. This differentiation is such that the school takes an active role in defining for poor children a role as outsiders and failures" (1970:198–199).

The bitter paradox is that such negative definition is not only, or even primarily, conveyed by punitive teachers in demoralized schools, particularly at the elementary level. In most cases, as in our study, it is conveyed by well-intentioned and hardworking teachers in reasonably well-run schools. An extensive literature, generated by the struggles over unequal education of the late fifties and the sixties, now documents the systemic nature of educational inequality that assures replication of existing class relations (e.g., Bowles and Gintis 1976; Ogbu 1978 and in this volume) and renders meaningless the search for new teaching methods as a panacea. Furthermore, a number of studies document the fact that it is the expectations teachers have for children's performance that are critical to their success or failure in the classroom (Rosenthal and Jacobson 1984; Rosenthal 1974). While an exceptionally good teacher can make an important difference to individual children (Pedersen et al. 1978), most teachers, like most people, are not exceptional. Most go along with the established patterns of school culture, and deeply embedded in these patterns are differential goals and expectations for children of different class and racial backgrounds.

The fact that lowered expectations for children are firmly built into educational practice helps explain some anomalies in the much-discussed Coleman Report (1966) and the later Jencks et al. (1972) restudy of educational inequities. Both Coleman and Jencks find surprisingly low correlations between children's achievement and the quality of schooling as measured by certain quantitative criteria such as teacher experience and school facilities. Both have been cited, therefore, in support of what Ogbu has labeled the "failure-of-socialization" hypothesis that shifts the blame for children's poor school performance on their families (1979:5). Missing from such studies, however, is reference to the qualitative dimensions of school input, via both teachers and curricula, and recognition of the complex ways in which schools as institutions project low goals for the achievement of children from poor and minority neighborhoods (John and Leacock 1979).

Through involvement in two kinds of community activities, I gained insight beyond that of my formal study into the indirect influences of factors external to education as such on the schooling process, and into the complex structure whereby even well-meaning and conscientious teachers fail to teach. First, I initiated a newsletter, *Facts for School Action*, designed to make available to community people in usable form the material on school policies and politicking that was buried in Board of Education and other documents. Second, I participated in a citywide council that was formed to coordinate activities of different neighborhood groups; to develop overall strategies in the attempt of ghetto communities to gain some say in their children's schooling; and to keep open, during a period of increasing tensions and bitterness, channels of communication between parent groups and those teachers who refused to be drawn into a union-organized confrontation with black parents (a confrontation that, with zealous assistance from the media, was deflecting attention from Board of Education responsibilities).

During the process of selecting study schools, I had become acquainted with the rigidity of the double-track system whereby "good" schools in "good" neighborhoods were college bound, while "bad" schools in poor and ghetto neighborhoods led to "drop-out" high schools; but becoming familiar with behind-the-scenes politicking made clear how neatly the system tied in with real estate and construction industry interests, local party politics, and, ultimately, the rigid, competitive, and discriminatory job market for which youngsters from different classes were being prepared (Rubinstein 1970).

I was also already familiar with the conservatism of training in schools of education and with something of the processes of selection and self-selection whereby more experienced and better-trained teachers (albeit not necessarily always better ones) end up in better schools. But getting to know activist teachers made clear how difficult it was for those who were committed to raising performance levels of their black students to challenge established school practices. By doing so, they would assert, in effect, that the school, and not the children's parents, was primarily responsible for children's performance. Furthermore, by trying to use appropriate texts, they would come up against the role of schools as an enormous market for publishing companies. In order to assure the widest market, school texts are designed to offend no one in a position of influence. Hence they blandly affirm the status quo with what Jerome Bruner (1959) has called the "pablum," which promulgates the myth Otto Klineberg (1963) has characterized as "Life is fun in a smiling, fair-skinned world." (That today some proportion of faces scattered through the illustrations in elementary school readers must be a vague, indeterminate brown merely underlines this characterization.)

Through the course of my school research, I had become familiar with the propensity of teachers in middle-income schools to see themselves as responsible for their students' performance, while teachers in low-income schools availed themselves of the rationale that failures were the result of the children's backgrounds. However, participation both in efforts to bridge gaps between parents and teachers in neighborhood settings, and in government-funded teacher training institutes focused on work with "disadvantaged" children, made clear how deeply tied to the maintenance of class and caste lines this differential attitude is. That teachers are commonly from working-class and/or black backgrounds need not ameliorate but rather can exacerbate their feeling of distance from children who are poor and/or black. Their training, the structure of schooling, concern with job security and advancement, all combine with dominant attitudes of class and race bias as they reassure themselves about their own hard-won climb to "middle-class" status by maintaining a clear divide between themselves and their low-status pupils.

It became clear that teachers are, in a sense, both victims and villains. As the primary instrument through which differential education is effected, their work is contradicted and their efforts to teach are frustrated. The liberating feeling of cutting through this tangle was expressed to an observer in one of the demonstration schools in New York's Ocean Hill–Brownsville district, a black community. The school was in the hands of a community board, and a teacher reported "that this was by far her best teaching experience in twelve years of parochial and public school teaching; that for the first time she felt the students really thought of themselves and the teachers as 'we' and felt they were working freely together" (Rubinstein 1970:232).

Such experiences were not to last, however. Ultimately "community control" was won in New York City, but as in the public health instance Schoepf analyzed, in such a form as to be ineffective. The significance of those experiments in one or another school or district across the country that had been successful was ignored or forgotten. Such children as were allowed leeway to "make it" served as evidence for the equal opportunity schools are supposed to offer; and meanwhile, for the overwhelming majority the double-track system remained as firmly entrenched as ever. Through research in classrooms, I had discovered how the double-track system affects teaching practices, but through involvement in community actions on behalf of equal schooling, I was able to piece together the complex processes mediating these effects and observe how they were being manipulated by people in positions of power in order to maintain the system itself. Involvement enabled me to view the object of my study in the totality of its context.

Commitment, Theory, and Teaching Urban Applied Anthropology

Personal involvement, then, may reveal aspects of a totality that "pure" research can choose to ignore. Far from leading to the avoidance of theoretical problems, it forces researchers who are serious and conscientious about their work to give the most careful attention to theory. This may take the form of criticizing extant formulations, and students who are interested in personal involvement should be encouraged to build on the theoretical implications of their work. A student of mine who wished to describe ways in which conflict between blacks and Puerto Ricans over control of a local school board was being generated by higher educational bodies complained of inadequacies in ethnic conflict theory. I thereupon suggested he write his paper as a critique of this theory. Another student expressed concern about the diagnostic categories being applied to the disturbed black and Hispanic youth she was teaching. I advised her to focus a paper on the nature of the evaluations themselves, the processes through which the behavior patterns they implied were being communicated to the young people, and the problems raised by the assumptions that anger at institutionalized racism was not valid and that all rebelliousness was necessarily pathological.

Although critiques of extant theory are important, they are limited. Advocacy research also calls for new theoretical formulations, for concepts that are adequate to the task of dealing with social complexity and social change. In the address cited above, Stavenhagen (1971:343) speaks of the obligation social scientists have "to create new models" in place of those they must discard, and Polgar (1971:356) comments that activist researchers are in a position to test these models directly for their scientific soundness. In a discussion on anthropology and colonialism, Diane Lewis points out that the important contribution to the discipline that Third World anthropologists engaged in advocacy research in their own countries can make is by helping "create conditions for a thorough-going and realistic understanding of processes of social change" (1973:590).

Speaking of the urban United States, Sue-Ellen Jacobs writes that the advocacy research in which she and her students became involved would not allow imposition of "traditional strictures to growth in theory and method," but instead called for broadened social science perspectives and the development of "a working paradigm for the humanization of social research" (1974:214). Stephen Schensul reports that contributing to the initiation and ongoing activities of a Chicano youth center in Chicago both afforded him great personal satisfaction and showed him the potential such work held for anthropology. The collation of information from anthropologists who have dealt with "bureaucracies, change programs, community groups, political forces, and other factors that constitute components of modern social change," Schensul writes, "can make a great contribution to the development of new concepts and theoretical models for all of anthropology" (1974:208).

What are the parameters of the new concepts and theoretical models referred to by advocacy researchers? "New" theories are never cut from whole cloth, of course, but involve reintegration and reinterpretation of the old. In this case, they involve the integration of established anthropological formulations with formulations drawn from other fields, such as economics, sociology, and, in particular, political economics and the focus on relations among production, class conflict, and power as initially defined by Marx. Established anthropological concepts emphasize the concept of culture as the rubric for analyzing interactions among economy, society, ideology, and individual personality within "tribal" enclaves that were presumed—in most cases erroneously—to be socially autonomous and economically self-contained. Therefore it might seem that anthropological theory has little relevance for the problems of urban industrial society. In my view, such is definitely not the case. Although I have criticized the antihistorical, functionalist, and psychological emphasis in anthropology that stresses equilibrium, turns attention away from contemporary realities of exploitation and conflict, and downplays possibilities for change, this does not mean I think anthropology has nothing to offer to urban applied studies.

To be adequate, a theory of society must take into account: first, economic and historical processes and their interrelations at a specifically societal level; second, social-psychological processes and their functioning at the level of the individual; and third, the interrelationships between the two. For this, the anthropological interest in relationships among different social-cultural processes, and in individual conformity to and deviance from established norms, is much needed. An adequate social theory must also deal with the sources and the effects of ideologies that inform individual attitudes and understandings. For this, the anthropological concern with value-attitude systems, with socialization processes, and with relations between belief and behavior is most useful. In both instances, I have contended in this paper, advocacy encourages theoretical innovation to an extent that attempted neutrality does not.

The commitment to assisting people who are moving to improve their situation calls for a reasoned appraisal of how they perceive their problems, needs, and choices for action, as well as of how their social-economic position both structures the choices realistically open to them and influences their perceptions and attitudes toward these choices. Such commitment rules out the tendency to categorize people in terms of narrow bipolar criteria (such as "modern" verses "traditional," or "middle-class values" versus "culture of poverty") according to which change is ultimately reduced to individual adaptation to the status quo. Furthermore, commitment requires specificity and necessitates the sorting out of those features that are particular to a given group or situation from those that are more general.

When combined with a broad historical orientation and an advocacy stance, anthropological perspectives make it possible to examine ways in which the conflicts and ambivalence people experience in their daily lives express fundamental social-economic conflicts that are impelling change. They offer the possibility for defining the potentials for action and the ambiguities that hinder it, as individuals and groups in part accept and in part resist the existing power relations that oppress them. Advocacy anthropology enhances the possibilities for delineating practical short-range steps and meaningful long-range goals for solutions to the problems urban people confront. Commitment makes it possible to work toward an effective—a practical—theory of social change.

Acknowledgment

This paper is based on "Applied Anthropology, Theory and Ethics," originally given at the 1975 Annual Meeting of the American Anthropological Association in a session on "Trends, Patterns, and Developments in the Science of Applied Anthropology" organized by James N. Kerri.

References

Bowles, Samuel and Herbert Gintis. 1976. *Schooling in Capitalist America*. New York: Basic.
Bruner, Jerome S. 1959. "Learning and Thinking." *Harvard Educational Review* 19 (3):186–190.

Coleman, James S. et al. 1966. *Equality of Educational Opportunity*. Washington, D.C.: U.S. Office of Education.

Fried, Morton H. 1972. *The Study of Anthropology*. New York: Crowell.

Fuchs, Estelle. 1969. *Teachers Talk: Views from Inside City Schools*. New York: Doubleday.

Gladwin, Thomas. 1971. "Modernization and Anthropology." *Newsletter of the American Anthropological Association* 12(8):9.

Gough, Kathleen. 1968. "New Proposals for Anthropologists." *Current Anthropology* 9 (5):403–407.

Horowitz, Irving, ed. 1967. *The Rise and Fall of Project Camelot*. Cambridge: MIT Press.

Huizer, Gerrit and Bruce Mannheim, eds. 1979. *The Politics of Anthropology*. The Hague: Mouton.

Jacobs, Sue-Ellen. 1974. "Action and Advocacy Anthropology." *Human Organization* 33(2):209–215.

Jencks, Christopher et al. 1972. *Inequality: A Reassessment of the Effect of Family and Schooling in America*. New York: Basic.

John, Vera P. and Eleanor Leacock. 1979. "Transforming the Structure of Failure." In Doxey A. Wilkerson, ed., *Educating All Our Children: An Imperative for Democracy*, pp. 76–91. Westport, Conn.: Mediax.

Jones, Delmos. 1971. "Social Responsibility and the Belief in Basic Research: An Example from Thailand." *Current Anthropology* 12(3):347–350.

Klineberg, Otto. 1963. "Life Is Fun in a Smiling Fair-Skinned World." *Saturday Review of Literature*, February 18.

Leacock, Eleanor. 1969. *Teaching and Learning in City Schools*. New York: Basic.

——1970. "Education, Socialization, and 'The Culture of Poverty.'" In Rubinstein, ed., *Schools Against Children*, pp. 192–210.

——1971. *The Culture of Poverty: A Critique*, ed. New York: Simon and Schuster.

——1980. "Politics, Theory, and Racism in the Study of Black Children." In Stanley Diamond, ed., *Theory and Practice: Essays to Gene Weltfish*, pp. 153–178. The Hague: Mouton.

Lewis, Diane. 1973. "Anthropology and Colonialism." *Current Anthropology* 14(5):581–591.

Lewis, Oscar. 1966. *La Vida*. New York: Random House.

Magubane, Bernard. 1971. "A Critical Look at Indices Used in the Study of Social Change in Colonial Africa." *Current Anthropology* 12(4–5):419–466.

Nader, Laura. 1972. "Up the Anthropologist—Perspectives Gained from Studying Up." In Dell H. Hymes, ed., *Reinventing Anthropology*, pp. 284–311. New York: Random House.

Ogbu, John U. 1978. *Minority Education and Caste: The American System in Cross-Cultural Perspective*. New York: Academic Press.

——1979. "Social Stratification and the Socialization of Competence." *Anthropology and Education Quarterly* 10(1):3–20.

Onoge, Omafune F. 1979. "The Counterrevolutionary Tradition in African Studies: The Case of Applied Anthropology." In Huizer and Mannheim, eds., *The Politics of Anthropology*, pp. 45–66.

Pederson, Eigil, Therese Annette Faucher, and William W. Eaton. 1978. "A New Perspective on the Effects of First-Grade Teachers on Children's Subsequent Adult Status." *Harvard Educational Review* 48(1):1–31.

Piven, Frances Fox and Richard A. Cloward. 1971. *Regulating the Poor*. New York: Vintage.

Polgar, Steven. 1971. "Comments." *Current Anthropology* 30(4):355–356.

Rosenthal, Robert. 1974. *On the Social Psychology of the Self-Fulfilling Prophecy: Further Evidence for Pygmalion Effects and Their Mediating Mechanisms*. MSS Modular Publication 53. New York: MSS Modular Publications.

Rosenthal, Robert and Lenore Jacobson, 1984. *Pygmalion in the Classroom.* New York: Irvington.

Rubinstein, Annette T., ed. 1970. *Schools Against Children: The Case for Community Control.* New York: Monthly Review Press.

Ryan, William. 1972. *Blaming the Victim.* New York: Random House.

Schensul, Stephen. 1974. "Skills Needed in Action Anthropology: Lessons from *El Centro de la Causa.*" *Human Organization* 33(2):203–209.

Schoepf, Brooke Grundfest. 1979. "Breaking Through the Looking Glass: The View from Below." In Huizer and Mannheim, eds., *The Politics of Anthropology,* pp. 325–342.

Stavenhagen, Rodolfo. 1971. "Decolonializing Applied Social Sciences." *Human Organization* 30(4):333–344.

Valentine, Charles A. 1968. *Culture and Poverty: Critique and Counterproposals.* Chicago: University of Chicago Press.

——1972. *Black Studies and Anthropology: Scholarly and Political Interests in Afro-American Culture.* Reading, Mass.: Addison-Wesley.

Valentine, Bettylou. 1978. *Hustling and Other Hard Work: Life Styles in the Ghetto.* Riverside, N.J.: Free Press.

Weaver, Thomas, ed. 1973. *To See Ourselves: Anthropology and Modern Social Issues.* Glenview, Ill.: Scott, Foresman.

Wolf, Eric and Joseph G. Jorgensen. 1970. "Anthropology on the Warpath in Thailand." *New York Review of Books,* November 19, pp. 26–35.

Index